the Comprehensive Guide to

Visual J ++

Windows 95 & Windows NT 4

the Comprehensive Guide to

Visual J++

Windows 95 & Windows NT 4

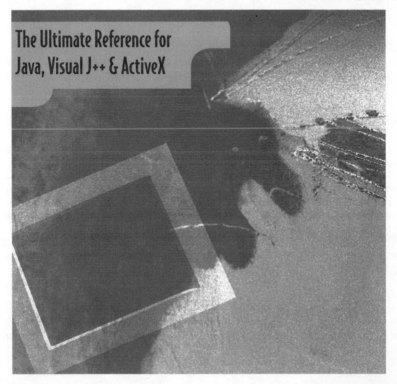

The Ultimate Reference for Java, Visual J++ & ActiveX

Daniel Joshi
Ramesh Chandak

VENTANA

The Comprehensive Guide to Visual J++
Copyright ©1997 by Daniel Joshi

Library of Congress Cataloging-in-Publication Data

Joshi, Daniel I.
       The Comprehensive Guide to Visual J++ / Daniel I. Joshi.
          p. cm.
       Includes index.
       ISBN 1-56604-533-9
       1. Java (Computer program language) 2. Microsoft Visual J++.
  I. Title.
  QA76.73.J38J67 1996
  005.13'3—dc20   96-35374
                                                 CIP

First Edition 9 8 7 6 5 4 3 2 1

Printed in the United States of America

Ventana Communications Group, Inc.
P.O. Box 13964
Research Triangle Park, NC 27709-3964
919.544.9404
FAX 919.544.9472
http://www.vmedia.com

Chief Executive Officer
Josef Woodman

**Vice President of
Content Development**
Karen A. Bluestein

Managing Editor
Lois J. Principe

Production Manager
John Cotterman

**Technology Operations
Manager**
Kerry L. B. Foster

Product Marketing Manager
Jamie Jaeger Fiocco

Creative Services Manager
Diane Lennox

Art Director
Marcia Webb

Acquisitions Editor
Neweleen A. Trebnik

Project Editor
Jennifer Rowe

Developmental Editor
Michelle Corbin Nichols

Copy Editors
Sandra Manheimer
Marie Dobson

Assistant Editor
Ginny Phelps

Technical Director
Dan Brown

Technical Reviewer
Pavel Vorobiev

Desktop Publisher
Lance Kozlowski

Proofreader
Kortney Trebnik

Indexer
Sharon Hilgenberg

Cover Illustrator
Laura Stalzer

About the Author

Daniel Joshi is a corporate developer for Fortune 500 companies and the managing partner for The Joshi Group (http://www.joshigroup.com), a Microsoft solution provider company. As a Java IDE expert, he was the lead author for *Teach Yourself Café in 21 Days* (Sams). He has also co-authored several best-selling computer books on Java and Web programming. Dan's first book was published when he was 19 and *The Comprehensive Guide to Visual J++* is the fourth book he has written while under the age of 21.

Acknowledgments

I think it is only fair that the foremost acknowledgment goes to Neweleen Trebnik. Her motivation and dedication to "the cause" was truly inspiring. Furthermore, I would like to thank Michelle Nichols, who was graced (or cursed) with a chance to develop my work. And last, but not least, I would like to thank project editor, Jennifer Rowe.

Thanks to Rodney Runolfson, my lunch partner on that insightful day that we were deliberating object-oriented programming, discussed in Chapter 3.

And to my father, whose four degrees and thirty years of focusing on education (and now the Internet) remind me I still have a long way go.

Contents

Introduction .... **xix**

1 Introduction to Java & Visual J++ **1**

What Is Java? 1

Where Did Java Come From? ■ Where Is Java Going?

Real-world Java 4

Applets, Applications & Appletcations ■ Capabilities &
Limitations of Java Applets ■ Examples of Java on the Net

Understanding Java 11

Java Is Based on C & C++ ■ Java Is Multithreaded ■ Java Is
Platform Independent ■ Java Is Secure ■ Java Is Dynamic

Visual J++: A Java IDE 20

Understanding Visual J++ 23

The Developer Studio ■ Developer Studio Wizards ■ The
Integrated Debugger

Creating Your First Java Program Using Visual J++ 27

Writing the Program ■ Building the Program ■ Executing
the Program

2 The Java Language Structure **39**

Keywords 40

Literals 41

Numerical Literals ■ Non-numerical Literals

Primitive Data Types 43

Integers ■ Tutorial: Declaring Data Types ■ Booleans
■ Tutorial: Declaring Boolean Variables ■ Characters
■ Tutorial: Declaring Character Data Types ■ Floating-
points ■ Casting ■ Tutorial: Casting Between Values

Operators 58

Arithmetic Operators ■ Tutorial: Arithmetic Operators
■ Assignment Operators ■ Comparison Operators
■ Tutorial: Comparison Operators ■ Logical Operators
■ Bitwise Operators ■ Tutorial: Bitwise Operators
■ Tutorial: Shifting Bitwise Operators

Operator Precedence 75

Operator Precedence in Algebra ■ Operator Precedence
in Java

Control Flow 77

Diagramming Control Flow ■ The If Conditional ■ Tutorial:
If Conditional ■ The ? Operator ■ The For Loop ■ Tutorial:
For Loop ■ The While & Do While Loop ■ Tutorial: While
Loop ■ The Switch Statement ■ Tutorial: Switch Statement
■ Breaking Out of Loops ■ Tutorial: Break Statement

3 Introduction to Object-Oriented Programming 113

Visual J++ Project Workspaces & Projects 114

The Project Workspace Window ■ Project Workspace Files
■ Organizing Your Project Workspaces ■ Tutorial: Creating
a Project Workspace

Object-oriented Programming 124

Programming, the Way It Used to Be ■ Working With
Objects ■ What Are Objects? ■ Implementing Objects in
Java With Classes ■ Instancing Classes ■ Class Variables
■ Class Methods ■ Method Overloading ■ Tutorial:
Creating Methods & Overloading Them

Complex Data Types 146

Strings ■ Arrays ■ Scope ■ Tutorial: Hiding Variables Using
Scope

More Operator Precedence 154

Inheritance 155

Method Overriding ■ Tutorial: Overriding Methods

Object Casting 168

Modifiers 170

Access Modifiers ■ Class Modifiers

Interfaces 173

4   Introducing Java Applets 179

Working With Applets 180

The Advantages of Applets ■ The Disadvantages of Applets
■ Java Applet Basics ■ The Life-Cycle Methods ■ Importing
Java Classes & Packages

Tutorial: Creating Your First Applet 186

HTML & Applets 200

Providing Alternate Text ■ Specifying the Location of an
Applet ■ Specifying How the Applet Displays

Enhancing Java Applets With Graphics 203

The paint() Method ■ The Graphics Class ■ The Graphics
Coordinate System ■ Fonts ■ Colors

Tutorial: Creating Your Second Applet 210

Viewing Your Applet in Netscape Navigator ■ Viewing Your
Applet in the JDK's AppletViewer

5   Working With Applets & the AppletWizard 219

The java.util Package 219

The Date Class

Introducing the AppletWizard 222

Starting the AppletWizard ■ Step 1 of 5 ■ Step 2 of 5
■ Step 3 of 5 ■ Step 4 of 5 ■ Step 5 of 5 ■ New Project
Information Dialog Box ■ Tutorial: Creating an Applet With
the AppletWizard

Passing Information to Java Programs 242

Passing Arguments (Parameters) to Java Applications ■
Tutorial: Passing Arguments in a Java Applet ■ Tutorial:
Passing Parameters in a Java Applet

Java Appletcations 266

How Are They Different? ■ Tutorial: Creating an
Appletcation in the AppletWizard

Introduction to Debugging in Visual J++ 277

6 Multithreading in Java 289

Review of the Multithreaded OS 290

Tutorial: Creating Your First Multithreaded Java Program 291

Threads 294

Multithreaded Java Programming Techniques 297

Subclassing the Thread Class ■ Tutorial: Subclassing
Threads ■ Implementing the Runnable Interface

Thread Life Cycle 308

The Spawned State ■ The Running State ■ The Blocked
State ■ The Dead State

Related Multithread Topics 314

Thread Priorities ■ Tutorial: Setting Thread Priorities
■ Thread Synchronization ■ Thread Groups ■ Daemon
Threads

7 The User Interface Using the AWT 327

Using the AWT Package 328

Introducing the AWT Components ■ Introducing the
AWT Containers ■ Introducing the AWT Layout Managers
■ Including Components

The AWT Components 332
    Button ■ Canvas ■ Checkbox ■ CheckboxGroup (Radio
    Buttons) ■ Choice (Combo Box) ■ Label ■ List ■ Scrollbar
    ■ TextComponent ■ TextArea

The AWT Containers 355
    Frame ■ Panel ■ Dialog ■ FileDialog ■ Menus

The AWT Layout Managers.. 374
    BorderLayout ■ CardLayout ■ FlowLayout ■ GridLayout
    ■ No Layout Manger

**8   DesigningUser Interfaces With
    the Resource Editors 387**

Introduction to the Resource Editors............................. 388
    The Graphic Resource Editor ■ The Dialog Resource
    Editor ■ Menu Resource Editor

Introducing the Java Resource Wizard 395
    Step 1 of 2 ■ Step 2 of 2 ■ The Confirmation Dialog Box

Tutorial: Developing a User Interface 398
    Understanding the Process ■ Creating the Project
    ■ Creating the Resource ■ Porting the Resource to Java
    ■ Adding the Files to the Project ■ Implementing the UI in
    the Application's Source Code ■ Building & Executing the
    Project

Tutorial: Adding a Menu to Your Java Applications 420
    Creating the Resource ■ Porting the Resource to Java
    ■ Adding the Files to the Project ■ Implementing the Menu
    in the Application's Source Code ■ Building & Executing
    the Project

Tutorial: Developing a UI for a Java Applet 438
    Creating the Project Using the AppletWizard ■ Creating
    the Resource ■ Porting the Resource to Java ■ Adding the
    Files to the Project ■ Implementing the UI in the Applet's
    Source Code ■ Building & Executing the Project

9 Event Handling **459**

How Java Handles Events 459

How the AWT Handles Events 461

Event Handling Techniques 465

The handleEvent() Technique ■ Tutorial: Overriding the
handleEvent() Method ■ Event Types ■ The Supporting
Method Technique

10 Debugging in Visual J++ **513**

Debugging Sessions in Visual J++ 513

Starting a Debugging Session ■ Breakpoints ■ Viewing
Information About Variables & Expressions ■ The Watch
Window ■ The Variables Window ■ The Call Stack Window ■ The Disassembly Window ■ The Exceptions Window ■ The Thread Window ■ Closing a Debugging Session

11 Using Streams to Handle I/O **533**

Understanding Streams 533

The InputStream Class 536

Methods of the InputStream Class ■ The
ByteArrayInputStream Class ■ The FileInputStream
Class ■ The SequenceInputStream Class ■ The
StringBufferInputStream Class ■ The FilterInputStream
Class ■ The PipedInputStream Class

The OutputStream Class 545

Methods of the OutputStream Class ■ The
ByteArrayOutputStream Class ■ The FileOutputStream
Class ■ The FilterOutputStream Class ■ The
PipedOutputStream Class

The File Class 551

GetInfo Methods ■ GetStatus Methods

The RandomAccessFile Class 553

The read() Methods ■ The write() Methods ■ Unique
Methods: seek(), getFilePointer() & length()

The FileDescriptor Class 555

The StreamTokenizer Class 556

java.io Exceptions 556

Tutorial: File I/O ■ Tutorial: ByteArray I/O
■ Tutorial: Data I/O

12 Network Programming 577

Introduction to Networking 577

TCP/IP Basics

Network Programming in Java 584

Communicating With Internet Protocols ■ Tutorial: Using
URLConnection ■ Communicating With the Browser
■ Communicating Between Applets ■ Communicating
With Servers

13 Java Database Connectivity (JDBC) 603

Open Database Connectivity (ODBC) 604

The Architecture of ODBC 605

ODBC API Conformance Levels

The JDBC Architecture 609

The java.sql Package ■ The java.sql Interfaces
■ The java.sql Classes

JDBC Implementation 616

Client-server Computing Using JDBC 618

Advantages & Disadvantages of Using JDBC

Overview of Structure Query Language (SQL) 621

Tutorial: Creating a JDBC Program

14 **Advanced Java Computing** **641**

The Java Virtual Machine (JVM) 642

Understanding Bytecodes 645

The .class File ■ Understanding the Bytecode Verifier

Native Methods 650

What Is a Dynamic Link Library ? ■ Accessing Windows
Native Methods ■ Creating Native Methods

Exception Handling 656

Throwing Java Exceptions ■ Catching Java Exceptions
■ Exceptions Thrown by Different Java Classes
■ Rethrowing Java Exceptions

15 **Using ActiveX With Java** **663**

What is ActiveX? 664

The ActiveX Internet Model ■ ActiveX Controls
■ ActiveX Scripting ■ ActiveX Objects in HTML
■ From ActiveX to BrandX

ActiveX & OLE 674

ActiveX Versus Java 675

ActiveX & COM 678

Why COM? ■ Why You Should Consider Using ActiveX
COM Objects

ActiveX COM Objects & Java 684

Using ActiveX COM Objects With Java Applets
■ Building ActiveX COM Objects in Java

Visual J++ ActiveX Samples 690

Real-world ActiveX on the Net 691

Appendix A About the Companion CD-ROM **699**

Appendix B Source Code Generated by the AppletWizard **701**

Index **719**

Introduction

The Comprehensive Guide to Visual J++ demystifies Java and separates the computer science from computer myth surrounding Java's capabilities, giving readers a clear understanding of the limitations of the Java language. In the past year, Java caught the attention of the development industry on the Internet and enterprise fronts. During that time, Java has received a lot of attention from the media. And, because of this, it is not surprising that a majority of people do not understand Java except through what the media has said about it.

All of this attention has also distorted Java's image. As a result, some assert that Java can do anything, and others say just the opposite. There are also two sides forming on the development front: the ActiveX community claiming that ActiveX is better, and the Java community claiming that Java is better. Both technologies, ActiveX and Java, have strong and weak points in different areas. That is what makes Microsoft's Visual J++ so powerful. Visual J++ gives Java developers a visual environment with which to develop Java programs. These programs are completely compatible with Java programs created using the Java Development Kit (JDK) from JavaSoft. Visual J++ also lets you work with Microsoft's ActiveX technology. ActiveX is an ever changing technology, put forth by Microsoft, that encompasses Object Linking and Embedding (OLE) funcationlity, among other things; however, it is focused specifically for the Net. In short, Visual J++ is one of the first products that seeks to bridge ActiveX and Java. Thus, Visual J++ is a unique product because it gives you the ability to utilize the best of both technologies.

There is no doubt about it, as long as the Internet is around, Java and ActiveX are here to stay. With Visual J++, at least these two technologies can get along. We only hope that the same will be true for the developers using them.

Who Needs This Book?

The Comprehensive Guide to Visual J++ gives a complete overview of Visual J++ along with useful tips. Please note that this book does not require you to have any prior Java programming experience.

You are among those who will find this book valuable if:

- You are a Java developer using the Java Development Kit, but you want to learn about Microsoft's Visual J++ to increase your productivity.

- You're an ActiveX developer interested in learning about Microsoft's Visual J++ and how using Java with Visual J++ can give you better ActiveX solutions.

- You have prior development experience in an older language, and you want to learn how to program in Java.

- You have experience programming in C or C++ or you have worked with Visual C++, and you are looking for an easy migration to Java and Visual J++.

The major shortcoming of books dealing with Java in the past is that they employed the Java Development Kit (JDK) and a text editor as their primary means of creating functional Java applets and applications. *The Comprehensive Guide to Visual J++* simplifies the process of creating real Java applets and applications, because it shows you how to use Visual J++ as your primary development environment.

In summary, *The Comprehensive Guide to Visual J++* painstakingly goes through all of the tips and techniques that will transform you into a serious Java developer. At the same time, it gives you hands-on experience with Microsoft Visual J++.

What's Inside?

The Comprehensive Guide to Visual J++ can basically be divided into three sections. The first is an introduction to the Java programming language and the Visual J++ environment. The second delves into programming techniques and capabilities of Java. And the last section introduces ActiveX as a technology and shows how to use ActiveX and Java as one solution with Visual J++.

Here is a profile of the material covered:

Chapter 1, "Introduction to Java & Visual J++": This chapter is designed to get your feet wet with Visual J++ and Java. It also covers the Java industry as a whole, highlighting the advantages of Java and dispelling some of the major myths.

Chapter 2, "The Java Language Structure": This is a very detailed chapter that goes over literals, primitive data types, and control flow structures of the Java programming language. All of the examples created in this chapter are compiled and tested in the Visual J++ environment.

Chapter 3, "Introduction to Object-Oriented Programming": This chapter provides a complete overview of object-oriented programming in Java and the object-oriented tools in Visual J++. From the very beginning, this chapter assumes that the reader knows nothing about objects. The chapter builds the foundation of knowledge necessary to create real-world, object-based Java applets and applications.

Chapter 4, "Introducing Java Applets": This chapter covers the Java applet model and useful applet programming techniques.

Chapter 5, "Working With Applets & the AppletWizard": Chapter 5 gives a detailed overview of the Visual J++ Applet-Wizard. This chapter also documents how to pass parameters to your Java applets or arguments to your Java applications. Finally, the chapter ends with an introduction to debugging, including a real-world Java program that has jury-rigged errors. The chapter then uses these jury-rigged examples, going through the step-by-step logic of a programmer, to show how to find and remove bugs using Visual J++.

Chapter 6, "Multithreading in Java": This chapter discusses all of the finer points of a multithreaded application on a modern operating system. Then, it moves to the real world, showing how to take full advantage of all the capabilities of Visual J++ and its wizards to create multithreaded Java applets and applications. Also included in this chapter are topics such as animations and optimization techniques inside of the Java language.

Chapter 7, "Understanding the Abstract Window Toolkit": In this chapter, there is a detailed overview of all of the components and their capabilities for creating a user interface in the Java class library.

Chapter 8, "Designing User Interfaces With the Resource Editors": Chapter 8 complements Chapter 7 in that it discusses how to design a user interface. However, this chapter shows how you can take advantage of several resource editors in Visual J++ to have the user interface automatically generated for you.

Chapter 9, "Event Handling": In this chapter, you learn how Java handles and catches events to make your program's user responsive. This also includes several of the most useful event handling programming techniques that you can implement in your Java programs.

Chapter 10, "Debugging in Visual J++": A very powerful chapter that discusses how to debug Java applets and applications in Visual J++. Note, this chapter also works with all of the debugging tools available in Visual J++.

Chapter 11, "Using Streams to Handle I/O": This chapter gives a comprehensive overview of how streams work in computers, why you need to know how to use streams, and real-world solutions that implement streams. This chapter also includes several tutorials, giving you a chance to read and write various types of data to a specified file.

Chapter 12, "Network Programming in Java": A complete chapter on all of the ways Java can network, this is a detailed discussion of some quick networking solutions and low-level socket programming, complete with an introduction to TCP/IP. Also included are other networking-related topics like interapplet communication and applet communication with the client's browser and the Net.

Chapter 13, "Java Database Connectivity (JDBC)": This chapter gives an introduction to the Java Database Connectivity (JDBC) API, highlighting strengths and weaknesses of the JDBC. Also included is a real-world Visual J++ project showing you how to use Java as your front end, and how to use the JDBC to connect to a SQL database on the back end.

Chapter 14, "Advanced Java Computing": A high-powered chapter exploring some less used, or very complex topics on Java. These topics include a detailed overview of bytecodes, advanced exception handling, and the implementation of native methods.

Chapter 15, "Using ActiveX With Java": This is a complete overview of ActiveX, how it relates to Java, and where Visual J++ fits in. It starts from the ground up, citing real-world examples and introducing development tools.

About the Companion CD-ROM

The companion CD-ROM included with this book contains all of the tutorials in the form of Visual J++ projects, thus giving you the ability to access all the examples directly from Visual J++. Smaller projects are in the msdev\projects directory, and larger projects have their own subdirectory off msdev\projects.

Hardware and Software Requirements

Visual J++ can be used on any system that currently supports Windows 95 or Windows NT 4.0. Note that this book is based on the full version of Visual J++ and not on any shareware versions that may become available.

Online Updates

As we all know, the Internet is constantly changing. As hard as we've tried to make our information current, the truth is that new sites will come online as soon as this book goes to press (and continually thereafter). Ventana provides an excellent way to tackle this problem and to keep the information in this book up-to-date: *The Comprehensive Guide to Visual J++ Online Updates.* You can access this valuable resource via Ventana's World Wide Web site at http://www.vmedia.com/updates.html. Once there, you'll find updated material relevant to *The Comprehensive Guide to Visual J++.*

Moving On

Some people are content to be tossed in the sea of hype regarding Java. Those who want to know what Java is really all about will get the most benefit out of this book. They will learn all about the great and not-so-great features of Java.

Visual J++ has revolutionized the Java industry. With a software giant like Microsoft embracing the Java language and releasing a very powerful development environment like Visual J++, Java has been reinvented yet again. And from this point forward, there is no turning back.

Introduction to Java & Visual J++

In this chapter you will receive a complete introduction to Java, including a formal definition of the Java language, where to find Java on the Net, and how Microsoft Visual J++ enlightens Java's future. First laying a foundation for Java, the chapter then turns specifically toward Visual J++, discussing its features and ending with a real-life example of building a Java program in Visual J++.

What Is Java?

Java is an *object-oriented* programming language. Object-oriented means that Java organizes its programs into a collection of objects. This is certainly not unique to Java; other programming languages like SmallTalk and C++ have been facilitating the use of object orientation in their language structure for years. However, Java does have the advantage of being easier to understand (particularly when compared to C or C++).

Java is modeled after the C++ programming language, which is very robust. C++ is used widely as the primary programming language for application development. Applications developed for environments ranging from UNIX to Macintosh to Windows all use one form of C++. The problem is that, at the linguistic and binary level, C++ is not easily portable across each of these platforms. Each of the operating systems mentioned above (and many others not mentioned) uses C++, but each uses it in a different way. This means that anytime you hop between platforms you have to rewrite the program and recompile it using a compiler specific to the environment you wish to run on. Sound complex? It is. Java, however, does not have these limitations; it is modeled with the robustness of C++ but inherently designed to be completely portable over many different platforms.

Aside from being platform-independent, Java is also easy to use. In fact, Java is very easy to learn—especially when compared to other languages like C++, SmallTalk, and Visual Basic. Java enhances the strengths of C++ and removes its overly complex parts.

The most intimidating part of Java to a programmer coming from older, nonobject-based programming languages (like Pascal and Visual Basic) is the fact that Java is object-oriented. Objects, not used in C, Visual Basic, and a host of scripting languages for the Net, can pose a threateningly complex way to organize programs. Nevertheless, objects are the future of programming, and once you learn to use one object-oriented language, you will find it easier to learn other object-oriented languages.

Where Did Java Come From?

In 1991, Sun Microsystems created a programming language that was known as Oak (named after a tree outside of the window of James Gosling, one of the language's most notable curators). That language, which we now call Java, was extremely portable and small, making it a perfect programming language to design software for portable electronic devices such as Personal Digital Assistants (PDAs) and television sets. While the Oak language was a revolutionary idea at the time, it didn't gain much acceptance in the consumer electronics industry.

It was not until the spring of 1995 that Java took hold. At that time, HotJava, the first Java-compliant browser written in the Java language, became available to the public. HotJava was designed to port the use of Java to the Internet by using a special type of Java application, known as an *applet*. Applets are a perfect fit to take advantage of Java's powerful and portable capabilities. It was not until the release of HotJava that Java broke into the Internet, gained public acceptance, and received endorsement by the top software and hardware companies in the industry. Today HotJava is not the only Internet browser to support Java applets. Giants in the Internet browser industry such as Netscape Navigator (as of version 2.0) and Microsoft's Internet Explorer (as of version 3.0) give users the ability to see Java applets or other Java-related technologies.

Other Flavors of Java

Java now comes in many flavors on the Net besides applets. The most notable is the JavaScript language (developed by Netscape), which is an object-based scripting language derived from Java. Because JavaScript provides more browser hooks, it acts as an enhancement to the HTML language.

Where Is Java Going?

Java has not been around for very long, but in the time since it was officially released, it has opened many doors. Last summer, Java moved forward with a full set of APIs (Application Programming Interfaces), known as the JDB, letting Java applets and applications interact with a SQL database

Since then, there have been two new sets of APIs: a set dealing with Java Electronic Commerce, letting Java have full transaction-based electronic commerce with which developers can work; and another set called Jeeves, which specifically deals with Java as a set of network-server APIs.

Other new technologies that spun off from Java are Integrated Development Environments (IDEs), specifically made for Java.

These are Windows-based programs that let you visually build and compile Java applets and applications. Modern Java IDEs also let you view your Java programs with object-viewer-type tools. There must be at least 30 Java IDEs available both commercially and over the Internet.

Visual J++ is Microsoft's version of an IDE for Java. Visual J++ is similar to any other Java-based IDE, except for the fact that it combines some of the enhanced capabilities of Java with a technology known as ActiveX. ActiveX is Microsoft's Internet development toolkit. This provides Visual J++ with a whole suite of Internet enabled technologies all based on Microsoft's original Object Linking and Embedding (OLE) theme. Before the announcement of Visual J++ (formerly known as Jakarta), Microsoft had not embraced the Java language.

As you go through this book, you will learn that Visual J++ lets you take the best of both worlds (ActiveX and Java) and use them to create one single Internet solution. Visual J++ takes much of the fear out of learning Java: with wizards, a visual development and integrated debugging environment, and online help at your fingertips, Java development has never been easier.

Real-world Java

In the beginning, people noting Java's rigid applet security model contested that although Java looks great in theory, it is impractical in the real world. However, now that Java has been out for some time, it has proven to be a very useful real-world solution for development problems. Furthermore, in the time that Java has been out, there have been many improvements to the Java language. Today, many companies endorse the use of Java for professional application development. The Internet development community has embraced it as a very important and practical tool for Java development, and the Net uses it for its programming problems as well. Let's look a little more closely at what types of Java are available.

Applets, Applications & Appletcations

The Java language has defined itself to have two different types of application formats: the applet and the application.

Naming Conventions for Java Programs

In Java, there is a naming convention for the type of software that you create. An applet represents the portable and Internet-enabled type of Java software. An application represents the more traditional Java software that follows the same paradigm as a C++ application. An *appletcation* means that your Java software can behave either as an applet or an application, depending on its host environment. Finally, you use the term "program" when you want to reference applets, applications, and appletcations all at the same time.

In Java, an applet is a special type of Java program. Applets are unique because HTML pages can call them. Applets have a different structure of invoking actions, based on various points in something known as the applet life. Various actions take place in an applet based upon a life-cycle model. Applets are designed to be much more secure than traditional applications, to ensure that they do can not pose a security risk to the Net.

Java applications are the more traditional Java programs in the sense that applications are similar to the programs you create using other programming languages. Java applications have fewer security restrictions than their applet counterparts, but applications are not accessible directly from the Internet.

Appletcations are a unique blend, creating a sort of half-breed between applets and applications. In this case, a Java program can be an applet or an application, depending on where it is invoked. Note that appletcations are merely programming techniques and do not change any of the definitions for applets and applications that you have just read about.

For most, the term application is very familiar. All types of programming languages (in particular C/C++) use a very similar application model. Conversely, the invention of the applet is unique to the Java language and probably not as well understood. So, the next section delves a little deeper into the inner anatomy and workings of Java applets.

Capabilities & Limitations of Java Applets

One of the biggest reasons behind the creation of the Java applet model stems from the fact that Java is so powerful. Such a powerful language, if used with malicious intent, could be potentially dangerous to its client's environment (the Web browser's hosting environment). To protect the client's system, the applet design is self-limiting. Furthermore, most Internet browsers also exercise increased security on Java applets to ensure that no harm—intentional or otherwise—can result from a Java applet. However, there is one major problem with all of this security—lack of versatility.

This leads to one of the ongoing debates in the Java industry over the security restrictions imposed on the Java applet. The Internet, an open-ended and potentially unsafe environment, requires Java to have a way to protect itself and anyone using it. Because the Java applet is self-contained, self-limiting, and self-verified, it cannot be susceptible to "the Trojan Horse attack" (where malicious code is hidden inside) or to the coder who tries to attach malicious code to the applet in transit to the client's environment.

In other words, the restrictions imposed to protect the client, limit the versatility of the applet and its ability to do useful things. In the end, the Java creators have erred on the side of conservatism. Also, most of the Java developers are content with this very conservative picture of the applet security model. A few developers do complain that Java is just "too secure" and thus too self-limiting. These people are certainly in the minority. After all, which would you rather have—an overly protective applet or hordes of angry users?

Examples of Java on the Net

On the Net it is very easy to spot Java applets. A number of these applets on the Net are shareware or freeware, which you can download and use on your own site. One of the very powerful features of Java is that, when dealing with already existing applets, you do not need any programming experience to use the applet in your pre-existing environment.

If you want to become a master of the Java language, then eventually you are going to need to roll up your sleeves and actually write some code. The following sections deal with a few sites totally involved with Java in one way or another, starting with the JavaSoft home page.

JavaSoft Home Page

If you want to know more about Java or if you want to stay on top of the latest Java breakthroughs, the best place to start is with the JavaSoft site. JavaSoft (http://www.javasoft.com) is part of the parent company, Sun Microsystems, but is specifically geared to manage all of the Java products for Sun. Not only can you find out information on the latest Java news, but you can download technical documentation for Java-related topics.

At JavaSoft you can also download the HotJava browser and the Java Development Kit (JDK). Figure 1-1 shows the JavaSoft main page.

Note

The JDK is the first tool to let you develop Java programs, but it is decidedly not user-friendly and relies on a proprietary text editor.

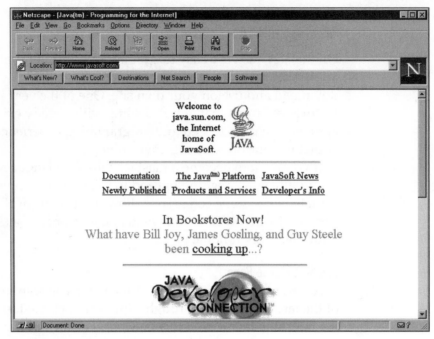

Figure 1-1: The JavaSoft site.

The GameLan Site

Another place to look for Java is the GameLan (pronounced "Gamma-Lahn") site. The GameLan site (http://www.gamelan.com) keeps a working directory of real-world Java applets and real-world JavaScript examples. The GameLan site, shown in Figure 1-2, is continually being updated and should be checked on a regular basis.

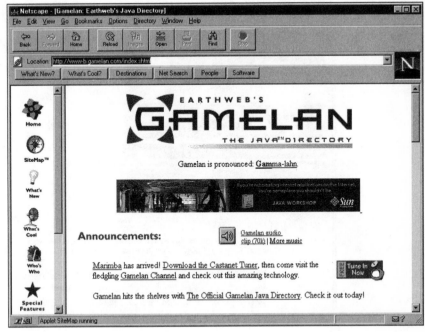

Figure 1-2: The GameLan site.

The Java Applet Rating Service

Another site that is very interesting and important to the Java community is the Java Applet Rating Service (JARS) site. The JARS site (http://www.jars.com) houses a list of the most outstanding Java applets published on the Internet. Each applet submitted for review receives a rating for various qualities (creativity, functionality, etc.) and receives a score. Based on the score, the applet receives a rating and is categorized by percentages (i.e., the top 1 percent represents the highest ranking). This site is probably one of the most useful in giving you immediate access to the absolutely best and coolest applets on the Net (see Figure 1-3).

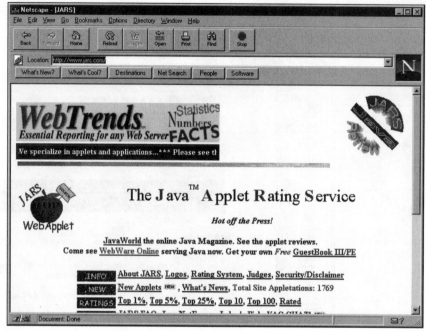

Figure 1-3: The Java Applet Rating Service (JARS) site.

JavaWorld

JavaWorld is actually an online magazine completely dedicated to Java. This site (http://www.javaworld.com) contains all of the components of a traditional magazine, such as press releases and articles. Most importantly, JavaWorld focuses heavily on Java programming, with articles on real-world programming techniques and overviews of new technologies and development products (see Figure 1-4). JavaWorld is definitely worth subscribing to.

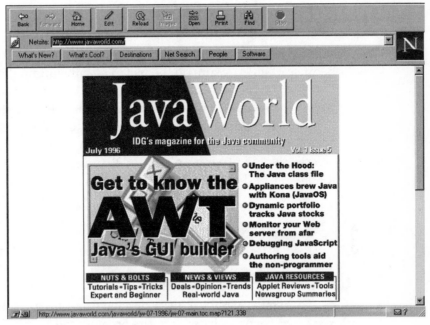

Figure 1-4: The JavaWorld site.

Understanding Java

Java is all over the Net. Java is all over the media. Java is being integrated into just about every Internet browser and every major C++ development environment. The next version of Windows 95 and Windows NT are going to have integrated Java support.

Knowing that Java is hot and understanding the key points that make Java so useful are two different topics. While the first part of this chapter told you the former, the following sections give you an understanding of some key points that make Java so powerful.

Java Is Based on C & C++

Most of the general public has a vague understanding of Java because of its exposure on the Net. Notwithstanding, it is safe to say that just about everyone outside of the development community has no idea what C or C++ even stands for. C++ and its predecessor C are programming languages (like Java). C is the structured programming language and C++ is an extension of C, adding an object-oriented programming model. C and C++ have been around for a while and are very important in the development community.

C and C++'s Usefulness in the Real World

The C/C++ language is the primary development language responsible for almost every Windows-based software program and it is also the language used to write the Windows 95 and NT operating systems.

Java is based on C++, but is specifically designed to be easier to use. Let's take a closer look at the similarities and differences between these two languages:

■ One of the more complex and potentially dangerous parts of C and C++, no longer supported in Java, is pointers.

Pointers

A pointer is a variable that contains the address (i.e., memory location) of another variable. Pointers can "point" to variables that contain data; also, it is not impossible for a pointer to "point" to another pointer.

Pointers are very powerful and useful tools; however, they are also extremely difficult to understand. Furthermore, pointers are major contributing factors to bugs in software. This is why Java does not support the direct use of pointers.

- In C and C++ you can have functions that stand on their own. Java, however, requires that every function be attached to a class. (Methods are the closest equivalent to functions in Java.)

- Other C/C++ items such as inline, typedef, enum, unions, and structures have also been removed.

- Object-oriented technologies such as multiple inheritance, found in C++, have been removed in creating the Java language. Chapter 3 discusses inheritance in further detail. The important thing to note is that multiple inheritance, while more versatile than single inheritance (which is what Java currently supports), can cause programs to become overcomplicated.

- Java does not support the use of templates.

- Java also does not support the preprocessor model used in C and C++, and Java does not have a const keyword.

Templates in C++

In C++ a *template* is a generic function that houses the overall framework for a set of similar functions, leaving it to the compiler to decide exactly which implementation of this generic function to use.

While this section covered at a high level just about every major discrepancy, you will learn more details about the differences and similarities between C/C++ and Java in Chapter 2.

Java Is Multithreaded

Many of you may have heard the statement "Java is multithreaded" thrown around in the past year. Its multithreaded nature has proven to be one of the strongest legs behind Java's success. Programming with threads is a very powerful programming technique, which can benefit almost any program you write. However, in order to understand and use threads effectively in your programs, you need to have at least an intuitive grasp of the concept behind multithreaded operating systems.

32-Bit Multithreaded Operating Systems

32-bit operating systems (OS) represent the current model for a modern operating system in the sense that it is able to have multiple threads running concurrently. Java is inherently designed to use multiple threads (even if you do not explicitly use them in your program) so it can only run on multithreaded operating systems. A number of 32-bit operating systems are on the market; however, our discussion will be limited to Windows 95 and Windows NT (an exemplar of the 32-bit operating system).

Windows 95 Versus Windows NT

Windows 95 and Windows NT look very similar on the outside. However, most of the differences between these two operating systems are on the interior architecture rather than the exterior user interface.

Window 95 is a 32-bit operating system hybrid, or half-breed, because Windows 95 works as a 32-bit operating system when programs running on it are also 32-bit. Unlike Windows NT, however, it reverts back to a 16-bit model when it is working with 16-bit programs. The idea behind Windows 95 is to make it a 32-bit operating system for today's programs, but retain a fully backward-compatible design for older programs. While most 16-bit programs work in Windows NT, that is most certainly not always the case.

Java Support for Windows 3.1x?

Windows 3.1x is an older 16-bit, single-thread operating system. Currently, there is no Java support for 16-bit operating systems, primarily because Java needs a multithread, 32-bit operating system like Windows 95 and NT. However, IBM has announced that it is going to provide a Windows 3.1 plug-in, enabling Java support.

On a 32-bit operating system, when you start a program, you are effectively creating a *process*. Process is the technical term for a program loaded into memory and prepared for further execution.

The process contains the code from the program. Each process starts with a single thread, but additional, independently executing threads can be created. Each thread works as an independent entity, and can be created and destroyed without ending the parent process (i.e., the program). Processes can create threads and threads can create threads; but, threads cannot create processes. The beauty of multithreaded operating systems comes into play when you realize that all of these threads can execute at the same time.

Multithreaded operating systems help create a better environment to develop in because they allow you to have more than one thread executing at a time. Thus, you can have more than one program executing at the same time, and you can have one program doing more than one thing at the same time as well.

Realistically, on a single-processor system, a 32-bit operating system only gives the illusion that more than one thread is executing at one time. It is only on Symmetric Multiprocessing Systems (SMP) that true multitasking at the processor level is taking place. On a single processor, the CPU cannot work with more than one thread at a time. What happens is that each of the active threads receives a slice (usually an extremely small amount) of CPU time and the available threads take turns.

Note

On the Windows NT environment, the time-slice quantum is approximately 20 milliseconds.

Think of it as a string of lights, where each bulb is a thread. Each of these bulbs lights up, one after the other, with only one bulb truly lit at any one point in time. Moreover, these lights are blinking so fast and continually looping so that to the human eye it looks like all the lights are on at the same time. Figure 1-5 shows a drawing of how several threads are sharing time and resources on a single machine.

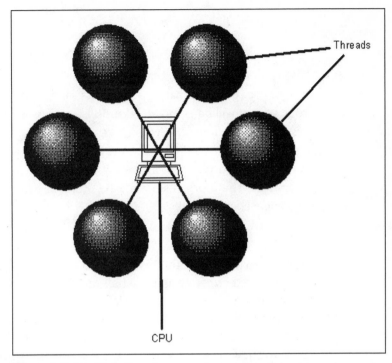

Figure 1-5: Multiple threads on a uni-processor system.

Key Features of Multithreaded Environments

Now, if multithreaded operating systems were just this simple, they might even be easy to understand. However, two key features of multithread systems need further discussion:

- **Preemptive multitasking** is the ability of the operating system (also known as the kernel) to interrupt a thread and assign the CPU to another waiting thread. Note that in certain situations this is not always possible.

  However, let's imagine that we are running a Windows NT box with Microsoft Word and Microsoft Excel loaded. In the middle of a long, CPU-intensive process in Excel, you (the user) get bored and switch over to Word. In this scenario, you can effectively preempt the thread currently running (which is Excel) and give it to a thread that belongs to Word. This is why the modern desktop stays responsive, so to speak.

Unresponsiveness on 32-Bit Operating Systems

Even with all of this resource sharing and multitasking, there is no guarantee that your system will be completely responsive. One reason could be that your system does not have enough resources (e.g., enough RAM, CPU power, etc.) or that you have too many programs open. Technically, this is a function of the number of threads running and the amount of resources available. The more resources, the more threads that can run without becoming encumbered.

■ **Thread priorities** is the last thing to mention here. When a program executes, it usually has several threads executing. Each thread is responsible for a specific task. For example, one thread handles mouse events and has a high priority; that way, it gets immediate attention from the CPU when it asks for it. This helps ensure that the mouse is not unresponsive every time a user starts a task that hogs CPU time.

Java Is Platform Independent

One of the really powerful features of the Java language is that it is platform independent. This means that Java programs port across different operating systems. You do not even need to reconfigure your Java applets at a high level to have them move from one environment to another. Java takes care of everything.

Note

Java is architecture neutral. This is a more technical term for platform independence, meaning that Java is 100 percent portable between platforms

Some critics have contested that Java's platform independence is useless because the operating system that dominates the market share is Windows. However, the truth of the matter is Java's platform independence improves its versatility. Moreover, Java's platform independence is perfect for the heterogeneous nature of the Net.

Java Is Secure

The technology that makes Java secure is *bytecodes*. Bytecodes are similar to machine language instructions. However, bytecodes are not specific to one particular machine environment.

Bytecodes give you the ability to verify your Java programs, assuring that when the program downloads from the Net to the client's environment, that it was not changed, distorted, or tampered with in transit.

Java Is Dynamic

Java is dynamic in the sense that it is garbage collected. In C/C++, you are responsible for memory management. Because Java does memory management automatically (unlike C++), Java alleviates the idea of *memory leaks* in its programs.

Memory leaks occur when a program takes free memory from the environment to construct its objects as it starts. Throughout the life of the program, it is creating and destroying many objects, thereby taking and freeing memory. Finally, the program quits releasing all the memory it used to the user's environment. This only happens to a perfect program that was able to keep track of every piece of used memory. All of the objects constructed need to be destroyed for all of the memory taken for the program to be released into the environment.

However, in the real world, perfect memory management is not always going to happen. In many cases, the program does not clean up after itself upon leaving the user's environment, and this results in poor memory management. The key difference between Java and C++ is that in C++ it is up to the programmer to keep track of the allocation of memory used for objects constructed. It is also up to the programmer to make sure his or her program releases memory that is no longer used by the program. The larger and more complex the program, the more room for errors in memory management. Memory leaks are a very real part of a program and occur eventually.

In C++ you have to keep track of all the objects you create and make sure that they are all properly destroyed; however, this is not so in Java. Java takes care of all the memory operations. It is really that simple.

Visual J++: A Java IDE

Throughout most of this chapter, the topics discussed have been based strictly on the Java language and not on Microsoft's Visual J++ in particular. That is because everything mentioned is not specific to Visual J++, but Visual J++ retains and uses every part of Java. So where does Microsoft's Visual J++ fit in? Visual J++ is a Java Integrated Development Environment (IDE). Visual J++ is not the first, nor is it the only, visual environment created solely for the development of Java programs. You will learn later on that Visual J++ does have some unique features that enable it to go beyond traditional Java IDEs.

Starting from the beginning, the JDK was the first tool made available for Java development. Not only can you create Java applets with the JDK, you can also create full-fledged Java applications (similar to those that you may have seen with C++). The JDK is also a free product, available directly from the JavaSoft site (http://www.javasoft.com). However, the JDK is by no means an easy or modern environment in which to develop Java solutions

The JDK is merely a set of command-line executables that you use to build, document, and debug your Java code. The JDK is also responsible for some of the media behind the statement "Java is hard to learn." Most of the people uttering that statement do so because they are using the JDK as their primary development tool.

Furthermore, the JDK requires the use of a proprietary third-party text editor (usually a word processor or text editor like Notepad) to author all your source code. This is very intimidating and creates an unsophisticated environment to develop Java solutions with. This is not the modern way to develop applications within any language. Why would anyone want to use the JDK to begin with? Well, it is free, and, in the beginning, it was the only development tool available specifically for the Java language.

However, not too long ago, the Java development industry made a big turn. The software development industry recognized that the JDK was not a practical tool, and companies like Borland, Symantec, and IBM each came out with an IDE for Java. An IDE basically takes all of the tools in the JDK and has them all work together as one big program utilizing one visual interface.

Figure 1-6 shows an example of a Java IDE. There are probably more than 30 IDEs for the Java language.

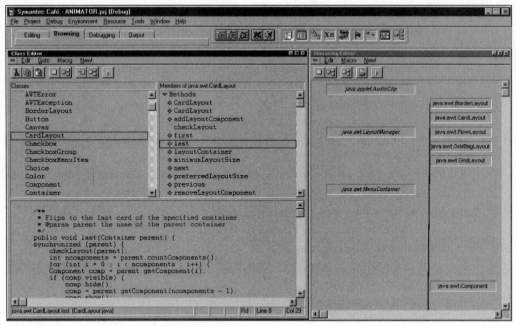

Figure 1-6: A Java Integrated Development Environment (IDE) called Symantec Café.

Visual J++ is a fully enabled Java IDE, containing all of the accessories that are common to any Java IDE. Plus, Visual J++ provides even more enhanced capabilities for using a development environment with which many developers (especially those using Visual C++) may already be familiar. Furthermore, Visual J++ gives you the ability to build ActiveX components from your Java programs, a procedure discussed in further detail in Chapter 14. Figure 1-7 shows an example of what Visual J++ looks like.

Figure 1-7: The Developer Studio in Visual J++.

In summary, Visual J++ gives you everything a professional IDE on Java would give you, and it contains several enhancements that are completely unique.

Understanding Visual J++

Visual J++, designed specifically for Java development, lets you create Java applets, applications, and appletcations. There are no proprietary tools or capabilities that Visual J++ uses to make your Java solutions any less versatile; nor does using Visual J++ encumber the platform-independent model described earlier. Visual J++

does contain some added tools to link to ActiveX that do not hamper Visual J++ as a Java development environment, including Developer Studio, Microsoft wizards, and an integrated debugger.

The Developer Studio

The Microsoft Developer Studio is the development environment for several other Microsoft development products. The Developer Studio is where you code your programs, invoke any wizards or help files, and debug or compile your projects. The Developer Studio used in Visual J++ is exactly the same as the one used in Microsoft Visual C++, Microsoft Visual SourceSafe, Microsoft Visual Test, Microsoft Development Library, and Microsoft Fortran PowerStation. Because the environment was kept the same, anyone who has used any of the previously mentioned products will immediately be comfortable with Visual J++.

Developer Studio Wizards

One of the more powerful features that a Java IDE like Visual J++ has over the older JDK is that it contains wizards.

Wizards

Wizards are miniprograms that are a part of Visual J++ specifically designed to simplify a complex or time-consuming process. Wizards give users a step-by-step set of options, and once they have finished taking input from the user, they perform the task based on the user's input.

Wizards take a fairly complex or time-consuming process, simplify it by merely asking the user for a few pieces of input in a step-by-step format, and then perform the task. Visual J++ contains one very powerful wizard called the AppletWizard, which is used extensively throughout this book. Figure 1-8 shows an example of the AppletWizard.

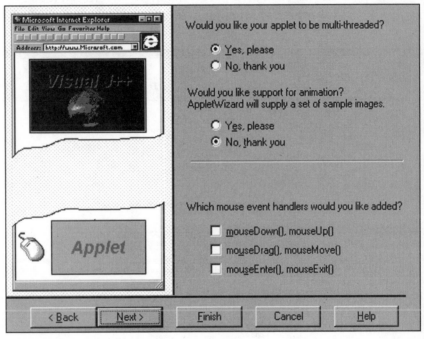

Figure 1-8: Microsoft Visual J++'s AppletWizard.

The Integrated Debugger

The Developer Studio for Visual J++ offers an integrated debugging environment in which you can choose to either debug your Java applets or applications in a debugging session or during execution. This provides an integrated way to create, test, and debug your Java programs more effectively. (See Figure 1-9 for an example of Visual J++'s integrated debugger.)

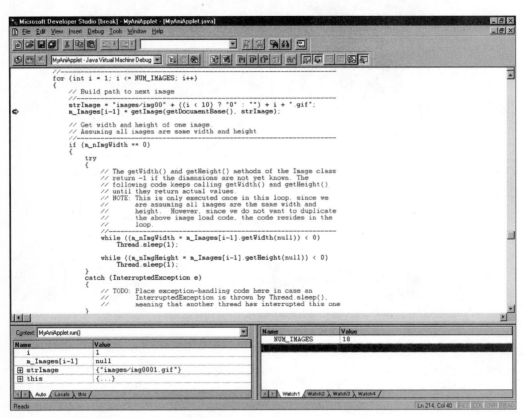

Figure 1-9: The Visual J++ integrated debugger.

The integrated debugger has several attractive features:

- You can specify breakpoints and step into or over a method.
- The debugger supports debugging sessions with exceptions.

- It provides a complete suite of tools that give you the ability to view variables and objects.

- You can trace and view all of the methods called by your Java program.

- Using the suite of dialog-based debugging tools, you can view individual threads, among other things.

Exceptions

Exception Handling is a method of programming by which you can programmatically set a net to catch a particular error. You will learn more about this in Chapter 14. Unlike many modern Java debuggers, Visual J++ supports the debugging of exceptions.

Creating Your First Java Program Using Visual J++

For a moment, let's leave the theoretical world behind and get our hands dirty with Visual J++ by creating a very simple Java program in Visual J++.

To create any program in Visual J++, follow these three simple steps:

1. Write the program. (Later on you will learn tips and tricks to let Visual J++ write parts of your programs for you.)

2. Compile or build the code into an executable format.

3. Execute the program.

Let's start by launching the Visual J++ environment for the first time. Do this by going to the Start menu, and, in the Visual J++ 1.0 folder, click on the Microsoft Developer Studio icon. Once the Developer Studio has successfully loaded, you will see something similar to Figure 1-10.

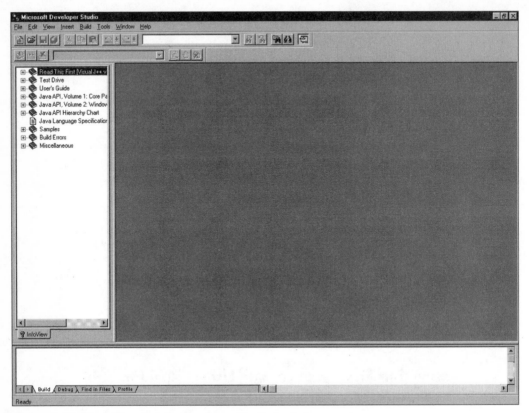

Figure 1-10: Visual J++ and the Developer Studio loaded.

Writing the Program

The example you are going to create, Welcome.java, is not discussed technically because you have not been introduced to the Java language structure yet. However, on a general level, Welcome.java is a console-based Java application that displays "Welcome to VJ++!" on the screen. At this point, Welcome.java gives you an introduction to working in Visual J++ and building your first Java program. Refer to Chapter 2 for information on the Java language.

Once you have loaded the Developer Studio, you are ready to begin developing. On the main menu bar in the Developer Studio, click on File I New.

When you click on New, a dialog box appears asking you what type of file you wish to create. At this point, click on the Text File item in the list box so that the Developer Studio can create a clean text file (see Figure 1-11).

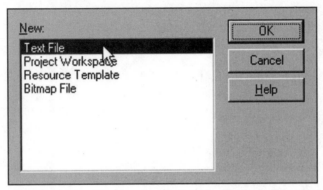

Figure 1-11: The New dialog box.

Note

If you have other development products that use the Developer Studio, your list shows more (or fewer) items than those shown in Figure 1-11.

Once you have clicked on the Text File item in the list box, click OK, and the Developer Studio loads a fresh text file in the Text Editor window (see Figure 1-12).

Figure 1-12: A new text file in the Developer Studio.

The Text Editor window is the large, right window pane in the Developer Studio (see Figure 1-12). You write and review all of the code in your Java programs in this window. On the right is the project workspace window that gives you a high level view of your project, files contained in your project, and a comprehensive set of online documentation for Java and Visual J++.

In the Text Editor window, type the following code:

```
class Welcome {

    public static void main(String argv[]) {
        // Print out the information
```

```
        System.out.println("");
        System.out.println("Welcome to VJ++!");
    }
}
```

Make sure that you have typed the code exactly as shown because it is crucial for the success of your example. Now, save the file by clicking on File | Save. The standard Save As dialog box appears, asking you what file type you want to save it as and where to save it. You should save the file as a text file called Welcome.java and put it in your ..\msdev\projects directory (see Figure 1-13).

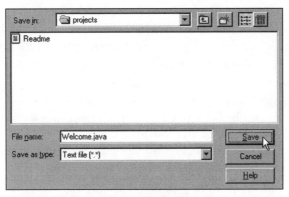

Figure 1-13: Saving Welcome.java.

Building the Program

Once you successfully save the file, you are ready for the next step in the development process: building the project. To do this, open the Build menu on the main menu bar and click on the Build item.

Colors in the Text Editor Window

Notice that when you saved your text file as Welcome.java, several parts of your program changed colors. This is part of the visual editing experience in Visual J++. Once you saved your file with the .java extension, the Developer Studio recognized it as a Java source code file and adjusted it accordingly. All of the blue parts of the code represent reserved keywords in the Java language. All code in green represents comments and are ignored by Visual J++.

You are then prompted to create a default active workspace (see Figure 1-14). Building a project workspace helps you organize your Java programs into projects that can be opened and closed. In Visual J++, you must have a project workspace open (or active) before you can build any of your Java programs. Click on Yes, as shown in Figure 1-14, to continue.

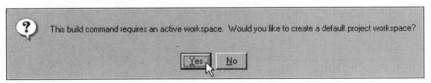

Figure 1-14: Creating a default project workspace.

Project Workspaces

When working with the Developer Studio in Visual J++, you always need to have an active workspace open in order to build your Java programs. Project workspaces help organize your Java programs more efficiently because you can link several source code files (i.e., files with a .java extension) to them before continuing. Unless you are creating a default project workspace, Visual J++ will put your project into a directory along with any other files that are specific to that project.

You can also create a project by going to the main menu bar and clicking on File menu and the New item. There, the dialog box shown in Figure 1-11 appears, and from it you can click on the Project Workspace item in the list box to create a new project.

Once you have successfully created a default project, Visual J++ automatically builds the project. For more information on Visual J++ projects and project workspaces reference Chapter 3. In the Output Window (the bottom window in Visual J++), you will be able to see the results of your build. If there are errors, it lists them with information regarding the nature of the error. However, in this case, if you typed everything in correctly, you see something similar to Figure 1-15.

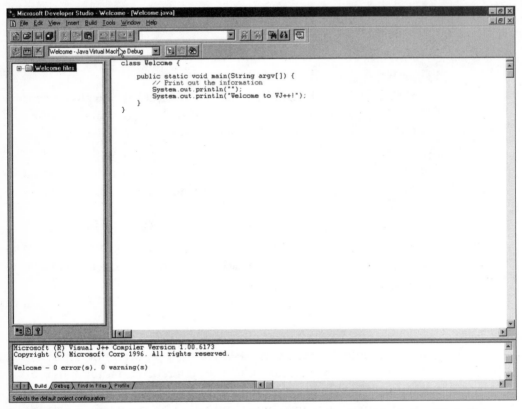

Figure 1-15: Building the project and viewing its progress in the Output window (the bottom window pane).

Naming Convention for Menu Items

When referencing a menu item during the remainder of this book, we will use the following naming convention: instead of using the statement "click on the File menu on the main menu bar, and the New menu item," we will write, "click on File|New."

Executing the Program

Now, to run the project, click on Build | Execute on the main menu bar. Since this is the first time you are attempting to execute this project, a dialog box appears asking you for more information on your project. In this case, enter the word **Welcome** into the text field that asks for Class filename. Use the defaults for the rest of the fields (see Figure 1-16), then click OK.

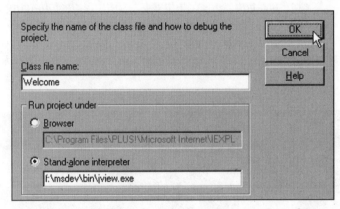

Figure 1-16: Dialog box for information on your Java class.

Now you can execute your Java program using Microsoft's JView.exe interpreter. In this case, we created a console-based Java application designed to say "Welcome to VJ++!" So, in this case, a DOS window should open up and execute the program as shown in Figure 1-17.

Tip

You may notice a problem viewing your Java application, because once your application has finished executing in the DOS window created by Visual J++, the window closes. In some cases, when executing your application, the DOS window may open and close without giving you a chance to actually view your application. If this is the case, you can circumvent it by opening a DOS window manually and executing your Java applications from there. For this example, you can execute it by running the following command line in the directory where Welcome.java is stored: jview.exe Welcome.

In this scenario, the DOS window executes the Welcome.java application and remains open until you manually close it.

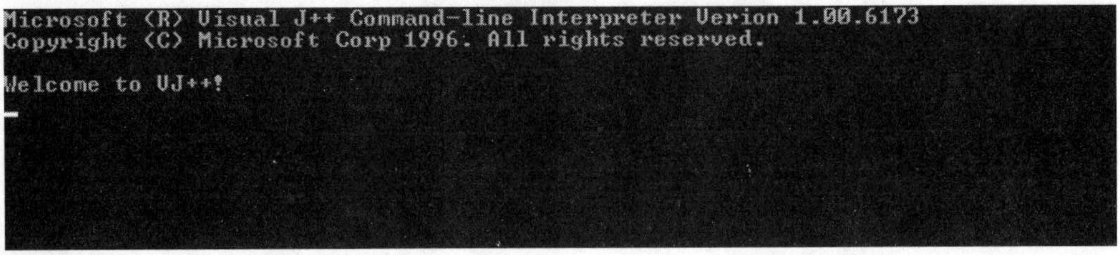

```
Microsoft (R) Visual J++ Command-line Interpreter Verion 1.00.6173
Copyright (C) Microsoft Corp 1996. All rights reserved.

Welcome to VJ++!
```

Figure 1-17: Executing Welcome.

At this point, you have successfully created, built, and executed your first Java application through Visual J++. You can test it as many times as you wish by simply re-executing your compiled project.

Moving On

In this chapter, you did more than break ground with Java and Visual J++. You had a chance to actually create a real-life Java application in Visual J++.

You learned that Java is an object-oriented programming language, including links to the ActiveX technologies. You also learned what makes Java so powerful and limiting. Finally, after becoming acquainted with the features of Visual J++, you created a real project in Visual J++.

In the next chapter, you begin to learn the Java language and build a foundation for understanding the Java structure. Specifically, Chapter 2 gives you a complete overview of the Java language structure using Visual J++ to exemplify everything discussed.

If you are already familiar with Java structure, you may want to move forward and start learning about objects in Chapter 3. And if you are already a competent Java programmer interested in moving directly to topics on Visual J++, go directly to Chapter 5.

2

The Java Language Structure

This chapter gives you a complete overview of the Java language structure. Topics covered include literals, data types, operators, and control-flow structures. Aside from the theoretical explanations, you will also have a chance to work with all of these topics in a real-world situation using Visual J++ projects.

You will breeze through this chapter if you have had any exposure to programming in other languages (especially C or C++). On the other hand, if you are not comfortable with your skills as a structured programmer or you do not have any experience programming, you can use this chapter to help build a foundation. The rest of the book relies on this chapter as the basic framework for understanding Java and Visual J++.

Structured programming was around before object-oriented programming. Java is an object-oriented programming language, but that does not mean that Java (and most other object-oriented programming languages) does not use structure. Before you can appreciate objects, you need to know about structures and how to use them inside of Java-based objects called classes.

Keywords

Java, just like the C/C++ programming language, has a somewhat small number of predefined *keywords*. Keywords represent reserved words in a programming language designated for a specific purpose. Table 2-1 shows a list of keywords for the Java language.

abstract	do	import	return	void
boolean	double	instanceof	short	while
break	else	int	static	throws
byte	extends	interface	super	
byvalue	false	long	switch	
case	final	native	synchronized	
catch	finally	new	this	
char	float	null	threadsafe	
class	for	package	throw	
const	goto	private	transient	
continue	if	protected	true	
default	implements	public	try	

Table 2-1: Keywords in the Java language.

The above table comprises the core building blocks that define the Java language. Throughout the next several chapters you will have a chance to use all of the functional keywords listed above.

Reserved Words With No Functionality in Java

The reserved keywords goto, byvalue, and const are part of the Java language, but do not have any specific functionality with this release of the Java language specification. Carried over from C/C++, they are no longer useful in the Java language.

Literals

A *literal* is any value expressed as itself. There are several types of literals: numerical literals, including integers, floating-point values, and booleans; and non-numerical literals, including characters and multiple-character literals (known as string literals).

Data types, discussed later in the chapter are values (a.k.a. variables) that represent or hold other values. This is very similar to algebra, where x can be more than just x; x could be 2, the square root of -5, or the gross national product. As you will learn later, Java has a specific set of data types for certain values.

Numerical Literals

In Java programs, numerical literals represent quantitative values. Java supports several different numerical systems, including *octal* (a numbering system with a base of 8) and *hexadecimal* (using a base of 16). However, most of what you see in this chapter will either be in decimal (base 10) or binary (base 2). An int is the default data type used for integer literals. If needed, you can specify the literal to be long by appending the letter "L": 24050000L

Note

Appended letters for specifying a particular data type when using literals are not case sensitive. For, example 10000l and 10000L both specify this literal to be a numerical type long. Extremely large values utilize the integer data type long

Floating-point values (numbers that have fractional parts, such as 3.14159) are automatically assumed to be a type double. However, if you wish to use the smaller floating-point type float, then you need to append a letter "f" to represent that data type: 2.313f

Note

Floating-point types also let you specify scientific notation by using the letter e (or E) to represent the exponential power. For example, the value 2.54 X 10^5 represented in Java is 2.54e5 or 2.54e5f housed in the float type.

Unlike C and C++, Java has boolean literals. Java booleans represent either the non-numerical value true or false.

Non-numerical Literals

There are two major non-numerical literals in Java. The first, a character literal, represents a single character surrounded by quotations. Some characters are not so obvious or simply cannot be encased in quotations. That is where character escapes come in. The following is a list of commonly used escape characters to print the not-so-obvious values:

\b Backspace

\f Form feed

\n New line

\t Tab

\\ Backslash

\' Single quote

\" Double quote

You worked with string literals, the second major non-numerical literals, to print statements on the screen in the example in the last chapter. String literals are merely collections of character literals. Java stores string literals in a more complex type known as a string object. This is very different from C or C++. In C, a string literal represents an array of characters (the char primitive data type). However, as you will learn in the next chapter, Java does not follow suit. The following code provides some examples of the use of a string literal and the \t escape characters:

```
"This is a test"
"This is a \t test"
```

The first line above simply prints out the statement "This is a test." The second line prints out the same thing, but places a tab where the \t is so, when printed, it will look something like "This is a   \t test."

Primitive Data Types

Literals are fairly simple concepts because they do nothing more than represent themselves. Nevertheless, in many instances, you may want to have a value represent something else, or you may need a variable where you can place values temporarily. In Java, you have two forms of variables (usually known as data types). The ones discussed in this chapter are primitive data types. There are a few complex data types, saved until the next chapter, that deal with object-oriented programming.

Primitive data types represent fundamental elements (denoted by keywords such as byte, int, short, long, boolean, and char) that let you hold a certain type of data in a specific range. You should use a data type that corresponds to the type of data and how large it is.

Java Is Strongly Typed

You may have heard the statement "Java is strongly typed." This means that you must explicitly declare all variables before you can use them in your Java programs. A variable declared but not assigned a value reverts to a default value.

In Java programs, you need to have a place to store data. For example, you store cars in parking lots and books in bookcases. If you were to switch the two around and park cars in bookcases and place books in parking lots, you would end up having a really big mess. The same is true when using data with data types. You need to be careful how and where your program is storing data, because storing it in the wrong data type can cause the values to become distorted or reported incorrectly.

And if your bookcase becomes full, you can do one of two things: remove some books to make more space or find a bigger bookcase. Variables follow exactly the same paradigm. Think of data as your books and variables (a.k.a. data types) as your bookcases. When used properly, they make a very efficient way to store data.

Integers

In mathematics, an integer is a whole number that can have either positive or negative values. Negative 10, 0, 5, and 2,040,506 are all examples of integers. Moreover, in mathematics, an integer can be any value from negative to positive infinity, with no theoretical limitations (except maybe the size of the chalkboard you are using). This is somewhat similar in data types. You can have a wide range of values for integer data types, but memory allocation inherently limits an integer's overall size.

All modern computers (at least the ones that support the use of Java) store their information in binary (a number of base 2) form. A *bit* is the smallest piece of information stored in a computer. "Bit" is a shortened name for the term "binary digit."

A *byte* is a series of eight bits and comprises the arrangement for how bits are stored in a computer. So, it should be no surprise to notice that byte is the smallest integer data type in Java. Since byte is the smallest size of the integers in Java, it is the most efficient to use. However, as a result, byte also has the smallest range. You can only assign a byte to have a value of -128 to 127. Below is an example of declaring a byte:

```
byte myVariable;
```

The next level up is the short data type, which is also an integer, but it is 16 bits in length. Plus, because short's bit width is twice as long as byte's it raises its range by a power of two. Thus, the integer data type short has a range of -32,768 to 32,767.

Int is probably the easiest to remember due to its name. This data type is a 32-bit value, twice the size of short, which makes its range rise from short by a power of 2. This is how Java organizes its integer data types so that each one increases in range by a power of 2. The range of int is -2,147,483,648 to 2,147,483,647. And the last and largest integer value that you can have in Java is the data type long. As you can probably guess, long is 64 bits in length, with a range of -9,223,372,036,854,775,808 to 9,223,372,036,854,775,807. Long is the single largest holding tank for integers in the Java language, and, hopefully you will never need to work with values nearly that size.

Table 2-2 summarizes all of the integer data types.

Keyword	Size in bits	Size in bytes	L. Range H. Range
byte	8	1	-128 to 127
short	16	2	-32,768 to 32,768
int	32	4	-2,147,483,648 to 2,147,483,647
long	64	8	9,223,372,036,854,775,808 to 9,223,372,036,854,775,807

Table 2-2: Integer Data Types.

Tutorial: Declaring Data Types

Let's go ahead and create a project in Visual J++, declaring various integer data types and assigning them values:

Note

You learned the process for creating a project, creating a text file, saving your work, and then building and executing your work in Chapter 1. The procedure is presented in detail here, and the rest of the tutorials in this chapter use this same process.

1. Make sure that you have Visual J++ loaded.

2. If you still have the previous project from Chapter 1 open, you need to close it. Do this by clicking on File I Close Workspace.

3. Open a new text file in the Developer Studio by clicking on File I New. On the dialog that appears, specify that you want to open a text file, and a fresh text file window appears, waiting for you to write your code (see Figure 2-1).

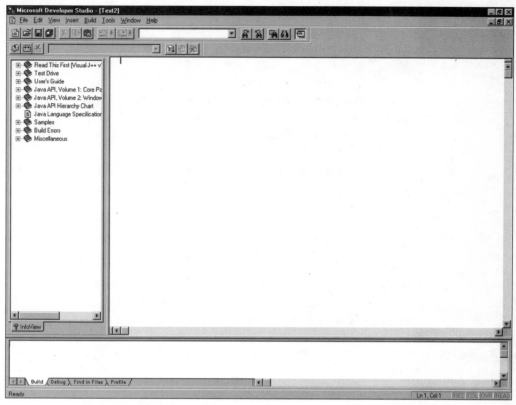

Figure 2-1: The Developer Studio with a fresh text file.

4. In that Text Editor window, type the following code:

```java
class myIntegerTest {

    public static void main(String argv[]) {

// Declare the variables
    byte myInteger1 =  25;

    int  myInteger2;

    // Declare and assign the value
    long myInteger3 = 500000000;
```

```
        //Assign a value
        myInteger2 = 5000;

        // Print out values
    System.out.println("The value of byte myInteger1 is " +
myInteger1);
    System.out.println("The value of int myInteger2 is " +
myInteger2);
    System.out.println("The value of long myInteger3 is " +
myInteger3);

    }
}
```

Notice in the above code that you are declaring three integer
data types: a byte called myInteger1, an int called myInteger2,
and a long called myInteger3. Then, you are using three lines of
code, each containing println() to print out the values for each of
these variables.

Note

*In the above code, just like in C/C++, the double backslash (//)
denotes a single line comment and the /* */ denotes multiline
comments.*

5. Save the text file by clicking on File | Save. A Save As dia-
   log box appears. Save this file as myIntegerTest.java in the
   msdev\projects directory on your system.
6. Build the project by clicking on Build | Build myIntegerTest
   to build the file. When prompted to create a default project
   workspace, click Yes. Figure 2-2 shows the Output window.

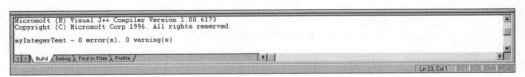

Figure 2-2: The Output window for myIntegerTest project.

7. Execute the project by clicking on Build I Execute. In the dialog box that appears (see Figure 2-3), type **myIntegerTest** in the Class file name field and click OK to continue. Figure 2-4 shows the DOS box that opens with the output displayed.

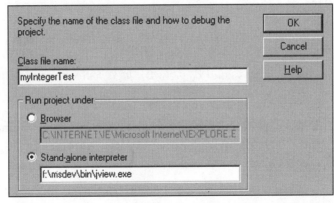

Figure 2-3: Dialog box (filled out) to execute the application.

```
Microsoft (R) Visual J++ Command-line Interpreter Verion 1.00.6173
Copyright (C) Microsoft Corp 1996. All rights reserved.
The value of byte myInteger1 is 25
The value of int myInteger2 is 5000
The value of long myInteger3 is 500000000
```

Figure 2-4: Executing the myIntegerTest application.

Integers are at the very heart of any programming language's structure. Java brings several key advantages to the programmer over other programming languages. The strong point with Java data types is that they are completely platform-independent so that you can use the same integer model just discussed on any platform currently supported by Java. Any programmer who has worked on more than one platform will recognize the simplicity of having a standard integer model.

Booleans

The next primitive data type we'll discuss is the boolean data type. Booleans are very simple in that they can contain only two values: either true or false.

Note

As you will learn later, data types can convert from one form to another (through casting). However, unlike the bool in C++ or boolean in Visual Basic (VB), Java booleans cannot convert to other data types.

Unless specified otherwise, declared booleans default to a value of false. The following shows several examples of declaring a boolean value:

```
boolean myfirstboolean = true //this variable is true
boolean mysecondboolean  //this variable defaults to false
boolean mythirdboolean = false //this variable is explicitly
set to false
```

In Java, you can declare a variable and assign it a value in the same line:

```
boolean myBool= true;
```

Tutorial: Declaring Boolean Variables

Now let's write a Visual J++ project based on the above snippet of code. In this tutorial, you are will have a chance to declare three boolean variables and assign them different values.

Load the Developer Studio and close the project workspace you created from the last example (closing all the document windows). Then, open a new text file and type the following code into the Text Editor window:

```java
public static void main(String argv[]) {

    // Declare the boolean.
    boolean myBool1;

    // Declare and assign the value to false.
    boolean myBool2 = false;

    // Declare and assign the value to true.
    boolean myBool3 = true;

    // Assign the first to false
    myBool1 = false;

    // Print out values
    System.out.println("The value of myBool1 is " + myBool1);
    System.out.println("The value of myBool2 is " + myBool2);
    System.out.println("The value of myBool3 is " + myBool3);

    }
}
```

Notice that in the above code you declare three boolean variables: myBool1, myBool2, and myBool3. Then, the last three lines of code each use println() to print out the value of each of the booleans.

Once you finish entering the above code, save the text file as myBoolTest.java in the msdev\projects directory. Then, build the code (creating a default workspace) and execute the code. When the program executes, you'll see something similar to Figure 2-5.

```
Microsoft (R) Visual J++ Command-line Interpreter Verion 1.00.6173
Copyright (C) Microsoft Corp 1996. All rights reserved.
The value of bool1 is false
The value of bool2 is false
The value of bool3 is true
```

Figure 2-5: Executing the myBoolTest application.

Booleans are a very useful data type in any language. However, the Java language enhances its capabilities by not giving it an integer-based compatibility like C and C++ have. This is an enhancement because it leaves less room for errors by having boolean be either true or false.

Characters

The keyword char denotes the character data type. The char type is exactly like char in C/C++ with only one major difference. The char type in Java stores its values using the 16-bit Unicode format.

Unicode

Unicode is a new coding format based on a 16-bit character. Unlike the older ANSI/ASCII standards used in C and C++ that are only 8 bits in length and can only contain a total of 255 characters, Unicode can contain 65,536 characters. Unicode contains symbols for almost every major dialect in the world. You can directly reference a Unicode character in Java by using the \uXXXX the X's representing a hexadecimal value.

The following is an example of a char. Notice that there are single quotation marks around the actual character. That denotes that X is a character literal, which was described earlier:

```
char mychar = 'X';
```

Some characters cannot be printed on the screen directly without some sort of assistance. For example, what if you wanted to have a single quotation as a value in the above snippet of code? In that case, you need to use a backslash and the quote to display it as shown below:

```
\'
```

The following example helps demonstrate using char data type, understanding how it relates to character and string literals, and using escape characters.

Tutorial: Declaring Character Data Types

Load the Developer Studio and close the project workspace you created from the last example (closing all the document windows). Then, open a new text file and type the following code into the Text Editor window:

```
class myCharTest {

  public static void main(String argv[]) {

    // Declare and assign a character
    char X = 'y';

      //Print out the literal value for X and the value
contained in X
      System.out.println("The character literal for X is " +
'X' + "\n But, the value inside of X is " + X);


    }
  }
```

In the above code, you are declaring the char called X to contain the value y. Then you are using the println() method to print out the value of X.

Once you finish entering the above code, save the text file as myCharTest.java in the msdev\projects directory. Then, build the code (creating a default workspace) and execute the code. When the program executes, you'll see something similar to Figure 2-6.

```
Microsoft (R) Visual J++ Command-line Interpreter Verion 1.00.6173
Copyright (C) Microsoft Corp 1996. All rights reserved.
The character literal for X is X
 But, the value inside of X is y
```

Figure 2-6: Executing the myCharTest application.

Once the application executes, you will see the following printed: "The character literal for X is X. But, the value inside of X is y."

Floating Points

Very large, very small, and any other noninteger decimal numbers use Java's floating-point type. There are two floating-point types in the Java language: a float and a double. Both of the floating-point data types in Java conform to the IEEE 754 specifications. (IEEE stands for the Institute of Electrical and Electronic Engineers, an organization noted for setting standards in the computer industry.) There are several formats for specifying a floating-point value, including using exponential notation:

    2.232   4.234e5   1.2E-56

Starting with the smaller of the two, the float is a 32-bit (4 byte) data type that contains seven significant digits (any significant digits after 7 are truncated). Float, known as a single-precision data type, is suitable for most calculations.

Tip

You can determine the number of significant digits in a value by finding the length of values that begin and end with nonzero values. For example, 4,500 has 2 significant digits, 1,001,000 has 4 significant digits, and 0.000123 has 3 significant digits.

However, in certain situations you may need to have a more precise way of keeping track of your values. In that case you use the double value. A double-precision floating-point value is 64 bits (8 bytes in length) and holds 15 significant digits. Table 2-3 shows a summary of the two floating-point types.

keyword	Size in Bits	Size in Bytes	L. Range H. Range
float	32	4	-3.40282347E+38 to +3.40282347E+38
double	64	8	1.79769313486231570E+308 to +1.79769313486231570E+308

Table 2-3: Floating point types.

Casting

One of the ways to manipulate a data type is to change the variable from one type to another. This form of conversion is known as *casting*. The actual syntax for casting between values is fairly simple. Put the data type you want to cast to in front of the variable, as shown below:

```
int A;
char B;
A = (int) B;
```

The idea behind casting is also very simple. However, there is a tricky part: you need to make sure that you understand all of the ins and outs of casting, because, if you are not careful, you could lose data during the cast. This is possible if the data type you are casting to is smaller than the original type. Technically speaking, not all of the bits will fit into the smaller type. Any bits left behind are truncated (i.e., ignored), resulting in an incorrect value. Probably the most common use for casting is to convert from an integer data type to a char or vice versa.

You can safely cast to a smaller data type, but only if the actual value does not exceed the smaller data type's range. Of course, if you are casting to a larger data type, then you can be sure that there will be no loss of data. Table 2-4 shows a list of all casts considered safe for any value of the original data type.

---

byte (8 bits) to **short**(16), **char**(16), **int**(32), **long**(64), **float**(32), **double**(64).

short (16 bits) to **int**(32), **long**(64) , **float**(32) and **double**(64).

char (16 bits) to **int**(32), **float**(32), and **double**(64).

int (32 bits) to **long**(64), **float**(32), and **double**(64).

float (32 bits) to **double**(64).

Table 2-4: Safe casts. data_type(bit_width).

Tutorial: Casting Between Values

Load the Developer Studio and close the project workspace you created from the last example (closing all the document windows). Then, open a new text file and type the following code into the Text Editor window:

```
class myCastTest {
    public static void main(String argv[]) {

        // Declare the variables
        short myShort;
        byte myByte;


        System.out.println("--No data is truncated in this
cast--");
```

```
// Assign a value
myShort = 20;

// Perform the Cast
myByte = (byte) myShort;

System.out.println("The value for myShort is " +
myShort);
System.out.println("the value for myByte after the
cast is " + myByte);

System.out.println("--Data is lost in this cast--");

//Assign a new value
myShort = 10000;

//Perform the cast
myByte = (byte) myShort;

System.out.println("The value for myShort is " +
myShort);
System.out.println("the value for myByte after the
cast is " + myByte);

    }
}
```

In the above code, you declare two integer variables: myShort and myBtye. Then, myShort is set to 20 and the following cast is performed:

```
myByte = (byte) myShort;
```

Since 20 is within myByte's range, no data will be lost, and myByte's value will become 20. Then, myShort is set to 10,000 and the cast is performed again; however, this time bits are truncated to fit into myByte, giving it an incorrect value.

Once you finish entering the above code, save the text file as myCastTest.java in the msdev\projects directory. Then, build the code (creating a default workspace) and execute the code. When the program executes, you'll see something similar to Figure 2-7.

```
Microsoft (R) Visual J++ Command-line Interpreter Verion 1.00.6173
Copyright (C) Microsoft Corp 1996. All rights reserved.
---No data is truncated in this cast----
The value for myShort is 20
the value for myByte after the cast is 20
---Data is lost in this cast---
The value for myShort is 10000
the value for myByte after the cast is 16
```

Figure 2-7: Executing the myCastTest application.

Executing the above application, you will see two casts performed. The first cast passes 20 from myShort to myByte and no data is lost. However, when myShort is set to 10,000 and the same cast is performed again, myByte returns a value of 16!

Casting can be a powerful, but tricky, programming technique. If used wisely it can come in very handy.

Operators

Operators are symbols that perform a specific task in various forms of expressions. Whenever you work with variables, literals, or combinations of the two, you need to understand all of the operators available to you.

Most of the operators in Java relate to the operators found in C and C++, with only very minor discrepancies.

Arithmetic Operators

Arithmetic operators are probably the easiest operators to understand because they deal directly with basic mathematical topics such as adding, subtracting, multiplying, and dividing. Table 2-5 gives an outline and an overview of each arithmetic operator.

Operator	Definition	Java Rep	Alg Rep	Sol.
+	Addition	5 + 7	5 + 7	12
-	Subtraction	5 - 6	5 - 6	-1
*	Multiplication	4 * 2	(4)(2)	8
/	Division	4 / 2	4 ÷ 2	2
%	Modulus	5 % 2	5 mod 2	1

Table 2-5: Arithmetic operators.

There are a few things to mention about the arithmetic operators before moving forward. First, notice that all of the arithmetic operators require you to have two operands (also known as values). This two-operand minimum is true for all the arithmetic operators except the minus sign, which can be used as a negation operator with one operand:

```
-5
```

Probably the only operator in the above table that may not be immediately recognizable is the modulus operator (the %). Modulus, carried over from mathematics, returns the remainder as the result from the division of the two operands. The following show some examples:

```
7 % 2; // results in 1
4 % 9; // results in 4
-20 % 5 // results in 0
```

When performing calculations you may not always receive a value that is of the same type as the original two. Java handles this in one of several ways. If the two operands are integers, then the resulting value will be an integer. If one or both of the two operands are floating-point values, the arithmetic expression returns a floating-point value after the nonfloating-point operand has been *promoted* to a floating-point. Promoted means it automatically casts to a data type containing a larger bit width. This is the same for double values as well. The default operand data type is int.

```
20 /* integer */ / 3; /* integer */ returns an integer value
of
20.0 /* floating */ / 3; /* integer */ returns a floating
value of 6.666666
```

It is important to understand exactly what value Java will return. The following Visual J++ project provides an example of using all of the arithmetic operators and gives an example showing the different returning data types for expressions using noninteger numerical data types.

Tutorial: Arithmetic Operators

Load the Developer Studio and close the project workspace you created from the last example (closing all the document windows). Then, open a new text file and type the following code into the Text Editor window:

```java
class myArithOperatorTest {

    public static void main(String argv[]) {

        // Declare and assign the variables
        int a = 5;
        int b = 13;
        float c = 2.5f;

        System.out.println("All of the following return an
integer.");

        System.out.println(a + "+" + b + "=" + (a + b));
        System.out.println(a + "-" + b + "=" + (a - b));
        System.out.println(a + "*" + b + "=" + a * b);
        System.out.println(a + "/" + b + "=" + a / b);
        System.out.println(a + "%" + b + "=" + a % b);

        System.out.println("All of the following return a
float.");
```

```
System.out.println(a + "+" + c + "=" + (a + c));
System.out.println(a + "-" + c + "=" + (a - c));
System.out.println(a + "*" + c + "=" + (a * c));
System.out.println(a + "/" + c + "=" + (a / c));
System.out.println(a + "%" + c + "=" + (a % c));


    }

}
```

In the above code, you are declaring three variables: a (with a value of 5), b (with a value of 13), and c (with a value of 2.5). Then you have two sets of println() statements. The first set performs arithmetic operations using the two integers (a and b), thus the result is an integer.

The second set of println() statements performs the same arithmetic operations, except this time c (a floating-point value) replaces b. Thus, the result of all these operations is a float.

Once you finish entering the above code, save the text file as myArithOperatorTest.java in the ..msdev\projects directory. Then, build the code (creating a default workspace) and then execute the code. When the program executes, you'll see something similar to Figure 2-8.

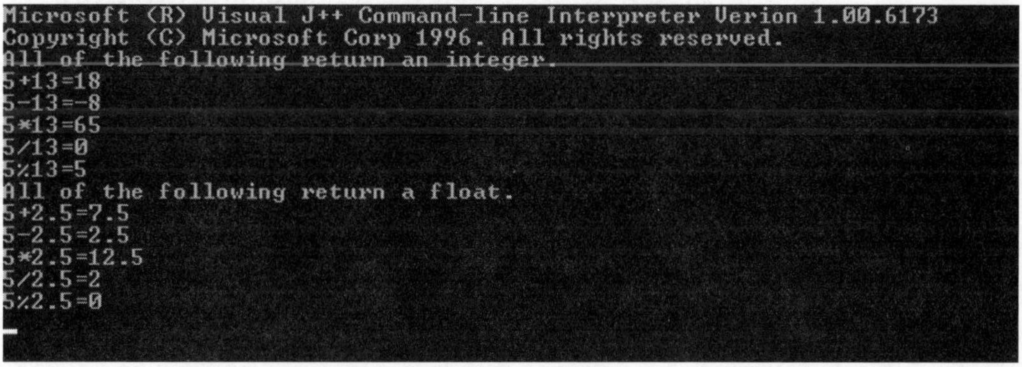

```
Microsoft (R) Visual J++ Command-line Interpreter Verion 1.00.6173
Copyright (C) Microsoft Corp 1996. All rights reserved.
All of the following return an integer.
5+13=18
5-13=-8
5*13=65
5/13=0
5%13=5
All of the following return a float.
5+2.5=7.5
5-2.5=2.5
5*2.5=12.5
5/2.5=2
5%2.5=0
```

Figure 2-8: Executing the myArithOperator application.

Assignment Operators

Assignment operators are fairly simple to understand because these operators are a specialized extension of the arithmetic operators. With an assignment operator, you can add values to variables. Table 2-6 gives a complete overview of assignment operators.

Op.	Java Rep.	Algebra	Ex.
+=	a += b	a = a + b	a += 5
-=	a -= b	a = a - b	a -= 5
*=	a *= b	a = a * b	a *= 5
/=	a /= b	a = a / b	a /= 5
%=	a %= b	a = a % b	a %= 5

Table 2-6: Assignment operators.

Comparison Operators

Sometimes you want to compare the relationship between two values. In Java, just like in C and C++, this can be done using a set of comparison operators. However, unlike in C and C++, the result of the comparison is not a numerical expression (0 for false and non0 for true). In Java, it returns a boolean type that has a value of either true or false. Table 2-7 shows the comparison operators and an example of using them.

Operator	Def.	Example	Result
Note: a equals 7 and b equals 3.			
==	equal to	a == 7	true
		b == 7	false
!=	not equal to	a != 7	false
		b != 7	true
<	less than	a < 7	false
		b < 7	true
>	greater than	a > 7	false
		b > 7	false
<=	less then or equal to	a <= 7	true
		b <= 7	true
>=	greater then or equal to	a >= 7	true
		b >= 7	false

Table 2-7: Comparison operators.

Tutorial: Comparison Operators

Load the Developer Studio and close the project workspace you created from the last example (closing all the document windows). Then, open a new text file and type the following code into the Text Editor window:

```
class myComparisionTest {
    public static void main(String argv[]) {
        // Declare and assign the values
        int x = 5;
        int y = 7;

        // Print out values
        System.out.println(x + "<" + y + " returns " + (x < 7));
        System.out.println(x + ">" + y + " returns " + (x > 7));
        System.out.println(x + "!=" + y + " returns " + (x !=
7));
        System.out.println(x + "==" + y + " returns " + (x ==
```

```
7));

    }
}
```

In the above code, you declare two integer variables: x (with a value of 5) and y (with a value of 7). Then, the next four println() statements contain an example using each of the four comparison operators.

Once you finish entering the above code, save the text file as my-ComparisionTest.java in the ..msdev\projects directory. Then, build the code (creating a default workspace) and execute the code. When the program executes, you'll see something similar to Figure 2-9.

```
Microsoft (R) Visual J++ Command-line Interpreter Version 1.00.6173
Copyright (C) Microsoft Corp 1996. All rights reserved.
5<7 returns true
5>7 returns false
5!=7 returns true
5==7 returns false
```

Figure 2-9: Executing the myComparisionTest application.

Once the application executes you will see each operation and a boolean value of true or false displayed as the result.

Logical Operators

Another set of operators that also return a boolean type are the logical operators (also known as boolean operators).

The && is the AND operator, and, just like in C/C++, it evaluates two operands and returns true only if both sides are true; otherwise it returns false.

The | | is the OR operator and behaves in a somewhat inverse fashion: it returns true if either side is true or if both sides are true. The only time it will return false if both sides are false.

The ! is the NOT operator and is used as a negation tool that inverses the value for a particular expression. Also, the logical NOT can be used for not equal to evaluations (!=). Table 2-8 shows an overview of the logical operators.

Operator Note: a = true and b = false	Def	Expression	Result
&&	AND	a && b	false
		b && a	false
		a && a	true
		b && b	false
||	OR	a || b	true
		b || a	true
		a || a	true
		b || b	false
!	NOT	!a	false
		!b	true

Table 2-8: Logical operators.

Note on Performance Tuning Using && and ||

The logical AND and OR (&& and || respectively) evaluate the left side of their expression first. If the left side returns false, then Java immediately returns false for the entire expression without evaluating the right side. The same is true for the OR; except in this case, if the left side evaluates to true, then the whole expression immediately returns true.

Java programs can leverage this subtle feature to improve their performance. You should place the evaluation of lesser intensity on the left side and leave the larger or more time-consuming evaluation for the right. By only calling the larger evaluation after the lesser evaluation has been performed, you can maximize efficiency.

Bitwise Operators

Bitwise operators are similar to the logical operators in the last section except, with bitwise operators, you are dealing at the binary level. As with the logical operators, there are assignment and comparison operators in the bitwise subset that perform their operations on the binary level.

Bitwise operators give you the ability to access data types at a very low level. This is useful for networking, operating systems, and performing other lower-level applications developed in Java.

Note

The operands for bitwise operators cannot be complex data types (such as float, double, etc.). And, they should only be used on the primitive data types that are integral in nature.

Bitwise operators, because they are at such a low level, are also able to perform certain mathematical tasks very efficiently. In fact, many compilers will take a higher-level operation and convert it to a more efficient bitwise operation during compilation.

Finally, bitwise operators come directly from C and C++. Since bitwise operations are inherently platform-independent, and in Java, the integer data types you deal with are also platform-independent, there is no problem using them in your Java applications.

Bitwise AND, OR, XOR & NOT

Remember the logical operators discussed earlier? The bitwise AND and OR look very similar to their logical counterparts. Bitwise operations use the & for bitwise AND and | for bitwise OR. There is also the logical exclusive or XOR in which only one of the operands can evaluate to true for it to return a true. Otherwise, it will return a false.

Bitwise operation is an advanced topic in any language. If you have trouble following along move to the next section. Otherwise look at Table 2-9 that shows a brief overview of each operator.

In the real world any bitwise operators are usually used to combine some flags (usually a power of 2) into a single value and perform a quick operations on that value.

Operator	Def	Expression	Result
Note: a is a bit with a value of 1, and b is a bit with a value of 0.			
&	AND	a & b	0
		b & a	0
		a & a	1
		b & b	0
I	OR	a I b	1
		b I a	1
		a I a	1
		b I b	0
^	XOR	a ^ b	1
		b ^ a	1
		a ^ a	0
		b ^ b	0
~	NOT	~a	0
		~b	1

Table 2-9: Bitwise AND, OR, XOR, and NOT operators.

Bitwise operations perform their evaluations with each binary value in the integral data type. To illustrate, let's take a look at a binary value of 40 that is (0000 0000 0010 1000) and the value 24 (0000 0000 0001 1000). Looking at Table 2-10, you see the result of the & operation on these two values.

Bit number	1	2	3	4	5	6	7	8	9	10	11	12	13	14	15	16
Value of 40	0	0	0	0	0	0	0	0	0	0	1	0	1	0	0	0
Value of 24	0	0	0	0	0	0	0	0	0	0	1	1	0	0	0	
Result 8	0	0	0	0	0	0	0	0	0	0	0	1	0	0	0	

Table 2-10: 40 & 24.

The above result for this operation is 8 (0000 0000 0000 1000). Table 2-11 performs the bitwise OR operation using the same values.

Bit number	1	2	3	4	5	6	7	8	9	10	11	12	13	14	15	16
Value of 40	0	0	0	0	0	0	0	0	0	0	1	0	1	0	0	0
Value of 24	0	0	0	0	0	0	0	0	0	0	0	1	1	0	0	0
Result 56	0	0	0	0	0	0	0	0	0	0	1	1	1	0	0	0

Table 2-11: 40 | 24.

You'll notice in Table 2-11 that even though you are using the same numbers as in the last example, you have a different result. This time, the result is 56 (0000 0000 0011 1000). Table 2-12 illustrates performing the XOR operation on the same values.

Bit number	1	2	3	4	5	6	7	8	9	10	11	12	13	14	15	16
Value of 40	0	0	0	0	0	0	0	0	0	0	1	0	1	0	0	0
Value of 24	0	0	0	0	0	0	0	0	0	0	0	1	1	0	0	0
Result 48	0	0	0	0	0	0	0	0	0	0	1	1	0	0	0	0

Table 2-12: 40 ^ 24.

Remember that the difference between OR and XOR is that with XOR one of the operands must be true and the other must be false in order for XOR to return a true. You can see in Table 2-12 that only line 13 is different from the last operation, using OR. The result for this operation is 48 (0000 0000 0011 0000).

The final bitwise operator left to discuss from the above table is the ~ bitwise NOT *unary operator* (meaning that it only works with one variable at a time). The bitwise NOT is very similar to the NOT (!) operator discussed with logical operators. However, when dealing with the bitwise NOT (~) operator, work at the binary level. So, if the binary value is 1, then it changes to 0 and vice versa with this operator. Table 2-13 shows an example of this reversal.

Bit number	1	2	3	4	5	6	7	8	9	10	11	12	13	14	15	16
Value of 40	0	0	0	0	0	0	0	0	0	0	1	0	1	0	0	0
V. of ~40	1	1	1	1	1	1	1	1	1	1	0	1	0	1	1	1
Value of 24	0	0	0	0	0	0	0	0	0	0	0	1	1	0	0	0
V. of ~24	1	1	1	1	1	1	1	1	1	1	1	0	0	1	1	1

Table 2-13: ~40 and ~24.

Look closely at the above table and you'll notice that the value for ~40, when converted to decimal, is -41 (1111 1111 1101 0111). And the value for ~24 is -25 (1111 1111 1110 0111).

Tutorial: Bitwise Operators

Load the Developer Studio and close the project workspace you created from the last example (closing all the document windows). Then, open a new text file and type the following code into the Text Editor window:

```
class myBitTest {

    public static void main(String argv[]) {

        //Declare and assign variables
        int x = 40;
    int y = 24;

        //Perform bitwise operations and print it out
        System.out.println("The value for x is " + x);
        System.out.println("The value for y is " + y);

        //Using the & operator
        System.out.println("Output for x & y " + (x & y));

         //Using the | operator
         System.out.println("Output for x | y " + (x | y));
```

```
//Using the ^ operator
System.out.println("Output for x ^ y " + (x ^ y));

//Using the ~ operator
System.out.println("Output for ~y " + ~y);
System.out.println("Output for ~y " + ~y);
    }
}
```

In the above code, you declare two integers: x (with a value of 40) and y (with a value of 24). The rest of the application contains a bunch of println() methods that perform various bitwise operations as described earlier.

Once you finish entering the above code, save the text file as myBitTest.java in the ..msdev\projects directory. Then, build the code (creating a default workspace) and execute the code. When the program executes, you'll see something similar to Figure 2-10.

```
Microsoft (R) Visual J++ Command-line Interpreter Verion 1.00.6173
Copyright (C) Microsoft Corp 1996. All rights reserved.
The value for x is 40
The value for y is 24
Output for x & y 8
Output for x | y 56
Output for x ^ y 48
Output for ~y -25
Output for ~y -25
```

Figure 2-10: Executing the myBitTest application.

Left & Right Shift Bitwise Operators

The shift operators move bits in one direction or another depending on which shift operator you choose and how many times you wish to shift it. << shifts to the left, and >> shifts to the right. Because shifting is done at the binary level, it is extremely fast and is sometimes preferred over traditional operations. Many operating systems, networking software, and any other low-level software use shifting techniques. Table 2-14 summarizes the shifting operators available for Java.

Operator	Def	Exp Syn.	Example
Note: a represents an integral number.			
<<	left shift	exp << num	a << 5
>>	right shift	exp >> num	a >> 2

Table 2-14: Bitwise shifting operators.

The << left shift moves the binary values to the left by the specified amount. Consequently, in the above table, the bits in a would be shifted left by one spot, adding a 0 to the right-hand side. Table 2-15 shows the binary interpretation for 75 before and after the shift.

Bit number	1	2	3	4	5	6	7	8	9	10	11	12	13	14	15	16
Value of 75	0	0	0	0	0	0	0	0	1	0	0	1	0	1	1	
Result 150	0	0	0	0	0	0	0	1	0	0	1	0	1	1	0	

Table 2-15: 75 << 1.

Notice that the bits were merely bumped to the left, a zero was added, and the decimal value for the result of the shift is 150 (0000 0000 1001 0110). If you were to have specified 2 for the number of shifts, it would result in the bits shifting 2 places to the left and 2 zeros being added to the right.

Now let's take a look at the binary level at an example of a right shift for the value 75 (see Table 2-16).

Bit number	1	2	3	4	5	6	7	8	9	10	11	12	13	14	15	16
Value of 75	0	0	0	0	0	0	0	0	1	0	0	1	0	1	1	
Result 37	0	0	0	0	0	0	0	0	0	1	0	0	1	0	1	

Table 2-16: 75 >> 1.

Since the above operation is a right shift, the bits are pushed to the right and a zero is added to the left-hand side. Notice that in the previous left shift the new decimal value for 75 was 150 or double the original value. This last table reveals that, using the right shift, the result is 37—half of 75 (truncating it to remain a whole number).

Signed Integral Types & Shifting

All of the examples in shifting thus far only deal with unsigned (i.e., positive) integral types. However, what if you were to shift a signed (i.e., negative) integer? The result is exactly the same—the bits for the specified value shift the specified number of times—except a 1 will be added to the left or right side instead of a 0.

For example, -50 >> 2 would result in -13. Looking at the binary level for the value 50 (1111 1111 1100 1110), you have shifted two spaces to the right and two ones are added to the left-hand side, resulting in -13 (1111 1111 1111 0011).

One of the important uses in shifting is to multiply by powers of 2 with left shifts and divide by powers of 2 if you right shift. The following shows the equations for both of these shifts:

$$X << A = X*2^A$$
$$X >> A = X/2^A$$

Notice, however, that in this shift there was a binary value of 1 cut off from the right-hand side. This can also happen to shifts that move the bits too far to the left. It is important to be aware of these losses in shifts. So, the above equations are only valid if there is no truncation during the shift.

Note

Java also supports the use of an unsigned right shift (>>>). The unsigned right shift performs unsigned right shifts using positive or negative integral values. However, Java does not have a <<< operator.

Tutorial: Shifting Bitwise Operators

Load the Developer Studio and close the project workspace you
created from the last example (closing all the document windows).
Then, open a new text file and type the following code into the
Text Editor window:

```java
class myShiftTest {
    public static void main(String argv[]) {
        //Declare and assign variables
        int x = 75;
        int y = 50;

        //Print out variables on the screen
        System.out.println("Value for x = " + x);
        System.out.println("Value for y = " + y);

        //left shifts
        System.out.println("Output for x << 1 = " + (x <<
1));
        System.out.println("Output for x << 2 = " + (x <<
2));

        System.out.println("Output for y << 1 = " + (y <<
1));
        System.out.println("Output for y << 2 = " + (y <<
2));

        //right shifts
        System.out.println("Output for x >> 1 = " + (x >>
1));
        System.out.println("Output for x >> 2 = " + (x >>
2));

        System.out.println("Output for y >> 1 = " + (y >>
1));
        System.out.println("Output for y >> 2 = " + (y >>
2));

    }
}
```

In the above code, you declare two integers: x (with a value of 75) and y (with a value of 25). The rest of the application contains a bunch of println() methods that perform various shift operations to both variables.

Once you finish entering the above code, save the text file as myShiftTest.java in the ..msdev\projects directory. Then, build the code (creating a default workspace) and execute the code. When the program executes, you'll see something similar to Figure 2-11.

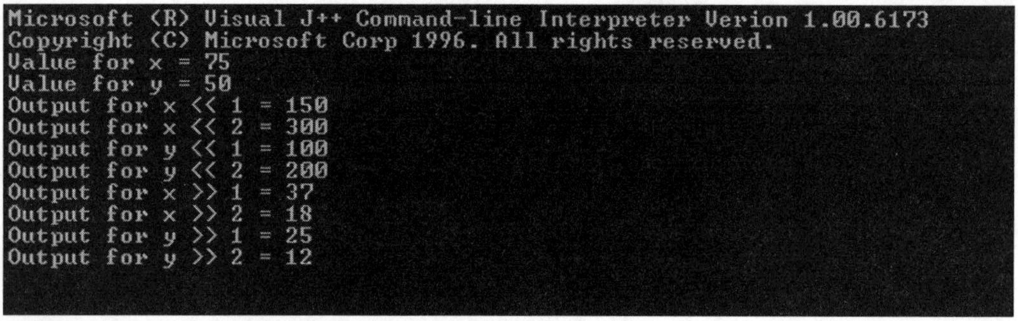

```
Microsoft (R) Visual J++ Command-line Interpreter Verion 1.00.6173
Copyright (C) Microsoft Corp 1996. All rights reserved.
Value for x = 75
Value for y = 50
Output for x << 1 = 150
Output for x << 2 = 300
Output for y << 1 = 100
Output for y << 2 = 200
Output for x >> 1 = 37
Output for x >> 2 = 18
Output for y >> 1 = 25
Output for y >> 2 = 12
```

Figure 2-11: Executing the myShiftTest application.

Bitwise Assignment Operators

The bitwise assignment operators behave just like the assignment operators reviewed in an earlier section. Table 2-17 shows a breakdown of the bitwise assignment operators available.

Operator	Def	Expression	Expanded Exp.
Note: a is a bit with a value of 1, and b is a bit with a value of 0.			
&=	AND	a &= b	a = a & b
|=	OR	a |= b	a = a | b
^=	XOR	a ^= b	a = a ^ b

Table 2-17: Bitwise assignment operators.

Note

There is a bitwise assignment operator for each respective bitwise operator except for the bitwise NOT (~) operator, because it is a unary operator.

Operator Precedence

At this point, you have reviewed all of the primitive data types in the Java language and have seen all of the operators you can employ to manipulate those data types. Before you rush into the real world to implement operators in your programs, it is important to know a little more about operator precedence. Operator precedence is a very easy-to-understand process of organizing operators to execute over other operators in the same expression. The idea behind operator precedence is very similar to that same concept in algebra.

Operator Precedence in Algebra

You'll recall that in algebra there are rules of operation that cause one operator to execute prior to others. To illustrate, let's take a look at the follow expression:

$$9 + 2 * 4 - 2 = y$$

Now, if you were not following the rules of operation as defined in algebra, you might be tempted to solve for y using the following methodology:

1. $9 + 2 * 4 - 2 = y$
2. $11 * 4 - 2 = y$
3. $44 - 2 = y$
4. $42 = y$

Naturally, this is incorrect. The correct answer is 15. You arrive at the correct answer if you remember that multiplication and division operations in algebra take priority over addition and subtraction operations. So, the correct procedure to solve this equation is:

1. $9 + 2 * 4 - 2 = y$
2. $9 + 8 - 2 = y$
3. $17 - 2 = y$
4. $15 = y$

At this point, it should be easy to understand why 15 is the correct answer and 42 is the incorrect one. Still, in algebra (and in Java as well) you have the ability to bend these rules and specify when certain operations should take priority over others. And that is done using parentheses. By surrounding a particular operation with parentheses, you are giving it precedence to execute first, regardless of what other operators are present.

Let's go ahead and make some changes to our algebraic equation so that 42 is the correct answer for y by adding some parenthetical citations:

$(9 + 2) * 4 - 2 = y$

If you now go through the logic of solving this equation, you will receive 42 as your correct answer:

1. $(9 + 2) * 4 - 2 = y$
2. $11 * 4 - 2 = y$
3. $44 - 2 = y$
4. $42 = y$

Operator Precedence in Java

Operator precedence in the Java language exactly mirrors the same methodology used in algebra, except in Java there are other types of operators. Table 2-18 shows list of operators discussed thus far, ordered by operator precedence. The first (or top) line has the highest priority; and in each line, the item to the far left has the highest priority for that line.

Note: The top, left has highest priority.
++ — ! - ~
* / %
+ -
<< >> >>>
< <= . >=
== !=
&
^
|
&&
||
= *= /= %= += -= <<= >>= &= |= ^=

Table 2-18: Operator precedence.

Note

The list in Table 2-18 is not complete. Chapter 3 contains the complete operator-precedence table for Java.

Control Flow

For most of this chapter, you are dealing with the details of operations in the Java language. However, one of the most important parts of structured programming is the use of control-flow structures to determine if a particular piece of code should be executed. Control-flow structures give you the ability to create all sorts of decision trees in your application.

Does Object-oriented Programming Replace Structured or Control-flow Programming?

No. Many people new to programming (in particular object-oriented programming) think that object-oriented programming languages like Java no longer need control-flow code as part of the programming language.

Control-flow is an integral part of object-oriented programming, composing much of the foundation behind the use of objects. As you will discover in the next chapter, all of the material you learn in this section wraps itself inside Java-based object classes.

Diagramming Control Flow

Diagramming control-flow (also referred to as pseudo-code) is a format for visually interpreting the programs you write without getting caught up in the actual details of how to write it in Java. Diagrams give you the ability to design your programs so that anyone (not just programmers) can view them. This provides a unique way for you to perform an analysis of your program and determine what it should (and should not) be doing. Figure 2-12 diagrams what to do when driving a vehicle approaching an intersection with a light.

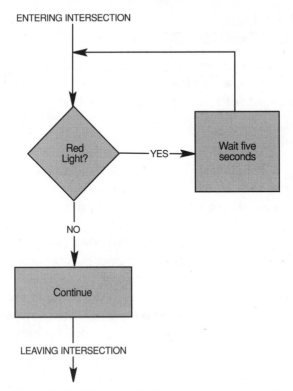

ENTERING INTERSECTION

Figure 2-12: Diagram of what to do when approaching an intersection.

In Figure 2-12, you come into an intersection and perform an evaluation, determining if the light is red; and if this is true, then you wait five seconds and perform the evaluation again. However, if this is false, then you continue through the intersection.

Notice that it does not matter what vehicle you are using nor at what exact intersection you are. In Figure 2-12, you have a relevant drawing showing a diagram for what to do at an intersection.

The If Conditional

The *if conditional* is a control statement that executes a line (or block) of code based on the result of an evaluation. The following shows the syntax for using a simple if statement:

```
if (conditional)
  statement;
```

Notice in the above code that if the conditional returns a true, then it causes the statement to execute. However, if the conditional returns a false, then it causes the statement not to execute, and the program continues.

For example, let's imagine that you are a programmer in a bank, and you are required to write a snippet of code determining if a customer's bank account contains more than $500. If the customer's balance is over $500, then the bank will waive the monthly charge. First, you need to draw out a diagram determining exactly what you want your code to do (see Figure 2-13).

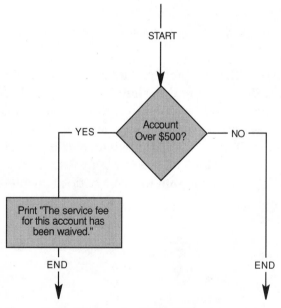

Figure 2-13: Diagram for the bank program.

Based on the above figure, let's write the actual code to implement in Java:

```
int account
//Body of Program
if (account > 500)
   System.out.println("The service fee for this account has
been waived.");
```

Using the if conditional, you have the ability to execute several lines of code. This is also true for just about all the other control-flow structures discussed in this chapter:

```
if (conditional) {
   statements;
}
```

In the above syntax, you are able to perform multiple statements (where *statements* represents a block of code) if the conditional returns a true.

Returning to our bank example, imagine that you now want to not only determine if a customer has at least $500 in an account, but you want to add $2 in interest as well. The if conditional stays the same, but the resulting code after it needs to be changed:

```
int account
Body of Program
if (account > 500) {
   System.out.println("The service fee for this account has
been wavied.");
   account += 2;
}
```

In the above code, using the += assignment operator adds 2 to the balance of the account. However, as with most banks, if the customer does not maintain a minimum balance, the bank imposes a fee on the account. In this case, you need somehow to add more functionality to your conditional so that if the balance is less then $500, you subtract $5 from it. You, the programmer, now need to determine how to make this possible. You could employ two separate if conditionals. However, another, more efficient, way would be to add functionality to the original if conditional by having it execute code if it returns a false (see Figure 2-14). That can be done by employing the else keyword in the if statement:

```
if (conditional) {
   statements;
} else {
   statements;
}
```

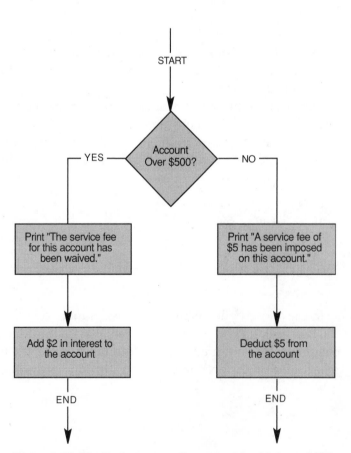

Figure 2-14: The bank program diagram with added capabilities.

Now, let's apply else to our bank example where you need to deduct $5 from accounts that have less than $500:

```java
int account
//Body of Program
if (account > 500) {
   System.out.println("The service fee for this account has been waived.");
   account += 2;
} else {
   System.out.println("A service fee of $5 has been imposed on this account.");
   account -= 5;
}
```

The above conditional has become fairly functional, leaving us with only one more topic concerning the if conditional (and one more example) before moving on: having more than one evaluation (i.e., conditional) taking place in the same if conditional:

```java
if (conditional) {
   statements;
} else if (conditional) {
   statements;
} else {
   statements;
}
```

So, looking back to our bank example let's imagine that if a customer's account is exactly equal to $500 dollars that there will be no fees nor interest added (see Figure 2-15).

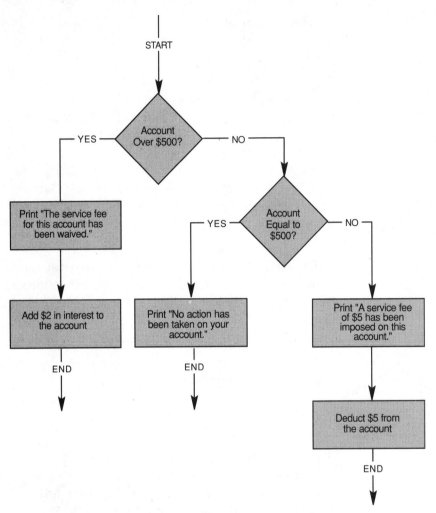

Figure 2-15: Diagram for the final bank program.

In Java, you could write Figure 2-15 as follows:

```java
int account
//Body of Program
if (account > 500) {
   System.out.println("The service fee for this account has
been waived.");
   account += 2;
} else if (account == 500) {
```

```
   System.out.println("No action has been taken on your
account");
} else {
   System.out.println("A service fee of $5 has been imposed on
this account.");
   account -= 5;
}
```

That is pretty much all there is to the if conditional.

Tutorial: If Conditional

Load the Developer Studio and close the project workspace you created from the last example (closing all the document windows). Then, open a new text file and type the following code into the Text Editor window:

```
class myIfTest {

   public static void main(String argv[]) {
   //Declare and assign a variable
   int account = 600;

      //Print out the beginning balance
   System.out.println("Your starting balance is $" + account);

      //The first if conditional
   if (account > 500) {
      System.out.println("The service fee for this account has
been waived.");
         account += 2;
      System.out.println("Your ending balance is $" +
account);
      } else if (account == 500) {
         System.out.println("No action has been taken on your
account");
   } else {
      System.out.println("A service fee of $5 has been imposed
on this account.");
         account -= 5;
```

```
        System.out.println("Your ending balance is $" +
account);
        }
    }
}
```

In the above code, you declare the integer account (with a value of 600). Then, there is an if conditional testing to see if this balance is greater than 500:

```
if (account > 500) {
```

If the above expression returns a true, then 2 is added to *account*. After the if conditional, there is an else-if conditional that checks to see if *account* is equal to 500:

```
} else if (account == 500) {
```

If the above expression returns true, then nothing is done to *account*. Finally, there is *else* that will be called if both of the above if conditionals return false, subtracting 5 from *account*.

Once you finish entering the above code, save the text file as myIfTest.java in the ..msdev\projects directory. Then, build the code (creating a default workspace) and execute the code. When the program executes, you'll see something similar to Figure 2-16.

```
F:\msdev\projects>jview myIfTest
Microsoft (R) Visual J++ Command-line Interpreter Verion 1.00.6173
Copyright (C) Microsoft Corp 1996. All rights reserved.
Your starting balance is $600
The service fee for this account has been waived.
Your ending balance is $602

F:\msdev\projects>jview myIfTest
Microsoft (R) Visual J++ Command-line Interpreter Verion 1.00.6173
Copyright (C) Microsoft Corp 1996. All rights reserved.
Your starting balance is $500
No action has been taken on your account

F:\msdev\projects>jview myIfTest
Microsoft (R) Visual J++ Command-line Interpreter Verion 1.00.6173
Copyright (C) Microsoft Corp 1996. All rights reserved.
Your starting balance is $400
A service fee of $5 has been imposed on this account.
Your ending balance is $395

F:\msdev\projects>_
```

Figure 2-16: Executing myIfTest application three times with 600, 500, and 400 for the account values, respectively.

In this example, the hard-coded balance amount of $600 is placed in the application. Go ahead and change the amount to $500; then recompile and execute. Then, finally, substitute $400 and recompile again and execute. In each of these executions, the program should behave in a different way. Test the application with different values of account to see different results.

The if conditional is a very useful and powerful tool to use in all of your Java programs. The next section discusses an operator that represents a sort of shorthand to the if conditionals you learned about in this section.

The ? Operator

The ? (known as the ternary) operator is something carried over from C/C++ language. The ternary operator could be considered an if shorthand notation. The following is the syntax for the ternary operator:

```
condition ? statement1 : statement2;
```

The ternary operator is very simple because it evaluates the condition, and if a true is returned, then statement1 is executed. On the other hand, if the condition is false, then statement2 is executed. Converting the above syntax of the ternary operator to an if conditional syntax looks like this:

```
if (condition) {
   statement1;
} else {
   statement2;
}
```

How the Ternary Operator Got Its Name
The ternary operator got its name from the fact that, according to the dictionary, ternary means the involvement of three, and the ternary operator has three terms.

The For Loop

The for loop behaves in a repetitious fashion, looping until it meets certain conditions. In every for loop there is an *initialization* that is called once when the for loop starts. Then the for loop continues to cycle between executing statements or block of statements, each time calling an incrementing or decrementing expression and retesting the conditional The following shows the general syntax of a for loop which only executes one statement:

```
for (initialization; conditional; expression)
    statement;
```

Or, if you wish to have a block of statements in your for loop, the following shows the syntax:

```
for (initialization; conditional; expression) {
    statements;
}
```

Note

All of the parts of the for loop are optional. In most cases, you can leave out any and/or all parts of the for loop. For example, leaving out the middle conditional would make the for loop cycle infinitely.

Let's take a look at an example. In this case, you need to print out all the even numbers contained between the numbers 1 and 10. Now, with what you have learned thus far, you can do this by using the following code:

```
System.out.println("2");
System.out.println("4");
System.out.println("6");
System.out.println("8");
System.out.println("10");
```

The above snippet of code does exactly what you need it to do. However, this brings up an important note about control-flow structures. Control-flow structures are here to help the programmer write less code and perform complex tasks in a more efficient manner. There is an easier and smarter way to do this same task. Let's start by looking at Figure 2-17 and understanding the exact logic of what you need the program to do.

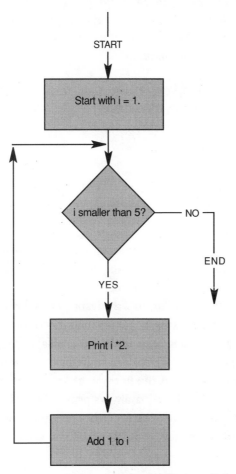

Figure 2-17: Diagram for displaying all the even numbers between 1 and 10.

Now, let's implement a for loop performing the same operation, but this time we'll write less code:

```
for (int i = 1; i < 5; i++)
    System.out.println(i * 2);
```

Note

Notice in the above code that you can declare variables inside the for loop. Also, note the variable i declared inside the for loop exists inside the loop only. This is part of variable scope that you will learn about later in the chapter.

In this case, the for loop cycles through, incrementing at every step, printing out another even number. Using a for loop, you were able to condense five lines of code into two; fairly impressive.

Code-writing Efficiency

In C, C++, and Java, it is possible to do the same function but with differing amounts of authored source code. It is not uncommon for some procedures to condense fifty lines of code into two.

The two lines of code may seem more advantageous; however, one of the problems with overly trite code is that it usually becomes much harder to understand. The key to writing code efficiently is balance and documentation. First, find a happy medium between the efficiency with which you wish to write your programs and the knowledge and needs of the audience who might view your code. Also, always provide ample documentation. By doing both of these things, you are protecting yourself in case you leave that program and come back to it later or if someone else needs to work with it.

With for loops you can also decrement so that with each cycle it goes in reverse. So, based on the above example, all of the even numbers between 1 and 10 are printed. The following snippet of code shows exactly the same task accomplished, except this time it prints each even number in reverse order:

```
for (int i = 5; i < 1; i--)
    System.out.println(i * 2);
```

This example prints all five even numbers on the screen in reverse order. Before leaving the topic of for loops, let's take a look at one more example. You have a loop that goes from 1 to 10, but this time you need to have the program test to see if the number is even or odd with each pass (see Figure 2-18).

Note

It is important to note that a for loop badly constructed may be infinite in nature. Thus, it will never quit looping. Or, the for loop will never start looping to begin with.

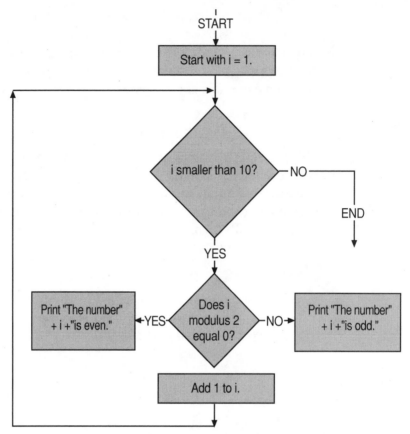

Figure 2-18: Diagram of a for loop displaying all the even and odd numbers between 1 and 10.

Review the above diagram; then consider the following code, which shows one technique for performing the above operation. In the example below, an if conditional is testing a modulus expression to see if the number is even or odd. Then it prints out its results:

```
for (int i = 1; i < 10; i++) {
  if ( i % 2 == 0)
    System.out.println("The number " + i + " is even");
  else System.out.println("The number " + i + " is odd");
}
```

The above code shows an example of having one control-flow structure inside another. This is a very common and useful programming practice.

Spacing

As you may have noticed throughout this chapter, a definitive spacing format is present in all the examples: statements inside a particular control-flow structure are indented. And, as you can see, a structure inside a structure is indented twice. Spaces in Java (also in C/C++) only benefit the programmer. The Java compiler does not recognize any of the spacing; all it looks for is the semicolon to know when a particular line of code has terminated.

Tutorial: For Loop

Load the Developer Studio and close the project workspace you created from the last example (closing all the document windows). Then, open a new text file and type the following code into the Text Editor window:

```
class myForTest {

    public static void main(String argv[]) {
        for (int i = 1; i < 10; i++) {
            if ( i % 2 == 0)
                System.out.println("The number " + i + " is even");
            else System.out.println("The number " + i + " is odd");
        }
    }
}
```

In the above code, you declare a for loop that will cycle 10 times, raising the variable i by 1 each time:

```
for (int i = 1; i < 10; i++) {
```

Inside the for loop is an if conditional checking to see if the current value of i is divisible by 2. If this is true, then the following println() method is invoked:

```
System.out.println("The number " + i + " is even");
```

If the current value of i is not divisible by 2, then the following println() method is invoked:

```
else System.out.println("The number " + i + " is odd");
```

Once you finish entering the above code, save the text file as myForTest.java in the ..msdev\projects directory. Then, build the code (creating a default workspace) and execute the code. When the program executes, you'll see something similar to Figure 2-19.

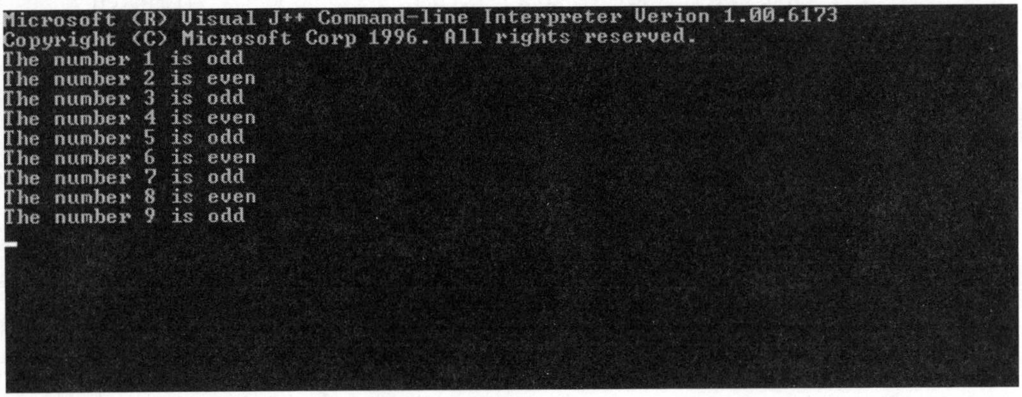

```
Microsoft (R) Visual J++ Command-line Interpreter Verion 1.00.6173
Copyright (C) Microsoft Corp 1996. All rights reserved.
The number 1 is odd
The number 2 is even
The number 3 is odd
The number 4 is even
The number 5 is odd
The number 6 is even
The number 7 is odd
The number 8 is even
The number 9 is odd
```

Figure 2-19: Executing the myForTest application.

Executing the application causes the numbers 1–10 to display, each with a corresponding "is even" or "is odd" reference.

The for loop is probably one of the most versatile of the control-flow structures in the Java language. The for loop is the backbone of most structured programming languages.

The While & Do While Loop

The while loop is similar to the for loop, except it does not have initialization or increment parts to it. Moreover, unless the body of the while loop eventually causes the condition to become false, it will continue looping forever. The following shows the syntax for a while loop with one statement and a while loop with a block of statements:

```
while (condition)
   statement;
```
Or,
```
while (condition) {
   statements;
}
```

While loops are very simple in the fact that they test for a particular condition: if true is returned, then they execute the statement(s) and finally go back and retest the condition. This will continue to loop until the condition sets to false.

Take a look at Figure 2-20. In the diagram, you have an account starting with a balance of $1000. Now, before withdrawing money, you are testing to make sure that there is at least $1 left in the account. If the test returns a true, then it will deduct $100 from the account and start over.

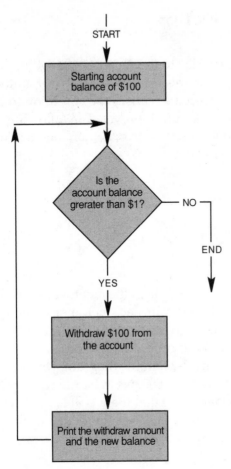

Figure 2-20: Diagram for withdrawing $100 from an account until it runs out of funds.

Let's translate the above diagram into a while loop in Java:

```java
int account = 1000;
Body of Program
while(account > 1) {
    account -= 100;
    System.out.println("You withdrew $100.");
    System.out.println("Your new balance is $" + account);
}
```

In the above snippet of code, you are looping through and deducting $100 with each loop.

Tutorial: While Loop

Load the Developer Studio and close the project workspace you created from the last example (closing all the document windows). Then, open a new text file and type the following code into the Text Editor window:

```
class myWhileTest {

    public static void main(String argv[]) {
        //Declare and assign $1000 to the account
        int account = 1000;
        System.out.println("Your starting balance is $" +
account);

        //Test to make sure there is at least $1 in the
account
        while(account > 1) {

            //Withdraw $100 from the account
            account -= 100;
            System.out.println("You withdrew $100.");
            System.out.println("Your new balance is $" +
account);

        }

        //At this point you are now out of the loop
        System.out.println("You are out of funds.");

    }
}
```

In the above code, you are declaring the integer account (with an initial value of 1000). Then you have a while loop that has been declared as follows:

```
while(account > 1) {
```

The while loop cycles, deducting 100 from account and displaying the new value for account until account is less than 1.

Once you finish entering the above code, save the text file as myWhileTest.java in the ..msdev\projects directory. Then, build the code (creating a default workspace) and execute the code. When the program executes, you'll see something similar to Figure 2-21.

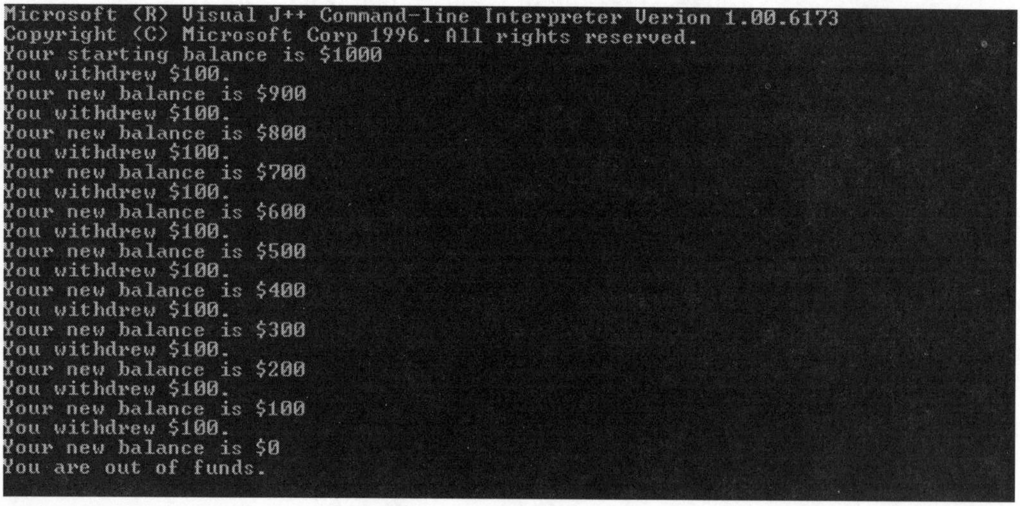

```
Microsoft (R) Visual J++ Command-line Interpreter Verion 1.00.6173
Copyright (C) Microsoft Corp 1996. All rights reserved.
Your starting balance is $1000
You withdrew $100.
Your new balance is $900
You withdrew $100.
Your new balance is $800
You withdrew $100.
Your new balance is $700
You withdrew $100.
Your new balance is $600
You withdrew $100.
Your new balance is $500
You withdrew $100.
Your new balance is $400
You withdrew $100.
Your new balance is $300
You withdrew $100.
Your new balance is $200
You withdrew $100.
Your new balance is $100
You withdrew $100.
Your new balance is $0
You are out of funds.
```

Figure 2-21: Executing the myWhileTest application.

Test the application with different values for account and you will see different results.

The other loop related to the while loop is the do while loop. Once you understand the while loop, the do while loop is very easy to understand. Simply stated, the only difference between a while loop and a do while loop is that with a do while loop the statement (or block of statements) executes first, then the condition is evaluated. In other words, the logical pattern followed is execute the statement(s) and then evaluate the condition. The following shows the syntax for the do while loop:

```
do
    statement;
while (condition);
```

And the following shows the syntax for the block method of using a do-while loop:

```
do {
    statements;
} while (condition);
```

That is pretty much all there is to a do while loop. However, this minor difference from the while loop can have major implications. In most cases, it does not really matter which loop you use, as they will both produce the same results. The only thing to keep in mind is that you should be consistent with which type of while loop you choose.

The Switch Statement

Sometimes, it is not convenient to have your conditional evaluate a true (or false) result for determining which way your program should flow. In these cases you can implement the switch statement. Carried over from C/C++, the switch statement is very useful for situations where you have multiple selections going at one time. The following is the syntax for a switch statement:

```
switch (expression) {

    case constant1:
        statement;
        break;
    case constant2:
        statement;
    case constant3:
        statement;
```

```
        break;

    .

    .

    .

    default:
        statement;
}
```

Tip

It is a good practice to always put a default statement in switch, since you might not always know for sure what data will come from expression.

The switch statement is very easy to understand. Starting from the top, the expression (that can be of type char, byte, short, or int) returns a value. Then the value matches itself to one of the case constants (e.g., constant1 or constant2). At this point, the statement contained inside that case executes and continues to execute down the switch statement until the keyword break is reached.

Breaks in Switch Statements

Notice in the above syntax for the switch statement that the break keyword is optional for each case. This means, however, that if a case does not contain a break, the program executes through other cases below it until it reaches a break statement or until it comes to the end of the switch statement.

The last part of the above syntax left to discuss is the default part. In the event that the expression returns a value that does not match any of the cases in the switch statement, the default and its corresponding statements execute. Note that the default is an optional part of the syntax for a switch statement.

Note

The entire switch statement itself comprises a block. Also, note that cases inside a switch statement cannot contain blocks.

Now let's try an example where you can use a switch statement to return a value and select among several options. In this case, you are a programmer working for a major college. The college wants you to write a segment of code to print out a response for students so they can determine if they have passed the class. If the students did not pass the class, then determine and print out if they qualify to retake it over the summer. The diagram in Figure 2-22 shows the logic for the program.

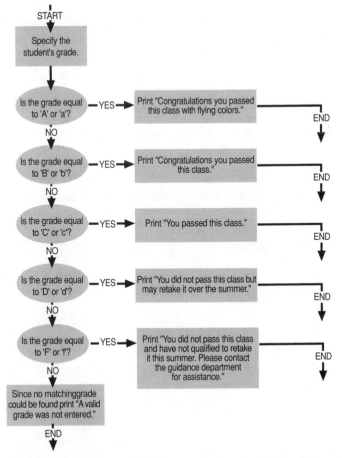

Figure 2-22: Diagram of a class program implemented with a switch statement.

```java
char grade;
//Body of Program
switch (grade) {
    case 'A':
    case 'a':
        System.out.println("Congratulations you passed this
class with flying colors.");
        break;
    case 'B':
    case 'b':
        System.out.println("Congratulations you passed this
class.");
        break;
    case 'C':
    case 'c':
        System.out.println("You passed this class.");
        break;
    case 'D':
    case 'd':
        System.out.println("You did not pass the class but
may retake it over the summer.");
        break;
    case 'F':
    case 'f':
        System.out.println("You did not pass the class and
have not qualified to retake it this summer.");
        System.out.println("Please contact the guidance
department for assistance.");
        break;
    default:
        System.out.println("A valid grade was not entered.");
        break;
}
```

Tip

*Two cases in one switch statement cannot have exactly the same
constant.*

Simply stated, the above will go through each step and determine which grade (regardless of case) and print the corresponding message to the student.

Tutorial: Switch Statement

Load the Developer Studio and close the project workspace you created from the last example (closing all the document windows). Then, open a new text file and type the following code into the Text Editor window:

```
class mySwitchTest {

    public static void main(String argv[]) {
        //Declare the variable and assign a grade
        char grade = 'A';
        System.out.println("You entered the grade: " +
grade);

        switch (grade) {
            case 'A':
            case 'a':
                //The grade was found to be an A (or a) so
print out the following
                System.out.println("Congratulations you
passed this class with flying colors.");
                break;
            case 'B':
            case 'b':
                //The grade was found to be an B (or b) so
print out the following
                System.out.println("Congratulations you
passed this class.");
                break;
            case 'C':
            case 'c':
                //The grade was found to be an C (or c) so
print out the following
                System.out.println("You passed the class.");
```

```
                break;
        case 'D':
        case 'd':
                //The grade was found to be an D (or d) so
print out the following
                System.out.println("You did not pass the
class but may retake it over the summer.");
                break;
        case 'F':
        case 'f':
                //The grade was found to be an F (or f) so
print out the following
                System.out.println("You did not pass the
class and have not qualified to retake it.");
                System.out.println("Please contact the
guidance department for assistance.");
                break;
        default:
                //Could not match a grade so execute the
default
                System.out.println("A valid grade was not
entered.");
                break;
        }
    }
}
```

In the above code, you declare the variable grade to have a value of A.

```
char grade = 'A';
    Then you have a switch statement that takes grade:switch
(grade) {
```

Then, the rest of the program comprises case statements, checking to see if there is a match, and printing an appropriate message.

Common Programming Error With Switch

A very common programming mistake for both new and veteran programmers is to forget to put a break to end the execution. If you are creating a switch statement, and it is either reporting errors or doing things incorrectly, always check to make sure that you placed the breaks in their proper places.

Once you finish entering the above code, save the text file as mySwitchTest.java in the ..msdev\projects directory. Then, build the code (creating a default workspace) and execute the code. When the program executes, you'll see something similar to Figure 2-23.

```
F:\msdev\projects>jview mySwitchTest
Microsoft (R) Visual J++ Command-line Interpreter Verion 1.00.6173
Copyright (C) Microsoft Corp 1996. All rights reserved.
You entered the grade: A
Congratulations you passed this class with flying colors.

F:\msdev\projects>jview mySwitchTest
Microsoft (R) Visual J++ Command-line Interpreter Verion 1.00.6173
Copyright (C) Microsoft Corp 1996. All rights reserved.
You entered the grade: f
You did not pass the class and have not qualified to retake it.
Please contact the guidance department for assistance.

F:\msdev\projects>jview mySwitchTest
Microsoft (R) Visual J++ Command-line Interpreter Verion 1.00.6173
Copyright (C) Microsoft Corp 1996. All rights reserved.
You entered the grade: x
A valid grade was not entered.

F:\msdev\projects>_
```

Figure 2-23: Executing the mySwitchTest application.

Test the application by entering different grade letters for grade in the application and you will see different results. The switch statement can be very useful when dealing with selections that are outside of the standard true and false paradigm.

Breaking Out of Loops

As mentioned in the keyword section, Java does not have any functional use for the goto keyword. As a result, Java has added extra functionality with labeled breaks.

In this section, we discuss three types of jumping that help you circumvent the need to use goto: breaking loops, breaking nested loops (using labels), and continuing.

The goto Controversy

One of the old controversies in the programming industry was whether to use goto in programs. Prior to the modern structured programming languages like Java, goto was the primary vehicle for executing control-flow structures. However, as programs became bigger, keeping track of all the gotos turned more of a challenge than an advantage. So, programmers employed more sophisticated techniques. During this transition, using goto became a bad programming practice. Today, there is still some debate questioning if things went too far, because, in certain situations, goto provides a very clean and efficient way to do certain tasks.

Java, with all of its advanced object-based features (that you will learn more about in Chapter 3) and breaking loops (that you will learn about in this section), no longer needs goto

Breaking

The first process to understand is the idea of breaking out of a loop. In these examples you are in a loop (e.g., a for loop) and you are cycling through. However, every time you cycle, you are testing for something. If that evaluation returns a true, then you call the break to jump out of the loop. The following snippet of code deducts a $100 loan payment from a customer's account 10 times. However, if the account runs out of funds, you need to print how much the customer still owes and break out of the loop so no more deductions take place. The following shows an example of how to do that using the break statement:

```java
int account;
Body of Program
for (int i = 1; i < 10; i++) {
    account -= 100;
    System.out.println("$100 has been deducted from your
account.");
    System.out.println("Your new balance is $" + account);

    if (account < 1) {
        System.out.println("Your account is out of money and you
still owe " + (1000 - 100 * i));
        break;
    }

}
```

None of the above code should be new to you. However, the key area to focus on for this section is the if conditional. Let's take a closer look at it:

```java
if (account < 1) {
    System.out.println("Your account is out of money and you
still owe " + (1000 - 100 * i);
    break;
}
```

Remember that in the above code you are inside the for loop. Notice that you are checking to see if the account balance is less than $1. If this evaluation returns true, then the next line prints out what the customer still owes. The remaining loan balance is determined by taking the customer's current location in the loop and multiplying it by $100 and subtracting that amount from the total loan balance of $1000. Finally, the last line inside this if conditional block is the break statement that stops the loop from executing any further, and the program continues outside of the loop. Sounds simple; however, let's take a look at a diagram showing how this flow works (see Figure 2-24).

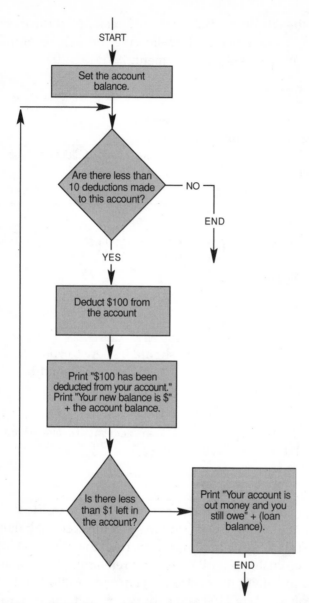

Figure 2-24: Diagram for the breaking-out-of-loops bank example.

Tutorial: Break Statement

Load the Developer Studio and close the project workspace you
created from the last example (closing all the document windows).
Then, open a new text file and type the following code into the
Text Editor window:

```java
class myBreakTest {

    public static void main(String argv[]) {

        //Declare the variable and assign an amount
        int account = 600;
        System.out.println("Your beginning balance is $" +
account);

        //Start Loop for 10 payments of $100
        for (int i = 1; i < 10; i++) {

    //Deduct $100 from the account
account -= 100;
    System.out.println("$100 has been deducted from your
account.");
    System.out.println("Your new balance is $" + account);

    //Check to make sure there is still money in the account
    if (account < 1) {
        System.out.println("Your account is out of money and you
still owe $" + (1000 - 100 * i));
            break;
    }
        }
    }
}
```

In the above code, you declare the variable account (with an
initial value of 600). Then you start a for loop that will cycle 10
times; each time, it subtracts 100 from account. The key part of
the application to notice is that in the for loop is an if conditional
that checks to see if account is less than 1.

```
if (account < 1) {
```

If this is true, then the following is invoked:

```
System.out.println("Your account is out of money and you
still owe $" + (1000 - 100 * i));
            break;
```

In the two lines of code above, the first displays a message telling you that you are out of money and then displays the remaining balance. The second line is a break statement that causes the program to immediately jump out of the loop.

Once you finish entering the above code, save the text file as myBreakTest.java in the ..msdev\projects directory. Then, build the code (creating a default workspace) and execute the code. When the program executes, you'll see something similar to Figure 2-25.

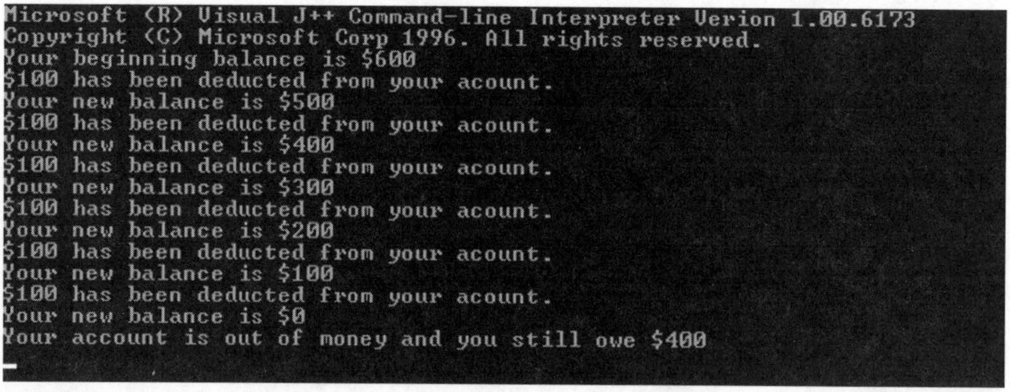

```
Microsoft (R) Visual J++ Command-line Interpreter Verion 1.00.6173
Copyright (C) Microsoft Corp 1996. All rights reserved.
Your beginning balance is $600
$100 has been deducted from your acount.
Your new balance is $500
$100 has been deducted from your acount.
Your new balance is $400
$100 has been deducted from your acount.
Your new balance is $300
$100 has been deducted from your acount.
Your new balance is $200
$100 has been deducted from your acount.
Your new balance is $100
$100 has been deducted from your acount.
Your new balance is $0
Your account is out of money and you still owe $400
```

Figure 2-25: Executing the myBreakTest application.

Executing the application causes it to loop through 6 times, deducting 100 from account each loop. However, when account is 0, myBreakTest breaks the loop and exits the application. Try executing account with different values, and you will see different results.

Notice in the program that you hard-coded the account to have a balance of $600. That means that this account defaults, and the break statement executes, leaving the customer left with a loan balance of $400 (see Figure 2-25).

Breaking With Labels

Sometimes, breaking out of a loop is just not that simple. In other languages such as C and C++, goto functionality is there in case you wish to use it to accomplish these tasks. However, in Java, goto is not an option. Instead, you can use a labeled break.

Before continuing, you need to understand how to create labels in the Java language:

```
label1:
```

A label is nothing more than a name (similar to a name you might give a variable) immediately followed by a colon. When performing a labeled break, you type the keyword break (just as you did in the last section to remove yourself from a loop), followed by the label you want to jump to:

```
HERE:

Body of Program

for (int I = 1; I < 100; I++) {
   Body of outer for Loop
   for (int a = 1; a < 10; a ++) {
      Body of inner for Loop
      break HERE;
   }
}
```

If you look closely at the above example, you will notice that if you were simply to specify break, you would only break out of the first for loop and not the second. Secondly, even if you were able to break out of both for loops by using two breaks, your program would continue execution at the end of the outer for loop and not at the specified label.

Labeled breaks are not the best solutions to a programming problem and should only be implemented as a last resort.

Continuing

The last technique to discuss in this chapter is how to prematurely advance in a for loop. This handy technique can prove quite useful. Simply stated, you have a loop that cycles through; inside that loop, you may have a situation arise where you want to advance to the next loop without executing all of the statements. Using the continue keyword and the following syntax you have your solution:

```
Beginning of a Loop {
    statement(s)1;
    Conditional (if true execute the following block) {
        statement(s);
        continue;
    }
    statement(s)2;
}
```

Notice in the above example that every time this loop cycles, statement(s)1 executes. However, statement(s)2 only executes if the conditional returns a false. Otherwise, the block inside the conditional executes the continue statement that automatically advances the loop to the next cycle without executing statement(s)2. Continue can be a very handy technique in certain situations.

Moving On

In this chapter, you learned about the overall structure of the Java language. Structured programming is a very important part of learning to program in any language. You also had a very healthy dose of using Visual J++. By now you should be able to create Visual J++ applications quite easily.

Chapter 3 continues to lay a foundation of Java understanding by focusing on the object side of the Java language. You will have a chance to learn more about other features of Visual J++ and how to take advantage of them.

3

Introduction to Object-Oriented Programming

One day I was having lunch with one of my colleagues. During that lunch, while everyone around discussed sports or weather, we were discussing the differences between object-oriented and structured programming (or procedural programming, as he termed it). My colleague is a structured programmer wanting to learn more about object-oriented programming, and I am an object-oriented programmer trying to sell him on the idea.

The discussion lasted well over an hour. Probably the single most important question he asked during that lunch was, "What does object-oriented programming do that structured programming doesn't?"

I thought about it and almost gave him a long-winded, technically inclined response discussing all the object-based programming techniques and new technologies that all object-oriented programming languages have in common. Then, I realized that this would not answer the question and would only cause confusion. So, in that instant I decided to answer him with the first thought that came to my mind: "It is a better way to organize your programs."

Indeed. Leaving behind all the technical advantages (and detailed discussions), at a very simplistic level, object-oriented programming organizes your programs in a more efficient and, more importantly, easier-to-understand format.

Java is an object-oriented programming language. Visual J++ is an object-conscious environment, which makes it easier to develop and test your object-based Java programs. Having an object-friendly environment is very important. The Visual J++ tools discussed in this chapter help you appreciate the advantages of using object-based programs.

To start off this chapter, you are going to learn more about the Visual J++ project environment, specifically, how to create custom project workspaces and what they do for you in Visual J++. After that, you will learn about all of the major object-based topics (such as inheritance and interfaces) and how to implement them in Java. Throughout the chapter, you will learn about features and tips available to you in Visual J++ to help you write object-based Java programs.

Visual J++ Project Workspaces & Projects

Project workspaces are the backbone for development in the Developer Studio. When you create a new project, you receive a Project Workspace window, directory, and compiling configurations. With the creation of the project workspace, Visual J++ provides a project that lets you create and edit other projects, subprojects, and, of course, Java programs.

Subprojects

A *subproject* (also known as a dependency project) is a project within a project. In Visual J++, you can create subprojects to extend from your current projects (or the main project workspace). Subprojects are very useful when you have more than one Java program working together.

On the inside, a project workspace consists of a special directory and several files. Visual J++ automatically creates both the directory and default files that belong to the project. You also have, by default, two project-compiling configurations (one for debugging and the other optimized for release) that determine how Visual J++ will build your programs. From there, your project workspace manages and maintains any project or subprojects that you create with this workspace open. Having a project workspace provides a much more efficient method of Visual J++ project management.

The Project Workspace Window

When you create a new project workspace, the first project for this workspace is automatically created for you. This window affords a comprehensive way of reviewing your projects and subsequent Java programs through the use of the different views. Figure 3-1 shows an example of a Project Workspace window.

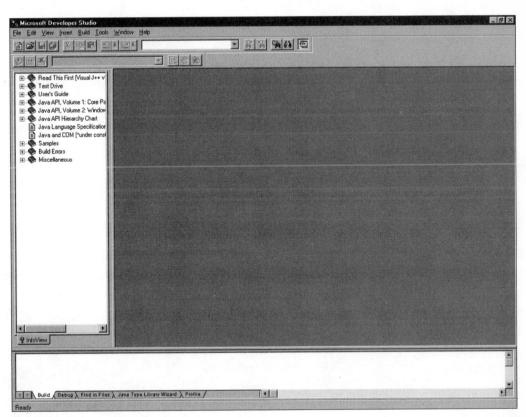

Figure 3-1 : Example of a Project Workspace window.

Basically, you have three views: FileView, ClassView, and InfoView. FileView displays any files and subprojects you created for this project workspace. This is useful when you have more than one subproject connected to the project workspace or if you have several source code files located in different areas (see Figure 3-2).

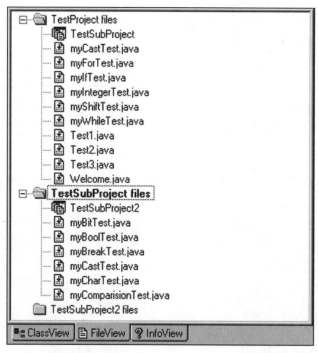

Figure 3-2: FileView in the Project Workspace pane.

Note

The bolded item in the FileView (see Figure 3-2) represents the default project for this project workspace.

ClassView displays an organization of all your Java classes. ClassView displays your project's class information in a very intuitive and logical format, including all the classes and any other projects contained in this project workspace (see Figure 3-3).

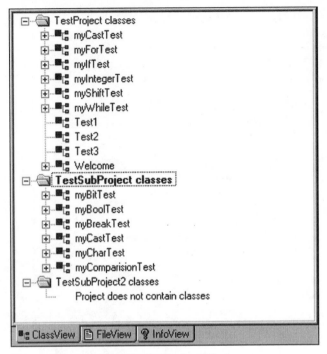

Figure 3-3: ClassView in the Project Workspace pane.

Finally, InfoView is an outline of all of the online information included with Visual J++, including online Java books, help, and the entire Java API specification. Since InfoView does not depend on any one project, you can use InfoView anytime by clicking on the InfoView Tab (shown in Figure 3-4) even if you do not have a project workspace open.

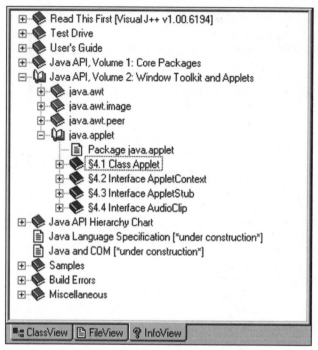

Figure 3-4: InfoView in the Project Workspace pane.

Project Workspace Files

When you create a new project workspace, Visual J++ also creates a new directory and project. Specifically, Visual J++ creates two basic files associated with the project workspace: an .MDP file (known as the Project Workspace file) and an .MAK file (known as the Project Workspace makefile). Essentially, when you create a new project workspace, Visual J++ creates a new file, using the name of your project workspace and adding the extension of .MDP for the first file and .MAK for the second.

The Project Workspace file (.MDP) is responsible for recording the generic environmental options dealing with your project workspace. This file also contains pertinent information for any breakpoints you may have specified in your debugging sessions (see Chapter 5 for more information on debugging). Also, the workspace file is responsible for any editing preferences (such as font type and size, color, etc.).

The Project Workspace makefile is responsible for the name and location of all the source code files. The makefile also stores any settings related to the compiler or other tools needed to build the project. The makefile is the lower-level, more detail-oriented of the two files.

Source Code Files

Unlike most project-related files, source code files do not need to be in their respective project (or project workspace) directory. The makefile (.MAK) from your project workspace keeps track of all project-related source code files and their respective directories.

This adds more versatility to your projects. As you will learn later on, you can link source code files from other projects and other directories.

The two files mentioned are not the only files created. There are many other files contained in the project workspace directory created by Visual J++ (either automatically or indirectly, as you continue to develop your Java programs). The project workspace directory is the holding tank for all of these files.

Organizing Your Project Workspaces

The overall purpose of having a project workspace to begin with is to help you better organize your Visual J++ projects and, on a deeper level, your Visual J++ programs.

Tip

One of the major advantages of using Visual J++ over the Java Development Kit (JDK), is that with Visual J++ you have complete professional project management capabilities that are not present in the JDK.

There are several ways in which you can organize your project workspaces (see Figure 3-5).

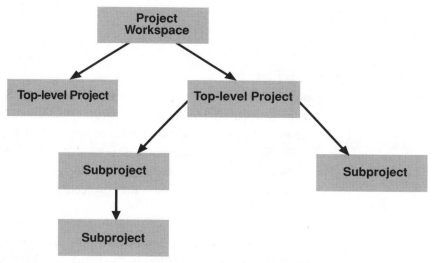

Figure 3-5: Diagram of the Visual J++ project structure.

Tutorial: Creating a Project Workspace

At this point, let's go ahead and create a new project workspace and, subsequently, a project. First, load Visual J++ so that it looks like Figure 3-6.

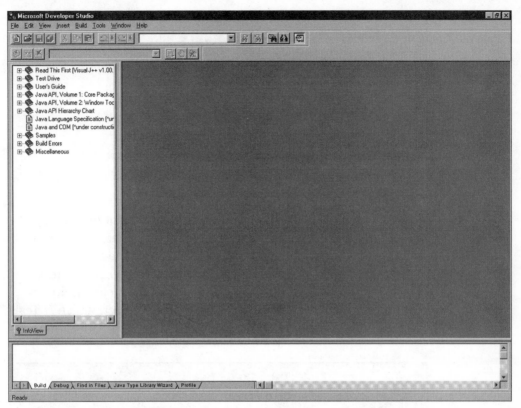

Figure 3-6: The Developer Studio loaded.

Now, click on File | New and the New dialog box appears. Note that, on your system, the dialog box may have more items from which to choose than those shown in Figure 3-7. Click on Project Workspace (as shown in Figure 3-7).

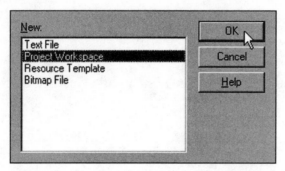

Figure 3-7: The New dialog box in the Developer Studio.

After you have clicked on Project Workspace, another dialog box opens, giving you options to set up your project workspace. In this example (as with all of them throughout the book), the Project Workspace directory is in the msdev\projects directory. However, you can put it in another location. In the text field, on the upper-left corner, enter the name for this project, which is **Test**. Figure 3-8 shows the dialog box filled out.

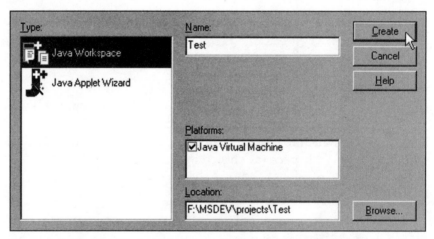

Figure 3-8: The New Project Workspace dialog box filled out.

Tip

Fill out the name of the project in the New Project Workspace dialog box, and Visual J++ automatically fills out the associated project workspace subdirectory in the Location field, as shown in Figure 3-8.

After you have filled out the New Project Workspace dialog box by adding Test to the Name field, you are ready to click Create to build the project workspace and its first project (see Figure 3-9).

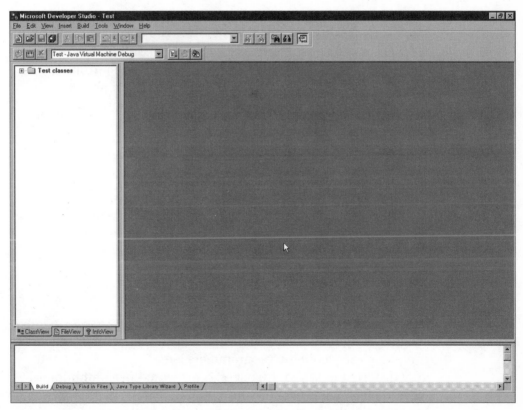

Figure 3-9: Visual J++ with a project workspace and associated project created.

At this point, you are ready to begin work in Visual J++. As you can see on the left side of Figure 3-9, the Project Workspace pane is open with the ClassView displaying information about your project, Test.

From now on, creating projects and their workspaces will not be very hard. Actually, many of the more common procedures in Visual J++ are not very hard. So, for the easier and more repetitive tasks, a table showing the step-by-step instructions is provided. For example, Table 3-1 shows what you did in the last section to create the project Test.

Step #	Location	Action
1	Developer Studio	Choose File|New.
2	New dialog box	Highlight Project Workspace, and click OK.
3	New Project Workspace dialog box	In the Name field, type **Test**, and click Create.

Table 3-1: Creating the Test Project Workspace.

This table shows you how to create a new project workspace and project in three simple steps. At this point, let's move forward and learn more about object-oriented programming in Java.

Object-oriented Programming

Java is an object-oriented programming language. Object-oriented programming may be one of the most misunderstood topics in computer science. Many programmers either have no idea or a very distorted idea about what object-oriented programming is. Nevertheless, regardless of your opinion, object-oriented programming is the future of programming as we know it.

Java is by no means the first (or last) programming language to be object-oriented. Java is special as an object-oriented programming language because it is easy to understand and even easier to implement when compared to other object-based programming languages. Once you learn how to program with objects in one language, you will find it easy to program in other object-oriented languages. Let's take a brief digression to learn a little more about structured programming design and how object-oriented design is better.

Programming, the Way It Used to Be

Structured programming languages, which you may be familiar with, include Pascal, C, and VB (though VB is becoming more object-based with every version upgrade). Essentially, structured programming, procedure-oriented programming, and function-oriented programming all represent the same type of programming: non-object-oriented. This book refers to all of them as structured programming.

Structured programming relies heavily upon the conceptual theme of a group of functions connected to one central location. In this model, there are two primary ways for functions to communicate with each other: either by going through a central location or by having a variable declared with a global status that is thus available to everything whether you want it to be or not. Figure 3-10 shows a diagram of a typical structured program.

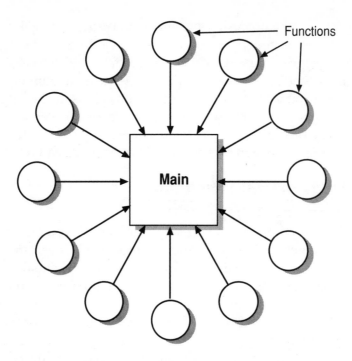

Figure 3-10: Diagram of a typical structured program with global variables available throughout the entire program.

Contrary to a myth floating around, structured programming does have reusable capabilities. Probably, the most common way to reuse structured programming is to create generic functions that you can implement in more than one program.

Working With Objects

Object-oriented programming designs itself around a more distributed theme in which there is no real focal point. In object-oriented programming, one key point is the ability to have more communication between the objects instead of just in one location. Also, you do not have any omnipresent global variables. You can grant certain parts of the classes to have complete exposure to everything and others to only be available inside their current class. Figure 3-11 shows a diagram of a distributed Java applet.

Implementing Objects in Java With Classes

Up to this point, we've dealt strictly with the theoretical topic of objects in any given object-oriented programming language. However, in Java, you do not implement objects; you implement classes (which embody objects). A *class* in Java is an implementation for the framework of an object that provides a generic holding tank for objects as well as other parts of a class.

Believe it or not, you have been creating classes since Chapter 1. You cannot write a non-object-based Java program. A class must encapsulate all your Java programs, which is why, in the last two chapters, the line of code at the top of the program was actually declaring a class. The following shows the syntax for a very basic class:

```
class classname {
Body of Class
}
```

Let's look at a sample real-world class called Book:

```
class Book {
}
```

Notice in the above code that *class* is part of the formal declaration for the class. Following that declaration is the class name. This class is called Book. Everything inside of the brackets is part of the class Book, in one way or another. At a very basic level, that is really all there is to creating a class. However, as you can see, the class Book does not have many capabilities. Frankly, that is because it is a class, but does not have any functionality.

Instancing Classes

Defining classes and actually implementing them are two different things. In the last section, you got a feel for what to do when you want to define a class. However, defining a class won't cause it to do anything but sit there and be defined. It is through the process of *instancing* that you actually get to use your classes. Instancing also gives you a more specific representation of the defined class.

For an illustration of class instancing, go back to the class Book. A book is pretty much anything that contains words or pictures and is bound with a cover. An instance of a book would be *Moby Dick*. In this case, you know more specific information about this book than just "bound with a cover." You know exactly how many words and what type of cover. Thus, you have a more specific representation of the class Book. The following shows how you would instance the class Book:

```
Book mobyDick = new Book();
```

On the left side of this line, you are basically declaring an instance variable in the same manner as you would a primitive data type that you worked with in the last chapter. Also, notice the keyword new. Technically speaking, *new* is an operator that constructs the instance of the Book class called MobyDick. Finally, note that the parentheses are not an optional part of the declaration, because they are acting as operators.

Tip

You can also specify variables when instancing, depending on the class definition. This variable information would go in parentheses. However, as shown in the above example, if there are no variables passed to this class, you still need to include the parentheses.

You now have an instance of Book reflected specifically toward the novel *Moby Dick*.

One of the nice features of Java over C/C++ is what is happening on the inside when you instance an object. In Java, you need to construct your objects using new. Unlike C++, however, Java handles the destruction of all your Java classes. This helps make Java programming that much easier and removes any chance for error related to memory management. The following shows the syntax for instancing classes:

```
ClassName variableName = new ClassName();
```

Throughout the rest of this chapter (and book), you will have a chance to create instances of classes.

Another tool that you can use is the instanceof operator that lets you check to see if one object is an instance of another class. The following shows the syntax for using the instanceof operator:

```
Object instanceof Class
```

If the object is an instance of Class on the right, then the expression returns a true. Consider the following:

```
Book myBook = new Book();
boolean test = myBook instanceof Book;
```

In these two lines of code, the first line creates myBook, which is an instance of the class Book. The second line uses the instanceof operator to check to see if myBook is an instance of Book. In this case, the second-line-of-code test would be true.

Right now, let's turn our attention back to understanding how to add functionality to classes.

Class Variables

Variables represent a holding tank for information that helps you save and access information within your Java programs. There are two important things to note about using variables in the Java language. First, every variable must be a member of a class. In other words, you cannot have a stand-alone variable in Java. Secondly, there are no global variables in Java. In the following code, you add an integer variable, numberOfPages, so that it is a member of our newly created class, Book:

```
class Book {
    int numberOfPages;
}
```

This is primarily all that you need to do in order to make a variable available to the entire class Book (i.e., this int variable could be used in any method belonging to this class). As you will learn later, other classes can access this variable; and, if you choose, you can specify restrictions for the types of classes that can access it. The declaration and use of variables should not be anything new to you, as Chapter 2 reviewed those subjects in detail. Although you may not have realized it, in the Visual J++ project examples in the last chapter, you were doing this exact thing.

Class Methods

Method is the object-oriented word for a function in structured-language talk. A method is exactly like a function, except that it wraps itself inside a class. Hence, the method is a member of the class it belongs to.

Tip

Java does not support stand-alone functions. The only way to employ a method is to wrap it inside a class. However, you can design your static class (e.g., Lib) and use its methods through all your programs (e.g, Lib.funct1()).

Methods, like functions, perform a set of actions when called. It is also not uncommon in Java for several classes to call one method. The code below shows the syntax for declaring a method:

```
returnType methodName( ) {

    // Body of Method

}
```

Just like a function, a method can have a return type. The *returnType* in front of the word *methodName()* represents the location where you designate a return type for this method. When you declare a method, you use the returnType to declare what type of data returns from this method. Unlike C, Java does not assume any default return type. Return type may be a primitive type (like int), an object, or even an array.

Tip

In some cases, you do not need to return a type. In those cases, place void for the returnType. That means nothing returns.

Notice the parentheses after methodName. Within these, you can place input variables to enter data to the method. When empty (as in the syntax above), it represents that you have no input variables for this method. Notice that even though you do not have any input variables, you still need the parentheses after the method name. Technically speaking, the parentheses are operators telling Java that this is a method. Using parentheses helps Java differentiate methods in your program.

Below is an example of a method with a return type of int that takes two declared input int variables:

```
class Test {
    int addTwoNumbers(int firstNumber, int secondNumber) {
        return firstNumber + secondNumber;
    }
}
```

First, notice the int in front of addTwoNumbers. That means that the method returns an integer value. The code inside the above method contains an expression with *return* just before the calculation. The keyword return is the method's cue to return the value of the expression immediately following return.

Method Overloading

One of the things that you can do with methods is overload them. Specifically, you can create methods that have similar functionality and the same name. Java automatically chooses the correct method to execute based on what was given in the method call. Method overloading in Java was carried over from C++. However, C++ refers to it as function overloading.

Tip

*In C++, you can overload operators (+, -, *, etc.) so that they perform different functions aside from their primary function in the language. However, because operator overloading can complicate a program, it is removed from the Java language.*

Method overloading can be very useful. Technically speaking, method overloading can be used to create several methods of the same name (with different input variables) to perform very similar tasks. Each overloaded method is designed to handle a different set of input variables, but perform similar functions. Method overloading is a very important part of the modern programming paradigm in Java.

Tutorial: Creating Methods & Overloading Them

In this tutorial, you are going to create the Java application WordAddition. This application will contain several overloaded combine() methods, thus, giving you a chance to work with overloaded methods. Let's try this in Visual J++. Create a project workspace called WordAddition (see Table 3-2 for the procedure).

Step #	Location	Action
1	Developer Studio	Choose File|New.
2	New dialog box	Highlight Project Workspace, then click OK.
3	New Project Workspace dialog box	In the Name field, type **WordAddition**; then click Create.

Table 3-2: Creating the WordAddition Project Workspace.

Once you have created a new project workspace, click on File | New. In the New dialog box, choose Text File and click OK. Once you have completed that task, the Developer Studio will look something like Figure 3-12.

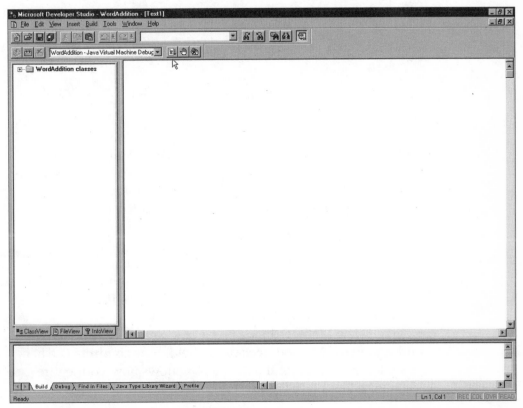

Figure 3-12: The Developer Studio with the WordAddition Project Workspace and a new text file open.

Now you need to create a new Java class called WordAddition. In the Developer Studio, click Insert | New Java Class. On the Create New Class dialog box, in the Name field, type **WordAddition** and click OK (see Figure 3-13).

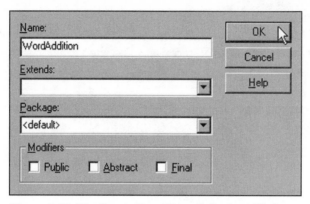

Figure 3-13: The Create New Class dialog box filled out.

The Developer Studio now shows the WordAddition Project Workspace (in the ClassView) with the WordAddition class in the left pane. Click on the WordAddition classes' folder to see the source code for WordAddition.java with its automatically generated code in the right pane.

Next, double-click on the WordAddition classes' folder in the ClassView to expand it. Notice that it has one item: the class WordAddition. You want to add a method, so highlight this class and right-click to open up the Context menu (see Figure 3-14). From the Context menu, select Add Method.

On the New Method dialog box, in the Return type field, type **void**; and in the Method declaration field, type **combine ()**. Then, click OK. The bottom of the dialog box shows how your entire declaration looks (see Figure 3-15).

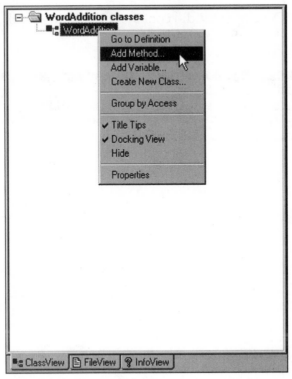

Figure 3-14: The menu in ClassView in the Project Workspace window for editing classes.

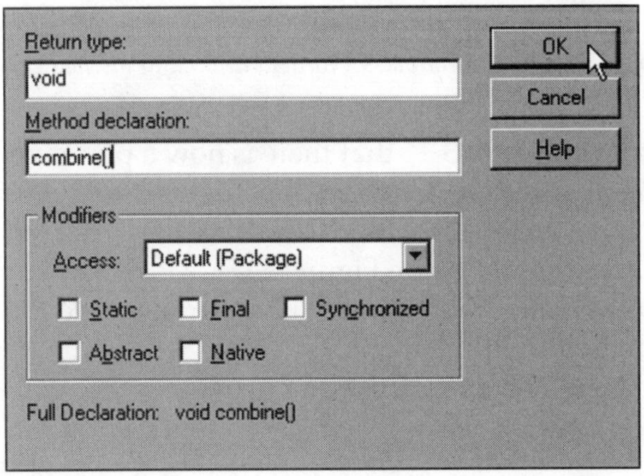

Figure 3-15: The Create New Method dialog box filled out for the first combine() method.

Your Developer Studio contains a definition for the method combine() (see Figure 3-16).

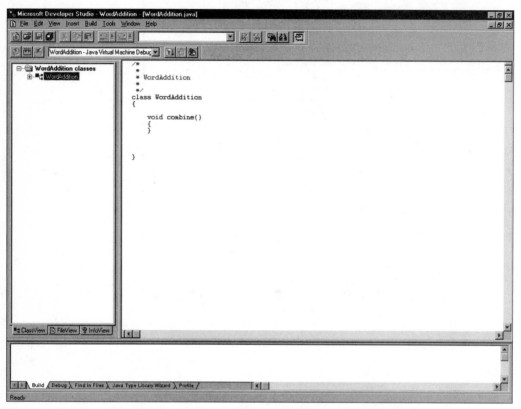

Figure 3-16: The Developer Studio with the class WordAddition and method combine() added.

Notice in Figure 3-16 that there is now a plus sign next to the class WordAddition. Click on the plus sign and you will open a list of members (i.e., methods and variables) that belong to the WordAddition class (see Figure 3-17).

Let's add another method with a parameter to the same class. The method should look like combine(String firstWord). Use Table 3-3 for step-by-step instructions.

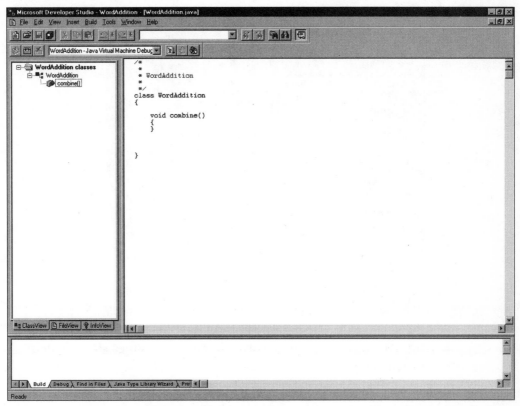

Figure 3-17: The Developer Studio with the class WordAddition expanded to show its members.

Step #	Location	Action
1	Left pane of WordAddition Project Workspace	On the WordAddition class, right-click and choose Add Method from the menu.
2	New Method dialog box	In the Return type field, type **void;** and in the Method declaration field, type **combine(String firstWord)**.
3	New Method dialog box	Verify that you typed the declaration correctly; then, click OK.

Table 3-3: Creating a combine() method with a parameter.

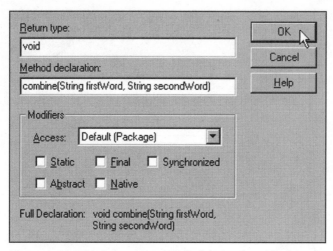

Figure 3-18: The Create New Method dialog box filled out for the second combine() method.

Now, let's add another method with multiple parameters to the same class. The method should look like combine(String firstWord, String secondWord). Table 3-4 provides step-by-step instructions:

Step #	Location	Action
1	Left pane of WordAddition Project Workspace	On the WordAddition class, right-click and choose Add Method from the menu.
2	New Method dialog box	In the Return type field, type **void**; and in the Method declaration field, type **combine(String firstWord, String secondWord)**.
3	New Method dialog box	Verify that you typed the declaration correctly; then, click OK.

Table 3-4 New Method table for combine() # 2.

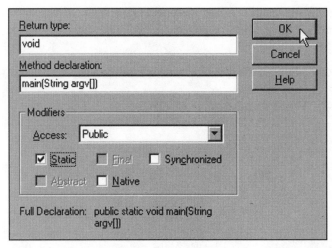

Figure 3-19: The Create New Method dialog box filled out for the third combine() method.

Now, let's add the final main() method to the same class. With this method, you define access and class modifiers, which is discussed in detail later in this chapter. The important thing to remember is that, just like in C/C++ applications, the main() method in Java is the central point for the action code in your application. Use Table 3-5 to add this final method.

Step #	Location	Action
1	Left pane of WordAddition Project Workspace	On the WordAddition class, right-click and choose Add Method from the menu.
2	New Method dialog box	In the Return type field, type **void**, and in the Method declaration field, type **main(String argv[])**.
3	New Method dialog box	In the Access box, choose public, and in the Modifiers box, check static.
4	New Method dialog box	Verify that you typed the declaration correctly; then click OK.

Table 3-5: Creating the main() method.

At this point, the Developer Studio should look something like Figure 3-20.

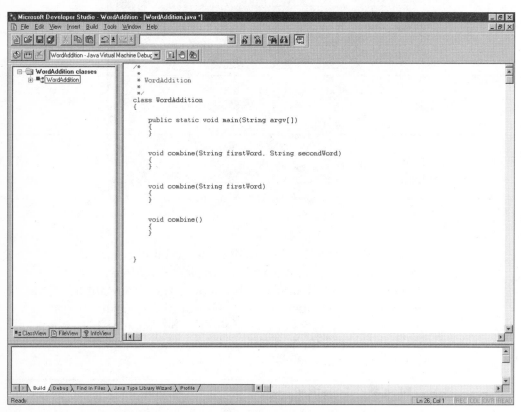

Figure 3-20: The Developer Studio with all the methods added.

In the following lines of code, the bolded lines are those that you need to add to the source file in the text file displayed in the right pane of the Developer Studio, as shown in Figure 3-20. The code that does not appear in bold is code generated by Visual J++ when adding classes and methods to the project workspace:

```
 *
 * WordAddition
 *
 */
class WordAddition
{

    public static void main(String argv[])
    {

    //My code starts here

        //Construct an instance of the class combining
        WordAddition myStatements = new WordAddition();

      //Run the method using the first overloaded method
        myStatements.combine();

      //Run the method using the third overloaded method
        myStatements.combine("The", "End");

      //Run the method using the second overloaded method
        myStatements.combine("Yes");

    //My code ends here


    }


    void combine(String firstWord, String secondWord)
    {

    //My code starts here

        System.out.println("Here are your combined words: " + firstWord +
secondWord);

    //My code ends here


    }
```

```
void combine(String firstWord)
{

//My code starts here

    System.out.println("You have only input one word: " + firstWord);

//My code ends here

}


void combine()
{

//My code starts here

    System.out.println("You did not specify anything to combine.");

//My code ends here

}


}
```

Tip

All the code you type in the examples in this book will always have a preface of the words "My code starts here" and an appending statement consisting of the words "My code ends here." That way, you always know what code you typed and what code Visual J++ automatically generated.

Once you finish typing the previous code, you are ready to save and build the Java application. To build the code, click on Build | Build WordAddition. Then, to execute the code, click on Build | Execute. Since you are executing this project for the first time, the Developer Studio displays a dialog box for you to specify the class filename (see Figure 3-21). In this dialog box, in the Class file-name field, type **WordAddition**. Also, underneath that, you have a choice of using either the jview interpreter or Internet Explorer to view the results. For this example, choose Stand-alone interpreter (which already has the jview program specified). Then, click OK.

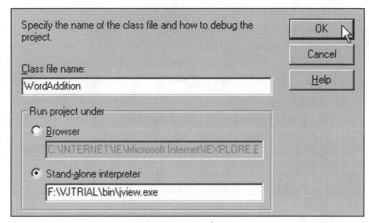

Figure 3-21: The Information for Running Class dialog box filled out.

Once the Java program executes, you should see something similar to Figure 3-22.

```
Microsoft (R) Visual J++ Command-line Interpreter Version 1.00.6194
Copyright (C) Microsoft Corp 1996. All rights reserved.
You did not specify anything to combine.
Here are your combined words: TheEnd
You have only input one word: Yes
```

Figure 3-22: Executing the WordAddition application.

WordAddition prints three lines. Each line is the result of Java calling an overloaded method based on the input parameters specified. Inherently, method overloading is not very hard to understand and is a very useful way to make your Java programs much easier to understand.

Complex Data Types

In the last chapter, you were introduced to a variety of primitive data types. However, there are a few data types in Java that we haven't covered yet because they are object-based. The two major data types not discussed until now are arrays and strings. Both of these are actually represented as Java classes.

In C/C++, an array is basically a set of memory addresses set in sequential order. A C/C++ string is merely an array of characters. Unfortunately, without the use of pointers, you lose the functionality of arrays (and ultimately strings) that exist in the C/C++ languages. That is why Java (which does not have pointers) must wrap these two data types in object-based classes. In essence, you treat them just like any other class in Java. Generally, it is not a very complicated topic to understand.

Tip

Strings and arrays are not the only data types to have object representations. In fact, every major primitive data type discussed in the last chapter has an object-based class representation.

Strings

Strings are a very important part of the Java language. You have been using string literals since Chapter 1. You declare a string in much the same way you declare a primitive data type. Consider the following:

```
String s = "This is a test";
```

You now have the variable s, which contains the string "This is a test". However, because strings are inherently object-based classes, you can construct one through instancing:

```
String s = new String();
s = "This is a test";
```

or:

```
String s = new String("This is a test");
```

The only tricky part to remember is that there is no string primitive data type. Anytime you want to use a string, you must use its wrapped class equivalent.

Arrays

In C/C++, an array is a consecutive group of memory locations that all have the same type. To refer to a particular location or element in the array, you specify the name of the array and/or the position number. In C++, there is no data type for a string variable, so a programmer would utilize an array of chars instead.

However, because of Java's pointerless environment and focus on simplicity, an array is represented as a Java class. And, just like any class in Java, you need to instance it in order to use it. The following example shows the declaration of an array of five integers called group:

```
int group[] = new int[5];
```

Now you have an array of five integer variables that can be accessed by reference to the location number of the variable in the brackets. The following example puts a value in the third element in the array:

```
group[2] = 10;
```

Tip

In C/C++, the index of the array starts with 0. This is also true for Java. To illustrate, look at the array in the following example. group[0] is the first index and the last is group[4].

An alternative way to declare an array group is to put the brackets next to the keyword int, as shown below:

```
int[] group = new int[5];
```

You can also declare and assign values to an array all in the same line. The following example of this uses the group example:

```
int group[] = {10, 2, 27, 32, 33};
```

One final note is that, in Java, you can create multidimensional arrays by declaring an array of arrays. Look at the following examples that demonstrate how you would declare a two-dimensional array implicitly and explicitly:

```
int multigroup[][] = new int[10][20];
int multi group[][] = {{1,2}, {2,4}, {4, 8}};
```

Arrays are a very basic and useful part of programming in any language. The important thing to keep in mind in Java, however, is that arrays that are built in Java are represented as classes.

Scope

Now that you have learned about all the major data types, we can address the idea of scope. When you declare and use a variable, you have a limited range in which it exists in Java.

The rules for variable scope are fairly easy to understand. Basically, a variable exists inside the block within which it has been declared. An excellent example of this is when you declare the int *i* inside a for loop:

```
for (int i = 1; i < 10; i++) {
  //Body of Loop
}
```

In this loop, the scope of the variable *i* is only inside the block for this loop, and you cannot access it outside of this for loop. Another thing to point out is that if you have a block that contains another block inside of it, a variable declared in the outer block is available to any inner blocks contained in that same block. To illustrate, look at the following example:

```java
void Test() {
int a;

   for (int i = 1; i < 10; i++) {
     //Body of Loop
     a++;
   }
}
```

In this example, notice that *a* is accessible inside the for loop because the for loop is inside the method block where int *a* resides.

One final note to discuss is the idea of hiding a variable. In certain situations, you can declare a variable in one block of code and declare that same variable inside another block, which in effect hides the first variable from your Java program. For example:

```java
void Test() {
// Declaring the original a
int a;

// A for loop containing another a
   for (int a = 1; a < 10; a++) {
     //Body of Loop
     // The original a has been hidden
   }
// The original a can now been seen
}
```

In this code, notice that inside the for loop the original variable *a* (declared outside the loop) replaces the one created inside the loop. However, the original *a* is not destroyed; it is only hidden from view, and when the loop ends you can access it again. It is important that you are careful to make your programs easy to understand by not declaring ambiguous variables with the same name within different blocks so that they hide each other.

Scope Resolution

One topic to introduce when dealing with scope is scope resolution. Scope resolution helps you specify what you are referring to in your Java programs by using the dot (.) operator. For example, the System.out.println() statement specifies that you are referring to the out variable contained in the System class, and the variable out is declared to be an instance of PrintStream. So, println() is a member of the PrintStream class.

For example, you have two classes, X and Y, and both of them have the method run(). In your Java program, if you did not specify scope resolution, Java would not know which method you were referring to.

Tutorial: Hiding Variables Using Scope

In this tutorial, you will create the application ScopeTest that will contain two String variables s. And, in the application, the first s will be hidden by the second s when it is in scope. Create a new project workspace called ScopeTest (see Table 3-6 for the step-by-step instructions).

Step #	Location	Action
1	Developer Studio	Choose File|New.
2	New dialog box	Highlight Project Workspace; then, click OK.
3	New Project Work-space dialog box	In the Name field, type **ScopeTest**; then click Create.

Table 3-6: Creating the ScopeTest Project Workspace.

First, you need to create a class. In the Developer Studio, click on Insert | New Java Class. On the Create New Class dialog box, in the Name field, type **ScopeTest**; then click OK.

Now, add a Show() method to the same class. See Table 3-7 for step-by-step instructions.

Step #	Location	Action
1	Left pane of ScopeTest project workspace	On the ScopeTest class, right-click and choose Add Method from the menu.
2	New Method dialog box	In the Return type field, type **void**; and in the Method declaration field, type **Show()**.
3	New Method dialog box	Verify that you typed the declaration correctly; then click OK.

Table 3-7: Creating the Show() method.

Next, add the final main() method to the same class. Again, you'll define access and class modifiers, which we'll discuss later. Use Table 3-8 to add this final method.

Step #	Location	Action
1	Left pane of ScopeTest Project Workspace	On the ScopeTest class, right-click and choose Add Method from the menu.
2	New Method dialog box	In the Return type field, type **void**; and in the Method declaration field, type **main(String argv[])**.
3	New Method dialog box	In the Access box, choose public; and in the Modifiers box, check static.
4	New Method dialog box	Verify that you typed the declaration correctly; then, click OK.

Table 3-8: Creating the main() method.

In the following lines of code, the bolded lines are those that you need to add to the source file in the text file displayed in the right pane of the Developer Studio:

```
/*
 *
 * ScopeTest
 *
 */
class ScopeTest
{

    public static void main(String argv[])
    {

    //My code starts here

        String s = "Another Test";

        //Construct a new instance of ScopeTest
        ScopeTest sTest = new ScopeTest();


        System.out.println("This is what s says before calling
Show(): " + s);

        sTest.Show(); //This will execute method Show()

        System.out.println("This is the what s says inside
after calling Show(): " + s);

    //My code ends here

    }


    void Show()
    {

    //My code starts here

        String s = "Testing";
        System.out.println("This is what s says inside of
Show(): " + s);
```

```
//My code ends here

    }



}
```

When you finish typing the above code, you are ready to save and build the Java application. To build the code, click on Build I Build ScopeTest. Then, to execute the code, click on Build I Execute. Since you are executing this project for the first time, Developer Studio displays a dialog box for you to specify the class filename (see Figure 3-23). On this dialog box, in the Class filename field, type **ScopeTest**. Also, underneath that, you have a choice of using either the jview interpreter or Internet Explorer to view the results. For this example, choose Stand-alone interpreter (which already has the jview program specified). Then, click OK.

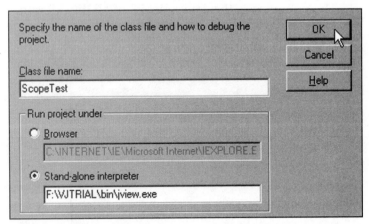

Figure 3-23: The Information for Running Class dialog box filled out.

Once the Java program executes, you will see something similar to Figure 3-24.

```
Microsoft (R) Visual J++ Command-line Interpreter Version 1.00.6194
Copyright (C) Microsoft Corp 1996. All rights reserved.
This is what s says before calling Show(): Another Test
This is what s says inside of Show(): Testing
This is the what s says inside after calling Show(): Another Test
```

Figure 3-24: Executing the ScopeTest application.

As you can see in Figure 3-24, there are two strings called s. The second string s hides the first s, only to reappear after the first one has gone out of scope. It is always important that you understand what scope variables your Java programs have.

More Operator Precedence

In the last chapter, you were introduced to the idea of operator precedence and given a list showing which operators would be executed first. However, in this chapter, there are several other object-related operators that weren't included in Chapter 2's list. The following is the complete list of all the operators in the Java language; the top left have the highest precedence, and the bottom right have the lowest.

. [] ()
++ — ! - ~ new (*cast*)
* / %
+ -
<< >> >>>
< <= . >= instanceof
== !=
&
^
|
&&
||
= *= /= %= += -= <<= >>= &= |= ^= >>>=

Table 3-9: The complete list of Java operators in order of precedence.

Inheritance

At this juncture, you should be familiar with building and using classes. However, that is only part of the object-oriented programming picture. The next step is creating a subclass. The important thing to understand is how to build a subclass that extends another class. This form of extending involves the idea of object-based inheritance. Inheritance is a unique and powerful tool behind object-oriented programming.

When you create a subclass, you are creating a more specific representation of the superclass that the subclass is inheriting from. Inheritance got its name because the subclass (think of it as the child class) inherits functionality from the superclass (think of it as the parent class).

You saw earlier that you can create your own classes as well as your own subclasses to extend from those classes and so on. Essentially, there are only two limiting factors to extending classes in the Java language. First, each subclass can only extend from one superclass. This means that Java only supports single inheritance. Secondly, you can specify how much access each class or its members can have from other classes by using access modifiers (something that we will discuss in further detail in the next section).

Tip

In C++, a subclass can extend from more than one superclass. Unfortunately, once you have more than two parent classes, you are extending your subclass until it becomes very confusing to keep track of all the functionality each superclass brings to the subclass. Thus, Java supports a much simpler version of inheritance—single inheritance.

Let's go back to the class Book we talked about earlier in this chapter and create a subclass Paperback. The logic that not all books are paperbacks, but all paperbacks are books makes this a good example of inheritance. In this logical relationship, the class Book is the superclass and class Paperback is the subclass. The following code creates class Book and the subclass Paperback:

```
class Book {
    int numberOfPages;
}

class Paperback extends book {

    String nameOfBook;

}
```

First, you have created a new class called Paperback. This class can have its own variables and methods. However, notice the keyword *extends*, and also notice the class name *Book* in the declaration line. This is how you subclass the functionality (i.e., the methods and variables) of class Book to class Paperback. You also created a string variable in class Paperback that is specific to that class. Figure 3-25 shows a diagram of the relationship and functionality between class Book and class Paperback.

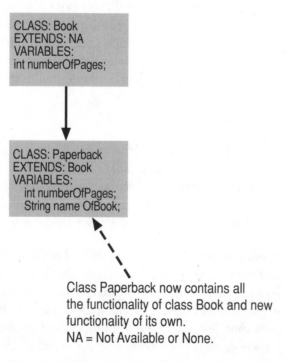

Figure 3-25: Diagram of class Book and class Paperback.

The keywords this and super let you reference certain classes' (or their parents') member variables or methods. They are used with the dot operator, along with the variable or method they are referencing. These two keywords provide a powerful way to indirectly point to another part of a class or its parent.

The Keyword this

The first one to discuss is the keyword this; you can use it to reference another variable or method inside the same class. The important thing to note is that the reference is taking place inside the class's definition. That is what makes using the keyword this so useful. Take a look at the following class:

```
class Sphere extends Circle {
   int dimensions;

   void properties() {
     this.dimensions = 3;
     // Body of properties() method
   }
   void displayProperties() {
     dimensions = 3;
     // Body of displayProperties() method


   }
}
```

You can also use the keyword this to pass a reference of the current class to another class by passing it through a method, as in the following:

```
class ABC {
   TestClass.testMethod(this);
   //Body of Class
}
```

In the above code, you are passing the class ABC with this method that is part of class TestClass. Once again, the keyword this is useful to the instance of that class.

The final usage for the keyword this goes back to the topic of scope, where you have two variables with the same name and you want to access both inside a certain block of statements. You can use the keyword this to specify the hidden variable. To illustrate, let's go back to our example from the section on scope:

```
void Test() {
// Declaring the original a
int a = 5;

// A for loop containing another a
   for (int a = 1; a < 10; a++) {
     //Body of Loop
     // The original a has been hidden

     System.out.println("The hidden a is " + this.a); //
Accessing and printing the hidden a

   }
// The original a can now been seen
}
```

The bolded code shows the code added to the example from the section on scope. Explicitly stating the keyword this, you can now access the original variable *a* that would normally be hidden by the *a* declared in the for loop.

The Keyword super

Use the keyword super to reference parts of the parent class (the keyword this references parts of the class it is within). So, for example, let's look at the parent class Circle for our class Sphere:

```
class Circle {
int dimensions = 2;
// Body of Class
}

class Sphere extends Circle {
   int dimensions;

   void properties() {
```

```
      this.dimensions = 3;
      // Body of properties() method
   }
  void displayProperties() {
    dimensions = 3;

    // References the number of dimensions for class Circle.
    System.out.println("Num. of dimensions " +
super.dimensions"); // Displays 2

    // References the number of dimensions for class Sphere.
    System.out.println("Num. of dimensions " +
this.dimensions); //Displays 3


   }
}
```

The bolded code is the code that was added to the original class Sphere. Notice that, in the above code, the first System.out.println() accesses the variable contained in the super (parent) class Circle and, as a result, prints 2. The second System.out.println() accesses the variable from the class Sphere and prints 3.

How to use the keywords this and super are topics that will likely require more than one pass before things begin to sink in. Nevertheless, they are both very useful tools that come with the Java language.

Method Overriding

Another interesting topic that follows inheritance is the idea of method overriding. Simply stated, method overriding is the ability for two methods, one located in the superclass and the other located in its subclass, to declare exactly the same method (unlike method overloading, discussed earlier). Keep in mind that they are both implemented in different ways. When you call the method, which one runs? The one in the subclass does, because it has overridden the method contained in the superclass. When you override a method, you hide the superclasses' method with a method in its subclass. (This is somewhat similar to the idea of scope with variables, discussed earlier.)

```
class Fruit {

   void eat() {
   //Body of Method
   }
}

class Oranges extend Fruit {
   void eat()
   //Body of Method
}
```

Looking at these two classes, you see that class Oranges extends class Fruit. Both of them have the same method, eat(). However, in class Oranges, the method eat() overrides the method eat() in class Fruit. Figure 3-26 shows a diagram of what the classes Fruit and Oranges look like.

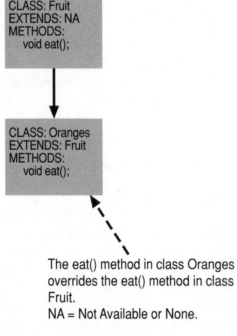

CLASS: Fruit
EXTENDS: NA
METHODS:
    void eat();

CLASS: Oranges
EXTENDS: Fruit
METHODS:
    void eat();

The eat() method in class Oranges overrides the eat() method in class Fruit.
NA = Not Available or None.

Figure 3-26: Diagram of the classes Fruit and Oranges.

Tip

Sometimes you may want to access the overridden method in the superclass. All you have to do is use the keyword super with the method call and you can access the overridden method in the superclass hidden by the method in the subclass.

Tutorial: Overriding Methods

In this tutorial, you are going to create two classes, one called Fruit and the other Oranges (which extends from Fruit). Both classes will contain an eat() method, giving you a chance to work with method overriding and the keyword super. Create a project workspace called MethodTest (see Table 3-10 for the procedure).

Step #	Location	Action
1	Developer Studio	Choose File|New.
2	New dialog box	Highlight Project Workspace; then click OK.
3	New Project Work-space dialog box	In the Name field, type **MethodTest**; then click Create.

Table 3-10: Creating the MethodTest Project Workspace.

First, you need to create a class. In the Developer Studio, click on Insert | New Java Class. On the Create New Class dialog box, in the Name field, type **MethodTest**; then click OK.

Now, let's add an eat() method to the same class. See Table 3-11 for step-by-step instructions.

Step #	Location	Action
1	Left pane of MethodTest Project Workspace	On the Fruit class, right-click and choose Add Method from the menu.
2	New Method dialog box	In the Return type field, type **void**, and in the Method declaration field, type **eat()**.
3	New Method dialog box	Verify that you typed the declaration correctly; then click OK.

Table 3-11: Creating the eat() method for the Fruit class.

Now, you need to create another Java class, Oranges, that will extend class Fruit for the project MethodTest. Click on Insert | New Java Class. In the Create New Class dialog box, in the Name field, type **Oranges**. Then, in the Extends field, choose (or type) **Fruit**. By doing this, you are creating a subclass called Oranges that extends from superclass Fruit. Finally, click OK to continue.

Now, add an eat() method to the Oranges class (see Table 3-12 for step-by-step instructions).

Step #	Location	Action
1	Left pane of MethodTest Project Workspace	In the Oranges class, right-click and choose Add Method from the menu.
2	New Method dialog box	In the Return type field, type **void**; and in the Method declaration field, type **eat()**.
3	New Method dialog box	Verify that you typed the declaration correctly; then, click OK.

Table 3-12: Creating the eat() method for the Oranges class.

Next, add the final main() method to the same class. Again, you'll define access and class modifiers, which we will discuss later. Use Table 3-13 to add this final method.

Step #	Location	Action
1	Left pane of MethodTest Project Workspace	On the Oranges class, right-click and choose Add Method from the menu.
2	New Method dialog box	In the Return type field, type **void**; and in the Method Declaration field, type **main(String argv[ ])**.
3	New Method dialog box	In the Access box, choose public; and in the Modifiers box, check static.
4	New Method dialog box	Verify that you typed the declaration correctly; then, click OK.

Table 3-13: Creating the main() method.

At this point, you are ready to begin editing your code. Looking at the project workspace ClassView, you see two classes (see Figure 3-27). Go to the class Fruit and double-click on it.

Figure 3-27: Project Workspace window for project MethodTest.

Now, you should have the source file for class Fruit open for editing in the text editor in the Developer Studio. Add the bolded code to the other code in the text editor:

```
/*
 *
 * Fruit
 *
 */
class Fruit
{

   void eat()
   {
```

```
//My code starts here
System.out.println("This method eats Fruit");
//My code ends here


    }


}
```

Finish editing the code for class Fruit, and, in the project workspace of the Developer Studio, double-click on the class Oranges to open it. Add the bolded code to the other code in the text editor:

```
import Fruit;

/*
 *
 * Oranges
 *
 */
class Oranges extends Fruit
{

    public static void main(String argv[])
    {

        //My code starts here
        Oranges o = new Oranges();

        o.eat(); //calls eat()
        //My code ends here


    }

    void eat()
    {

        //My code starts here
        System.out.println("This method eats Oranges");
        super.eat(); //calls eat() from Fruit
```

```
//My code ends here

    }


  }
```

Notice in the code above that the method eat() in this class contains the statement:

```
System.out.println("This method eats Oranges");
```

When called, it prints "This method eats Oranges." However, also notice, in the method eat(), the following statement:

```
super.eat(); //calls eat() from Fruit
```

Taking advantage of the keyword super, this statement calls the overridden method eat() contained in the superclass Fruit that prints "This method eats Fruit." Generally, you should have two lines printed on the screen for this project.

Tip

Notice that the first line in the above code, which was automatically generated when you created the Oranges class, uses import to import the class Fruit for class Oranges. You use import statements to make classes and groups of classes (known as packages) available to your Java programs; import statements in Java are the equivalent of include statements in C/C++.

To build the code, click on Build | Build MethodTest. Then, to execute the code, click on Build | Execute. Since you are executing this project for the first time, the Developer Studio displays a dialog box for you to specify the class filename (see Figure 3-28). In this dialog box, in the Class filename field, type **Oranges**. Also, underneath that you have a choice of using either the jview interpreter or Internet Explorer to view the results. For this example, choose Stand-alone interpreter (which already has the jview program specified). Then, click OK.

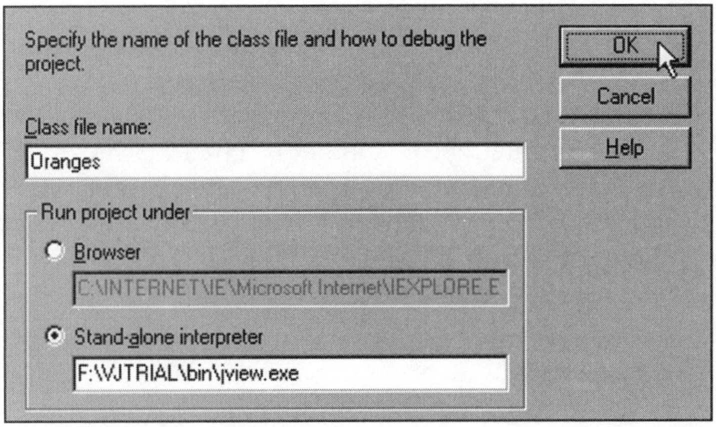

Figure 3-28: The Information for Running Class dialog box filled out.

Once the project has executed, you should see something similar to Figure 3-29.

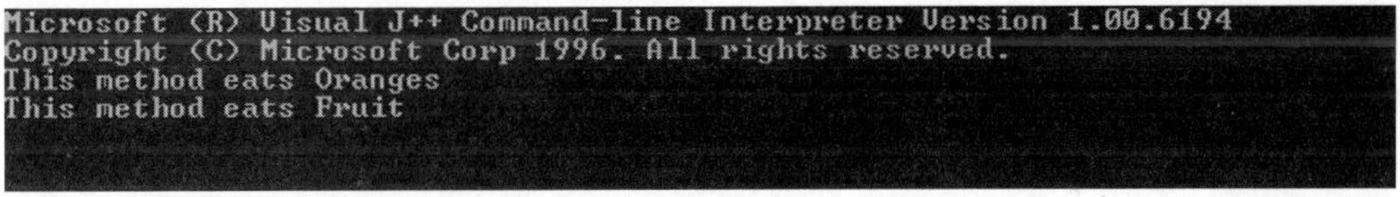

Figure 3-29: Executing the MethodTest application.

As you can see in Figure 3-29, when you execute the method eat(), it prints the statement "This method eats Oranges." Since the eat() method in class Oranges also contains a super reference to the method in the superclass Fruit, it also executes that method that prints "This method eats Fruit."

Method overriding is very useful when you have a subclass that needs to enhance the functionality of a particular method higher up in its class hierarchy. Just remember that method overriding works for any superclass above the current class, not just the class directly extending from it. Also, remember that method overriding does not mean that the hidden method no longer exists. It is quite accessible through the use of the keyword super.

Object Casting

In the last chapter, you learned that you can explicitly convert from one data type to another by entering the data type you want to cast to in parentheses in front of the current data type. For review, suppose you have a data type int, and you want to cast to a data type byte. The following shows an example of casting variable myInt to myByte:

```
//Declare the variables
int myInt = 50;
byte myByte;

//Perform the Cast
myByte = (byte) myInt;
```

Another, more complex version of casting is the ability to cast between classes. In Java, you can perform a class-based cast from a superclass to its more functional subclass. You can cast to the subclass directly under it or to any class that is below it in its class hierarchy.

Tip

You can use the instanceof operator to avoid potentially dangerous problems with casting one object reference to another class.

Probably the only time you may need to perform class-based casts is when you have instanced a class in the beginning of your Java program and later when you need the added functionality of one of its subclasses (or any other class below it).

When you cast between objects, it is syntactically the same as casting between data types, as mentioned earlier. To illustrate, suppose you had a class Tree and its subclass Maple:

```
class Tree {
   //Body of Class
}
class Maple extends Tree {
   //Body of Class
}
```

Now, imagine that you created an instance of the class Tree called myTree:

```
Tree myTree = new Tree();
```

Later in your program, you decide that the instance myTree is actually a Maple that needs the added functionality of changing colors in the fall. So, you cast the instance of class Tree (called myTree) to its subclass Maple, as shown in the following:

```
Maple myMapleTree;
myMapleTree = (Maple) myTree;
```

In the above code, you are declaring the instance myMapleTree and then, in the next line, casting myTree to class Maple, calling it myMapleTree. Figure 3-30 diagrams where Maple and Tree fit into a class hierarchy and the cast of myTree to myMapleTree.

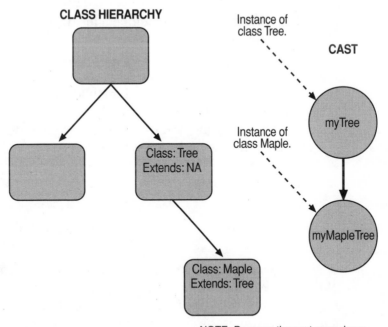

Figure 3-30: Diagram of the Tree cast.

Unlike casting primitive data types with casting classes, you cannot lose data, because the Java language does not let you perform any "sometimes" casts. Because of this, the major point to remember is that you can only cast if you are moving down the class hierarchy for a given class.

Modifiers

Modifiers help to regulate how much access you want to grant to a particular class or its members. The following sections introduce these topics, and you will have a chance to work with them in more depth later on in the book.

Access Modifiers

Access modifiers work with members inside a class. Using access modifiers, you can increase or decrease the level of accessibility a variable or method can have from other classes. Continue to work with subclasses and superclasses and you will find that there is a way to restrict some variables and methods to be overridden by other classes (using the keyword final). In addition, you can also restrict a variable or method from being seen outside of its own class through the use of the keyword private.

To illustrate, let's take a look at the following example:

```
class ABC {
   private int A;
   //Body of Class
}
```

The keyword private in the above code snippet located in front of the variable declaration makes this variable private; it is the most restrictive of all the access modifiers available in the Java language. Below is the class XYZ that extends ABC:

```
class XYZ extends ABC {
   //Body of Class
}
```

Based on the definition of inheritance, the functionality from ABC is now part of class XYZ. However, because A has been declared private, class XYZ will not be able to see or use it. This simple example shows how to declare an access modifier and what one does.

Access modifiers define the accessibility of the variable and methods in their own class as they relate to other classes. Access modifiers include the following:

- **private**   Placing private in front of a method or variable declaration allows it to be accessed only by the original class that declared it.

- **protected**   Placing protected allows its variable or method access in the class that declared it and any subclasses inherited from it; it is accessible by code in the same package.

- **public**   This access modifier is the least restrictive in the sense that it makes the variable and method accessible by any class no matter which package it belongs to.

- **final**   The final methods cannot be overridden by another method in a subclass. A final variable means that the variable is going to be a constant, and the value assigned to it will not change.

- **synchronized**   This deals specifically with threads and multithreading. It helps regulate how a method is accessed by each thread. For more information, refer to Chapter 6.

- No modifier means that this method is accessible in the same package.

Tip

A package is a group of related classes and interfaces. Interfaces are formally introduced later in this chapter. Packages will be formally discussed in Chapter 13.

Specifying the type of access your variables have in Visual J++ is very simple. When you used the New Method dialog box, it had various access rules which we declared for a couple of the methods.

Class Modifiers

Class modifiers, just like variable and method modifiers, determine a set of regulations and/or access restrictions for classes and how they are to interact with other classes. You can specify one access modifier and several class modifiers. The following shows the syntax for declaring a class using class modifiers:

```
[access modifier(s)] [class modifiers] class className {
}
```

Every method and variable you declare uses the default class modifier of friendly even though you did not specify it explicitly. The default access modifier for classes is friendly; that makes this class available to any of the other classes in the same package or group. Class modifiers include:

- **abstract**   Declaring your class abstract means that the class is going to be a holding tank of definitions to be implemented in a later subclass down the hierarchy. In the single inheritance model (which is what Java uses), abstract classes are at the root of a hierarchy of classes. These classes cannot be instanced, contain at least one method (or variable declaration, and cannot be modified with private or final. Finally, an abstract class must contain at least one abstract method to be implemented by a later class in the hierarchy.

- **final**   This class is the final class (i.e., the last) in any overall class hierarchy. In other words, by declaring a class final, you are specifying that this class cannot have any subclasses extending from it.

- **public**   This denotes that the program is accessible to any class outside of the package. However, only one public class can be put in a source-code file at a time. Plus, the file must be called the same name as the class, with the extension of

.java. You may have more than one class in a single file of program code, but only one of them will be accessible via the import clause. So, the file must have the same name as this public class.

Native Methods

Another modifier available strictly for methods is *native*. When a method is declared with the modifier native, it is anything but native. These methods are actually C/C++ functions ported to your Java program through the use of native. The advantage of having native methods is the ability to link C/C++ code to your Java program. The disadvantage of having a native method is that you lose much of the enhanced functionality (multiplatformed, bytecode verified, etc.) because of the added baggage.

You can specify a modifier for your class when you create it in the Developer Studio. When you create a new class using the Create New Class dialog box, you can choose what modifiers you want enabled. Class modifiers (like variable and method modifiers) have only been touched upon. Later, in Chapter 14, you will have a chance to get a more in-depth look at modifiers in the Java language.

Interfaces

The idea behind interfaces is to make up for the functionality lost when multiple inheritance was removed from the Java language. By definition, interfaces are abstract and cannot contain any implementationary code. Interfaces provide the set of common method definitions that you implement in your Java classes. Moreover, in Java, you can implement as many interfaces as you need, and you can use the same interface on several classes, even if they do not belong to the same package.

Starting with inheritance, the major difference between inheriting a class and implementing (note the word "implementing") an interface is that Java supports multiple inheritance of interfaces. Also, as you look at a typical class hierarchy in Java, notice that, because of the single inheritance rule, it is fairly monolithic. Interfaces provide you with the ability to connect to several classes anywhere in the hierarchy.

Interfaces behave in a very similar fashion to classes. They are declared and can also be extended within themselves, so you could feasibly have a superinterface parenting a subinterface. The following shows the syntax for declaring an interface:

```
interfaceModifier interface interfaceName {
    //Body of interface
    //including method declarations and variables
}
```

The interfaceModifier can be either public or the default, friendly.

You can also declare an interface to extend another interface, and, when a class implements the subinterface, it gets all the superinterfaces extended from the subinterface:

```
interfaceModifier interface interfaceName extends
interfaceName2 {
    //Body of interface
    //including method declarations and variables
}
```

Notice in the above code that interfaces extend just like classes extend.

Declaring interfaces is only half the story, because interfaces only contain method definitions and variables that are effectively constants. The other half is implementing them into your Java-based classes. The following shows the syntax for declaring a class with an interface implemented:

```
class className implements interfaceName [, interfaceName2] {
Body of Class
}
```

Or, if this class has a superclass connected to it:

```
class className extends superClassName implements
interfaceName [, interfaceName2] {
Body of Class
}
```

Notice the use of the word implements in the above syntax declaration. This is how you declare an interface in your class. Furthermore, implements is a fitting word, because that is exactly what you will be doing with the interface in this class. Additionally, as the above syntax shows, you can implement as many interfaces as needed.

Tip

When one of your classes implements an interface, you must override every method declared inside that interface and provide an implementation for it (assuming the class implementing the interface is not abstract itself).

Interfaces provide an excellent way to inherit multiple frameworks to one Java class. Consider the following; you have a class VCR and a class TV:

```
class VCR extends CassettePlayer {
   //Body of Class
}
```

```
class TV extends Receiver{
   //Body of Class
}
```

Now, assuming that you want to have the buttons for each of these electronic component Java classes to be the same, you want to create a similar interface for each. One way to do this would be to create two separate interfaces and include them in each respective class (one interface for the class TV and the other, for class VCR). Each one of the two interfaces are specifically designed to only be used with its respective class. On the other hand, you could create one interface class that contains an abstract overview of the buttons to be used on these two classes (TV and VCR). Furthermore, you could use this same interface on any other classes you may want to add or create later. The following shows the interface for class UniversalButtons:

```
public interface UniversalButtons {
  // Body of Interface
  //Including static final variables (constants)
  //and method definitions
}
```

At this point, you have created the classes TV and VCR, and the interface UniversalButtons. All that is left is to implement the interface as follows:

```
class VCR extends CassettePlayer implements UniversalButtons
{
  //Body of Class

  //Implementation code for the interface
}

class TV implements UniversalButtons {
  //Body of Class

  //Implementation code for the interface
}
```

Notice that what you have done is declare that you are implementing the interface, and then you are actually implementing all the methods later on in each class. The fact that Java supports multiple interface implementations means that you have the added flexibility to implement other interfaces in the above classes. Also, you have the added flexibility to use the interface you already created on other classes as well. Figure 3-31 shows a diagram of this example and how interfaces connect to each of the classes.

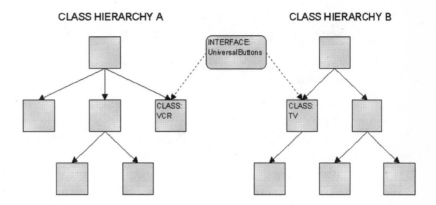

CLASS HIERARCHY A   CLASS HIERARCHY B

Figure 3-31: Diagram of the VCR, TV, and UniversalButtons interface example.

Comparing Abstract Classes & Interfaces

If abstract classes and interfaces are so similar, what is the difference between the two?

Abstract classes are usually designed to be at the top of one of Java's single inheritance hierarchies, handling only methods, variables, and method definitions. Interfaces, while also designed to be a holding tank for definitions, can be used in a multiple inheritance paradigm and can be implemented anywhere in a Java class hierarchy (not just at the top).

Finally, it is important to note that abstract classes can hold some implemented methods/variables, but interfaces cannot.

Interfaces provide an excellent way to take advantage of C++'s multiple inheritance without having all the added baggage. Because interfaces can only contain definitions, they are very similar to abstract classes. However, interfaces have a different functionality than abstract classes, because they can be implemented just about anywhere (not just at the top of a class hierarchy).

Moving On

In this chapter you learned about many object-oriented topics in the Java language. Because Java is an object-based language, topics discussed here will be exemplified or reinforced throughout the rest of this book. Chapter 6, for example, explores interfaces in a real-world setting. And Chapter 14 discusses some of the topics just introduced in more detail and covers other, more complex object-based topics. The next chapter introduces the Java AppletWizard in Visual J++ and also gives an overview of some of the built-in classes that come with the Java language.

4

Introducing Java Applets

Up to this point, everything discussed dealt specifically with the creation and use of Java applications. However, (as discussed in Chapter 1) there is another breed of Java programs that you can create using Visual J++ called Java applets.

In this chapter, you will learn about Java applet—how they work and how they are different from applications. You will also learn how to code applets from scratch in Visual J++ and view them in an HTML page in Microsoft's Internet Explorer, Netscape Navigator, and the Java Development Kit's (JDK's) AppletViewer. Furthermore, you will discover some of the capabilities behind the built-in Java class library.

Defining Class Library

A class library is a group of related classes (and interfaces) grouped together because of a common similarity. Java comes with a set of built-in class libraries that you can use or you can create your own.

Finally, you are going to learn about displaying text and other types of graphics in your applets. First, we'll review the strengths and weaknesses of applets.

Working With Applets

Because applets have been designed for the Net, people are probably more familiar with them than they are with regular Java applications. Applets give you the ability to create specialized Java programs and publish them on the Net. Much debate surrounds the usefulness of applets, but it is awfully hard to find weaknesses in their design.

The Advantages of Applets

The advantages of applets include:

- Java applets compile into binary class files so there is no source code on the server. You simply use an <APPLET> tag, specifying how the browser should load the applet.

- Applets are completely configurable and reusable. So, you can create a useful Java applet and distribute it as a shareware (or freeware) program on the Net.

- Anyone using Netscape Navigator (version 2.0 or later) or Internet Explorer (version 3.0 or later) and a 32-bit operating system (Windows95, PowerPC, UNIX, or other) can view Java applets. Remember that Java applets contain all of the inherent functionality of Java; so that means that Java applets are 100 percent portable (from the ground up).

- Java applets follow a very secure programming model, so users do not have to worry about having their networks or computers hacked into by malignant applets.

Java applets are a very useful Internet development solution. Visual J++ helps automate the creation of applets and provides a set of state-of-the-art debugging tools for Java applets.

The Disadvantages of Applets

While applets can be very useful, there are certain limitations that you should be aware of before continuing. Still, these limiting factors of applets have not put a damper on the applet industry. The disadvantages include:

■ Java applets are said to be too secure and are therefore limiting (see Chapter 1 for more information on this topic). Interestingly enough, security is a double-edged topic that is seen as both an advantage and disadvantage.

■ Applets are said to be too slow. There are two reasons for this. The first issue may be more of a bandwidth issue than a Java issue. If a user has a low bandwidth connection to the Internet, everything will be slow, not just the applet. Secondly, Java applets are verified and interpreted when they download to the user's system. Thus, it causes the applet to be slower than a typical C/C++ compiled program. The solution to this is to use a Just In Time (JIT) compiler that speeds up execution by as much as1000 percent. Currently, several development environments (including Visual J++) have a JIT compiler. Netscape Navigator 3.0 also uses a speedier JIT compiler for viewing applets.

Aside from the above mentioned, there are a few other issues that are not discussed here primarily because they are more opinion than fact. Java applets are not perfect for every solution. The next section briefly discusses technologies. Some have roots back to Java.

Java Applet Basics

Technically speaking, there are two major differences between a Java applet and a Java application. You could, in fact, define a Java applet by these two properties:

■ As you know, when you create a Java application, there is one method that contains the action code for your application. That method is the main() method. However, applets do not use the main() method. Instead, they use a set of four life-cycle methods, init(), start(), stop(), and destroy(), that are browser-invoked methods you override to create your applet.

■ When you create the class that makes up your Java applet, you subclass it from the built-in Java class java.applet.Applet. With this inheritance, your Java applet receives all of the properties that make a Java applet different from a regular Java application.

While there are several other smaller things that also make applets unique, the two above are the most prevalent and most universal. Without following the above guidelines, you cannot create a Java applet. Starting with the life-cycle methods, let's get a better understanding of how to implement these two things to create real-world Java applets.

The Life-Cycle Methods

Figure 4-1 shows a diagram of how the four methods init(), start(), stop(), and destroy() relate to each other. It also shows where their place is in the overall applet life cycle.

Each one of the four aforementioned methods has a particular place and meaning. When you write your Java applet, you place the appropriate action code in the appropriate method. The init() method always gets called first in the applet life cycle. The next method called is start().The stop() method is called when the user leaves the HTML page containing the applet or if the applet is physically unloaded. The last method called in the applet life-cycle scenario is the method destroy(). This method is responsible for cleaning up after the applet. Let's take a closer look at each of these methods.

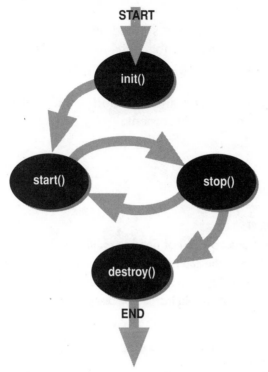

Figure 4-1: A diagram of the life-cycle methods for the Java applet.

Do I Need to Use Every Life-Cycle Method in My Java Applet?

No. Technically speaking, when you put a life-cycle method in your applet, you are actually overriding it from the java.applet.Applet class. If you do not override the life-cycle method in your Java applet, then, when your applet runs, it will use the method provided in the java.applet.Applet class. However, in order for your applet to have some functionality you need to at least override init() or start().

init()

This is the first method that is called when your applet loads for the first time. Usually, it is not called again unless the applet is completely reloaded.

In this method, you should include any initializations, including the loading of images and sound files and the passing of any parameters from the environment.

Constructing Applets

Unlike Java applications, you do not need to explicitly construct applets. Usually, the browser loading the applet automatically constructs it. Thus, you don't need to have a new MyApplet(...) clause. Plus, any variables that need to be constructed along with it should instead be placed in the init() method.

start()

The second method that is automatically called by the browser after method init() is the start() method. The most important points to remember with this method are that it can be called more than once and it works in conjunction with stop(). Basically, anything that may need to be reinitialized when the user returns to the applet should be included here.

You will have a chance to work with the start() method in Chapter 6 on multithreading and creating an animation. When the user leaves the applet (but does not unload it), you want to suspend the animation to conserve resources. The start() method also contains any reinstating code needed to start up the animation when the user returns to the applet.

stop()

Used in conjunction with start(), the stop() method is very similar to the start() method in the fact that it can be called multiple times, depending on the user's activities. Usually, it gets called when a user leaves the site. The code to suspend anything that is not needed while the user is not looking at the applet (such as an animation mentioned in the last section) is placed here.

destroy()

The last method to call after the stop() method is destroy(). This method automatically performs a routine form of garbage collection, releasing any resource held by the applet. Once this method finishes, your applet has been unloaded. The only way to see your applet again is to reload it. This method is seldom needed and is not usually overridden in your Java applets.

These four methods compose a more complex version of the main() method used in a Java application. The browser automatically invokes (or reinvokes) all of these methods throughout the life of your applet. At this point, let's create your first Java applet, exemplifying these four methods.

Importing Java Classes & Packages

You can import built-in classes, third-party classes, or classes of your own design by using import and the name of the class at the beginning of your Java program:

```
import java.awt.Graphics;
```

However, you can also import the entire package by using the asterisk. The following shows how you would import the entire awt package:

```
import java.awt.*;
```

Now all of the public classes in the package java.awt are available to your Java program.

Packages in the Java Class Library

There are many built-in classes that you can import or extend to your Java classes. There are six groupings or packages that help to better organize all the built-in classes available from the Java language:

- java.applet   The applet package is the package that contains the Applet class. It contains all of the pertinent classes that relate to Java applets.

- java.awt   The Abstract Window Toolkit gives you the ability to design complete user interfaces, work with images, and print graphics on the screen.

- java.io   This package deals with input and output of data streams. Chapter 11 provides a complete overview of this topic.

- java.lang   The core package for your Java programs, java.lang is the default package that is responsible for housing the String, Array, and System classes that you have worked with.

- java.net   This package provides you a complete set of classes to implement high- or low-level network programming. Any Web-based protocols or other related functionality are also included as part of this package (see Chapter 12 for more information

- java.util   This package comprises a group of utility and miscellaneous classes such as the Date class.

Tutorial: Creating Your First Applet

In this tutorial you will create an applet that has all four of the life-cycle methods overridden. Each life-cycle method displays a comment in its browser's status bar, giving you a chance to see when each life-cycle method invokes. At this point, let's go to Visual J++ and construct our first Java applet. First, create a project workspace called LifeCycle (see Table 4-1 for the procedure).

Step #	Location	Action
1	Developer Studio	Choose File|New.
2	New dialog box	Highlight Project Workspace and click OK.
3	New dialog box	In the Name field, type **LifeCycle** and click Create.

Table 4-1: Creating the LifeCycle Project Workspace.

Now you need to create a new Java class called Cycle. In the Developer Studio, click Insert \| New Java Class. On the Create New Class dialog box, do the following:

1. In the Name field, type **Cycle**.

2. In the Extends field, type **java.applet.Applet**.

3. In the Modifiers area, choose public.

Then, click OK (see Figure 4-2).

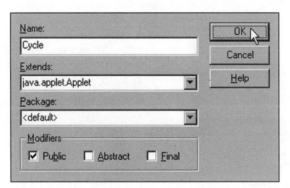

Figure 4-2: The Create New Class dialog box filled out.

Let's start by creating our first public method called paint() (see Table 4-2 for step-by-step instructions).

Step #	Location	Action
1	Left pane of LifeCycle Project Workspace	On the Cycle class, right-click and choose Add Method from the menu.
2	New Method dialog box	In the Return type field, type **void**, and in the Method declaration field, type **paint()**.
3	New Method dialog box	In the Access box, choose Public.
4	New Method dialog box	Verify that you typed the declaration correctly; then click OK.

Table 4-2: Creating the paint() method.

Next, we want to add a pause() method (see Table 4-3 for step-by-step instructions).

Step #	Location	Action
1	Left pane of LifeCycle Project Workspace	On the Cycle class, right-click and choose Add Method from the menu.
2	New Method dialog box	In the Return type field, type **void**, and in the Method declaration field, type **pause()**.
4	New Method dialog box	Verify that you typed the declaration correctly; then click OK.

Table 4-3: Creating the pause() method.

Now let's create a public method and override the life-cycle method destroy() (see Table 4-4 for step-by-step instructions).

Step #	Location	Action
1	Left pane of LifeCycle Project Workspace	On the Cycle class, right-click and choose Add Method from the menu.
2	New Method dialog box	In the Return type field, type **void**, and in the Method declaration field, type **destroy()**.
4	New Method dialog box	Verify that you typed the declaration correctly; then click OK.

Table 4-4: Creating the destroy() method, overriding the existing destroy() method.

Now let's create another public method and override the life-cycle method stop() (see Table 4-5 for step-by-step instructions).

Step #	Location	Action
1	Left pane of LifeCycle Project Workspace	On the Cycle class, right-click and choose Add Method from the menu.
2	New Method dialog box	In the Return type field, type **void**, and in the Method declaration field, type **stop()**.
4	New Method dialog box	Verify that you typed the declaration correctly; then click OK.

Table 4-5: Creating the stop() method, overriding the existing stop() method.

Now let's create another public method and override the life-cycle method start() (see Table 4-6 for step-by-step instructions).

Step #	Location	Action
1	Left pane of LifeCycle Project Workspace	On the Cycle class, right-click and choose Add Method from the menu.
2	New Method dialog box	In the Return type field, type **void**, and in the Method declaration field, type **start()**.
4	New Method dialog box	Verify that you typed the declaration correctly; then click OK.

Table 4-6: Creating the start() method, overriding the existing start() method.

Now let's create another public method and override the life-cycle method init() (see Table 4.7 for step-by-step instructions).

Step #	Location	Action
1	Left pane of LifeCycle Project Workspace	On the Cycle class, right-click and choose Add Method from the menu.
2	New Method dialog box	In the Return type field, type **void**, and in the Method declaration field, type **init()**.
4	New Method dialog box	Verify that you typed the declaration correctly; then click OK.

Table 4-7: Creating the init() method, overriding the existing init() method.

At this point, your Developer Studio should look something like Figure 4-3. If you do not see the source code file for the class Cycle, then, in the ClassView, expand the LifeCycle Classes folder and double-click on the Cycle class.

Figure 4-3: The Developer Studio with the source open for project LifeCycle.

Edit the code as shown below. Remember that the bolded code is material you need to add and the regular code listed below is code automatically generated by Visual J++:

```
import java.applet.Applet;

//My code starts here
import java.awt.Graphics;
//My code ends here

/*
 *
 * Cycle
 *
```

```java
     */
public class Cycle extends Applet
{

   public void init()
   {

      //My code starts here
      //Display in the Status bar
      showStatus("Now in the init() method.");

      //Pause so the user can read the Status message
      pause();
      //My code ends here

   }


   public void start()
   {

      //My code starts here
      //Display in the Status bar
      showStatus("Now in the start() method.");

      //Pause so the user can read the Status message
      pause();
      //My code ends here

   }


   public void stop()
   {

      //My code starts here
      //Display in the Status bar
      showStatus("Now in the stop() method.");
```

```
        //Pause so the user can read the Status message
        pause();
        //My code ends here


    }

public void destroy()
{

    //My code starts here
    //Display in the Status bar
    showStatus("Now in the destroy() method.");

    //Pause so the user can read the Status message
    pause();
    //My code ends here


    }


public void pause()
{
    //My code starts here
    // Wait for 5000 ms = 5 sec
    long x = System.currentTimeMillis();
    while(x + 5000 > System.currentTimeMillis()) {
    }
    //My code ends here

    }


public void paint(Graphics g)
{

//My code starts here
g.drawString("MY FIRST APPLET.", 5, 10);
//My code ends here
```

```
        }


    }
```

Let's take a closer look at some of the above code, starting with the import statements at the top of the program:

```
import java.applet.Applet;

//My code starts here
import java.awt.Graphics;
//My code ends here
```

The two statements above (comments excluded) use the keyword import to effectively make these two classes available to the class Cycle. They are built-in classes that are part of the built-in Java class library. The first *import* statement gives us access to the class Applet so we can use it to extend to the Cycle class. The second *import* makes the class Graphics available. This class is needed by the paint() method that is discussed a little later on.

The next major part is the class declaration for Cycle. Notice that it extends the class Applet imported earlier. Then there is the first life-cycle method init(). Notice that it does two things. First it uses a method showStatus() to print the statement "Now in the init() method." If you look at the entire program above you will not see a declaration for the method showStatus(). That is because it comes from the class Applet. What it effectively does is let you display information in the status bar at the bottom of whatever applet is running it. The second method, pause(), forces Java to hold, giving readers a chance to read the message displayed in the status bar. The other methods, start(), stop(), and destroy(), follow the same format as init() in that they all contain the same two method calls.

Now let's turn our attention to the pause() method to see exactly how it is pausing the Java program. Essentially, the pause() method does two things. It uses the method currentTimeMillis(), which returns the number of milliseconds since January 1, 1970, and it places that value into the variable x:

```
long x = System.currentTimeMillis();
```

Then it goes into a while loop until the current time (as returned by currentTimeMillis()) equals the value of x + 5000:

```
while(x + 5000 > System.currentTimeMillis()) {
}
```

In other words, it takes the value of x and adds 5000 milliseconds to it. So, this empty loop will continue to cycle for at least five seconds. Thus, the method pause() effectively pauses for five seconds before returning.

The last method to look at is the paint() method. This method is discussed in more detail later on. The important thing to note here is that it is a built-in method (like main()) that lets you display all types of graphics inside your applet; in this case, you'll display the statement:

```
g.drawString("MY FIRST APPLET.", 5, 10);
```

The above snippet of code prints out the line "MY FIRST APPLET" inside your applet using the coordinates above.

Now you are ready to save and build your code. To save all the files for your project, click on File | Save All. To build the code, click on Build | Build LifeCycle. Then, to execute the code, click on Build | Execute.

Since you are executing this project for the first time in the Developer Studio, a dialog box displays for you to specify the class file name (see Figure 4-4). On this dialog box, in the Class filename field, type **Cycle**. Also, underneath that you have a choice of using either the jview interpreter or Internet Explorer to view the results. For this example, choose Browser (which already has the Internet Explorer program specified). Then, click OK.

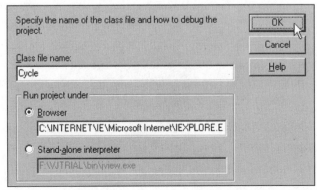

Figure 4-4: The Information for the Running Class dialog box filled out.

Now your program will execute by automatically generating an HTML file and loading Microsoft Internet Explorer (your screen should appear similar to Figure 4-5). Once Explorer finishes loading, you will not see anything in the main window. However, focus your attention on the status bar at the bottom.

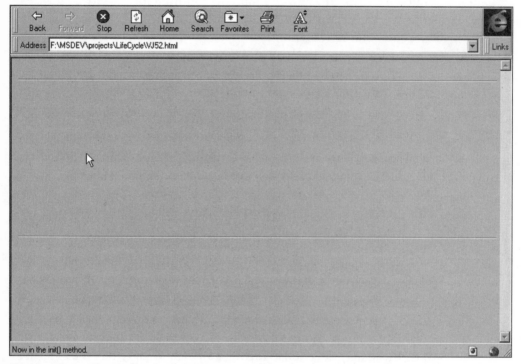

Figure 4-5: Loading applet Cycle in Internet Explorer.

Tip

Make sure your cursor is over the Internet Explorer window inbetween the two bars. That way, it is over the applet and not another part of Internet Explorer (see Figure 4-8).

Notice that the status bar at the bottom is displaying "Now in the init() method." Then, after about five seconds, it displays "Now in the start() method." Once the applet has started, Internet Explorer displays the message "Applet Started" and the words "MY FIRST APPLET" appear in the top left corner of the browser window (see Figure 4-6).

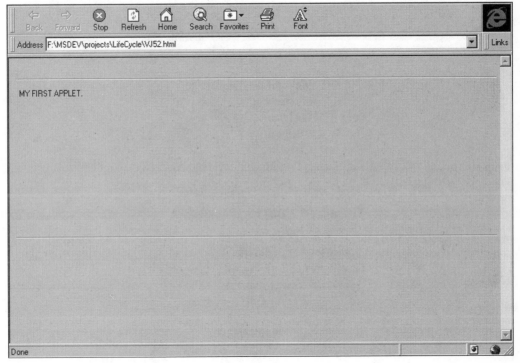

Figure 4-6: The loaded Cycle applet in Internet Explorer.

Tip

If you do not have a status bar showing up at the bottom of the Internet Explorer window, then check the menu item View | Status Bar.

Now, if you are connected to the Internet, let's go ahead and move off the page by loading the JavaSoft site (http://www.javasoft.com) shown in Figure 4-7. If you are not connected to the Internet, you can supplement loading the JavaSoft site with any other HTML site that is local to your system. The important thing is that you are leaving the HTML page with the Cycle applet.

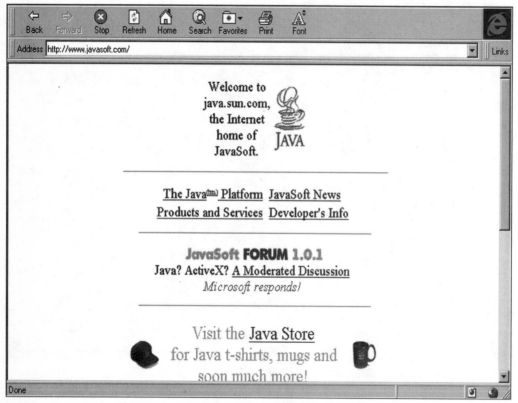

Figure 4-7: Leaving Cycle applet and loading the JavaSoft home page.

Now, even though you cannot see it, the Cycle applet is in the stop() method.

Tip

In order to see the Cycle applet in the stop() method, load the JavaSoft site so that it is in cache. Then quickly go to the Cycle applet site and go back to the JavaSoft site. This time, immediately go back and you will see the Cycle applet in the stop() method.

The important thing to note is that, in order for you to see the stop() method, you must leave and return to the Cycle applet HTML page in less than five seconds, which is the duration of the method pause().

However, if you click on the Back icon to go back to the Cycle applet and look at the status bar, you will see it start() again and call the start method. After doing so, it will display "Now in the start() method." See Figure 4-8.

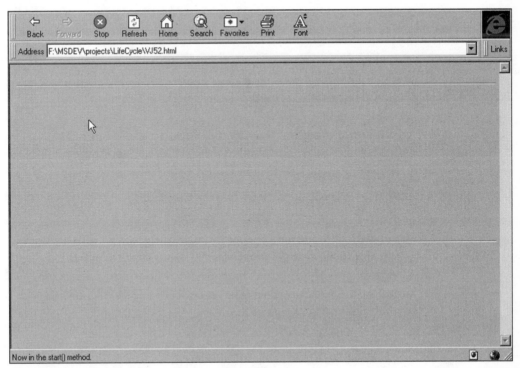

Figure 4-8: The Cycle applet restarting in Internet Explorer.

This example, while very basic, does show how the life-cycle methods work. You can experiment with this example as much as you want. Try clicking on the Refresh icon, and you will see your applet end with destroy() and reinitialize with init().

HTML & Applets

Embedding a Java applet in an HTML page is very similar to embedding a graphic. This section briefly discusses the HTML aspect of embedding a Java applet. However, the section does assume that you have at least a working knowledge of HTML syntax.

When creating applets in Visual J++, the program automatically generates an HTML page on the fly for you to view your applets. However, the applets you create in Visual J++ can be used in any HTML page, not just the ones created by Visual J++.

Tip

> *This section provides you with a high-level overview of HTML, specifically dealing with embedding applets. It requires that you have at least a working knowledge of HTML.*

To illustrate, imagine you created the applet ABClass.class. Now you want to embed this into an HTML page. In the HTML file, you would use the <APPLET> tag, as follows:

```
<APPLET CODE=ABClass.class WIDTH=300 HEIGHT=300>
</APPLET>
```

Essentially, the above snippet of code is what Visual J++ generates automatically for you every time you execute your Java applet project using Internet Explorer. The following discussion examines other options that you can add to the <APPLET> tag to customize how the applet is loaded.

Providing Alternate Text

As you learned earlier, you need to have a Java compliant browser to view Java applets. If your browser is not Java-compliant, it will simply ignore the <APPLET> tags and read the HTML code between the <APPLET> and </APPLET> tags. If there is nothing there then the <APPLET> tag is completely ignored. This provides a useful way for displaying a message in the event a user accesses your HTML page without a Java-compliant browser. The following shows an example of displaying a message or alternative HTML code in place of the applet if the browser is not Java-compliant:

```
<APPLET CODE=ABClass.class WIDTH=300 HEIGHT=300>
You do not have applet viewing capabilities. <P>
</APPLET>
```

Sometimes a user may have a Java-compliant browser, but for some other reason the Java applet is unable to load. For these cases you should use the ALT attribute to specify a message to be displayed. Below is an example using the ALT with our applet ABClass.class:

```
<APPLET CODE=ABClass.class WIDTH=300 HEIGHT=300>
ALT= "Could not load applet ABClass"
You do not have applet viewing capabilities. <P>
</APPLET>
```

Specifying the Location of an Applet

CODEBASE is useful when your HTML page and Java applet class files reside in different directories. In certain situations you may want to create a special directory for your Java applets. You then need to use the attribute CODEBASE. CODEBASE accepts full and partial URLs. The following lines show several examples of CODEBASE:

```
CODEBASE = "http://www.myserver.com/htm/java/ABClass.class
CODEBASE = "http://www.myserver.com/htm/java/"
```

```
CODEBASE = "../java/"
CODEBASE = "java/"
```

Notice that all of the above references are pointing to relatively the same location. Extending our example of the HTML code for the fictitious applet ABClass.class is another example of using CODEBASE:

```
<APPLET CODE=ABClass.class CODEBASE = "applet/" WIDTH=300
HEIGHT=300>
<PARAM NAME=Color VALUE="red">
ALT= "Applet could not be loaded"
Your browser does not support Java Applets. <P>
</APPLET>
```

Specifying How the Applet Displays

Other HTML code sets various display attributes for Java applets. Two that we have already used are the WIDTH and the HEIGHT properties. These are two fairly self-explanatory attributes for a browser. One deals with the width and the other deals with the height of a Java applet. By using these two attributes, you can set the display size for the Java applet.

You can also specify the alignment of where the Java applet is placed by using the ALIGN attribute. The following table shows the various states that ALIGN can be in and their meanings, as interpreted by the browser:

Attribute	Explanation
ALIGN = TEXTTOP	Aligns the applet to the tallest text in the line.
ALIGN = TOP	Aligns to the topmost item in the line.
ALIGN = ABSMIDDLE	Aligns to the middle of the largest item in the line.
ALIGN = MIDDLE	Aligns the middle of the applet to the middle of the baseline.
ALIGN = BASELINE	Aligns with the baseline of the line.
ALIGN = BOTTOM	This is the same as specifying ALIGN = BASELINE.
ALIGN = ABSBOTTOM	Aligns the bottom of the applet to the bottom of the line.

Table 4-8: ALIGN options.

The last two parameters are HSPACE and VSPACE. These attributes deal with specifying the amount of space (in pixels) between the applet and other elements in the HTML site. HSPACE represents the horizontal spacing, and VSPACE represents the vertical spacing.

Enhancing Java Applets With Graphics

An important part of the Java applet programming model is to be able to create text and graphics that stand out. Including several shapes, sizes, and colors over a plain format (like the one you used in the LifeCycle example where you displayed the text "MY FIRST APPLET") helps make your applet much more eye-catching.

Displaying anything inside a Java applet requires the use of two key points. First, you need to override the paint() method. Secondly, you need an understanding of the Graphics class. In a nutshell, the Graphics class is intimately tied with the paint() method and is very resourceful in containing all kinds of methods to create all kinds of graphics. Aside from the Graphics class, there are only a few other built-in classes that you may use when displaying things in your Java applets, including an introduction to the Color and Font classes that are part of the java.awt package.

The paint() Method

You override paint() in your applet to draw anything in the applet's window. The paint() method can and will be called many times in one applet session. For example, the paint() method gets called when the applet loads, reloads, if the user leaves the applet (or covers it up with another window) and then comes back, and if the user resizes the applet; finally, if you can call paint() externally in your applet by calling the method repaint().

The Graphics Class

The Graphics class contains a plethora of public methods that are at your disposal to draw just about every kind of text or object. Included in the Graphics class is the ability to create lines, rectangles, polygons of any number of sides, arcs, and, of course, all kinds of text.

The Graphics class, as you already know, comes from the Abstract Window Toolkit (AWT) package that is also responsible for building user interfaces in Java. You had a chance to work with the Graphics class because the paint() method uses it as well. The important thing to remember about the Graphics class is that it needs to be imported at the beginning of your Java programs before it can be used:

```
import java.applet.Applet;
import java.awt.Graphics;

public class Test extends Applet {
  //Body of Class
}
```

Table 4-9 shows a list of the most useful methods available to you in the Graphics class:

Methods	Explanation
drawString (String str, int x, int y)	Draws the specified String str at the specified coordinates x and y.
getColor()	Gets the current Color.
getFont()	Gets the Font.
getFontMetrics()	Gets the FontMetrics.
getFontMetrics(Font f)	Returns the FontMetrics from the specified f.
setColor(Color c)	Changes the current color to the specified c.
setFont(Font f)	Sets the font to the specified f.
toString()	Returns a String representing this Graphic's value.

Table 4-9: Useful methods in the Graphics class.

The above table only displays a few of the methods contained in the Graphics class. These methods are the most common Graphics methods that you'll use throughout this book.

This book does not give you a complete overview of every method contained in the Graphics class. However, all of these methods are documented (along with every other built-in class in Java) in Visual J++'s InfoView.

Tip

You can query all the online material, including Visual J++ help and the entire Java API specification, by clicking on Help | Search in the Developer Studio.

The Graphics Coordinate System

One thing to note about the Graphics class is the coordinate system it uses. Let's take a closer look at the method drawString() that you used in the Visual J++ project earlier in the chapter:

```
g.drawString("MY FIRST APPLET.", 5, 10);
```

As you know from the example, the first parameter passed to this method is the string to be printed in your applet. However, the second and third parameter specify the x coordinate and y coordinate where the string should start printing.

Java uses a specific coordinate system for all of its methods that use x and y. However, in the coordinate system used by Java the origin is at the top left corner of the applet pane (the border of the applet). So, in the above method drawString(), the second parameter represents x. In this case, it is specified to be 5 points to the right from the y-axis origin, and y is specified to be 10 points down from the x-axis. It is at that precise location where the string "MY FIRST APPLET" begins.

The diagram in Figure 4-9 shows the coordinate system used in the Java language. Be sure to base all your x and y coordinates on this system.

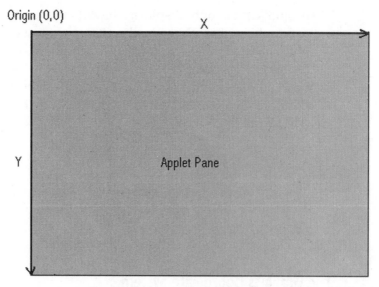

Figure 4-9: Diagram of the Graphics coordinate system.

Note

This book specifies all Graphics coordinates in terms of x and y point spacing. A point is equivalent to a pixel on a computer screen.

It is important to understand exactly where your text and graphics will be placed. With Java, this process is greatly simplified because you do not need to test each platform that your application may run on.

Fonts

Another built-in class that is part of the AWT package is the Font class. The Font class, used in conjunction with the paint() method, lets you specify a font with a specific size, type, and any attributes (bold, etc.) for all the text you display in your applet.

Let's start by constructing an instance of the Font class:

```
Font f = new Font("Helvetica", Font.PLAIN, 36);
```

Notice that the constructor for the Font object takes three parameters. The first input variable lets you specify the font name you want to use for this instance of the Font class. Java currently supports five fonts:

- Dialog
- Helvetica
- TimesRoman
- Courier
- Symbol

With the second variable, you specify the font attributes, which include the following:

```
Font.BOLD
Font.ITALIC
Font.PLAIN
```

Note

Font does not support the underline or strike through style.

The third and final input variable takes an integer that represents font size. Whenever you create a new font, you must specify all three items.

The second thing that you need to do is to set the font in the Graphics class so that it uses the class variable f by default. Specifically, there is a method in the Graphics class called setFont() that you can utilize to set the font. You do all of this inside the paint() method of your applet:

```
public void paint(Graphics g) {
    Font f = new Font("Helvetica", Font.PLAIN, 36);
    g.setFont(f);
    g.drawString("This is a customized font", 5, 50);
}
```

Essentially, that is all that you need to do in order to customize your fonts inside an applet. The following table, Table 4-10, shows a list of useful methods that are all part of the Font class.

Being able to customize fonts is a very important part of the Java programming experience, and this book touches upon it again later.

Colors

Another part of creating very splashy text and graphics is to display them in many different colors. That is why the Color class is part of the java.awt package.

The class Color actually has several different constructors (overloaded constructors) that you can use to specify various attributes. Java uses a 24-bit, abstract color model, including RGB and HSB color formats. However, you do not have to construct an instance of the Color class in order to use it. The following shows an example where you can specify a color by merely using one of its constants:

```
g.setColor(Color.red);
```

Using the setColor() method from the Graphics class, you can set the default color that all graphics and text are displayed in. Looking at the above example, you can see that you can pass a color without creating an instance of it. This provides a great convenience if you only need to use default colors. The following list shows all the basic colors available to you:

```
Color.blue
Color.cyan
Color.green
Color.magenta
Color.orange
Color.pink
Color.red
Color.yellow
```

However, if you need to have a more specific color, you can construct a class variable using the following color and the RGB color format:

```
Color c1 = new Color(255, 200, 0);
```

As you can see, RGB gets its name from red, green, and blue. And each of the three parameters specifies an intensity for each of these colors, respectively. Note that 255 specifies full intensity. The above color specifies the color orange.

Another constructor lets you specify three floating point values representing the RGB format, with 1 equal to 255:

```
Color c2 = new Color(1, 0.78, 0);
```

This one also specifies the color orange.

Tutorial: Creating Your Second Applet

You have been introduced to several new built-in classes with Java. At this point, let's go to Visual J++ and construct our second Java applet.

First, create a project workspace called Second (see Table 4-10 for the procedure).

Step #	Location	Action
1	Developer Studio	Choose File|New.
2	New dialog box	Highlight Project Workspace and click OK.
3	New dialog box	In the Name field, type **Second**, and click Create.

Table 4-10: Creating the Second Project Workspace.

Now you need to create a new Java class called SecondApplet. In the Developer Studio, click Insert | New Java Class. On the Create New Class dialog box, do the following:

1. In the Name field, type **SecondApplet**.

2. In the Extends field, type **java.applet.Applet**.

3. In the Modifiers area, choose public.

Then, click OK (see Figure 4-10).

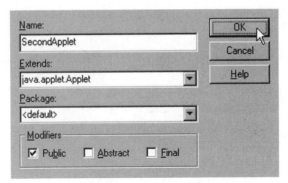

Figure 4-10: The Create New Class dialog box filled out.

Next, you need to add the public method paint() (see Table 4-11 for step-by-step instructions).

Step #	Location	Action
1	Left pane of Second Project Workspace	On the SecondApplet class, right-click and choose Add Method from the menu.
2	New Method dialog box	In the Return type field, type **void**, and in the Method declaration field, type **paint()**.
3	New Method dialog box	In the Access box, choose Public.
4	New Method dialog box	Verify that you typed the declaration correctly; then click OK.

Table 4-11: Creating the paint() method.

At this point, your Developer Studio should look something like Figure 4-11. If you do not see the source code file for the class SecondApplet in the ClassView, expand the Second Classes folder and double-click on the Second class.

Figure 4-11: The Developer Studio with the source code open for Second.

Edit the code as shown in the code below. Remember that the bolded code is material you need to add, and the regular code listed below is code automatically generated by Visual J++:

```
import java.applet.Applet;

//My code starts here
import java.awt.Font;
import java.awt.Color;
import java.awt.Graphics;
//My code ends here

/*
 *
 * SecondApplet
```

```
     *
     */
public class SecondApplet extends Applet
{

     //My code starts here
     Font f = new Font("Courier", Font.BOLD, 20);
     //My code ends here


     public void paint(Graphics g)
     {

     //My code starts here
     g.setFont(f);
     g.setColor(Color.blue);
     g.drawString("My Second Applet", 5, 36);
     //My code ends here


     }



}
```

As you can see in the above code, you used the Graphics class methods setFont() and setColor() to set both the color and font for the text displayed in drawString().

Once you have finished entering the above code, you are ready to save and build the project Second. To save all the files for your project, click on File | Save All. To build the code, click on Build | Build Second. Then, to execute the code, click on Build | Execute. Since you are executing this project for the first time in the Developer Studio, a dialog box displays for you to specify the Class file name (see Figure 4-12). On this dialog box, in the Class name field, type **SecondApplet**. Also, underneath that, you have a choice of using either the jview interpreter or Internet Explorer to view the results. For this example, choose Browser (which already has the Internet Explorer program specified). Then, click OK.

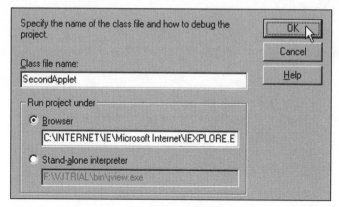

Figure 4-12: The Information for the Running Class dialog box filled out.

At this point, Internet Explorer automatically loads and you see something similar to Figure 4-13.

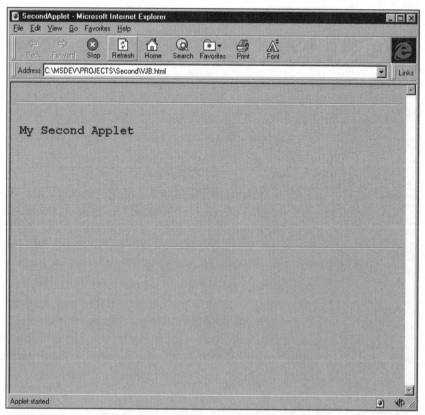

Figure 4-13: Executing the project Second in Internet Explorer.

While Internet Explorer is intimately tied in with Visual J++, it is not the only browser on the Net. Actually, it is dwarfed in overall market share by the Netscape Navigator browser. The following sections provide a brief overview of how to view your applet from other browsers.

Viewing Your Applet in Netscape Navigator

At this point Netscape Navigator is the most common browser used on the Net. As of version 2.0, Java support was added, and as of 3.0, a much faster Borland-based JIT compiler was also included. In order to see applets in Netscape Navigator you need to have at least version 2.0, and make sure that you have enabled Java support.

When you develop a Java applet, it, in itself, is platform-independent. This means that you do not have to worry that some components (or graphics) you have won't be available to all browsers. However, the browsers themselves sometimes make changes to external things such as the coloring and other things related to how the applet embeds in the HTML page. This is not so much a Java issue as an HTML issue. Each browser interprets HTML code in its own way. Albeit most of the time they are extremely similar, there are times when one browser may deviate from another. That is why it is usually a good idea to test your applet in the browsers that you think people are most likely to use to display your applet. Obviously, Netscape Navigator should be at the top of your list. Let's go ahead and view the applet SecondApplet in Netscape Navigator.

When you executed the Visual J++ project in the last section, it created a default HTML file for you to view the applet in Internet Explorer. You can use that HTML file to view your applet in Netscape Navigator. However, the name of the HTML file is automatically generated by Visual J++ and may be different from the one used in this book.

All that you need to do is go to the directory containing the project Second. In that directory, open the only HTML file there in Netscape Navigator and you'll see something like Figure 4-14.

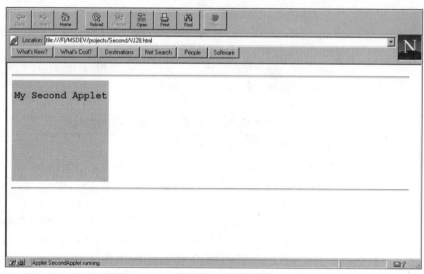

Figure 4-14: Viewing your applet in Netscape Navigator.

As you can see in the figure above, that applet is exactly the same. However, notice that Netscape Navigator uses a gray applet background on a white page (which is different than the gray on gray used in Internet Explorer).

Viewing Your Applet in the JDK's AppletViewer

The last "browser" that you are going to view your applet in is the AppletViewer. The AppletViewer is a utility included in the Java Development Kit (freely available at http://www.java.com) that you can use to view your applets.

The important thing to note is that the AppletViewer is not a browser in the sense that it will load HTML pages. It is essentially a browser that can only read the <APPLET> tag, making it useful for testing your Java applets. However, the AppletViewer suffers in two major areas when compared to Visual J++. First, it is a command-line utility, so you need to enter command lines every time you wish to execute it:

```
appletviewer test.html
```

Secondly, while the AppletViewer is great for testing applets, it is not as effective when you want to test your applet in an HTML page. This is what makes Visual J++ and Internet Explorer shine, because of their seamless integration.

In order to run the AppletViewer you must have downloaded and installed the JDK. Secondly, you must enter the correct command-line parameters in the AppletViewer. Note that, since you most likely have a different directory and HTML file name, it is irrelevant to specify it here. Figure 4-15 shows the AppletViewer running SecondApplet using exactly the same HTML page used in Internet Explorer and Netscape Navigator.

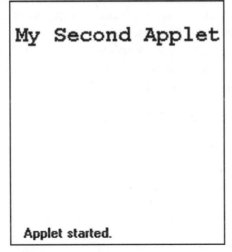

Figure 4-15: Viewing your applet in the AppletViewer.

It is important to be familiar with the browsers and how they interpret the HTML tag <APPLET> because it almost always affects how the browser displays your applet.

Moving On

In this chapter you were introduced to Java applets, starting from a high-level overview and list of alternative solutions and progressing to a detailed explanation of its anatomy. Java applets have a definite fit in the Internet Development community.

You were also introduced to other topics that relate to applets such as the <APPLET> tag and several built-in Java classes that help you display information. This chapter is not the only place that you will hear about applets. However, this chapter does mark a turning point in the book, as you will continue to use what was introduced here, but in much more detail.

The next chapter continues with the discussion of applets, but goes deeper into other topics, including how to pass parameters from your HTML page to your applet and other techniques that are available to you. The next chapter also introduces one of the most powerful tools in Visual J++, the AppletWizard.

5

Working With Applets & the AppletWizard

In this chapter, you are going to continue working with Java applets, learning such information as how to pass information from HTML pages to applets and how to pass command-line arguments to applications. Also, you will learn how to create the appletcation hybrid that was introduced in Chapter 1. There is also a brief introduction to the java.util package.

This chapter also introduces the Visual J++ AppletWizard and shows you, step-by-step, how easy it can be to create Java applets and appletcations. The AppletWizard is one of the most powerful features of Visual J++, and this chapter starts by presenting its capabilities.

The java.util Package

The java.util package contains a number of useful classes that you can use to store data in other, more sophisticated, array-like complex data types and other "stuff." Basically, it contains several other odds and ends that are useful. The following paragraphs introduce several classes contained in the java.util package.

The java.util.Vector class, contained in the java.util package, is a useful class for the storage and retrieval of information because it has the ability to dynamically grow (and shrink) based on its need.

The Observable abstract class and Observer interface class allow you to observe an observable object. If an object implements the interface Observer or it subclasses the abstract class Observable, then the object is observable. Observing is a way for objects to communicate changes to one another.

Another array-like class extends from the Vector class called java.util.Stack class. This class lets you set up a data structure in a LIFO (Last In First Out) format. Usually, you do not work with stacks directly. However, Java does support direct manipulation through the use of several methods.

The Random class comes with the java.util package. It lets you retrieve pseudo-random numbers. Pseudo-random numbers repeat the same numbers after some finite period of steps. This period is extremely large and not essential for calculations. For a detailed explanation of any (and all) of these classes, check the API specification included in Visual J++.

The Date Class

One class that is very useful in the java.util package is the Date class. This class can retrieve today's date (as determined by your computer's internal clock) or any date that you specify and provides functionality to operate dates and times. The time can also be a part of the date retrieved from the Date class. The following shows the default constructor for the Date class:

```
Date d = new Date();
```

In the above code, the value for *d* contains the current date.

Java provides five other constructors for the Date class:

- **Date(long time)** Dates in Java using the Date class can be constructed in the form of Greenwich Mean Time (GMT):

    ```
    Date d = new Date(822202489752L);
    ```

You can also specify a date based in Universal Time Coordinated (UTC).

Note

GMT is an international date standard based on the Greenwich meridian. (The mean solar time for the meridian at Greenwich, England is used as a basis for calculating time throughout the world.)

UTC is a time standard based on an atomic clock that calculates the number of seconds from a given point. For UNIX systems, this counter started at midnight, GMT, January 1, 1970. For IBM and compatible PCs, this counter started at midnight, GMT, January 1, 1980.

The following are constructors you can use to create instances of the Date class, passing them parameters as follows shown in Table 5-1.

Type	Format	Example	Value Passed
year	Year - 1900	1956	56
month	0-11	Jun	5
date	1-31	15	15
day	0-6	Sunday	0
hour	0-23	9:00 PM	21
minute	0-59	25 min. past the hr.	25
second	0-59	30 sec. past the min.	30

Table 5-1: Format for Date Constructors.

The following syntax shows the constructors that you can use in conjunction with the above table:

- Date *classVariable* = new Date(*year, month, date*)
- Date *classVariable* = new Date(*year, month, date, hours, minutes*)
- Date *classVariable* = new Date(*year, month, date, hours, minutes, seconds*)

Note

All of the above constructors for the Date class take integers (int) as their input variables for year, month, date, and so forth.

In addition, you can pass a String variable to construct a Date object:

```
Date classVariable = new Date(Jun Jun5, 1976).
```

The fields in all forms of constructors are normalized before the Date object is created. The argument does not have to be in the correct range. For example, the 32nd of January is correctly interpreted as the 1st of February. You can use this feature to figure out on what day a particular date falls.

Along with several constructors, the Date class comes with a host of methods that you can use to calculate and manipulate Dates in Java.

The Date class is very useful and will be implemented in the Visual J++ project coming up a little later in the chapter. For more information on the methods contained in it, reference InfoView in Visual J++.

Introducing the AppletWizard

The AppletWizard is one of the most sophisticated tools available to you in Visual J++. A Microsoft wizard is a miniprogram that takes information from the user in a step-by-step process and then performs a complex (or extremely redundant) process automatically. Wizards usually involve some sort of automatic code generation on the back end.

Note

The AppletWizard in Visual J++ is very similar to the AppWizard in Visual C++ (another development environment that uses Microsoft's Developer Studio), which can be used to create Windows-based C++ programs.

You can find wizards everywhere, not just in the Developer Studio. Microsoft has used wizards all over the place in Windows 95. Other software you buy usually comes with an install wizard to set up the program. Generally, wizards look the same in the sense that they are a gray dialog box with a picture on the left and information (including options) on the right. Finally, the bottom of the Wizard window is the location for any command buttons, usually including Next, Back, Finish, and Cancel.

Note

A Microsoft wizard in the Developer Studio is very similar to an Express Agent in Symantec (in particular Symantec Café, a Java IDE). Specifically, the AppExpress in Café corresponds to the AppletWizard in Visual J++.

Aside from the fact that wizards perform complex tasks automatically, they are also very powerful in the way they query information. Wizards use the step-by-step approach that allows you to go back and make revisions to some of your earlier decisions.

The AppletWizard allows you to choose from a variety of options. It gives you the ability to create applets and appletcations that can have built-in multithreaded support automatically included. You can also specify what parameters you want to pass to the applet and have them automatically included in the HTML page. The AppletWizard is a very powerful tool for creating the framework to a variety of Java applets.

Starting the AppletWizard

You invoke the AppletWizard exactly the same way that you create a new project—by clicking on File | New in the Developer Studio. Then, in the New dialog box that appears, you choose the Project Workspace item. That opens the New Project Workspace dialog box, which you've used before. However, this time you want to highlight the item Java AppletWizard on the left (see Figure 5-1).

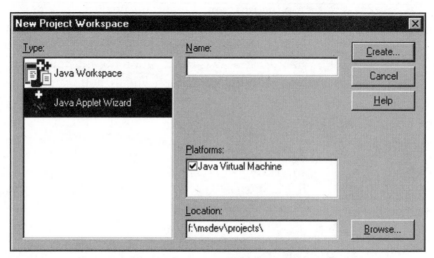

Figure 5-1: New Project Workspace with the Java AppletWizard chosen.

When you click on Create, instead of simply creating the project workspace, the AppletWizard starts.

Step 1 of 5

Step 1 asks you to specify the type of applet you want to create and other general information about the applet (see Figure 5-2).

Tip

Looking at the bottom of Figure 5-2, notice the command button Finish. As you continue to work with the AppletWizard, you will become familiar with the default options. Then, at any step, you can click on Finish to automatically jump to the end of step 5, thereby going with the defaults.

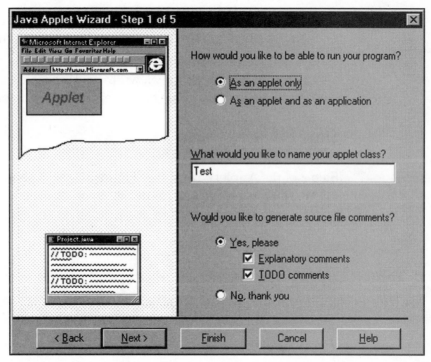

Figure 5-2: Java AppletWizard—Step 1 of 5.

First, the AppletWizard asks you what type of program you want to create. You can create an applet, which runs only in a browser, or what is called an appletcation, which can run in a browser or stand alone.

Second, the AppletWizard asks you to name the class you are creating. By default, the AppletWizard puts the name you entered for the project in the New Project Workspace dialog. However, if you wish, you can change it here.

Finally, you must decide if you want comments included in the applet and if so, what types of comments:

- **Explanatory comments** add descriptive comments into the applet before each method or class they automatically generate.

- **TODO comments** place "TODO" comments, letting you know where you may want to add more implementation code.

You can move back to the New Project Workspace dialog box by clicking on Back or continue on to step 2 by clicking on Next.

Step 2 of 5

Step 2 of the AppletWizard (see Figure 5-3) asks about specific HTML files and related attributes that you can use to test your applet.

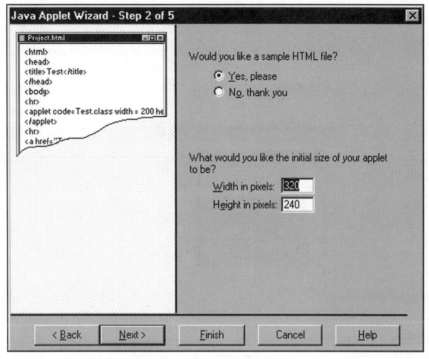

Figure 5-3: Java AppletWizard—Step 2 of 5.

The AppletWizard first asks if you would like to have an HTML page automatically generated and included in the project. Usually, you'll click Yes, please.

Next, the AppletWizard asks what overall size you would like to have for the border of your applet. These two text fields, Width in pixels and Height in pixels, represent the values that will go into the WIDTH and HEIGHT attributes in the <APPLET> tag of the automatically generated HTML file.

You can move back to step 1 by clicking on Back or move to step 3 by clicking on Next.

Step 3 of 5

Step 3 deals with two different topics separated by a line (as shown in Figure 5-4). Here you can customize how your Java applet handles animations and responds to mouse events.

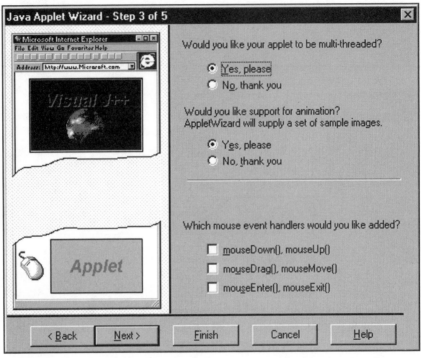

Figure 5-4: Java AppletWizard—Step 3 of 5.

Figure 5-4 starts by asking you whether you would like to have multithreaded support for your Java program. This is a topic that is discussed in further detail in the next chapter. The second question relies heavily on the first, asking you if you would like to have a set of default images loaded with your applet. The animation that the AppletWizard is actually referring to is being shown on the left side with the rotating globe.

The second question under the line asks if you want to provide support for any or all of the listed mouse events. For more information on event handling, check out Chapter 9.

You can move back to step 2 by clicking on Back or move to step 4 by clicking on Next.

Step 4 of 5

Step 4 works with the idea of passing parameters from the HTML page containing the Java applet to the applet itself (see Figure 5-5). This is a very important programming feature of the Java language and the <APPLET> tag. Passing parameters helps to make your Java applets much more versatile, because you do not need to recompile the Java applet every time you change a parameter. Instead, all that you need to do is reload the HTML page containing the applet.

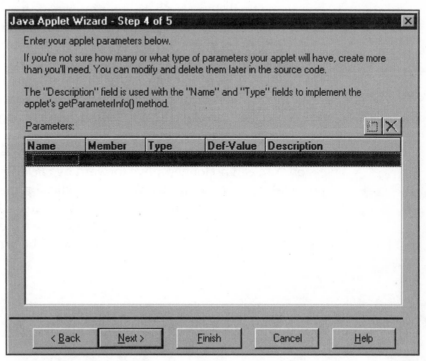

Figure 5-5: Java AppletWizard—Step 4 of 5.

Click on the first toolbar button on the left to add a new parameter to the list, or click on the toolbar button with the red X to delete the parameter. With each addition, you can change the values for each of the columns to create the custom parameter you want. You will learn more about this topic later in this chapter.

Tip

The two buttons described in step 4 may be hard to recognize. They are the two small buttons just above the text field, aligned to the right.

You can move back to step 3 by clicking on Back or move to step 5 by clicking on Next.

Step 5 of 5

You use the final step, step 5, to enter information about the applet, your company, and yourself. This information can be retrieved by users to find out more information about your applet (see Figure 5-6).

In Figure 5-6, note that you can edit the entire area in white (including the highlighted items) as if this were a text editor such as Notepad. So, you can edit, add, and delete as you wish to give any information you choose.

At this point, you have reached the end of the AppletWizard session. You can no longer move forward by clicking on Next. Your final step for the AppletWizard is to click on the Finish button to load a confirmation screen called New Project Information. On the other hand, you can move back and take a look at the changes you made all the way back to the very beginning with the New Project Workspace dialog box.

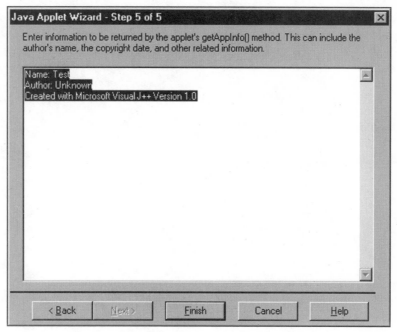

Figure 5-6: Java AppletWizard—Step 5 of 5.

New Project Information Dialog Box

The New Project Information dialog box is the last step between the AppletWizard and the actual creation of your project. This dialog box gives you information regarding your applet that is either the default information chosen by the AppletWizard or options you explicitly asked for (see Figure 5-7).

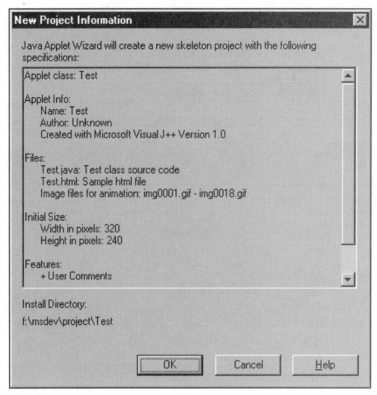

Figure 5-7: The New Project Information dialog box.

The New Project Information dialog box is strictly for your review; you cannot edit any of the information or make changes to the Install directory from this dialog box. Furthermore, if you look behind the New Project Information dialog box, you notice that the AppletWizard is still there. If you click Cancel in the New Project Information dialog box, you return to step 5. On the other hand, if you click on OK, then the AppletWizard creates your applet with an accompanying project workspace. You are now ready to develop.

Tutorial: Creating an Applet With the AppletWizard

So far in this chapter, you have been introduced to the Visual J++ AppletWizard and the java.util package. Now, let's turn our attention to actually creating a Java applet that uses the Date and Random classes from the java.util package.

Go to the Developer Studio and click on File I New to open the New dialog box. Choose the item Project Workspace; then click OK to continue. In the New Project Workspace dialog, highlight the item Java AppletWizard. Then type **Welcome** for the name of the project. Click Create to continue.

The AppletWizard opens to step 1. There are no changes that need to be made to this step, so click on Next to move to step 2.

Tip

The AppletWizard contains a set of default options selected for you. This same set of defaults is used every time you execute the AppletWizard no matter what you specified in a past session.

In step 2, you need to change the Width in pixels to 700 and the Height in pixels to 200 for the second question.

In step 3, you need to select No, thank you as the answer to the first question, "Would you like your applet to be multi-threaded?" Then click Next to continue.

For step 4, you will not be passing any parameters to this applet, so you do not need to make any changes. Click Next to move to step 5.

In step 5, the final step, you can add information about your applet and yourself. For example, you can include the name of the applet, name of the author, and what development environment created the applet.

Once you have finished filling out your information, click Finish to open the New Project Information confirmation dialog box. Check to make sure that the information you entered in each of the five steps is consistent with the information displayed in this dialog box. If everything looks in order, click OK to create the project and corresponding applet.

At this point, your Developer Studio should look similar to Figure 5-8. Go to the ClassView on the left and double-click on the folder Welcome. There you see the class Welcome that the AppletWizard of Visual J++ automatically generated.

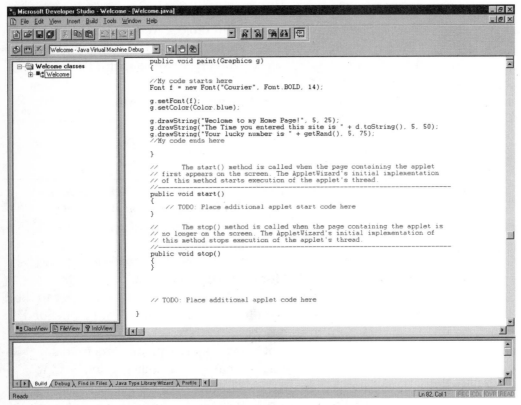

Figure 5-8: The Developer Studio.

Next, you need to add a getRand() method to the Welcome class (see Table 5-2 for step-by-step instructions).

At this point, you are ready to edit the automatically generated class Welcome with implementation code.

Tip

If you cannot see the source code for class Welcome, go to ClassView and find the Welcome class. Then double-click on it and the source code for it will open on the right.

Step #	Location	Action
1	Left pane of Welcome Project Workspace	On the Welcome class, right-click and choose Add Method from the menu.
2	New Method dialog box	In the Return type field, type **int**, and in the Method declaration field, type **getRand()**.
3	New Method dialog box	In the Access box, choose Public.
4	New Method dialog box	Verify that you typed the declaration correctly; then click OK.

Table 5-2: Creating the getRand() method.

Edit the code as shown below. Remember that the bolded code is material you need to add and the regular code listed below is code automatically generated by Visual J++:

```
//**********************************************************
// Welcome.java:    Applet
//
//**********************************************************
import java.applet.*;
import java.awt.*;

//My code starts here
import java.util.*;
//My code ends here


//==========================================================
// Main Class for applet Welcome
//
//==========================================================
public class Welcome extends Applet
{
```

```
//My code starts here
Date d = new Date();
Random r = new Random();
//My code ends here

public int getRand()
{

//My code starts here
return Math.abs(r.nextInt() % 10) + 1;
//My code ends here

}

// Welcome Class Constructor
// This standard text is a bit misleading since it welcome's
to Class Constructor instead of declare the Constructor of
class "Welcome"
//----------------------------------------------------------
public Welcome()
{
    // TODO: Add constructor code here
}

// APPLET INFO SUPPORT:
//    The getAppletInfo() method returns a string describing
the applet's
// author, copyright date, or miscellaneous information.
//----------------------------------------------------------
public String getAppletInfo()
{
    return "Name: Welcome\r\n" +
            "Author: Daniel Joshi\r\n" +
            "Created with Microsoft Visual J++ Version
1.0\r\n" +
            "Note: My first applet using the AppletWizard";
}
```

```
    // The init() method is called by the AWT when an applet is
first loaded or
    // reloaded.  Override this method to perform whatever
initialization your
    // applet needs, such as initializing data structures,
loading images or
    // fonts, creating frame windows, setting the layout
manager, or adding UI
    // components.
    //-------------------------------------------------------
    public void init()
    {
        // If you use a ResourceWizard-generated "control
creator" class to
        // arrange controls in your applet, you may want to
call its
        // CreateControls() method from within this method.
Remove the following
        // call to resize() before adding the call to
CreateControls();
        // CreateControls() does its own resizing.
        //-----------------------------------------------
        resize(700, 200);

        // TODO: Place additional initialization code here
    }


    // Place additional applet clean up code here.  destroy()
is called then
    // when your applet is terminating and being unloaded.
    //-------------------------------------------------------
    public void destroy()
    {
        // TODO: Place applet cleanup code here
    }


    // Welcome Paint Handler
    //-------------------------------------------------------
    public void paint(Graphics g)
    {
```

```
//My code starts here
Font f = new Font("Courier", Font.BOLD, 14);

g.setFont(f);
g.setColor(Color.blue);

  g.drawString("Welcome to my Home Page!", 5, 25);
  g.drawString("The Time you entered this site is " +
d.toString(), 5, 50);
  g.drawString("Your lucky number is " + getRand(), 5, 75);
  //My code ends here


  }


// 	The start() method is called when the page containing
the applet
// first appears on the screen. The AppletWizard's initial
implementation
// of this method starts execution of the applet's thread.
//-------------------------------------------------------
public void start()
{
   // TODO: Place additional applet start code here
}


// 	The stop() method is called when the page containing
the applet is
// no longer on the screen. The AppletWizard's initial
implementation of
// this method stops execution of the applet's thread.
//-------------------------------------------------------
public void stop()
{
}
```

```
// TODO: Place additional applet code here
```

```
}
```

Let's look more closely at the above code. Starting from the beginning, you have the import statements bringing in the java.applet, java.awt, and java.util packages. From there, you begin the main class Welcome. Let's look at the following snippet of code you added right underneath the Welcome applet:

```
Date d = new Date();
Random r = new Random();
```

In the above code, you are creating *d*, which is an instance of class Date, using the default constructor. Thus, *d* contains the current date. *r* is an instance of class Random, and since you are declaring them in the class Welcome they are available to any other member of that class.

After that, you have the method getRand(), which you created to call later in the Java applet to retrieve a random number. Basically, there is only one line contained in the method; it is as follows:

```
return Math.abs(r.nextInt() % 10) + 1;
```

The keyword return should not be new to you. It merely returns the value of the expression following it for the return value of the whole method. The method Math.abs() is a method that comes from Math class, which is part of the java.lang package. It merely takes any numerical value inside its parentheses and returns the absolute value for it.

Tip

The java.lang package automatically imports to any Java program you create. So, you do not need to explicitly import it.

Delving deeper into the line, you have the nextInt() method that comes from *r*, a member of the Random class, and returns a random integer-based value. The modulus, 10, is there to make whatever value returned be between -9 and 9. Then, the absolute value makes any negatives positive. So, in effect, the getRand() method only returns values between 1 and 10.

Tip

Using the modulus, as mentioned above, is a very useful way to retrieve a uniform set of random numbers in your Java programs.

After getRand(), you have the default constructor for the class Welcome which is automatically generated by the AppletWizard. Then there is the getAppletInfo() method that contains the information you entered in step 5 of the AppletWizard. Continuing down the code, you have the init() life-cycle method overridden and containing the resize() method which comes from the Applet class. The resize() method resizes the applet to the specified values (in this case, 700 by 200). Finally, you have the destroy() method, left untouched.

Underneath the destroy() method is the method paint() that contains all the graphics for the applet. The first thing you did in the applet was create an instance, f, of the Font class:

```
Font f = new Font("Courier", Font.BOLD, 14);
```

In the above code, you specified *f* to be Courier bold with a font size of 14. Then, you used the two methods from the Graphics class, setFont() and setColor(), to specify the font and color for everything printed in the applet pane:

```
g.setFont(f);
g.setColor(Color.blue);
```

In the above code, you set the font to be of the instance f and the color to be blue.

The next three drawString() methods are responsible for the actual drawing of the text on the screen:

```
g.drawString("Welcome to my Home Page!", 5, 25);
    g.drawString("The Time you entered this site is " +
d.toString(), 5, 50);
    g.drawString("Your lucky number is " + getRand(), 5, 75);
```

The first drawString() prints a title at the top of the applet. The second drawString() uses a method, the toString(), from the Date class to convert the instance of Date to a String and print the current time and date. The final drawString() calls the method getRand() and prints the number returned on the screen.

The last lines of code in the above applet are the default code created by the AppletWizard for the life-cycle methods start() and stop().

Now you are ready to save and build your code. To save all the files for your project, click on File I Save All. To build the code, click on Build I Build LifeCycle. Then, to execute the code, click on Build I Execute.

Tip

The AppletWizard automatically filled in the Running Class dialog box with the information the Developer Studio needs to run the applet. So, you no longer need to explicitly enter any information about the class to execute or the environment to run it in.

Since this is an applet and you had the AppletWizard automatically generate the HTML file for it, Visual J++ invokes Internet Explorer (see Figure 5-9).

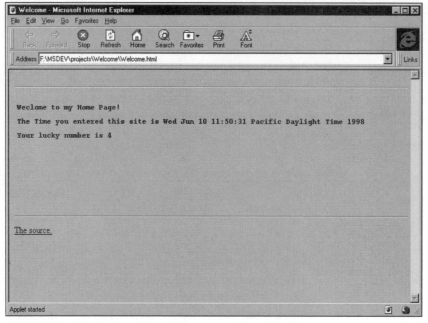

Figure 5-9: Running the Welcome applet in Internet Explorer.

As you can see in Figure 5-9, the applet prints three lines: the first is a welcome line; the second prints the date; and the third line prints a random number between 1 and 10.

Passing Information to Java Programs

Passing information from the environment to your Java programs is an extremely useful way of creating programs that are *customizable*. Customizable means that an applet can receive certain information and run accordingly without the need to recompile each time. That is what this section shows you how to do for both applications and applets.

Passing Arguments (Parameters) to Java Applications

Just like in C/C++, in Java, you have the ability to pass command-line arguments to a given application. For example, imagine that you have an application called myApp and you want to pass the statement "test" to it. Using Visual J++'s interpreter called jview, the following shows what you would type in a command prompt when you run the application:

```
jview myApp test
```

Now, you cannot just pass the argument without programming your application to accept it on the back end. Starting from the beginning, the first thing to point out is where the argument goes when you pass it. To find out, let's take a closer look at the signature for the main() method:

```
public static void main(String argv[]) {

    //Body of Method
}
```

Note

Signature is another name for the declaration.

When you pass an argument to a program, it goes into the String array argv[] declared in the main() method. The main() method is the central location for your action code; it is also where you receive any arguments passed to it.

Tip

You can name the String array in the main() method declaration anything you want. The most common names are args, argv, and arg.

Essentially, each argument you specify goes as an index value in the String array argv. So, if you want to pass two arguments to the myApp application:

```
jview myApp test test2
```

The *test* string would go into the main() method as argv[0]; *test2* would go into argv[1] and so on if you had more arguments passed to it.

Note

Unlike in C/C++, the name of the application is not stored as the first element in the array argv[].

Another topic to discuss about passing arguments to the main() method is what to do if you want to pass spaces inside a String argument. You accomplish this by surrounding all the arguments in quotations:

```
jview myApp "one arg" two arg
```

Looking at the above snippet of code, notice that *one arg* will be placed as a String in argv[0], *two* will be put in argv[1], and *arg* will be placed in argv[2].

Finally, the last thing to note is that argv[] is an array of Strings. So, if you want to accept any other data type you need to convert the inputted arguments accordingly.

Tutorial: Passing Arguments in a Java Applet

Let's create a Visual J++ sample application that can accept input arguments. First, create a project workspace called ArgTest (see Table 5-3 for the procedure).

Step #	Location	Action
1	Developer Studio	Choose File|New.
2	New dialog box	Highlight Project Workspace and click OK.
3	New Project Workspace dialog box	In the Name field, type **ArgTest** and click Create.

Table 5-3: Creating the ArgTest Project Workspace.

Tip

Remember you are creating a Java application, so do not use the Java AppletWizard.

Go to the main menu and click on Insert I New Java Class. When you have done this, Visual J++'s Create New Class dialog box opens; all you need to fill in is the Name field with ArgTest. Then, in the Modifiers panel, be sure Public is checked. When you finish, click on OK (see Figure 5-10).

Now you need to create a new Java class called ArgTest. In the Developer Studio click Insert I New Java Class. On the Create New Class dialog box, do the following:

1. In the Name field, type **ArgTest**.

2. In the Modifiers area, choose Public.

Then, click OK (see Figure 5-10).

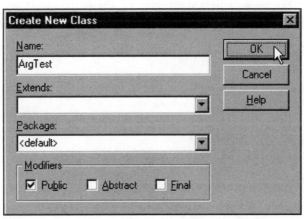

Figure 5-10: The Create New Class dialog box filled out.

Let's start by creating our first public method called main() (see Table 5-4 for step-by-step instructions).

Step #	Location	Action
1	Left pane of ArgTest Project Workspace	On the ArgTest class, right-click and choose Add Method from the menu.
2	New Method dialog box	In the Return type field, type **void**, and in the Method declaration field, type main(String argv[]).
3	New Method dialog box	In the Access box, choose Public. In the Modifiers area, choose Static.
4	New Method dialog box	Verify that you typed declaration correctly; then click OK.

Table 5-4: Creating the main() method.

At this point, the Developer Studio automatically opens the class ArgTest for editing. Edit it so that it looks like the following code. Remember that the bolded code is material you need to add and the regular code listed below is code automatically generated by Visual J++:

```
/*
 *
 * ArgTest
 *
 */
public class ArgTest
{

    public static void main(String argv[])
    {

        //My code starts here
        //Check to see if an argument was passed
        if (argv.length == 0) {
            System.out.println("You did not enter anything.");
            System.exit(0);
        }
```

```
      //Print out the arguments are passed
      for (int i = 0; i < argv.length; i++) {
          System.out.println("You entered " + argv[i] + " as
argument #" + i );
      }
      //My code ends here


}
```

Now you are ready to save and build your code. To save all the files for your project, click on File I Save All. To build the code, click on Build I Build ArgTest. Then, to execute the code, click on Build I Execute. Since you are executing this project for the first time in the Developer Studio, a dialog box displays for you to specify the class file name (see Figure 5-11). On this dialog, in the Class name field, type **ArgTest**. Also, underneath that, you have a choice of using either the jview interpreter or Internet Explorer to view the results. For this example, choose Stand-alone interpreter. Then, click OK.

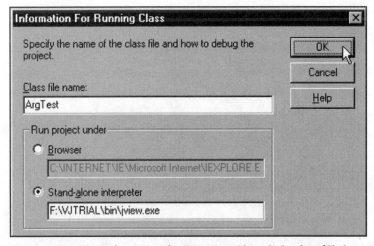

Figure 5-11: The Information for Running Class dialog box filled out.

Once you execute ArgTest, you should see something similar to Figure 5-12.

Figure 5-12: Executing ArgTest with no arguments passed.

In Figure 5-12 you executed ArgTest without passing any arguments. Now, go to a command prompt and execute the ArgTest application by typing the following:

```
jview ArgTest One Two Three
```

In the above code, you are executing ArgTest passing three arguments (see Figure 5-13).

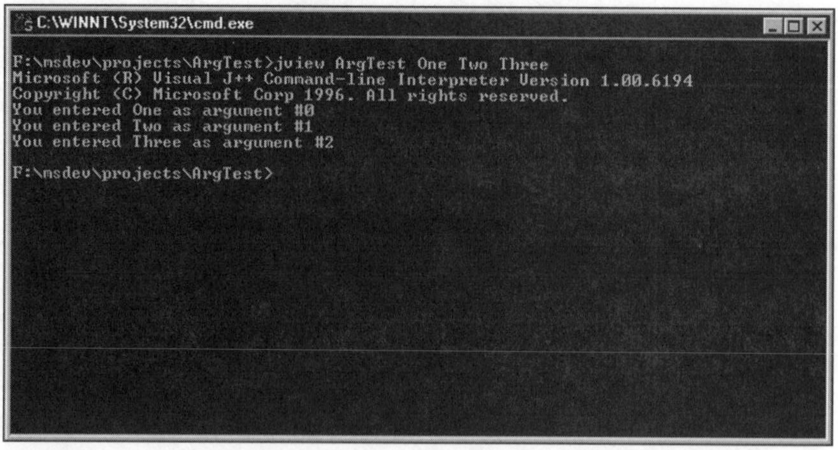

Figure 5-13: Executing ArgTest with three arguments passed.

Now go ahead and execute ArgTest from the command prompt again, but this time type the following:

```
jview ArgTest "One Two" Three
```

When ArgTest is executed you should see Figure 5-14.

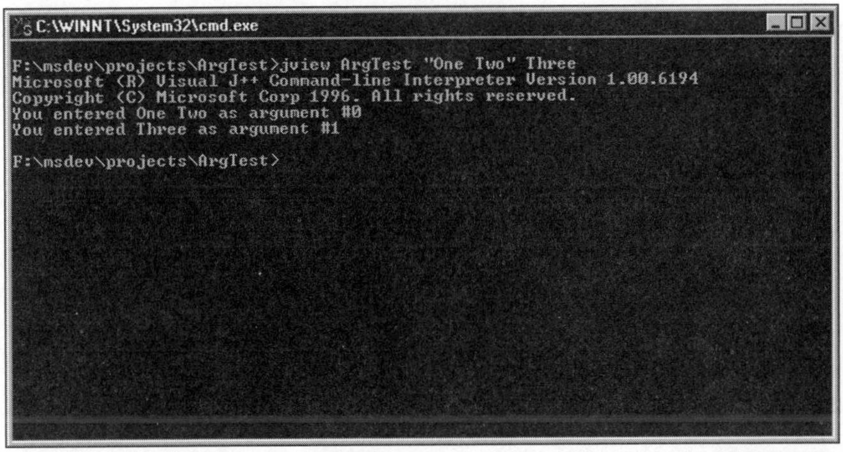

Figure 5-14: Executing ArgTest with two arguments passed.

This tutorial showed you how to specify arguments from the command line. However, You can specify arguments to be passed in the Developer Studio by going to Build | Settings. Then, go to the Debug tab and enter any arguments you want to pass to the application executing in this project in the Arguments text field Passing Parameters to Java Applets.

Passing a parameter to a Java applet is a little more sophisticated than passing an argument to a Java application. However, the idea is the same. Basically, you need to have two things in place in order to pass information to a Java applet.

First, you need to have an HTML page designed with the appropriate tags and attributes. Then, in this HTML page, you can specify that you are passing a parameter NAME and its corresponding VALUE. Second, you need to have code in the Java applet to retrieve this information. If both sides are not in place, then it won't work.

The HTML Side of Passing Parameters

Starting with the HTML side, let's take a closer look at what you need to do in order to specify a parameter for a particular Java applet.

Consider the following example: You have a Java applet called myApplet and you have an HTML page where you want to have a parameter to specify the background color for the applet. The following shows what the <APPLET> tag in the HTML file would look like:

```
<APPLET CODE =myApplet WIDTH=200 HEIGHT=200>
<PARAM NAME=Background VALUE="white">
</APPLET>
```

First, notice that the <PARAM is put inside the <APPLET> tag. Second, notice that, on the line containing the parameter, there is a NAME and VALUE attribute. Both of these send case-sensitive values back to the Java applet. The NAME gives the applet the parameter name and the VALUE gives the Java applet the corresponding value.

You can specify as many parameters as you want. However, unless there is a Java applet programmed to pull the information off the HTML page, it is ignored by the browser and the Java applet loading. The next section describes at the programmatic level how to retrieve parameter information off an HTML page.

The Java Side of Passing Parameters

The Java side of passing parameters is not very difficult to understand. You need to be aware of a few methods and a few techniques and from there you should be fine.

Anytime you want to retrieve information from an HTML page, you need to use the getParameter() method which is a member of the java.applet.Applet class. Then you need to have a local variable to put it into. Consider the following:

```
private String test = "white";

//Body of Class

public void init() {
```

```
   String param;

param = getParameter("Background");
if (param != null)
   test = param;
}
```

All getParameter() methods that you use should be placed in the init() life-cycle method of your Java applet. Looking closely at the above, notice that you declared the member variable *test* earlier in the class. Then, when you get to the init() method, create a temporary holding tank *String param*. The getParameter() always returns a String (no matter what data type you include for the VALUE attribute). Finally, notice that the input variable for the getParameter() method is the name as it is specified by the corresponding NAME attribute in the HTML page.

Then you have the if statement that checks to make sure something was returned. If nothing returns, then it uses the default which in this case is white.

Now, let's take another look at a getParameter() method; but this time, it is going to read in an integer value. Here is the HTML page:

```
<APPLET CODE=XYClass WIDTH=200 HEIGHT=200>
<PARAM NAME=Images VALUE="10">
</APPLET>
```

Now, let's take a look on the applet side for how you would retrieve this information:

```
private int numOfImages = 5;

//Body of Class

public void init() {
   String param;

param = getParameter("Images");
if (param != null)
   numOfImages = Integer.parseInt(param);
}
```

Looking the above code, notice that nothing has changed from the last example except for the member variable's data type which is an int called numOfImages. Also, the line inside the if statement uses the method parseInt() to convert the String param into an integer value. parseInt() is a member of the java.lang.Integer class. There are class representations for all the primitive data types introduced in Chapter 2. Each of these class-based primitive data types contains methods such as the one used here that allows you to do more sophisticated manipulations with your data.

That is pretty much all there is on the Java side to retrieving a parameter. There is, however, another method from the java.applet.Applet class related to passing information about possible parameters called getParameterInfo(). Basically, its function is to provide other people with information about the parameters you programmed your applet to take. The following shows an example:

```
public String[][] getParameterInfo()
{
  String[][] info =
  {
    { "Background", "String", "Background color" },
    { "Images", "int", "Number of Images" },
  };
  return info;
}
```

Looking at the example above, you can see that you actually override this method, which returns a two-dimensional String array. For each parameter, you specify three values: the name of the parameter, the data type, and a description of what the parameter does.

Tutorial: Passing Parameters in a Java Applet

At this point, you have a feel for what needs to be done on the Java level to retrieve a <PARAM statement in HTML. Let's create a Visual J++ project and unleash the power of the AppletWizard.

Not only does the AppletWizard automatically generate all the source code to pass a parameter, it also creates all of the HTML code as well.

Let's use the AppletWizard to create a JavaApplet called CustApplet. Use Table 5-5 to follow step-by-step instructions on the details of the applet.

Step #	Location	Action
1	Developer Studio	Choose File|New.
2	New dialog box	Highlight Project Workspace and click OK.
3	New Project Workspace dialog box	Highlight Java AppletWizard. Then, in the Name field, type **CustApplet** and click Create.
4	AppletWizard, step 1	Click Next.
5	AppletWizard, step 2	Click Next.
6	AppletWizard, step 3	For the "Would you like your applet to be multi-threaded?" question, click No, thank you. Then, click Next.
7	AppletWizard, step 4	Click the New icon. In the Name field, type **Color**; in the Member field, type **theColor**; and in the DefValue field, type **black**. Then, click Next.
8	AppletWizard, step 5	Type any applet or copyright information here, then click Finish.
9	New Project Information dialog box	Verify the information is correct (see Figure 5-15); then click OK.

Table 5-5: Creating the CustApplet using the AppletWizard.

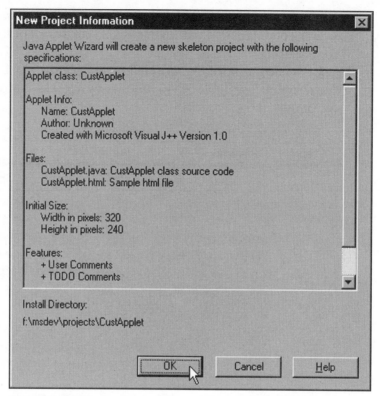

Figure 5-15: New Project Information for project CustApplet.

Next, you need to add the method colorFromString() to the CustApplet class (see Table 5-6 for step-by-step instructions).

Step #	Location	Action
1	Left pane of CustApplet Project Workspace	On the CustApplet class, right-click and choose Add Method from the menu.
2	New Method dialog box	In the Return type field, type **Color**, and in the Method declaration field, type **colorFromString()**.
3	New Method dialog box	In the Access box, choose Public.
4	New Method dialog box	Verify that you typed the declaration correctly; then click OK.

Table 5-6: Creating the colorFromString() method.

Now, edit the code as shown below. Remember that the bolded code is material you need to add and the regular code listed below is code automatically generated by the AppletWizard of Visual J++:

```
//***********************************************************
// CustApplet.java: Applet
//
//***********************************************************
import java.applet.*;
import java.awt.*;


//===========================================================
// Main Class for applet CustApplet
//
//===========================================================
public class CustApplet extends Applet
{

    public Color colorFromString(String s)
    {
```

```
//My code starts here
if (s.equalsIgnoreCase("red")) {
    return Color.red;
  } else if (s.equalsIgnoreCase("green")) {
    return Color.green;
  }  else if (s.equalsIgnoreCase("blue")) {
    return Color.blue;
  } else if (s.equalsIgnoreCase("black")) {
    return Color.black;
  } else if (s.equalsIgnoreCase("white")){
    return Color.white;
  } else if (s.equalsIgnoreCase("gray")) {
    return Color.gray;
  } else if (s.equalsIgnoreCase("lightgray")) {
    return Color.lightGray;
  } else if (s.equalsIgnoreCase("darkgray")) {
    return Color.darkGray;
  } else {
   return Color.black;
  }
//My code ends here


}


// PARAMETER SUPPORT:
//    Parameters allow an HTML author to pass information to
the applet;
// the HTML author specifies them using the <PARAM> tag
within the <APPLET>
// tag.  The following variables are used to store the
values of the
// parameters.
//-----------------------------------------------------

// Members for applet parameters
// <type>         <MemberVar>    = <Default Value>
//-----------------------------------------------------
private String theColor = "black";
```

```
    // Parameter names.  To change a name of a parameter, you
need only make
    // a single change.  Simply modify the value of the
parameter string below.
    //---------------------------------------------------------
    private final String PARAM_Color = "Color";

    // CustApplet Class Constructor
    //---------------------------------------------------------
    public CustApplet()
    {
      // TODO: Add constructor code here
    }

    // APPLET INFO SUPPORT:
    //   The getAppletInfo() method returns a string describing
the applet's
    // author, copyright date, or miscellaneous information.
    //---------------------------------------------------------
    public String getAppletInfo()
    {
      return "Name: CustApplet\r\n" +
             "Author: Daniel Joshi\r\n" +
             "Created with Microsoft Visual J++ Version 1.0";
    }

    // PARAMETER SUPPORT
    //   The getParameterInfo() method returns an array of
strings describing
    // the parameters understood by this applet.
    //
    // CustApplet Parameter Information:
    //   { "Name", "Type", "Description" },
    //---------------------------------------------------------
    public String[][] getParameterInfo()
    {
      String[][] info =
      {
```

```
        { PARAM_Color, "String", "Parameter description" },
      };
      return info;
  }


    // The init() method is called by the AWT when an applet is
first loaded or
    // reloaded.  Override this method to perform whatever
initialization your
    // applet needs, such as initializing data structures,
loading images or
    // fonts, creating frame windows, setting the layout
manager, or adding UI
    // components.
    //-------------------------------------------------------------
  public void init()
  {
    // PARAMETER SUPPORT
    //    The following code retrieves the value of each
parameter
    // specified with the <PARAM> tag and stores it in a
member
    // variable.
    //-------------------------------------------------------------
    String param;

    // Color: Parameter description
    //-------------------------------------------------------------
    param = getParameter(PARAM_Color);
    if (param != null)
      theColor = param;


        // If you use a ResourceWizard-generated "control
creator" class to
        // arrange controls in your applet, you may want to
call its
        // CreateControls() method from within this method.
Remove the following
```

```
        // call to resize() before adding the call to
CreateControls();
        // CreateControls() does its own resizing.
        //------------------------------------------------
    resize(320, 240);

    // TODO: Place additional initialization code here
  }

    // Place additional applet clean up code here.  destroy()
is called when
    // when your applet is terminating and being unloaded.
    //------------------------------------------------------
    public void destroy()
    {
      // TODO: Place applet cleanup code here
    }

    // CustApplet Paint Handler
    //------------------------------------------------------
    public void paint(Graphics g)
    {

    //My code starts here
    Font f = new Font("Courier", Font.BOLD, 24);

    g.setFont(f);
    g.setColor(colorFromString(theColor));

    g.drawString("My Customizable Applet", 5, 25);
    //My code ends here

    }

    //   The start() method is called when the page containing
the applet
    // first appears on the screen. The AppletWizard's initial
implementation
    // of this method starts execution of the applet's thread.
```

```
//----------------------------------------------------------
public void start()
{
    // TODO: Place additional applet start code here
}


//   The stop() method is called when the page containing
the applet is
// no longer on the screen. The AppletWizard's initial
implementation of
// this method stops execution of the applet's thread.
//----------------------------------------------------------
public void stop()
{
}




    // TODO: Place additional applet code here

}
```

Analyzing the above code, you can see that the AppletWizard generated most of the program for you. There are only two specific areas where you need to add extra code. Starting at the top, you are importing the packages java.awt and java.applet. Underneath that is the signature for the class CustApplet that extends the class Applet. The first thing contained inside the class is the method colorFromString(). This method takes a String as input and returns a reference to static Color object. The following shows a snippet of code from the method body:

```
if (s.equalsIgnoreCase("red")) {
    return Color.red;
} else if (s.equalsIgnoreCase("green")) {
    return Color.green;
```

Looking at the above code, you see there is a series of else-if statements that are performing comparisons using the equalsIgnoreCase() method. The equalsIgnoreCase() method comes from the String class and is used to compare two strings and returns a true if they are the same. The nice feature about this method in particular is that it disregards case when making a determination. This helps to make your applet a little more user-friendly. If the comparison returns a true, then the method colorFromString() returns a Color object represented by the comparison.

After the method, you have a series of comments. Then you have the declaration for the variable theColor:

```
private String theColor = "black";
```

This is the variable you will use throughout your applet to specify the color passed from the <PARAM in the HTML page.

Tip

Notice that Visual J++ declares the variable theColor with the default color you specified in the AppletWizard.

After that, you have the declaration of the String variable PARAM_Color:

```
private final String PARAM_Color = "Color";
```

This is the variable that your applet uses to specify the NAME of the parameter. The purpose of this variable is to make sure that through all the program you'll only need one reference to this variable. A little later, you have the overridden getParameterInfo() giving all the information about the parameters available for this applet. In the init() life-cycle method underneath it, you have the getParameter() method that actually attempts to retrieve the VALUE for Color from the HTML page in the <PARAM line.:

```
param = getParameter(PARAM_Color);
if (param != null)
   theColor = param;
```

The above code should not be new to you, as it was discussed in the last section. The actual retrieving takes place with the getParameter() method. The following if statement checks to see if anything was returned; and, if so, then it puts that result for new value of theColor.

The rest of the applet should contain nothing new to you. Moreover, the only other area to focus on is in the pain() method:

```
Font f = new Font("Courier", Font.BOLD, 24);

g.setFont(f);
g.setColor(colorFromString(theColor));

g.drawString("My Customizable Applet", 5, 25);
```

Looking at the above code, you see that you are creating a Font and setting it as the default font with the setFont(). Then, after that, you call the method colorFromString() and pass to it the variable theColor. At this point, theColor now contains the value passed from the getParameter() called in the init() method (or if nothing returned from the getParameter(), then it will have the default value of black).

After the paint() method are the life-cycle methods start() and stop() that are not used in this applet.

Now you are ready to save and build your code. To save all the files for your project, click on File I Save All. To build the code, click on Build I Build CustApplet. Then, to execute the code, click on Build I Execute. Since this is an applet and the AppletWizard automatically generates the HTML file, Visual J++ uses Internet Explorer to load the applet (see Figure 5-16).

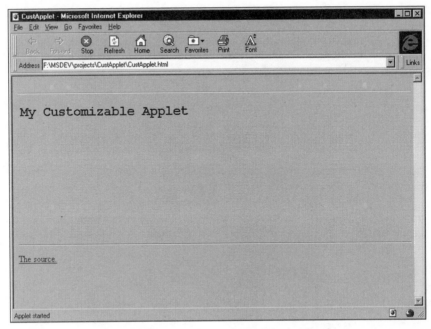

Figure 5-16: Running the CustApplet applet in Internet Explorer.

As you can see in Figure 5-16, the color for the text is black. Let's now go back to the Developer Studio and edit the HTML page CustApplet.html. In the Developer Studio, click File | Open. By default, the Developer Studio opens in the directory for the current project that is, in this case, CustApplet. Then change the Files of type to HTML files, and you will see the CustApplet.html file listed. Open it in the Developer Studio (see Figure 5-17). Notice that all of the HTML syntax is color coded.

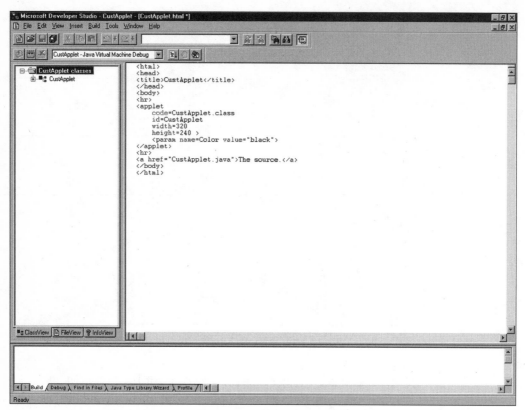

Figure 5-17: Editing the CustApplet.html in the Developer Studio.

Tip

You can edit HTML files in Visual J++. Visual J++ supports the HTML 2.0, Internet Explorer 2, and Internet Explorer 3 extensions (with Internet Explorer 3 extensions specified as the default). You can change the HTML extensions specifications by right-clicking on the open HTML file in the Developer Studio and choosing Properties.

Let's take a closer look at the <PARAM line inside the <APPLET> tag in the CustApplet.html file:

```
<param name=Color value="black">
```

Here is the parameter that the AppletWizard automatically generated. Go ahead and change the value from black to green so that the <PARAM line looks like the following:

```
<param name=Color value="green">
```

Is HTML Case-Sensitive?
When working with HTML, you may notice several different forms of case for the extensions, tags, and attributes. Technically speaking, browsers read these extensions without regard to case. However, you should always use a case consistently to make your code easier to understand.

Now, save the HTML file by clicking on File | Save. Then execute the applet again by clicking Build | Execute CustApplet. This time, you will see the same text printed, but in bright green (see Figure 5-18).

Try other colors in the HTML file and even try entering a value that is totally incorrect to test the default color. Passing parameters is an integral part of making your applet customizable. Many applets can have 10 or more parameters that let users (not just programmers) decide what the applet should do.

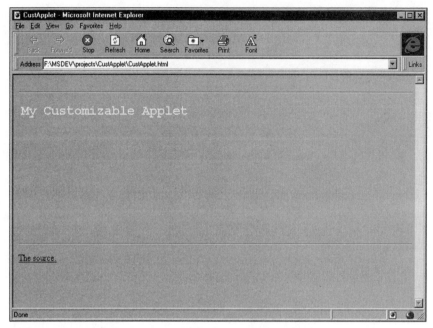

Figure 5-18: Executing the CustApplet applet again with green passed for the color.

Java Appletcations

The last thing to introduce in this chapter is the idea of Appletcations. As you learned earlier, an appletcation is a Java program designed to run either as an applet or application depending upon its environment. So, if the appletcation is invoked in a browser, it loads as an applet; if the appletcation is invoked at a command prompt, it runs as an application.

How Are They Different?

There are two important things to note about appletcations. First, they are not a new breed of a Java program (like applets are). Instead, they are merely a programming technique for you to use.

Second, concerning the applet security model, they do not offer a workaround for circumventing the security restrictions imposed on Java applets. For appletcations to work, the following need to be in place:

- Another class that extends from the Frame class for application support. This is needed because, when you run an applet, it already contains code built-in to construct a Frame.

Note

The Frame class is part of the java.awt package and is responsible for constructing the parent window for any of your Java applications. For more information, reference Chapter 8 on User Interfaces.

- A Java applet that contains all of the life-cycle methods and a main() method. If the class runs as an applet, the main() method is completely ignored. However, if the applet runs as an application, the main() method is called by the environment. Furthermore, inside the main() method is the code to construct the supporting Frame class. The main() method also contains code to embed the applet itself inside the newly constructed Frame, and it calls the life-cycle methods init() and start() (in that order).

- An optional boolean flag specifying if the appletcation is running as an applet or application to help you determine the actions the appletcation should take.

Basically, when you create an appletcation, you are creating an applet with a main() method and a supporting Frame class to put it in. Fortunately, the Visual J++ AppletWizard comes with the functionality to create an appletcation for you.

Tutorial: Creating an Appletcation in the AppletWizard

Let's use the AppletWizard to create an appletcation called AppletCation. Use Table 5-7 to follow step-by-step instructions on the details of the applet.

Step #	Location	Action
1	Developer Studio	Choose File|New.
2	New dialog box	Highlight Project Workspace and click OK.
3	New dialog box	Highlight Java AppletWizard. Then, in the Name field, type AppletCation and click Create.
4	AppletWizard, step 1	For the "How would you like to be able to run your applet?" question, check As an applet and an application. Then, click Next.
5	AppletWizard, step 2	Click Next.
6	AppletWizard, step 3	For the "Would you like your applet to be multi-threaded?" question, click No, thank you. Then, click Next.
7	AppletWizard, step 4	Click Next.
8	AppletWizard, step 5	Type any applet or copyright information here, then click Finish.
9	New Project Information dialog box	Verify the information is correct (see Figure 5-19), then click OK.

Table 5-7: Creating the AppletCation appletcation using the AppletWizard.

At this point, you are ready to edit the source code for the AppletCation applet. Go to the ClassView; expand it and you see two classes. Double-click on the AppletCation class, not the AppletCationFrame class.

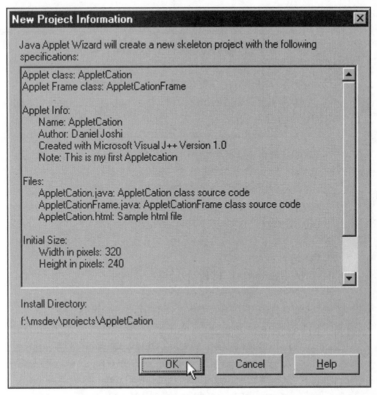

Figure 5-19: The New Project Information dialog box for project CustApplet.

Edit the code as shown below. Remember that the bolded code is material you need to add and the regular code listed below is code automatically generated by the AppletWizard of Visual J++:

```
//******************************************************
// AppletCation.java:      Applet
//
//******************************************************
import java.applet.*;
import java.awt.*;
import AppletCationFrame;


//=====================================================
// Main Class for applet AppletCation
```

```
//
//==============================================================
public class AppletCation extends Applet
{
   // STANDALONE APPLICATION SUPPORT:
   //   m_fStandAlone will be set to true if applet is run
standalone
   //-----------------------------------------------------------
   boolean m_fStandAlone = false;

   // STANDALONE APPLICATION SUPPORT
   // The main() method acts as the applet's entry point when
it is run
   // as a standalone application. It is ignored if the applet
is run from
   // within an HTML page.
   //-----------------------------------------------------------
   public static void main(String args[])
   {
      // Create Toplevel Window to contain applet AppletCation
      //--------------------------------------------------------
      AppletCationFrame frame = new
AppletCationFrame("AppletCation");

      // Must show Frame before we size it so insets() will
return valid values
      //--------------------------------------------------------
      frame.show();
         frame.hide();
      frame.resize(frame.insets().left + frame.insets().right
+ 320,
               frame.insets().top  + frame.insets().bottom +
240);

      // The following code starts the applet running within
the frame window.
      // It also calls GetParameters() to retrieve parameter
values from the
```

```
    // command line, and sets m_fStandAlone to true to
prevent init() from
    // trying to get them from the HTML page.
    //------------------------------------------------------
    AppletCation applet_AppletCation = new AppletCation();

    frame.add("Center", applet_AppletCation);
    applet_AppletCation.m_fStandAlone = true;
    applet_AppletCation.init();
    applet_AppletCation.start();
        frame.show();
    }


    // AppletCation Class Constructor
    //------------------------------------------------------
    public AppletCation()
    {
        // TODO: Add constructor code here
    }


    // APPLET INFO SUPPORT:
    //   The getAppletInfo() method returns a string describing
the applet's
    // author, copyright date, or miscellaneous information.
    //------------------------------------------------------
    public String getAppletInfo()
    {
        return "Name: AppletCation\r\n" +
               "Author: Daniel Joshi\r\n" +
               "Created with Microsoft Visual J++ Version
1.0\r\n" +
               "Note: This is my first Appletcation";
    }


    // The init() method is called by the AWT when an applet is
first loaded or
```

```java
// reloaded.  Override this method to perform whatever
initialization your
// applet needs, such as initializing data structures,
loading images or
// fonts, creating frame windows, setting the layout
manager, or adding UI
// components.
//--------------------------------------------------------
public void init()
{
        // If you use a ResourceWizard-generated "control
creator" class to
        // arrange controls in your applet, you may want to
call its
        // CreateControls() method from within this method.
Remove the following
        // call to resize() before adding the call to
CreateControls();
        // CreateControls() does its own resizing.
        //------------------------------------------------
    resize(320, 240);

    // TODO: Place additional initialization code here
  }


    // Place additional applet clean up code here.  destroy()
is called when
    // when your applet is terminating and being unloaded.
    //--------------------------------------------------------
  public void destroy()
  {
    // TODO: Place applet cleanup code here
  }


    // AppletCation Paint Handler
    //--------------------------------------------------------
  public void paint(Graphics g)
  {
```

```
    //My code starts here
    Font f = new Font("Courier", Font.BOLD, 18);

    g.setFont(f);
    if (m_fStandAlone)
        g.drawString("This is my first Appletcation", 2, 25);
    else
        g.drawString("This Appletcation runs as an Applet", 2,
25);
//My code ends here


    }


    //   The start() method is called when the page containing
the applet
    // first appears on the screen. The AppletWizard's initial
implementation
    // of this method starts execution of the applet's thread.
    //-----------------------------------------------------------
    public void start()
    {
        // TODO: Place additional applet start code here
    }


    //   The stop() method is called when the page containing
the applet is
    // no longer on the screen. The AppletWizard's initial
implementation of
    // this method stops execution of the applet's thread.
    //-----------------------------------------------------------
    public void stop()
    {
    }




    // TODO: Place additional applet code here


}
```

Note

The AppletCationFrame class is the supporting class discussed earlier. Essentially, it contains the code to construct and destroy a window because, when you run as an application you do not have the browser to load your applet into.

In analyzing the above code, you should see nothing that is new to you. However, there are a few details left to discuss. The first is the import statements at the top of the java.awt and java.applet packages. Also, the third import statement imports the class AppletCationFrame that is the supporting class for application compatibility for the project.

Also notice that the class AppletCation extends the Applet class and behaves just like an applet with all the life-cycle methods. Inside the AppletCation class you have the following variable declaration:

```
boolean m_fStandAlone = false;
```

This *boolean m_fStandAlone* will be changed to true if the main() method is called. That, of course, only happens if the appletcation is invoked outside an HTML page. You can use this variable to toggle between application-specific and applet-specific code.

The main() method contains constructors for the class AppletCationFrame and AppletCation. It also contains code to resize this application window to use the same specifications if the AppletCation were executed as an applet in a browser. The following is a snippet of code from the main() method:

```
AppletCation applet_AppletCation = new AppletCation();

frame.add("Center", applet_AppletCation);
applet_AppletCation.m_fStandAlone = true;
applet_AppletCation.init();
applet_AppletCation.start();
    frame.show();
```

Looking at the above code, you see that you are creating applet_AppletCation, an instance of the AppletCation class. Then, in the next line, you are loading it in the window using the add() method (this method is discussed in more detail in Chapter 8 on User Interfaces). The next line of code changes the boolean m_fStandAlone talked about earlier to true. The next two method calls are used to initialize and start the applet in this application window. The last method call is another user interface method that actually displays the window on the user's screen.

Now you are ready to save and build your code. To save all the files for your project, click on File | Save All. To build the code, click on Build | Build CustApplet. Then, to execute the code, click on Build | Execute. Since this is an applet and you had the AppletWizard automatically generate the HTML file, Visual J++ invokes Internet Explorer that invokes and loads the applet (see Figure 5-20).

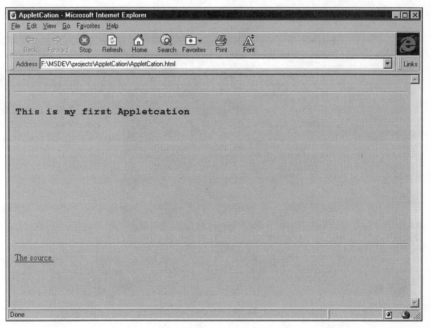

Figure 5-20: Running the AppletCation applet in Internet Explorer.

However, this is also an application. To prove it, open a command prompt and go to the directory containing the project (which in the example for this book is f:\msdev\projects\ AppletCation), and run jview by typing the following:

```
jview AppletCation
```

Tip

If you attempted to run jview to execute the application and, for some reason, it did not work, check to make sure you are in the proper directory and you have built the project successfully.

Figure 5-21 shows a command prompt as the applet loaded as an application in the supporting Frame.

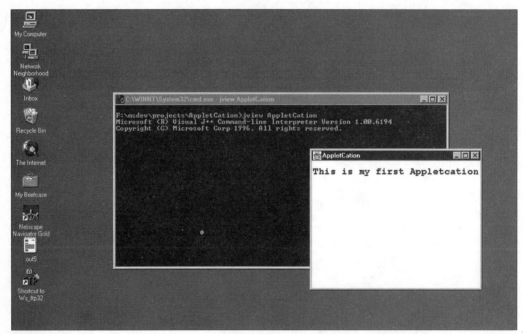

Figure 5-21: The AppletCation run as an application.

Introduction to Debugging in Visual J++

The debugging project in this section gives those who have never used a professional debugger before, a chance to work with one. The project also gives those who have more experience programming, a chance to see how Java handles errors. You also get a look at the debugging tools available to you in Visual J++. The premise this section makes is that in the real world when you develop applications you receive errors. Thus, it is sometimes more important for a programmer to know how to deal with these errors than to attempt to write perfect code the first time.

The following project contains a "broken" Java application for you to fix using Visual J++. In this section you will create a project that contains jury-rigged bugs, then you will attempt to debug your program. Let's start by creating the project DebugTest using Table 5-8.

Step #	Location	Action
1	Developer Studio	Choose File|New.
2	New dialog box	Highlight Project Workspace and click OK.
3	New Project Workspace dialog box	Highlight Java AppletWizard. Then, in the Name field, type **DebugTest** and click Create.
4	AppletWizard, step 1	For the "Would you like to generate source file comments?" question, click No, thank you. Then, click Next.
5	AppletWizard, step 2	Click Next.
6	AppletWizard, step 3	For the "Would you like your applet to be multi-threaded?" question, click No, thank you. Then, click Next.
7	AppletWizard, step 4	Click Next.
8	AppletWizard, step 5	Type applet information, then click Finish.
9	New Project Information dialog box	Verify the information is correct (see Figure 5-22), then click OK.

Table 5-8: Creating the DebugTest using the AppletWizard.

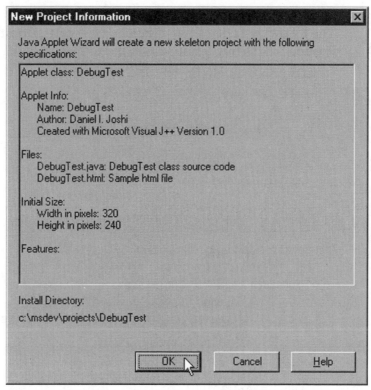

Figure 5-22: The New Project Information dialog box for project DebugTest.

Tip

In step 1 of the AppletWizard you specified to not have source-file comments included in the DebugTest applet. Not including all the comments in the source file for DebugTest makes it less cluttered and easier for you to sift through when you try to debug the test code. Not including comments is all right because this is just a simple example. However, in the real world it is always a good idea to include ample comments in your code.

Click OK and the AppletWizard creates the project and applet. The following code shows the DebugTest class. Add the bolded code so that DebugTest looks similar to the following:

```
import java.applet.*;
import java.awt.*;

public class DebugTest extends Applet
{

  public DebugTest()
  {
  }

  public String getAppletInfo()
  {
    return "Name: DebugTest\r\n" +
           "Author: Daniel I. Joshi\r\n" +
           "Created with Microsoft Visual J++ Version 1.0";
  }


  public void init()
  {

      //My code starts here
    Font f = new Font("Courier", Font.ITALIC, 26)
    setFont(f);
    //My code ends here

      // If you use a ResourceWizard-generated "control
creator" class to
      // arrange controls in your applet, you may want to
call its
      // CreateControls() method from within this method.
Remove the following
      // call to resize() before adding the call to
CreateControls();
      // CreateControls() does its own resizing.
      //-------------------------------------------------
    resize(320, 240);
```

```
      }

      public void destroy()
      {
      }

      public void paint(Graphics g)
      {

         //My code starts here
         //g.drawString("Created with Microsoft Visual J++
Version 1.0", 10, 20);
         g.drawString("This is a Test, 50, 100);
         //My code ends here

      }

      public void start()
      {
      }

      public void stop()
      {
      }


   }
```

Looking at the above code you may have already noticed that there are two errors. The first error is in the line you added in the init() method:

```
Font f = new Font("Courier", Font.ITALIC, 36)
```

Look closely at the above line and notice that there is no semicolon terminating the statement. The second error is in the paint() method in the drawString() line you added:

```
g.drawString("This is a Test, 50, 100);
```

In the above line of code, look at the sentence "This is a Test." Notice that there are unpaired quotation marks. Do not attempt to fix this error or the statement termination error above—they will give you a chance to debug your Java program.

Obviously, this example is jury rigged because you know where the errors are ahead of time. However, if you do not have a lot of experience programming you might conclude that when you try to build the DebugTest project you will get two build errors. As you will see, this is incorrect.

Note

The DebugTest applet contains two errors in its code and will not compile.

At this point let's go ahead and try to build the project DebugTest by clicking Build | Build DebugTest. Figure 5-23 shows the Output window of the Developer Studio.

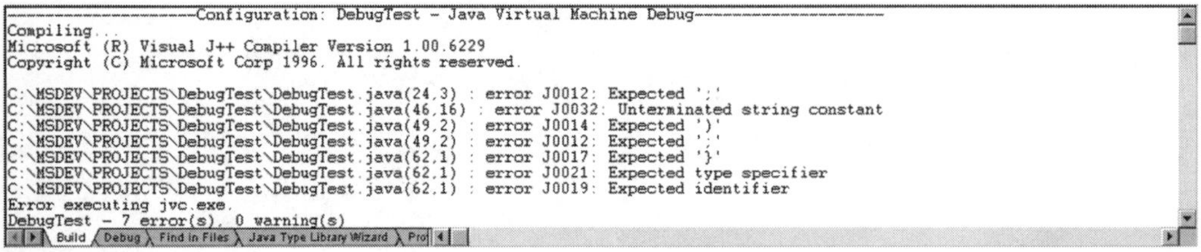

```
-------------------Configuration: DebugTest - Java Virtual Machine Debug-------------------
Compiling...
Microsoft (R) Visual J++ Compiler Version 1.00.6229
Copyright (C) Microsoft Corp 1996. All rights reserved.

C:\MSDEV\PROJECTS\DebugTest\DebugTest.java(24,3) : error J0012: Expected ';'
C:\MSDEV\PROJECTS\DebugTest\DebugTest.java(46,16) : error J0032: Unterminated string constant
C:\MSDEV\PROJECTS\DebugTest\DebugTest.java(49,2) : error J0014: Expected ')'
C:\MSDEV\PROJECTS\DebugTest\DebugTest.java(49,2) : error J0012: Expected ';'
C:\MSDEV\PROJECTS\DebugTest\DebugTest.java(62,1) : error J0017: Expected '}'
C:\MSDEV\PROJECTS\DebugTest\DebugTest.java(62,1) : error J0021: Expected type specifier
C:\MSDEV\PROJECTS\DebugTest\DebugTest.java(62,1) : error J0019: Expected identifier
Error executing jvc.exe.
DebugTest - 7 error(s), 0 warning(s)
```

Figure 5-23: Output window for project DebugTest.

Unless you have not been trying the examples, or you keyed in the code for the examples *correctly*, you have probably seen something like this show up when you tried building a project in Visual J++.

Either way, Table 5-9 discusses all the parts of the first error message printed in the above Output window.

Let's dissect the error C:\MSDEV\PROJECTS\DebugTest\ DebugTest.java(24,3) : error J0012: Expected ';' using Table 5-10.

Part	Meaning
C:\MSDEV\PROJECTS\ DebugTest\DebugTest.java	The location and filename where this error originates.
(24,3)	The column and row specifying where the compiler tripped.
Error J0012	Visual J++ compiler error code that lets you know the error type.
Expected ';'	A brief error description.

Table 5-9: Syntax of a Visual J++ error message.

Notice that the compiler returned seven errors for the DebugTest project. Furthermore, if you look at the location of these error messages, some are positioned in *assumed* bug free locations. The first thing to remember is that compilers usually do not give you a one-to-one relationship between the number of actual errors (in this case, two) and the number of reported errors. The solution is to not take each error at face value. Instead look for a pattern.

Tip

The larger and more complex your programs become, the larger a gap in the error-to-error message ratio your compiler reports. To illustrate, it is not uncommon for a compiler to report 100 errors when there is only one error in a declaration referenced 99 times throughout your program.

Below is the first error message:

```
C:\MSDEV\PROJECTS\DebugTest\DebugTest.java(24,3) : error
J0012: Expected ';'
```

With every error in Visual J++ there are two things that you can do. First, you can go to the line of code referenced in the error messaged by double-clicking the error message in the Output window. Figure 5-24 shows an arrow where Visual J++ positions you when the above error is detected.

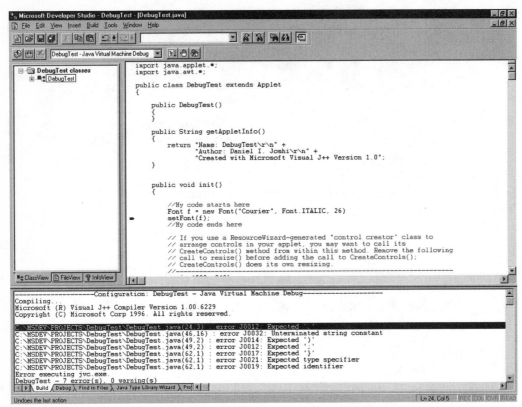

Figure 5-24: Finding the location of the error message in the source.

By placing the cursor over the Visual J++ compiler error code (in this case J10012) and pressing the F1 key, Visual J++ opens an InfoView article giving more information on the error. Figure 5-25 shows InfoView open for the above error message.

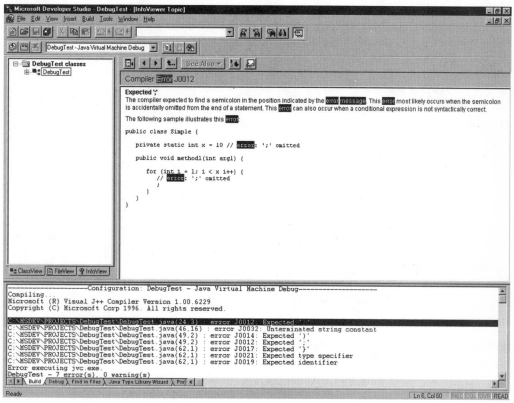

Figure 5-25: Finding help using Visual J++ error codes.

Thus far it appears the Visual J++ compiler expects a ; (semicolon) and did not find one. It also appears the compiler brought you to an incorrect location. However, your position in the code does give you a very important clue. Look at the line of code just before the setFont() line the compiler brought you. See that the Font constructor is missing a ; (semicolon). You can deduct that the Visual J++ compiler was building the project when it came to the end of the Font constructor line and did not find a semicolon. However, the compiler did not trip until it hit the next line of code. How can you prove this? Put the semicolon in and rebuild the project by clicking Build | Build DebugTest (see Figure 5-26).

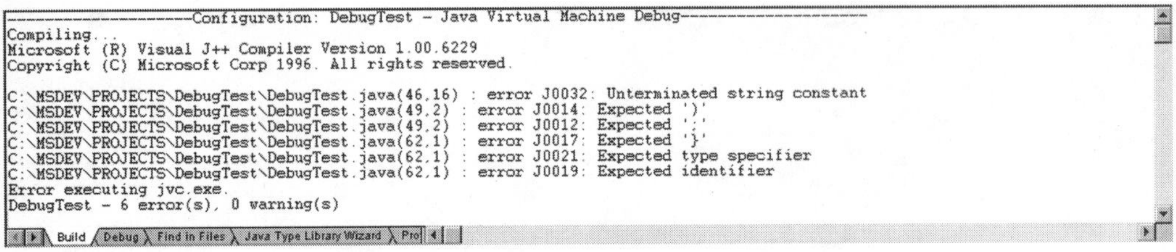

```
-----------------Configuration: DebugTest - Java Virtual Machine Debug-----------------
Compiling...
Microsoft (R) Visual J++ Compiler Version 1.00.6229
Copyright (C) Microsoft Corp 1996. All rights reserved.

C:\MSDEV\PROJECTS\DebugTest\DebugTest.java(46,16) : error J0032: Unterminated string constant
C:\MSDEV\PROJECTS\DebugTest\DebugTest.java(49,2)  : error J0014: Expected ')'
C:\MSDEV\PROJECTS\DebugTest\DebugTest.java(49,2)  : error J0012: Expected ';'
C:\MSDEV\PROJECTS\DebugTest\DebugTest.java(62,1)  : error J0017: Expected '}'
C:\MSDEV\PROJECTS\DebugTest\DebugTest.java(62,1)  : error J0021: Expected type specifier
C:\MSDEV\PROJECTS\DebugTest\DebugTest.java(62,1)  : error J0019: Expected identifier
Error executing jvc.exe.
DebugTest - 6 error(s), 0 warning(s)
```
Build / Debug \ Find in Files \ Java Type Library Wizard \ Pro

Figure 5-26: Building the project DebugTest—try number two.

Look at the Output window in Figure 5-26. You can see that on the second try there are now six errors as opposed to seven. Look at the first message on top. You can see in the brief description there is a problem with line 46. In addition, the message tells you there is "Unterminated String constant," meaning there is an imbalance in the quotation marks for a string literal in your code. Take a closer look at line 46:

```
g.drawString("This is a Test, 50, 100);
```

It should look familiar because it is the line of code that contains the second jury-rigged bugs. Go ahead and review all the errors after this one. However, this imbalance in quotation marks is causing all six of the errors. To prove this, add the other quotation marks in the above line of code and rebuild the project by clicking Build | Build DebugTest.

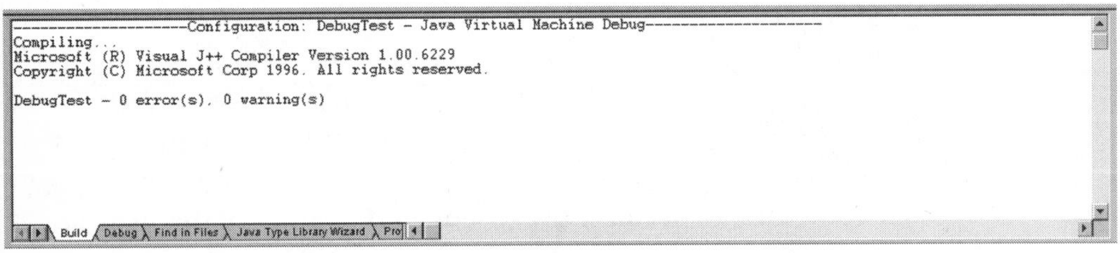

```
-----------------Configuration: DebugTest - Java Virtual Machine Debug-----------------
Compiling...
Microsoft (R) Visual J++ Compiler Version 1.00.6229
Copyright (C) Microsoft Corp 1996. All rights reserved.

DebugTest - 0 error(s), 0 warning(s)
```
Build / Debug \ Find in Files \ Java Type Library Wizard \ Pro

Figure 5-27: Building the DebugTest project—try number three.

At this point you have isolated the two errors and found patterns in the error messages that the Visual J++ compiler displays. You are now ready to execute the project. Click Build | Execute DebugTest. Figure 5-28 shows what you will see in Internet Explorer.

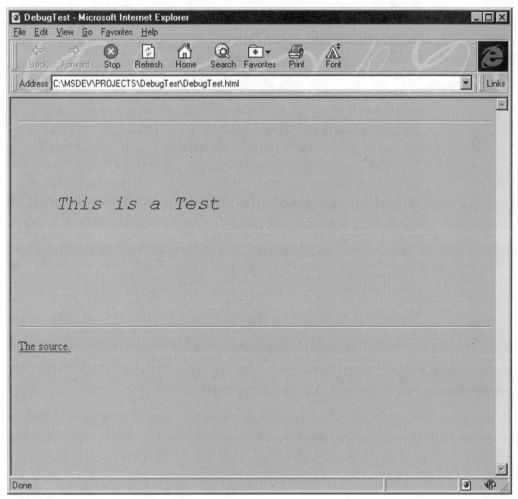

Figure 5-28: Executing the DebugTest project.

Moving On

In this chapter, you learned about the AppletWizard and had a chance to create three very different Java applets (or appletcations) using the AppletWizard. You were also introduced to the java.util package and you learned about other applet programming tips and techniques like passing parameters and creating appletcations. Finally, you had a chance to debug a jury-rigged project using Visual J++.

The next chapter marks another turning point in the book. Moreover, most of the material discussed in the last two chapters has been introductory material building a foundation for the next several chapters. The next chapter teaches you all about multi-threaded Java programming. While you did not know it, you have been using programming with threads since day one. However, Chapter 6 teaches you how to unleash the full power of threads in the Java language, and once again the Visual J++ AppletWizard plays a key role.

Finally, Chapter 10 gives you a more comprehensive overview of the debugging tools available to you in Visual J++.

6

Multithreading in Java

In Chapter 1 you received a fairly comprehensive description of multithreading in the modern 32-bit operating system and how it relates to Java. Chapter 1, however, did not cover the specifics of how to program multiple threads in Java. The purpose of this chapter is to provide a complete description of multithreaded Java at the programmatic level by briefly reviewing the multithreaded model discussed in Chapter 1. In addition you'll learn that the Visual J++ AppletWizard includes several options to make your applet multithreaded and to make you a more productive Java programmer.

This chapter provides an overview of the classes and techniques needed to effectively program in threads. Most of the examples deal with animations of one form or another. However, multithreaded programming is an extremely valuable asset for many other areas.

Note

As you read through this chapter, you will notice terminology such as the following used when discussing threads: "spawning a new thread," "killing a thread," and "invoking is Alive()." In just about any programming language, thread discussion uses this "lifelike" terminology.

By the end of this chapter, you should have an understanding of what threads are in the Java language. You will also learn how to program threads into your Java programs and how to take advantage of the AppletWizard to assist you in the process.

Review of the Multithreaded OS

In a 32-bit modern OS environment, you can have several tasks that appear to execute at the same time. Windows 95 and Windows NT are both 32-bit operating systems. However, Windows 95 is more of a hybrid 32-bit operating system that can revert back to a 16-bit OS (where only one thread can execute at a time) if the need arises. You'll recall from earlier chapters that, on a multiprocessor system, more than one task can execute at the same time.

Every time you load an application it creates a new process. This is true for the OS as well. Each process can have one or more threads executing under it. *Threads* are smaller, independently executing entities that a process or another thread can spawn (be created). Once a thread has spawned, it goes into a queue. A thread scheduler that is part of the OS manages this queue, acting like a daisy wheel, giving each thread execution time with the CPU (albeit an extremely small amount). However, based on a thread's various attributes (e.g., priority, spawned by the kernel in the OS, etc.) it may receive more or less overall execution time than its peers.

The Car Analogy

One analogy that may make the idea of threads easier to understand is to think of them as cars on a highway. From one perspective you have a finite number of different cars on the road and each one can be categorized as belonging to Ford, Chevy, and so forth. On the other hand, every car is unique; if you attempt to look for exactly the same driver in two or more cars you will quickly realize that each car is unique. Finally, some cars can have a higher priority over the road than others. For example, a police car with its lights on has the higher priority, causing the other cars on the road to stop and let it pass.

Threads are very similar in behavior. In one sense, threads all relate to each other and can be categorized as belonging to a parent process—or another thread. On the other hand, each thread spawned is a unique entity and has a completely unique identity. Preemptive multitasking, discussed in Chapter 1, and thread priorities can cause some threads (like the kernel belonging to the OS) to have priority over other threads executing. These higher priority threads can force the current thread executing to stand down and let it execute.

Tutorial: Creating Your First Multithreaded Java Program

Let's move forward and unleash the power of the AppletWizard. You are about to create your first multithreaded Java program without writing one line of code!

The Java applet that you are going to create is an animation that runs on its own thread. When you leave the page the thread automatically stops, and when you return to the page it automatically restarts. By executing this applet, you will see the power of multithreading. In particular, notice the smooth animation with no sluggishness with any of the other programs running, resources loaded, or devices such as your mouse and keyboard.

Use the AppletWizard to create a JavaApplet called MyAniApplet. Use Table 6-1 to follow step-by-step instructions on the details of the applet.

Step #	Location	Action
1	Developer Studio	Choose File|New.
2	New dialog box	Highlight Project Workspace and click OK.
3	New Project Workspace dialog box	Highlight JavaAppletWizard. Then, in the Name field, type **MyAniApplet** and click Create.
4	AppletWizard, step 1	Click Next.
5	AppletWizard, step 2	Click Next.
6	AppletWizard, step 3	Click Next.
7	AppletWizard, step 4	Click Next.
8	AppletWizard, step 5	Type applet and copyright information here, then click Finish.
9	New Project Information dialog box	Verify the information is correct (see Figure 6-1); then click OK.

Table 6-1: Creating the MyAniApplet using the AppletWizard.

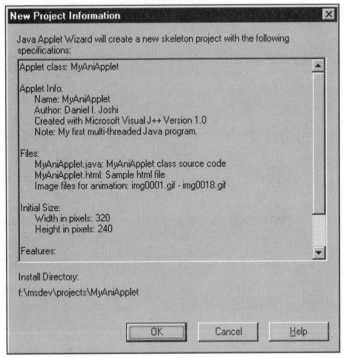

Figure 6-1: The New Project Information dialog box for project CustApplet.

You do not need to do any coding; once the AppletWizard finishes creating your project, you are ready to build and execute it.

To save all the files for your project, click on File I Save All. To build the code, click on Build I Build MyAniApplet. Then, to execute the code, click on Build I Execute MyAniApplet.

Tip

Appendix B provides a detailed analysis of the code generated by the AppletWizard for the MyAniApplet. In Appendix B, notice that the AppletWizard generated over three hundred lines of code.

Since this is an applet and the AppletWizard automatically generated the HTML file, Visual J++ invokes Internet Explorer and loads the applet (see Figure 6-2). You should see a globe rotating.

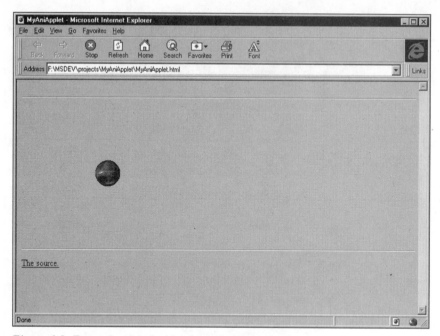

Figure 6-2: Executing MyAniApplet in Internet Explorer.

Using the Visual J++ AppletWizard (in about five minutes), you created a multithreaded Java applet or, more precisely, a multithreaded animation. Move your mouse around and notice that there is no drag in either the mouse or the animation going on inside the applet. That is multithreading at its finest: everything working in tandem.

Threads

Threads are the building blocks of multithreaded programming. Although you have not programmed with threads explicitly, all Java programs are internally multithreaded. Typically, Java creates a thread for the user interface and another for the main body of the program. You do not have to do anything; programmatically speaking, everything is done implicitly.

However, Java also gives you the ability to directly work with the creation (or spawning) and destruction (or death) of threads.

Java has wrapped all this functionality into one class in the Java class library: java.lang.Thread.

You will learn later that there are two ways to incorporate threads into your Java programs. One form is by subclassing the Thread class and the other is to instance the Thread class and implement the Runnable interface. Table 6-2 contains all the available methods that belong to the java.lang.Thread class.

activeCount()	Returns an integer value that represents the number of active threads in a particular thread group.
checkAccess()	Performs a check to see if the current Thread is allowed to modify this Thread.
countStackFrames()	Returns an integer value that represents the number of stack frames in this suspended Thread.
currentThread()	References the currently executing Thread.
destroy()	Removes an active Thread. This is a last resort method as it does not clean up the thread after it is disposed of.
dumpStack()	A debugging procedure to print a stack trace for this Thread.
enumerate(Thread[] threadArray)	Copies, into the specified array, references to every active thread in this Thread's group.
getName()	Returns a String that contains this Thread's name.
getPriority()	Returns an integer value that represents the Thread's priority.
getThreadGroup()	Returns ThreadGroup object for this Thread.
interrupt()	Send an interrupt to this Thread.
interrupted()	Returns a boolean value based on if the current Thread has been interrupted.
isAlive()	Returns a boolean indicating if the Thread is active (i.e. the thread has been successfully started and has not been stopped).

isDaemon()	Returns a boolean that evaluates if this Thread is a daemon.
isInterrupted()	Returns a boolean value based on if a Thread has been interrupted.
join()	An overloaded method that waits indefinitely for this Thread to die.
join(long milliseconds)	This synchronized method waits for this Thread to die.
join(long millisec, nanosec)	An overloaded method that waits for this int Thread to die.
resume()	Resumes this Thread's execution. This method is used only after a Thread has been suspend()ed.
run()	The actual action code for the Thread. This method is usually overridden.
setDaemon (boolean x)	Marks this Thread as a daemon Thread (user Thread).
setName(String name)	Sets this Thread's name.
setPriority(int Priority)	Sets this Thread's priority.
sleep(long milliseconds)	This method causes the currently executing Thread to become inactive for a period of time.
sleep(long, int) start()	Sleep, in milliseconds and additional nanosecond. Starts the Thread and calls the run() method.
stop()	Stops a Thread by calling ThreadDeath.
stop(Throwable obj)	An overloaded method that stops the Thread by throwing the specified obj object instead of the object ThreadDeath.
suspend()	Causes a Thread to be in a blocked state and remain that way until resume() is called in it.
toString()	Returns a String that represents the object Thread, including the Thread's name, priority, and Thread group.
yield()	Causes the currently executing Thread to yield to other Threads.

Table 6-2: java.lang.Thread.

Multithreaded Java Programming Techniques

Now that you have a little more information about the Thread class, the first thing you need to be able to do is create an instance of it. The simplest way to construct a Thread is to use the default constructor as follows:

```
Thread myThread = new Thread();
```

Another way you can construct a Thread is by passing it a name. This is useful for several reasons. First, it gives your Thread a readable name that you can reference throughout your Java program. Also, it provides an easy way to reference a particular thread by giving it a user-friendly name. The following shows an example of declaring a thread with a name:

```
Thread myThread = new Thread("Test");
```

Typically, when you create a new Thread, you need to pass it an object. However, the object passed needs to implement the interface Runnable. Thus, you will typically hear the term "Runnable objects." The following shows an example of an instance of a class ABC that implements the Runnable class and how you would construct a Thread with it:

```
ABC ABCInstance = new ABC();
Thread myThread = new Thread(ABCInstance);
```

Or,

```
ABC ABCInstance = new ABC();
Thread myThread = new Thread(ABCInstance, "Test");
```

The second example shows the constructor that lets you pass a Runnable object and a name to construct the Thread.

Working with threads in Java involves two specific techniques you can use to integrate multithreaded programming into your Java programs. You can do this either by subclassing the Thread class or implementing the Runnable interface.

Subclassing the Thread Class

One method that only works if your Java application does not need a superclass is to subclass the Thread object, thereby inheriting all the functionality of the Thread object. The following shows an example of subclassing the Thread class:

```
class CarThread extends Thread {
//Body of Class
}
```

Tip

The subclassing Thread technique can be used with applets. Going back to the definition of a Java applet, you need to subclass java.applet.Applet. Because Java does not support multiple inheritance, you have already used up your one inheritance slot. Thus, this technique is only beneficial to Java applications.

The next thing that you need to do in the main() method of your class (in this case CarThread) is construct an instance of your class. Then, construct an instance of a Thread class passing a reference of the instance you just constructed:

```
public static void main(String args[]) {
   CarThread honda = new CarThread();
   Thread h1Thread = new Thread(honda);

//Body of main()

}
```

The above code constructs a new Thread h1Thread that invokes the run() method of the CarThread class.

What About Passing a Runnable Object Rule?

You learned that you can only pass objects to a Thread constructor that implements the Runnable interface. How does this still hold in the example above?

The reason the above example is legal stems from the fact that the Thread class itself implements the Runnable interface. Thus, when you inherit the Thread class to your own class, you also inherit the Runnable interface implementation (along with other functionality). That is how you can define a class and subclass it from the Thread class and not directly implement the Runnable interface, but still pass it to a Thread

Another important point about multithreading is the ability to create several threads based on the same object that have an individuality from each other aside from just having a different name.

Another important point about multithreading is the ability to create several threads based on the same object that have an individuality from each other aside from just having a different name:

```java
public static void main(String args[]) {
    CarThread honda = new CarsThread();
    Thread h1Thread = new Thread(honda);
    Thread h2Thread = new Thread(honda);

    //Body of main()

}
```

Looking at this code, notice that the only thing added is the instance *h2Thread* that has the instance *honda* passed to it. The important thing to note here is that *h1Thread* and *h2Thread* are independently executing entities. For example, even though you constructed *h2Thread* after *h1Thread*, it could finish execution and die before *h1Thread*. This exemplifies one of the key concepts of concurrent programming and shows you the power of multithreaded programming.

Tutorial: Subclassing Threads

At this point, let's create a very simple Java application in Visual J++ to demonstrate the subclassing Thread multithreaded programming technique. You need to create a project workspace called CarThread (see Table 6-3 for instructions).

Step #	Location	Action
1	Developer Studio	Choose File|New.
2	New dialog dialog box	Highlight Project Workspace and click OK.
3	New Project Workspace dialog box	In the Name field, type **CarThread**, and click Create.

Table 6-3: Creating the CarThread Project Workspace.

Tip

Remember that you are creating a Java application, so do not use the Java AppletWizard.

Go to the main menu; click on Insert | New Java Class. On the Create New Class dialog box that displays, do the following:

1. In the Name field, type **CarThread**.

2. In the Extends field, type **Thread**.

3. In the Modifiers area, check Public.

When you finish, click OK.

Let's start by creating a public method called main() (see Table 6-4 for step-by-step instructions).

Step #	Location	Action
1	Left pane of CarThread	On the CarThread class, right-click Project Workspace and choose Add Method from the menu.
2	New Method dialog box	In the Return type field, type **void**, and in the Method declaration field, type **main(String argv[ ])**.
3	New Method dialog box	In the Access box, choose Public. In the Modifiers area, choose Static.
4	New Method dialog box	Verify that you typed the declaration correctly; then click OK.

Table 6-4: Creating the main() method.

Now, you need to add the method run() (see Table 6-5 for step-by-step instructions).

Step #	Location	Action
1	Left pane of CarThread Project Workspace	On the CarThread class, right-click and choose Add Method from the menu.
2	New Method dialog box	In the Return type field, type **void**, and in the Method declaration field, type **run()**.
3	New Method dialog box	In the Access box, choose Public.
4	New Method dialog box	Verify that you typed the declaration correctly; then click OK.

Table 6-5: Creating the run() method.

At this point the Developer Studio automatically opens the class CarThread for editing. Edit it so that it looks like the following code. Remember that the bolded code is material you need to add and the regular code listed below is code automatically generated by Visual J++:

```
import java.lang.Thread;

/*
 *
 * CarThread
 *
 */
public class CarThread extends Thread
{

  public void run()
   {

     //My code starts here
       System.out.println("Thread " +
Thread.currentThread().getName() + " is running.");
     //My code ends here


   }


  public static void main(String args[])
   {

     //My code starts here
   CarThread honda = new CarThread();
       System.out.println("honda constructed\n");

       Thread h1Thread = new Thread(honda, "h1Thread");
       System.out.println("h1Thread spawned");

       Thread h2Thread = new Thread(honda, "h2Thread");
       System.out.println("h2Thread spawned\n");

       //Start each thread (which implicitly calls run())
       h2Thread.start();
       System.out.println("h2Thread started");

       h1Thread.start();
```

```
        System.out.println("h1Thread started\n");

        int i = 0;
        while (h1Thread.isAlive())
            i++;

        //Stop each thread
        System.out.println();
        h2Thread.stop();
        System.out.println("h2Thread stopped");

        h1Thread.stop();
        System.out.println("h1Thread stopped\n");
    //My code ends here



    }



}
```

Analyzing the above code, let's see what is going on. Starting from the top, notice that the class definition extends the Thread class. Now, at the top of the source-code file, the Visual J++ generated import of java.lang.Thread is unnecessary because the java.lang is the default package imported to every Java program. However, it does not hurt to have it in there.

Underneath the class definition CarThread is the run() method. You will learn about this method later, but at this point only note that it is automatically called whenever you start a Thread. The following shows the body of the run() method:

```
    //My code starts here
        System.out.println("Thread " +
Thread.currentThread().getName() + " is running.");
    //My code ends here
```

Looking at the single line contained in the above method, notice the interesting combination of methods used to retrieve the name of the thread to print on the screen. Referencing the table of methods for the Thread class, you see that the currentThread() method returns a Thread for the current Thread executing. Then, getName() returns the name of the currently running Thread returned in the currentThread() method. Hence, you receive the name of the current Thread executing.

Tip

The currentThread() method can be very useful because it can return the threads created by the Java Virtual Machine (JVM) (for more information on the JVM reference Chapter 14) not just the threads you create. The only stipulation is that it must be the currently executing Thread.

The main() method contains the remainder of this Java application. The first section of code constructs honda that is an instance of the CarThread class. Then, underneath it are the constructors for two threads h1Thread and h2Thread that both receive honda for the object reference. The next section of code starts both threads:

```
//Start each thread (which implicitly calls run())
        h2Thread.start();
        System.out.println("h2Thread started");

        h1Thread.start();
        System.out.println("h1Thread started\n");
```

Looking at this code, the most important thing to note is that even though you constructed h2Thread after h1Thread, it is a separate entity and can start before h1Thread.

Tip

Anytime you invoke the start() method for a Thread, it automatically calls the run() method.

The following while loop pauses execution long enough for both the threads to access the method run() and return to main():

```
int i = 0;
        while (h1Thread.isAlive())
            i++;
```

Notice that the while loop uses the isAlive() method contained in the Thread class to determine if h1Thread is still alive.

The last piece of code in the main() method contains the code to stop both of the threads from executing. That finishes the Java application. stop() is another method part of the Thread class discussed in more detail later. But, the important thing to note is that stop() actually is more destructive than it sounds; stop() effectively kills the Thread. Once you have stopped a Thread, you must reinstance it to use it again.

Now you are ready to save and build your code. To save all the files for your project, click on File | Save All. To build the code, click on Build | Build CarThread. Then, to execute the code, click on Build | Execute.

Since you are executing this project for the first time in the Developer Studio, a dialog box displays for you to specify the class file name (see Figure 6-3). On this dialog box, in the Class name field, type **CarThread**. Also, underneath that, you have a choice of using either the jview interpreter or Internet Explorer to view the results. For this example, choose Stand-alone interpreter. Then, click OK.

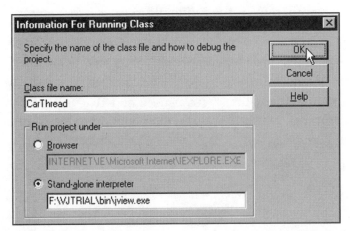

Figure 6-3: The Information for Running Class dialog box filled out.

Once the project has executed, you should see something similar to Figure 6-4.

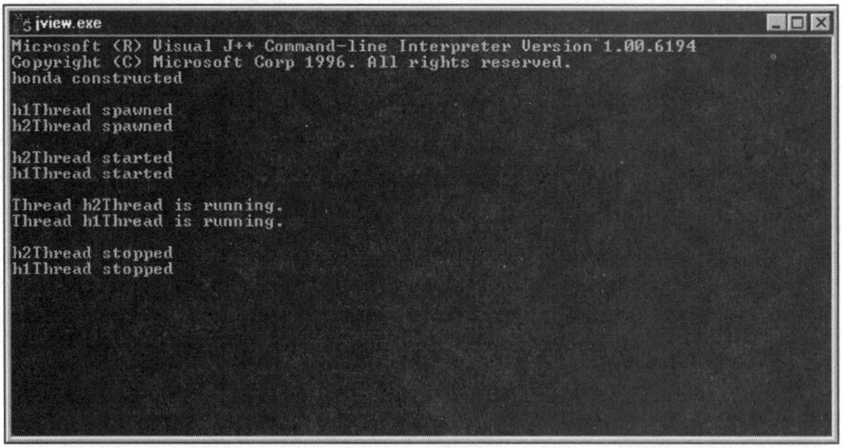

Figure 6-4: Executing CarThread.

Notice in the above example that h2Thread starts before h1Thread, proving that each thread behaves as its own entity. This is the power of multithreaded programming: having your Java program do more than one thing at the same time.

Implementing the Runnable Interface

Another multithread programming technique you can use in your Java programs is the Runnable interface. As you will learn later, by implementing the Runnable interface you provide a much more versatile solution than the subclass Thread technique discussed in the last section.

Remember that you can only subclass once, but you can implement as many interfaces as necessary. The following shows an example of a class declaration implementing the Runnable interface:

```
class myApplet extends Applet implements Runnable {
  //Body of Class
}
```

However, applets do not have a single main() method available to you, but instead a set of life-cycle methods. Recalling what you learned about the life-cycle methods, you know the start() and stop() methods can be invoked more than once throughout an applet's life. Anytime a user leaves, your applet stop() invokes; and if they return, the start() is invoked (or reinvoked).

When working with threads, you want to maintain as much efficiency as possible. So, that when a user loads the applet, a Thread spawns in the start() method. The following shows an example of a start() method for an applet that creates a Thread called myAppletThread:

```
Thread myAppletThread;

public void start() {
   if (myAppletThread == null) {
     myAppletThread = new Thread(this);
     myAppletThread.start();
}
```

Looking at the above you can see that you are checking to see if a Thread object exists; if not, then you construct a new one. Notice *this* is placed as the input for the Thread constructor. That signifies that you are passing the Runnable class of the applet invoking the *this* reference. Finally, you call the start() method from the Thread class that invokes the run() method that is overridden in class myApplet from the implementation of the Runnable interface.

If the user unloads the applet, start() always invokes before destroy(). Also, if the user leaves the applet (but does not unload it) stop() is invoked. For both of these cases in the stop() method, you want to kill the thread because the applet is being unloaded or you want to conserve system resources. If the user only left your applet and returns later, start() invokes again and creates a new thread (as shown above). The following shows a stop() method for the Thread myAppletThread:

```
public static void stop() {
   if (myAppletThread != null) {
   myAppletThread.stop();
   myApplteThread = null;
}
```

Looking at the above code, note that when you call stop() from the Thread class you are not pausing the thread; you are killing it and then setting it equal to null.

Implementing multithreaded programming techniques into your applet can be very easy and give you more versatility. Now, when a user leaves your applet, the Thread stops to conserve resources; when the user returns, a new Thread spawns when the life-cycle start() is invoked. All of this is done so fast that, to the user, it appears as if the Thread never died in the first place.

Tip

You can implement the Runnable interface on Java applications as well. The only major difference is that, instead of having Thread code in both the life-cycle start() and stop() methods (which do not exist in applications), you condense it all into one main() method.

Thread Life Cycle

You learned that applets have a life cycle that you can utilize to execute various things at various times. A Thread does follow a path. However, unlike applets, there are several paths that a thread's life can take. This is probably one reason Threads can be hard to understand. Figure 6-5 shows a diagram of a Thread's potential life cycle.

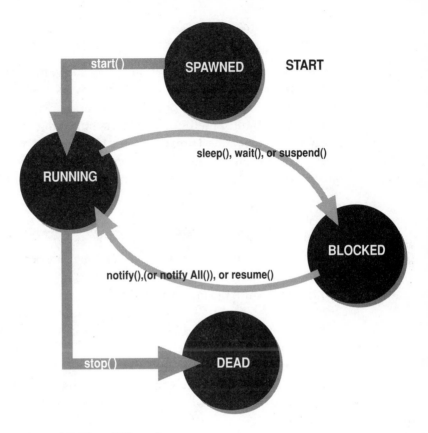

Figure 6-5: Thread life cycle.

Looking at the above diagram, notice that, just as there are four life-cycle methods of a Java applet, there are four states a Thread can be in: spawned, running, blocked, and dead. Note that these are not methods you override, but states that your Thread can be in throughout its life.

Tip

You can use the method isAlive() from the Thread class to return a boolean determining the Thread state (spawned, running, blocked, or dead). You used this method in the Visual J++ project CarThread.

The Spawned State

Anytime you spawn a Thread in Java you can recognize it by the new operator's presence. Typically the spawn stage can occur in the start() method for an applet. Or, in an application the Thread is created in the main() method. The important thing to remember is that when you create a Thread, it is sent to the system and does not execute immediately. The system then does some record keeping before the Thread can start execution and enter the running state.

The Running State

When a Thread enters a running state, this does not mean that it actually runs. Technically, it means that it is spawned and accounted for by the OS and is then thrown into a queue with all the other threads executing. As you will learn later, your Thread may be bumped up to the front of the line, or pushed to the back, depending on its priority.

It is important that you know the reality of multithreaded environments. (Recall the discussion of the multithreaded multitasking with regards to a uniprocessor system.) In short, only one Thread can execute at one time. The point is that just because your Thread is in a running state does not mean it is executing. Your Thread is one of many running threads executing at this stage. However, when your Thread is in this state, it is usually running code in the run() method defined in your Java program.

The Blocked State

When your Thread is in a blocked state, it is not able to run for several reasons. When a Thread enters a blocked state it is no longer in the queue of running threads until it is put back in a running state.

Looking back at the diagram in Figure 6-5, you see that there are several methods you can invoke at the programmatic level to block a Thread's execution. For each method that causes a blocked state there often is another method that puts it back in the running state.

Tip

There are other ways that a Thread can be put in a blocked state that do not always have to come directly from the programmer. For example, during Input Output (I/O) operations, a Thread can be put in a blocked state waiting for the I/O procedure to complete. For more information, go to Chapter 11 on Streams.

sleep()

Using the sleep() method causes the Thread to go to a blocked state for a specified number of milliseconds and then jump back to a running state. The following shows an example of putting the current Thread to sleep for 500 milliseconds:

```
try {
   Thread.currentThread().sleep(500);
} catch (InterruptedException e) {}
```

Tip

In Java, you can use exception handling to catch potential errors (usually called exceptions) as well as handle these exceptions. Use the keyword try and a pair of brackets to encircle potentially problematic parts of code. Furthermore, in the second pair of brackets (located on the catch line), you can put code in to do special things in the event that there is an exception. You will learn more about this in Chapter 14.

wait() & notify(), or notifyAll()

The wait() method defined in the java.lang.Object class can be called by a Thread that is the owner of the object monitor. Thus, having it release ownership of the object monitor and putting the thread into a blocked state. It remains blocked until the Thread now owning the object monitor calls the notify() method and so causes the Thread to be put back into a running state. Thus, receiving ownership of the object monitor again. You use the notifyAll() method if you have more than one Thread waiting on the object monitor. You will learn more about this in the section on Thread synchronization later in this chapter.

Note

The java.lang.Object class is the root class for all classes in the Java class library and, consequently, classes you create that subclass a built-in class

suspend() and resume()

The suspend() method from the Thread class is similar to sleep(), except that it causes the Thread to remain blocked for an indefinite amount of time—until its counterpart method, resume(), is called to bring it back to a running state. To illustrate, the following shows an example of suspending and resuming a thread called theThread:

```
if (i < 100)
   theThread.suspend();
 else
   theThread.resume();
```

Looking at this code, notice that you are checking to see if i is less than 100, and, if so, suspend() theThread. On the other hand, if theThread is not less than 100, then resume() it.

yield()

The yield() method causes a Thread to be put in a blocked state for a specified amount of time and sends it to the back of the line (or queue) of running threads.

The yield() method can be invoked on a Thread to put it in a blocked state and push it to the back of the line (or queue) to let all the other running threads execute:

```
if (i < 100)
   .yield();
```

In the above example, if the *i* is less than 100 the currently executing Thread will yield().

Tip

Unfortunately, using yield() on your threads may not be the smartest choice for all situations because your Thread does not execute again until the other threads that are now in front of it have finished. So, when you call yield() you do not really know when your Thread will get a chance to execute again. Furthermore, if the Thread is has a high priority it may force the current Thread to lose control and start executing again.

State Exceptions

You can use all of the above techniques to block Thread execution. If, for some reason, you invoke a method when it is in the wrong state for that method (i.e., calling resume() on a Thread that has not been suspend()ed), Java throws the exception IllegalStateExecption.

The Dead State

The final cycle a Thread comes to is dead. A Thread can die (or be killed) in the following ways:

- When it reaches the end of the run() method.

- If someone (or something) invokes stop() on it.

- If you call the destroy() method. Typically, the destroy() method is used as a last resort, because it kills the Thread without cleaning up any resources used by the Thread..

The important thing to know about Thread death is that death once invoked is *not* always immediate (destroy() excluded). Usually, what happens is an object ThreadDeath is passed to the Thread before it can be sent to the OS to be unloaded from memory.

Related Multithread Topics

The following sections discuss several topics that relate to multithreaded programming in the Java language. When working with threads you can specify attributes, such as priorities, for handling potential conflicts when several different threads attempt to access the same information. You can also give threads the ability to exist outside the life of your Java program and impose thread management with the ThreadGroup class.

Thread Priorities

Several times you saw the term *queue* concerning thread scheduling. In particular, the Thread Scheduling queue utilizes the First In First Out (FIFO) format and is how the OS manages all the threads related to the system and to applications. Chapter 1 touched upon the idea of Thread priority. By default, anytime you create a Thread, it automatically inherits the priority from its parent Thread. However, you can increase or decrease the priority by using the setPriority() method defined in the Thread class.

Note

Another method related to Thread priority is getPriority(), which lets you get the priority for a given Thread.

Setting the priority of a Thread is based on a scale of 1 to 10 (10 being highest). There are also three constants defined in the Thread class: MAX_PRIORITY (equal to 10), NORM_PRIORITY (equal to 5), and MIN_PRIORITY (equal to 1). The following illustrates several examples of setting priority:

```
myFirstThread.setPriority(Thread.MAX_PRIORITY -2); //Set to 8
mySecondThread.setPriority(Thread.NORM_PRIORITY); //Set to 5
myThirdThread.setPriority(Thread.MIN_PRIORITY +3); //Set to 4
```

Looking at this code, you can see that the first line sets the priority of myFirstThread to 8, the second sets mySecondThread to 5, and the third sets myThirdThread to 4.

Tip

If two threads have the same priority, then they are put on the same level and share equal execution time based on their mutual priority level.

Tutorial: Setting Thread Priorities

Setting the priority of a Thread can make a big difference. To prove it, let's create a very simple Java application in Visual J++.

You need to create a project workspace called ThreadTest (see Table 6-6 for instructions).

Step #	Location	Action
1	Developer Studio	Choose File|New.
2	New dialog box	Highlight Project Workspace and click OK.
3	New Project Work-space dialog box	In the Name field, type **ThreadTest** and click Create.

Table 6-6: Creating the ThreadTest Project Workspace.

Tip

Remember you are creating a Java application so do not use the Java AppletWizard.

Go to the main menu; click on Insert I New Java Class. On the Create New Class dialog box that displays, do the following:

1. In the Name field, type **ThreadTest**.

2. In the Extends field, type **Thread**.

3. In the Modifiers area, check Public.

When you finish, click OK.

Let's start by creating a public method called main() (see Table 6-7 for step-by-step instructions).

Step #	Location	Action
1	Left pane of ThreadTest Project Workspace	On the ThreadTest class, right-click and choose Add Method from the menu.
2	New Method dialog box	In the Return type field, type **void**, and in the Method declaration field, type **main(String argv[])**.
3	New Method dialog box	In the Access box, choose Public. In the Modifiers area, choose Static.
4	New Method dialog box	Verify that you typed the declaration correctly; then click OK.

Table 6-7: Creating the main() method.

Now you need to add the method run() (see Table 6-8 for step-by-step instructions).

Step #	Location	Action
1	Left pane of ThreadTest Project Workspace	On the ThreadTest class, right-click and choose Add Method from the menu.
2	New Method dialog box	In the Return type field, type **void**, and in the Method declaration field, type **run()**.
3	New Method dialog box	In the Access box, choose Public.
4	New Method dialog box	Verify that you typed the declaration correctly; then click OK.

Table 6-8: Creating the run() method.

At this point the Developer Studio automatically opens the class ThreadTest for editing. Edit it so that it looks like the following code. Remember that the bolded code is material you need to add and the regular code listed below is code automatically generated by Visual J++:

```java
import java.lang.Thread;

/*
 *
 * ThreadTest
 *
 */
public class ThreadTest extends Thread
{

    public void run()
    {

    //My code starts here
    System.out.println(Thread.currentThread().getName() + "
entered run() at " + System.currentTimeMillis());
    //My code ends here

    }


    public static void main(String args[])
    {

    //My code starts here
      ThreadTest A = new ThreadTest();

      Thread ThreadA = new Thread(A, "ThreadA");
      Thread ThreadB = new Thread(A, "ThreadB");


      ThreadA.setPriority(Thread.MIN_PRIORITY);
      ThreadB.setPriority(Thread.MAX_PRIORITY);
```

```
    ThreadA.start();
    ThreadB.start();

    int i = 0;
    while (ThreadA.isAlive() || ThreadB.isAlive()) {
        i++;
    }

    ThreadA.stop();
    ThreadB.stop();
//My code ends here


    }



}
```

Analyzing the above code, notice that the class ThreadTest extends Thread. Then in the run() method you have one long statement that basically retrieves the current thread executing and the current time (in UTC):

```
System.out.println(Thread.currentThread().getName() + "
entered run() at " + System.currentTimeMillis());
```

Underneath, run() is the main() method where you create an instance of TheadTest called A. And in the two lines following it, you create two Threads, ThreadA and ThreadB, both being passed to A. After that, the next two lines set the priority for the threads:

```
ThreadA.setPriority(Thread.MIN_PRIORITY);
ThreadB.setPriority(Thread.MAX_PRIORITY);
```

As you can see by looking at the above code, ThreadA is set with the minimum priority setting a Thread can have, *MIN_PRIORITY* (aka1). ThreadB has the highest setting a Thread can have, *MAX_PRIORITY* (aka 10).

Below the priority setting lines are the two lines to start both of the threads. Then you have a while statement cycling until ThreadA dies. This gives both threads time to start() and run() before coming back to main() and executing the last two lines of code that kill both threads:

```
ThreadA.stop();
ThreadB.stop();
```

Now you are ready to save and build your code. To save all the files for your project, click on File | Save All. To build the code, click on Build | Build ThreadTest. Then, to execute the code, click on Build | Execute.

Since you are executing this project for the first time in the Developer Studio, a dialog box displays for you to specify the class file name (see Figure 6-6). On this dialog box, in the Class file name field, type **ThreadTest**. Also, underneath that, you have a choice of using either the jview interpreter or Internet Explorer to view the results. For this example, choose Stand-alone interpreter. Then click OK.

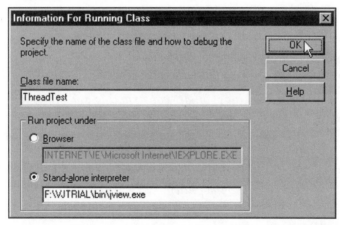

Figure 6-6: The Information for Running Class dialog box filled out.

Once the project is executed, you should see something similar to Figure 6-7.

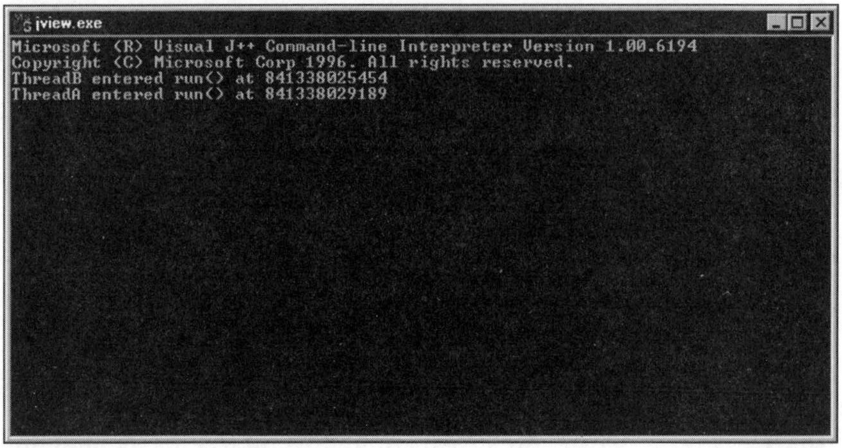

Figure 6-7: Executing ThreadTest.

Looking at Figure 6-7, you can see that ThreadB (set with a priority of MAX_PRIORITY) entered run() at 841338025454. And ThreadA (set with a priority of MIN_PRIORITY) entered at 841338029189. Subtracting those two numbers and dividing by 1,000 gives you a 3.7 seconds time lapse before the lower priority thread was allowed to execute and run.

Note

You could argue that the above test is inaccurate because, technically speaking, you are constructing and starting the two threads at different times. However, if you look at the code, you'll notice that ThreadA is constructed and started before *ThreadB. Yet ThreadB, with its higher priority ranking, got to run() before ThreadA. So, even after giving ThreadA a head start, ThreadB still beat it to the punch.*

Thread Synchronization

As you continue to work with threads you may run across a situation where you have several threads attempting to access more than one object at the same time. In certain situations this can be a big problem. Now if you think about it, you may wonder what the big deal is. The point to remember is (go back to the last section) that when you create several threads you are not guaranteed in what particular order they will execute.

Volatile Variables

Java supports modifying a variable to be volatile. By specifying a variable volatile, you are telling the Java compiler that this variable may be accessed asynchronously (that is, accessed by more than one thread) and should not be optimized.

However, Java has a solution in the keyword synchronized, which tells the Java Virtual Machine to set up a monitor that only blocks a resource or method, letting only one thread enter and execute at a time. The following shows an example of a method declared with synchronized:

```
synchronized void Test() {
  //Body of Method
}
```

wait() & notify(), or notifyAll() Revisited

Sometimes you may want to stop the current Thread executing inside a synchronized method. You can do this by using the wait(), notify(), and notifyAll() discussed earlier.

For example, you have two threads called x and y. Thread x enters a synchronized method and, part of the way through it, you need Thread y to execute in this same method. What you can do is invoke wait() inside the synchronized method that causes the current Thread to stop executing. In our example, this causes Thread x to stop executing and, therefore, lets Thread y execute. Then, later on, the synchronized method calls notify() (or notifyAll() if more than one Thread is blocked by a wait()ing state) and Thread x will continue to execute.

Thread Groups

The ThreadGroup class that is part of the Java class library lets you define a sort of management class for your threads. This is very similar to the project workspace paradigm used in Visual J++. ThreadGroups are sort of your managers for your threads.

There are several advantages to utilizing ThreadGroup to manage your threads. For example, you can specify things with one ThreadGroup and it will, accordingly, make the changes to all the threads that belong to it. This is much more efficient than the alternative of going to each and every thread. Basically, implementing a ThreadGroup is a two-step process.

The first step is to construct an instance of a ThreadGroup. The following shows an example of a constructor:

```
ThreadGroup threadGrp = new ThreadGroup("Manager");
```

This code constructs a ThreadGroup called threadGrp with the name Manager.

The second step is to use a special constructor from the Thread class that has not been introduced until now. This constructor, Thread, is just like all the others you worked with in this chapter, except it has one extra input parameter in front for passing a ThreadGroup object it will belong to:

```
Thread xThread = new Thread(threadGrp, "Employee1");
Thread yThread = new Thread(threadGrp "Employee2");
```

In the above code, you constructed two threads, xThread labeled Employee1 and yThread labeled Employee2. Both of these threads belong to the ThreadGroup threadGrp.

Creating SubThreadGroups

Just like in Visual J++, you can create subprojects that connect to a top-level project or to a project workspace. You can connect a subThreadGroup to another ThreadGroup by passing an object reference of the parent ThreadGroup to the subThreadGroup:

```
ThreadGroup threadGrp2 = new ThreadGroup(threadGrp,
"Assistant Manager");
```

ThreadGroups are very useful if your Java programs deal with more than three or four threads at one time.

Daemon Threads

Daemon threads (aka user threads) are threads with a specific purpose: to support other threads executing.

Note

When the only threads left executing in your Java program are daemon threads, your program exits.

In Java, you can specify some of your threads to be daemon threads. Once you do this, you are essentially giving those threads a "life after death," meaning that, even if the Java program that created those threads exits, the threads can continue to live. To illustrate, let's look at the Windows environment and printing with the word processor Microsoft Word. You execute the print command in Word for a large document. Word creates a daemon thread that executes the print process. Then, even if Word no longer exists, the daemon thread goes to the system and will continue to live. Hence, your document will continue to print.

In the Thread class, there are two methods that deal with daemon threads. The first method, setDaemon(), let's you set or unset a Thread with a daemon status based on the boolean you pass to it:

```
myThread.setDaemon(true); //myThread is a daemon thread
myThread.setDaemon(false); //myThread is not a daemon thread
```

The above code shows two examples, one setting the Thread myThread to a daemon thread and the other unsetting myThread as a daemon Thread. The second method, getDaemon(), lets you check to see if a particular Thread has daemon status.

Tip

In Visual J++, you can debug your Java programs in such a way as to view and manipulate all the threads currently executing in the program at a given breakpoint. Chapter 10, on debugging, gives you a chance to debug threads in a Visual J++ project in real time.

Moving On

In this chapter, you learned about the Thread class and how to program threads in your Java programs. You also learned more about how a multithreaded program works in any language, including topics such as the Thread life cycle and related multithreaded topics.

In this chapter you had a chance to unleash the power of the AppletWizard by creating a multithreaded animation with no coding whatsoever. As you continue to work in Java with Visual J++, you can benefit from its automatic code generation of multithreaded programs or multithreaded animation-based programs.

The next two chapters discuss two very related topics. Chapter 7 and 8 both begin covering how to design front ends in Java. Chapter 7 delves into the java.awt package, discussing the classes and methods needed to design a front end. Then Chapter 8 shows how you can use Visual J++ and its resource editors to do it for you.

7

The User Interface Using the AWT

This chapter is the first part of a two-chapter series on designing User Interfaces (UI). It is a reference chapter discussing how to design front ends using Java and the Abstract Window Toolkit (AWT). All the Visual J++ examples have been saved for the next chapter, building on what you learn here, but focusing more on how to do it using the AWT, the Developer Studio's Resource Editor, and Visual J++'s Resource Wizard. Thus, you can let Visual J++ automatically construct your UI without having to code everything from scratch.

With version 1.0 of the Java User Interface (UI), the key strength is providing a compatible UI environment for all platforms supported by Java. Java developers only need to create one UI that is essentially the same on any platform supported by Java. From a multiplatform developer's perspective this is a blessing, because it reinforces the cross-platform environment that has made Java famous. On the flip side, many of the UI bells and whistles are not present. A Windows developer, for example, will be familiar with several UI components that are not present, appear in a watered down state, or are simply harder to implement.

Note

The next version of Java (version 1.1) includes major enhancements to the current (version 1.0) set of AWT classes. The JDK 1.1, scheduled for release sometime in the fourth quarter of 1996, will house these new features. No doubt, an updated version of Visual J++, including these enhancements will follow.

Unfortunately, the AWT package is extremely large, so this chapter is geared to be more of an introduction, or quick review, than a complete overview of the AWT.

Tip

If you cannot find a particular tool from the AWT package to match your needs, you can always create your own class that subclasses a component nearest to matching your needs. Your class would contain any new functionality built upon the functionality of the superclass that you inherited.

Using the AWT Package

The java.awt package, called the AWT, can be divided up into the following: components, containers, and layout managers. Most of these classes subclass off of java.awt.Component, the main class of the AWT package. A few subclass off of other package classes and will be noted as such in the text.

Introducing the AWT Components

Throughout the chapter you will notice that Java uses specific UI terminology that is not always the same in other programming languages or environments. For example, Java jargon refers to a UI object as a *component*. The Java components belonging to the AWT are: Button, Canvas, Checkbox, CheckboxGroup, Choice, Label, List, Scrollbar, TextComponent, and TextArea.

Note

All of the above classes subclass from java.awt.Component except for CheckboxGroup.

Now, the key to designing front ends (or UIs) in Java is to be able to understand and use all of the components listed above. However, Java has defined a class that subclasses component, called java.awt.Container. The idea behind containers is extremely simple—create a UI component, or several components, and put them in a container. Let the container handle displaying the components.

Introducing the AWT Containers

Java also defines several classes that you can use to hold UI components. All of these classes are subclasses from java.awt.Container. A *container* is a sort of hybrid AWT component used to house other components. Probably the easiest way to think of containers is to associate them with windows and panels in the Windows 95 and Windows NT environments. The primary difference between a window and a panel in the Windows environment is that a panel is a sort of subcontainer for a window. Furthermore, a window can contain several panels, giving you increased flexibility for displaying components. Figure 7-1 shows a Java program with a window full of components.

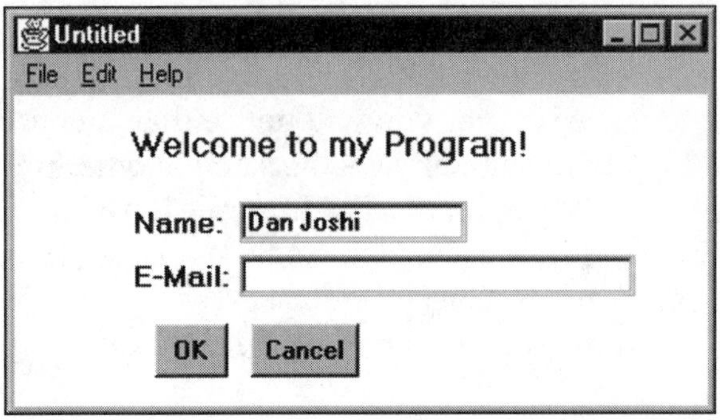

Figure 7-1: A Java program with a container full of components.

Panel, Frame, Dialog, and FileDialog have roots that go back to java.awt.Container. Menu, MenuBar, MenuItem, and CheckboxMenuItem all derive from the abstract class java.awt.MenuComponent.

Introducing the AWT Layout Managers

When working with components and containers, it is important to understand that unlike other programming languages, Java uses a special set of classes from the AWT package. They are called *layout managers* because they oversee how components are displayed in a container. A layout manager does pretty much what it says, in the sense that it manages how components look in their container. You can choose from several styles of layout managers to get the right look and feel for your Java programs.

At this point, you may be wondering what advantage there is to utilizing a layout manager. The reason that Java has layout management stems from the fact that Java programs are platform-independent. If you have ever compared UNIX, Mac, and Windows UI formats, you will notice that each one has its own set of standards, and different versions of standards within itself. Layout managers adapt to the platform and desktop of the user executing the program. Hence, layout managers are very useful in Java's heterogeneous environment.

Tip

You do not have to use a layout manager. Later you will have a chance to learn about programming techniques that circumvent layout management, if needed.

BorderLayout, CardLayout, FlowLayout, GridLayout, and GridBagLayout are layout managers that are currently available. All of the layout managers mentioned above extend from the interface LayoutManager. LayoutManager is part of the AWT package.

Creating Your Own Layout Managers

You can create your own layout managers that will do just about anything you want them to. All you need to do is create a class that implements the LayoutManager interface and overrides the five methods defined in the LayoutManager interface.

Those five methods are addLayoutComponent(), removeLayoutComponent(), preferredLayoutSize(), minimumLayoutSize(), and layoutContainer(). Check the Java API spec using InfoView in Visual J++ for more information.

Including Components

Including components is a very simple process. Essentially, you have a layout manager specified for a given container, and you have component(s) to add to the layout manager. As you will learn later, there are two specific techniques for adding and using components between Java applets and applications. Consider the following example:

```
Button myTestButton = new Button("Test");
add(myTestButton);
```

Above is a snippet of code that you would use in either a Java application or an applet. The key is that you create an instance of the component you want to use. In the above case, you are constructing a button with a label of Test. Secondly, you use the method add() to add it to the layout manager, which is the default FlowLayout in this case. From this point forward, the layout manager is responsible for displaying it on the screen.

Naming Conventions

If you have any experience programming in other languages (in particular VB), you know that there is a fairly uniform set of standards to use when naming your variables. Usually, it is a three letter contraction for the object or component type in front of the variable name. For example, a name for a button in VB might be btnTest (*btn* stands for button and *Test* stands for the variable name).

At this point Java is still new enough that it does not have a completely uniform set of standards to use for naming; however, that is changing. At this point, the best thing to do is to find out if there are any standards in your area (e.g., organization, company, etc.). Whatever you decide to do, be religiously consistent about it.

The AWT Components

The first set of tools to discuss is the components. Each mini-section provides you with a complete description of the components, all of the constructors available to it, a table of useful methods for the class, and a figure showing you what it looks like on the Windows 95/NT platforms. Starting with Buttons, let's take a closer look at these components.

Button

Definition

A button is nothing more than a box that looks like a button on the computer screen. When pushed, it sends a message to its owner, which executes a block of code in response.

Syntax

The following shows two examples of instancing the Button class:

```
Button myOKButton = new Button("OK");
Button = myButton = new Button();
```

In looking at the above constructors, the first one should not be new to you. It creates an instance of a Button with the label, OK. The second one shows the default constructor for a button that does not have a label.

Note

A button in Java is equivalent to a Command button in Windows.

Example

Figure 7-2 shows an example of what buttons look like. Remember, the buttons shown here represent what a Java button looks like on the Windows 95/NT platforms. However, these same buttons will not look like Figure 7-2 on a UNIX or Mac platform.

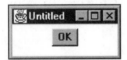

Figure 7-2 : An example of a button in Java.

The following shows a snippet of code for the above button:

```
setLayout(new FlowLayout());
Button myOKButton = new Button("OK");
add(myOKButton);
show();
```

Useful Methods

Table 7-1 shows useful methods that are members of the Button class.

Method	Explanation
getLabel()	Returns a String containing the label of the button.
setLabel(String name)	Sets the label for the button using the specified string.

Table 7-1: java.awt.Button.

Canvas

Definition

Canvas is a component with little functionality, allowing you to draw things from the Graphics class and include it as a component. Instead of drawing directly to the pane of the applet (or window if it is a Java application), you can use a canvas and treat the whole thing like a component.

Syntax

The only constructor for a Canvas is the default constructor shown in the following example:

```
Canvas myCanvas = new Canvas();
```

A very common technique used in Java for canvases is to create a subclass of it and add your own functionality.

Useful Methods

The only useful method included in the Canvas class is the paint() method; it accepts a Graphics parameter just like the paint() method you worked with for drawing things on an applet pane.

Canvases are also useful because they can catch and handle events. You will learn more about event handling in Chapter 9.

Checkbox

Definition

Checkboxes are used to set to a state of true or false for a given option. Usually, checkboxes are best suited for a particular user preference, as they provide an option for the user to toggle "on" or "off".

Syntax

Below are several examples of how to declare a checkbox:

```
Checkbox myCheck = new Checkbox();
Checkbox myEarthCheck = new Checkbox("Earth Inhabitant");
```

Note

The default value for a checkbox is false or off.

The first line of code represents the default constructor for a checkbox with no label. The second represents another constructor for a checkbox, allowing you to specify a label of "Earth Inhabitant." Note that on the inside, Checkboxes retain their state with a boolean value of true or false. On the outside, the user sees a corresponding on or off for the Checkbox.

Note

The checkbox in Java is equivalent to check boxes in Windows.

Example

```
setLayout(new FlowLayout());
Checkbox myRedCheck = new Checkbox("Red");
Checkbox myWhiteCheck = new Checkbox("White);
Checkbox myBlueCheck = new Checkbox("Blue);
add(myRedCheck);
add(myWhiteCheck);
add(myBlueCheck);
show();
```

Figure 7-3 shows three checkboxes based on the above code.

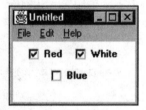

Figure 7-3 : Example of three checkboxes.

Useful Methods

Table 7-2 shows a list of useful methods available in the Checkbox class.

Method	Explanation
getCheckboxGroup()	Returns the group that this Checkbox belongs to in the form of the object CheckboxGroup.
getLabel()	Returns a String containing the label of this Checkbox.
getState()	Returns a boolean value representing if the Checkbox is check or not (i.e., true or false).
setCheckboxGroup (CheckboxGroup mygroup)	Changes the CheckboxGroup that this Checkbox belongs to the specified group.
setLabel(String txt)	Sets the label of this Checkbox to the specified text.
setState(boolean state)	Changes the state of this Checkbox to the specified state.

Table 7-2: java.awt.Checkbox.

CheckboxGroup (Radio Buttons)

Definition

A checkbox group is a collection of checkboxes grouped together using the CheckboxGroup class. The CheckboxGroup class allows you to group several checkboxes, yet have only one checkbox that can be true (i.e. checked) at any one time.

Syntax

Consider the following:

```
CheckboxGroup myCheckGroupRank = new CheckboxGroup();

Checkbox myHighCheck = new Checkbox("High", myCheckGroupRank,
false);
Checkbox myMeduimCheck = new Checkbox("Medium",
myCheckGroupRank, false);
Checkbox myLowCheck = new Checkbox("Low", myCheckGroupRank,
true);
```

Looking at the above code, notice that the first constructor builds the CheckboxGroup called myCheckGroupRank. Then, using a special constructor from the Checkbox class, the next three lines construct a checkbox but passes the object for the checkboxgroup that this checkbox will belong to.

Note

A checkbox group is equivalent to a radio button in Windows.

Example
The following is a pseudo-example of a CheckboxGroup:

```
setLayout(new FlowLayout());
CheckboxGroup myCheckGroupNumbers = new CheckboxGroup();

Checkbox myFirstCheck = new Checkbox("00-10",
myCheckGroupNumbers, false);
add(myFirstCheck);
Checkbox mySecondCheck = new Checkbox("11-20",
myCheckGroupNumbers, false);
add(mySecondCheck);
Checkbox myThirdCheck = new Checkbox("21-30",
```

```
myCheckGroupNumbers, true);
add(myThirdCheck);
Checkbox myFourthCheck = new Checkbox("31-40",
myCheckGroupNumbers, false);
add(myFourthCheck);
Checkbox myFifthCheck = new Checkbox("41-50",
myCheckGroupNumbers, false);
add(myFifthCheck);
show();
```

Figure 7-4 shows the above snippet of code in action.

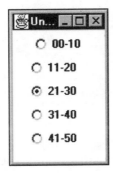

Figure 7-4 : Example of a checkbox group.

Looking at Figure 7-4, notice that the checkboxes that are part of a group differ cosmetically because they are round, instead of square like the checkboxes discussed in the last section. Also, unlike the checkboxes in Figure 7-3, these have more than one item checked. With a CheckboxGroup, there can be only one item checked at a time.

Tip

There is not a specific constructor to make a checkbox that is not part of a group, but will automatically toggle true; however, there is one option for doing this:

```
Checkbox myTestCheck = new Checkbox("Test", null, true);
```

This constructs a checkbox that is not linked to any CheckboxGroup, but defaults to true, or on.

Choice (Combo Box)

Definition

Choice allows you to create a drop-down list of items for the user to choose from. It does not take up much space on the screen though, because it can hide its list.

Syntax

Looking at the following code, the default constructor is the only constructor for Choice:

```
Choice myChoice = new Choice();
```

Note

A choice in Java is equivalent to a combo box in Windows.

Example

Unlike other components, just constructing an instance of the class is not enough for Choice. You now need to populate it with items using the addItem() method. The following shows an example of how you would add items to myChoice, which we constructed above:

```
myChoice.addItem("Windows NT");
myChoice.addItem("Windows 95");
myChoice.addItem("PowerMac");
myChoice.addItem("Unix");
add(myChoice);
```

Looking at the above code, notice that each of the items added will appear as an item in the drop-down list for the Choice myChoice. The last line uses the add() method to add the item to the current layout manager. Figure 7-5 shows two versions of the same choice component created from the above code.

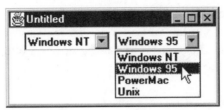

Figure 7-5: The example choice on the left is closed. The example choice on the right is open.

Useful Methods

Table 7-3 shows a list of useful methods for Choice.

Method	Explanation
addItem(String item)	Adds the specified item.
countItems()	Returns the number of items.
getItem(int index)	Returns a String that represents the specified index.
getSelectedIndex()	Returns an integer representing the index of the currently selected item.
getSelectedItem()	Returns a String that represents the current selected item.
select(int index)	Selects the item in this Choice base on the specified index.
select(String value)	An overloaded method that selects the item based on the specified value.

Table 7-3: java.awt.Choice.

Label

Definition

A label is a string of text displayed as a component in a container of your Java program. In essence, it is the same as using the drawString() method that you worked with to print text on the applet pane. The advantage a Label has over drawString(), however, is that it is a component and can be housed with other UI components, making it more versatile.

Syntax

Below are two examples of constructing a label:

```
Label myHelloLabel  = new Label("Hello World");
Label myHelloAgainLabel = new Label ("Hello again",
Label.LEFT);
```

The above code shows two constructors for the Label class. The first constructs a label with the parameter *Hello World*. Using the default, the first label constructs to be left justified. The second label uses the constructor that lets you also define the justification for the label. Table 7-4 shows all of the available justifications for the Label class.

Input Variable	Explanation
Label.CENTER	Specifies the center alignment (integer value of 0).
Label.LEFT	Specifies the left alignment (integer value of 1).
Label.RIGHT	Specifies the right alignment (integer value of 2).

Table 7-4: Static variables for the java.awt.Label class.

Note

Just in case you were wondering, labels in Java are just like labels in Windows.

Example

Consider the following:

```
setLayout(new FlowLayout());
Label myWelcomeLabel = new Label("Welcome to Java");
add(myWelcomeLabel);
show();
```

Figure 7-6 shows what the above code looks like in Java.

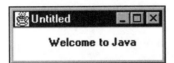

Figure 7-6 : An example of a label in Java.

Note

To a user, a label looks very similar to the text that is printed when you use the drawString() method inside of the paint() method. Remember that labels are components and can belong to a layout manager. However, drawString() text cannot.

Useful Methods

Table 7-5 shows a list of useful methods for Label.

Method	Explanation
getAlignment()	Returns an integer specifying the alignment for this Label.
getText()	Returns a String specifying the Label.
setAlignment(int align)	Sets the alignment.
setText(String label)	Changes the text to be displayed for this label based on the specified String.

Table 7-5: java.awt.Label.

List

Definition

List displays a list of items in a scrolling format. The functionality of Lists is very similar to Choices, which was described earlier. However, a list is always in a drop-down state. What makes lists unique is that a list can be configured to have more than one selection in one box at one time.

Syntax

The following shows examples of constructing two lists:

```
List myList = new List();
List myMultiList = new List(5, true);
```

The first line of code above is the default list constructor that builds the List myList with no lines or items. The second constructor for the List class takes two parameters, one for the number of lines, and the second to indicate if multiple selection is enabled.

Note

A list is equivalent to a list box in Windows.

Example

Just like Choice, List has an addItem() method that you can use to populate your list:

```
myMultiList.addItem("CD-ROM");
myMultiList.addItem("Sound Card");
myMultiList.addItem("modem");
myMultiList.addItem("SCSI controller");
myMultiList.addItem("EIDE controller");
myMultiList.addItem("16 MB RAM");
myMultiList.addItem("32 MB RAM");
myMultiList.addItem("64 MB RAM");
add(mylist);
show();
```

As you can see in the above lines of code, you are adding various items by using the addItem() method from the List class. Figure 7-7 shows what the above list looks like.

Figure 7-7: An example of a list with multiple selections set to true.

Useful Methods

Table 7-6 shows a breakdown of all the useful methods for the class List.

Method	Explanation
addItem(String item)	Adds the specified item.
addItem(String item, index)	An overloaded method that adds the int specified item at the specified location index.
allowsMultiple Selections()	Returns a boolean representing multiple selection is available.
clear()	Clears the List.
countItems()	Returns an integer representing the number of items in this List.
delItem(int index)	Removes the specified item.
delItems(int startIndex, endIndex)	A method used to delete a series of int items.
deselect(int index)	Deselects the item at the specified index.
getItem(int index)	Returns a String representing the item at the specified index.
getRows()	Returns an integer representing the number of visible lines.

Method	Explanation
getSelectedIndex()	Returns an integer representing the selected item (-1 if no item was selected).
getSelectedIndexs()	A method that returns an array of integers that represents the selected items.
getSelectedItem()	Returns a String containing the selected item.
getSelectedItems()	A method that returns an array of Strings that contain all of the selected items.
getVisibleIndex()	Returns an integer representing the index value for the last item that was made visible by the method makeVisible().
isSelected(int index)	Returns a boolean based on the evaluation of if the specified index is in a selected state.
makeVisible(int index)	Makes the item with the specified index visible.
minimumSize()	Returns the object Dimension that contains the minimum dimensions needed.
minimumSize (int numofRows)	An overloaded method that returns the object Dimension that holds the minimum dimensions needed for a List with the specified number of items.
paramString()	Returns a String that contains the parameter of this List.
preferredSize()	Returns the object Dimension that holds the preferrred dimensions needed for this List.
preferredSize (int numofRows)	An overloaded method that returns the object Dimension that holds the preferred dimensions needed for this List with the specified number of rows.
replaceItem(string item, int index)	Replaces the item at the specified index with the specified item.
select(int index)	Selects the item at the specified index.
setMulipleSelections (boolean bool)	Specifies the state of multiple selection.

Table 7-6: java.awt.List.

Scrollbar

Definition

Scrollbar lets a user scroll through a continuous range of predetermined integer values. You can create stand-alone scrollbars. You can also create ones that are dependent on other components in your UI, just like the scrollbars that appear on the corner of your Microsoft Word documents when your document grows larger than one page.

Syntax

The following code shows several examples of constructing a scrollbar:

```
Scrollbar myScroll = new Scrollbar();
Scrollbar myHScroll = new Scrollbar(Scrollbar.HORIZONTAL);
Scrollbar myVScroll = new Scrollbar(Scrollbar.VERTICAL, 500,
50, 10, 1000);
```

The above code shows three constructors for the Scrollbar class. The first is the default constructor for the scrollbar that builds a vertical scrollbar. The second constructor for the Scrollbar class lets you specify if the scrollbar is vertical or horizontal, using the static variables Scrollbar.HORIZONTAL and Scrollbar.VERTICAL respectively. The final constructor takes several parameters. Table 7-2 describes what each one does.

Input Variable	Explanation
orientation	Specifies if this Scrollbar will be VERTICAL or HORIZONTAL.
value	The initial value for this Scrollbar.
visible	The size of the visible scrollable area.
minimum	The minimum value for this Scrollbar.
maximum	The maximum value for this Scrollbar.

Table 7-7: The Scrollbar constructor: scrollbar(int orientation, int value, int visible, int minimum, int maximum).

Note

A scrollbar in Java actually represents two objects in Visual Basic: the Vertical Scrollbar and the Horizontal Scrollbar.

Example
Figure 7-8 shows an example of a scrollbar.

Figure 7-8: An example of a scrollbar in Java.

Useful Methods
Table 7-8 shows a list of useful methods for the Scrollbar class.

Method	Explanation
getLineIncrement()	Returns an integer value for the increment of this Scrollbar.
getMaximum()	Returns an integer that represents the maximum value for this Scrollbar.
getMinimum()	Returns an integer that represents the minimum value for this Scrollbar.
getOrientation()	Returns an integer value representing this Scrollbar's orientation.
getPageIncrement()	Returns an integer value for the page increment (or decrement) of this Scrollbar. This value is fired when the user clicks in the area between the thumb and the arrows. ➡

Method	Explanation
getValue()	Returns an integer representation for the value of this Scrollbar.
getVisible()	Returns an integer representation that represents the visible amount of the Scrollbar.
setLineIncrement (int value)	Sets the line increment (or decrement).
setPageIncrement (int value)	Changes the page increment (or decrement).
setValue(int value)	Changes the value of the Scrollbar to the specified value.
setValues(int value, int visible, int min, int max)	Changes the values for the Scrollbar.

Table 7-8: java.awt.Scrollbar.

TextComponent

Definition
The TextComponent class is a superclass to two subclasses: TextField and TextArea. The TextField and TextArea subclasses are discussed in the next two sections. They are extremely similar and even have some methods in common; these methods come from the TextComponent class.

Useful Methods

Table 7-9 shows available methods for the TextComponent class.

Method	Explanation
getSelectedText ()	Returns a String representing the selected text contained.
getSelectionEnd()	Returns an int with the selected text's end position.
getSelectionStart()	Returns an int with the selected text's start position.
getText()	Returns a String representing the text contained in this TextComponent.
isEditable()	Returns the boolean indicating if this TextComponent is editable.
paramString()	Returns a String containing a list of parameters for this TextComponent.
select(int selstart, int selEnd)	Selects the text found between the specified start and end locations.
selectAll()	Selects all the text in the TextComponent.
setEditable (boolean txtbool)	Sets this TextComponent if it is editiable based on the specified boolean txtbool.
setText(String txt)	Sets the text of this TextComponent to the specified text.

Table 7-9: java.awt.TextCompnent.

Tip

You cannot use TextComponent directly in your Java UI because it does not have any constructors. Instead, use the two subclasses, TextField and TextArea, that are discussed in the next two sections.

TextField

Definition

The TextField class represents an area for a user to enter data. A text field can be thought of as an editable label designed for input. Note that a text field can be a maximum of one row in height. However, the number of columns (i.e., width) of a text field is customizable.

Syntax

Consider the following code:

```
TextField myField1 = new TextField(20);
TextField myField2 = new TextField("This is my TextField!");
TextField myField3 = new TextField ("This is my TextField!",
20);
```

As you can see in the above code, there are three different ways to construct a TextField. The first input specifies the number of columns that this text field will have. The second line constructs a text field with the specified String as default text to be typed in it. Finally, the third text field constructor shows how to implement a combination of the first two constructs, giving you maximum extendibility.

Example

Figure 7-9 shows an example of a text field.

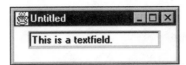

Figure 7-9: An example of a text field.

The following is a snippet of code for Figure 7-9:

```
setLayout(new FlowLayout());
TextField myField1 =new TextField("This is a textfield.", 18);
add(myField1);
show();
```

Useful Methods

Table 7-10 shows a list of methods available for the TextField.

Method	Explanation
echoCharIsSet()	Returns a boolean based on if this TextField has a character set for echoing.
getColumns()	Returns an integer that represents the number of columns.
getEchoChar()	Returns the char that is being used for echoing.
minimumSize()	Returns the object Dimension that contains the minimum dimensions.
minimumSize (int cols)	An overloaded method that returns the object Dimension that contains the minimum dimensions for a TextField with the specified number of columns.
preferredSize()	Returns the object Dimension that contains the preferred dimensions for this TextField.
preferredSize (int cols)	An overloaded method that returns the object Dimension that contains the dimensions for a TextField with the specified number of columns.
setEchoCharacter (char c)	Changes the echo character for this TextField.

Table 7-10: java.awt.TextField.

Echoing Characters in Your TextFields

Several methods talk about echoing characters. Echoing characters gives you the capability to build text fields that do not display the user's text. Instead it echoes the characters with one place holder character. Passwords are the most common example of an echoed text field.

TextArea

Definition
A TextArea is nothing more than a TextField that can have more than one row for inputting information.

Syntax
There are three constructors for the TextArea class:

```
TextArea myTextArea1 = new TextArea(10, 30);
// TextArea
TextArea myTextArea2 = new TextArea("User input goes here.");
// TxtArea, rows, cols
TextArea myTextArea3 = new TextArea("User input goes here.",
20, 40);
```

Looking at the above code, notice three TextArea constructor examples. The first constructs myTextArea1 with 10 rows, 30 columns, and no text initially loaded. The second constructs myTextArea2 wrapped around the size of the default text passed to it. The final constructor builds myTextArea3 that constructs the TextArea with 20 rows, 40 columns, and the default text, "User input goes here."

The three constructors for TextArea give you the flexibility to create the text area most suited for your needs. The constructs for TextArea are almost the same as the ones for TextField, except that there is one more input variable to specify the number of rows in a TextArea.

Example
Figure 7-10 shows an example of a text area.

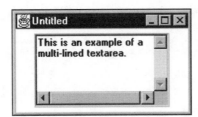

Figure 7-10: An example of a textarea.

The following shows the code for the above component:

```
setLayout(FlowLayout());
TextArea myFirstTextArea =new TextArea(5,18);
add(myFirstTextArea);
show();
```

Useful Methods

Table 7-11 shows a list of available methods for TextArea.

Method	Explanation
appendText(String txt)	Adds the specified text to the end.
getComlumns()	Returns an integer that represents the number of columns in this TextArea.
getRows()	Returns an integer that represents the number of rows in this TextArea.
insertText (String txt, int pos)	Inserts the specified text at the specified point.
minimumSize()	Returns the object Dimension that contains the minimum dimensions.
minimumSize (int rows, int cols)	An overloaded method that returns the object paramString().
preferredSize()	Returns the object Dimension that contains the preferred dimensions.
preferredSize (int rows, int cols)	An overloaded method that returns the object Dimension that contains the dimensions for a TextArea with the specified number of columns.
replaceText(String txt, int start, int end)	Replaces text from the indicated start to end position with the new text specified.

Table 7-11: java.awt.TextArea.

The AWT Containers

The AWT package includes several classes that you can instance or subclass to best fit your needs for containing the components discussed earlier. The Frame, Dialog, FileDialog, and Panel classes give you the ability to add components quite easily.

This section also discusses other classes from the AWT package that are not containers, but relate to them. MenuBar, Menu, MenuItem, and CheckboxMenuItem are a complete set of classes that you can use to create menus for your containers.

Frame

The Frame class comes from the abstract class Window that is the primary window in any and all of your UI based Java applications. Frames include a top-level window, a title, and a border that you can customize or disable depending on your needs. The Frame class contains two constructors as follows:

```
Frame myFrame = new Frame();
Frame myNewFrame = new Frame("This is a new Window");
```

The above shows examples of the two constructors for the Frame class. The first is the default and the second takes a String for the title.

Note

A frame in Java is equivalent to a top-level window on the Windows 95/NT platforms. Be careful not to confuse the abstract class Window as the actual object to implement.

Useful Methods

Table 7-12 shows all of the most used methods for the Frame class.

Method	Explanation
addNotify ()	Creates the Frame's peer.
dispose()	Disposes of the Frame.
getCursorType()	Returns the cursor type.
getIconImage()	Returns the icon image for this Frame.
getMenuBar()	Gets the menubar for this Frame.
getTitle()	Gets the title of the Frame.
isResizable()	Returns true if the user can resize the Frame.
paramString()	Returns the parameter String of this Frame.
remove (MenuComponent menuCom)	Removes the specified menuCom menu bar from this Frame.
setCursor(int type)	Sets the cursor image to the specified type.
setIconImage (Image img)	Sets the image to display when this Frame is iconized.
setMenuBar (MenuBar menuBar)	Sets the menubar for this Frame to the specified menuBar.
setResizable (boolean bool)	Sets the resizeable flag.
setTitle(String txt)	Sets the title for this Frame to the specified text.

Table 7-12: java.awt.Frame.

Let's now take a look at some examples of a Frame. Three topics of note for Frames are: instancing frames, subclassing frames, and adding component frames.

Instancing Frames

```
Frame myNameFrame = new Frame();
myNameFrame.resize(300,200);
myNameFrame.show();
```

Notice that you are creating an instance of the Frame class. Secondly, the resize() method coming from the java.awt.Component class specifies the size of the frame to a width of 300 and a height of 200. Finally, you are using the method show() to display it on the screen. Figure 7-11 shows the frame.

Figure 7-11: A basic instance of a frame.

Subclassing Frames

The other way you can incorporate Frame functionality into your Java applications is to create a subclass of it. Then add any customizations you want to the Frame.

```
class TestFrame extends Frame {
   public void TestFrame() {
      resize(300, 200);
   }
   public static void main(String args[]) {
    TestFrame myTestFrame= new TestFrame();
         myTestFrame.show();
   }
//Rest of Class
}
```

Looking at the above code, you see that the first line constructs the class TestFrame that inherits from the Frame class. The method located under the class declaration is the default constructor for the TextFrame class. Essentially, the only thing you are doing for the constructor is resizing the frame to 300 X 200. The next method is the main() method that creates an instance of TestFrame called myTestFrame, and the line under the declaration uses the show() method to display the frame on the screen.

The frame constructed above is exactly the same as the frame you instanced in Figure 7-11.

Adding Components to Frames

You can also add components to a Frame using the add() method from the Component class and a layout manager. The following shows an example of a subclassed Frame that has several components added to it:

```
class myComponentFrameTest extends Frame {
   public void myComponentFrameTest() {
      Label myWelLabel=new Label("Welcome to my Program!",
Label.CENTER);
      myWelLabel.setFont(new Font("Dialog",Font.BOLD,16));
      add(myWelLabel);

      Label myNameLabel=new Label("Name:");
      myNameLabel.setFont(new Font("Dialog",Font.BOLD,14));
      add(myNameLabel);

      TextField myNameField = new TextField(13);
      add(myNameField);

      Label myEmailLabel = new Label("E-Mail:");
      myEmailLabel.setFont(new Font("Dialog",Font.BOLD,14));
      add(myEmailLabel);

      TextField myEmailField=new TextField(24);
      add(myEmailField);

      Button myOKButton=new Button("OK");
      add(myOKButton);
      Button myCancelButton=new Button("Cancel");
      add(myCancelButton);
   }
}
```

Looking at the above code, you construct the class myComponentClassFrameTest extending Frame:

```
class myComponentFrameTest extends Frame
```

Then the rest of the application creates and adds various components. Figure 7-11 shows what myComponentTest looks like.

Tip

You can use the paint() method that you used with applets and canvases to draw all kinds of graphics on the screen. You do it by creating a subclass of Frame and overriding its paint() method.

Panel

Panels give you the ability to specify certain areas on a frame or applet pane to have specific properties. This is an excellent way to describe one area of components. Panels can even include other panels. The Panel class is the simplest of the containers having only a default constructor:

```
Panel myPanel = new Panel();
```

Usually, you construct a Panel inside a Frame and construct your components in the Panel as opposed to the Frame itself. Then you can add the Panel (or panels) to the Frame.

Dialog

The Dialog class represents a tool that you can use to create dialog boxes. Dialogs are temporary windows that display an important message or perform specific tasks for the user of your Java program. The following shows several examples of constructing a dialog:

```
Dialog myDialog = new Dialog(myFrame, true);
Dialog mySecondDialog = new Dialog(myFrame, "WARNING!",
false);
```

Looking at the above, notice that the first constructor requires you to pass a Frame object, and the second is a boolean specifying whether the Dialog is *modal* or not. Modal means that the user must be finished with dialog (usually pressing the OK or Cancel buttons) before continuing in the Java program. The second constructor for Dialog building mySecondDialog is the same as the first. However, it adds another parameter for the title of the dialog.

Tip

Whenever you construct a Dialog, you must attach it to a Frame. Thus, there is no default Dialog constructor.

It is important to remember on the modern OSs of Windows 95/NT, a modal dialog only locks out your program. However, the user can do anything they want outside the program (such as access any other tasks currently running or load new tasks).

Useful Methods

Table 7-13 lists useful methods for the Dialog class.

Method	Explanation
getTitle()	Returns a String representing the title of the Dialog.
isModal()	Returns a boolean that is true if the Dialog is modal.
isResizable()	Returns a boolean that is true if the user can resize the frame.
paramString()	Returns a String representing the parameter String of this Dialog.
setResizable (boolean bool)	Sets the resizable flag based on the specified boolean bool.
setTitle (String title)	Sets the title of the Dialog based on the specified String title.

Table 7-13: java.awt.Dialog.

FileDialog

Another type of dialog that you can use in Java is the FileDialog class. This dialog is actually a link to the set of system dialogs that are part of the OS. In Windows 95 and NT, the two system dialogs that you can interact with are the Open dialog, as shown in Figure 7-12, and the Save As dialog, shown in Figure 7-13.

Note

If you tried these examples of FileDialog on a Mac or UNIX-based platform, you would see different dialogs based on the respective operating system, even though it is the exact same Java program executing.

Figure 7-12: Open dialog box in Windows 95/NT.

Note

All FileDialogs are modal.

Figure 7-13: Save As dialog box in Windows 95/NT.

The advantage of using a system based dialog is that it changes with each platform, but the functionality is essentially the same. This lets you spend less time trying to understand a new interface and more time being productive with your Java application. The following shows examples of the two constructors for the FileDialog class:

```
FileDialog myOpenDialog = new FileDialog(myFrame, "Please
choose a File.");
FileDialog mySaveAsDialog = new FileDialog(myFrame, "Save As
Dialog", FileDialog.SAVE);
FileDialog myOpenDialog2 = new FileDialog(myFrame, "Please
chose Another File.", FileDialog.LOAD);
```

Looking at all the constructor examples to build FileDialogs, notice that you need to pass them a Frame object (which you learned about in the last section) with the Dialog class. In particular, the first constructor (building myOpenDialog) defaults to a FileDialog.LOAD state for the FileDialog using the string as the title for the dialog. The second constructor (building mySaveAsDialog) acts just as the first except that there is another boolean parameter specifying that you want a FileDialog.SAVE state for this FileDialog. The final constructor (building myOpenDialog2) is exactly like the one before it. However, you are explicitly stating a FileDialog.LOAD state for the FileDialog.

Tip

The third constructor example is redundant in specifying the FileDialog.LOAD state. If you do not specify a state for a file dialog, it defaults to a FileDialog.LOAD state.

Useful Methods

When using file dialogs, it is imperative that you use the methods in Table 7-14 to retrieve the information and specify certain options for your FileDialog class.

Method	Explanation
getDirectory()	Returns a String representing the directory of the FileDialog.
getFile()	Returns a String representing the file of the Dialog.
getFilenameFilter()	Returns the class FileNameFilter containing the filter for this Dialog.
getMode()	Returns an int for the mode of this FileDialog. If 0 returns then the FileDialog is the mode LOAD. If 1 returns then the FileDialog is the mode SAVE.
paramString()	Returns a String containing the parameter String of this FileDialog.
setDirectory(String dir)	Sets the directory of the Dialog to the specified directory using String dir.
setFile(String file)	Sets the file for this Dialog to the specified file using String file.
setFilenameFilter (FilenameFilter filter)	Sets the filter for this Dialog to the specified filter object FilenameFilter filter.

Table 7-14: java.awt.FileDialog.

Note

The next version of Java should have enhanced capabilities for constructing standard Print dialogs in your Java programs.

Using the FileDialog is a very important and useful tool that gives your Java programs a professional look. Remember though, that due to the security restrictions imposed on Java applets, FileDialog is only useful with Java applications.

Menus

The last topic to discuss concerning containers is the idea of menus. Java contains four classes that you can use to create menus for your frames or dialogs.

You know from your experience in Visual J++ how to use and work with menus. For example, File | Save lets you save the current file in Visual J++ (see Figure 7-14).

Figure 7-14: File | Save in Visual J++.

Let's take a closer look at the terminology. If the menu in Figure 7-14 were created in Java (and not C/C++), you would use the MenuBar class to create the main menu bar. Then you would use the Menu class for each of the menus in the menu bar. Finally, you would add MenuItems and CheckboxMenuItems to the Menus. The cursor in the above figure is positioned above the Save menu item.

Figure 7-15 shows an example of a CheckboxMenuItem in Visual J++. In the Window menu you have a list of all of the open windows for editing. The checked item (in this case AppletCation.java) is the source file displayed as the top file in the Developer Studio.

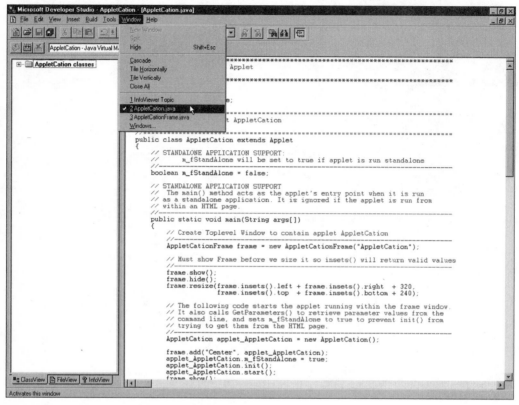

Figure 7-15: Window.AppletCation.java in Visual J++.

Note that in the Window menu you have three separators (i.e. lines), creating three distinct sections for this menu. That, too, is functionality that you can add to Java created menus. Let's take a closer look at each class and see how to implement it to create a menu in your Java programs.

MenuBar

The first class that you need to work with is the java.awt.MenuBar. Declare a MenuBar and add it to a particular Frame using the setMenubar() method from the Frame class. MenuBar only contains the default constructor shown as follows:

```
MenuBar myBar = new MenuBar();
myFrame.setMenuBar(myBar);
```

The above code constructs the menu bar called myBar and—using the setMenuBar()—adds it to the given Frame. However, now you have a menu bar, but there is no residual functionality, such as menus or menu items. All of these components need to be constructed and added to the menu bar by using the add() method from the MenuBar class.

Useful Methods

Table 7-15 lists all of the useful methods for MenuBar.

Method	Explanation
add(Menu menuitem)	Adds the specified MenuItem to the MenuBar.
countMenus()	Returns an int for the number of menus on the MenuBar.
getHelpMenu()	Returns a Menu object representing the help menu on the MenuBar.
getMenu(int menuloc)	Retrieves the specified menu based on its position using the specified int menuloc.
remove(int menuloc)	Removes the menu specified at location menuloc from the MenuBar.
remove(MenuComponent menu)	An overloaded method that removes the specified MenuComponent menu from the MenuBar.
setHelpMenu(Menu menu)	Sets the Help menu to the specified Menu menu on the MenuBar.

Table 7-15: java.awt.MenuBar.

Notice that most of the above methods are those that you use to add() and remove() menus from the menu bar. Let's now take a closer look at how to create and add menus to your menu bars.

Menu

The Menu class lets you create objects that represent the actual menus for your menu bar. So, for example:

```
Menu myFileMenu = new Menu("File");
myMenuBar.add(myFileMenu);
Menu myHelpMenu = new Menu("Help");
myMenuBar.add(myHelpMenu);
myMenuBar.setHelpMenu(myHelpMenu);
```

Starting from the top, you are constructing an instance of Menu labeled "File," which you add() to the MenuBar myMenuBar in the next line. The third line is the constructor for another instance of Menu called myHelpMenu. Also, just like the first Menu, you use the add() method to add it to the MenuBar myMenuBar. The last line shows how you could use the setHelpMenu() method to set myHelpMenu as the application's standard help menu.

Useful Methods

Table 7-16 shows the useful methods for MenuItem.

Method	Explanation
add (MenuItem item)	Adds the specified item to this Menu.
add(String label)	Adds an item with the specified label to this Menu.
addSeparator()	Adds a separator line, or a hypen, to the Menu at the current position.
countItems()	Returns an int representing the number of elements in this Menu.
getItem(int loc)	Returns a MenuItem object containing the item located at the loc of this Menu.
remove(int loc)	Deletes the item from this Menu at the specified index int loc.
remove (MenuComponent menuItem)	Deletes the specified item from this Menu.

Table 7-16: java.awt.MenuItem.

By this point, you have been introduced to creating a MenuBar and adding it to Frame. And you just saw how to add menus to the menu bar. The next section discusses how to populate your menus with items (and even other menus).

MenuItem and CheckboxMenuItem

There are several types of menu items that you can add to a menu. The first and easiest to add is a basic MenuItem. The MenuItem class contains very few methods and only one constructor. The following shows an example of constructing and adding a MenuItem to the Menu myMenu:

```
Menu myMenu = new Menu("File");
MenuItem mySaveItem = new MenuItem("Save");
myMenu.add(mySaveItem);
```

Notice that the first line of code constructs the Menu myMenu. The second line constructs the MenuItem mySaveItem, and the final line uses the add() method from the Menu class to add mySaveItem to myMenu.

Adding a CheckboxMenuItem is almost exactly the same as adding a menu. You construct an instance of CheckboxMenuItem; then you add it to the current Menu:

```
Menu myMenu = new Menu("File");
CheckboxMenuItem myCheckItalicsItem = new
CheckboxMenuItem("Italics");
myMenu.add(myCheckItalicsItem);
```

Essentially, the logic for this segment of code is unchanged from the last example, except that here you are constructing a CheckboxItem and adding it to Menu myMenu.

Tip

When creating a CheckboxMenuItem, you can decide if you want it to be checked by using the setState() method contained in the CheckboxMenuItem class.

Another item you can add to a Menu is a separator. Adding a separator lets you define certain sections in your menus. Going back to Figure 7-15, notice that there are three separators. You can add a separator to your menu one of two ways:

```
MenuItem myFileItem = new MenuItem("File");
myMenu.add(myFileItem);
MenuItem mySaveItem = new MenuItem("Save");
myMenu.add(mySaveItem);

myMenu.add(new MenuItem("-");

MenuItem myRunItem = new MenuItem("Run");
myMenu.add(myRunItem);
```

Or,

```
MenuItem myFileItem = new MenuItem("File");
myMenu.add(myFileItem);
MenuItem mySaveItem = new MenuItem("Save");
myMenu.add(mySaveItem);

myMenu.addSeparator();

MenuItem myRunItem = new MenuItem("Run");
myMenu.add(myRunItem);
```

These snippets of code each create the same menu. However, the first uses a constructor for the MenuItem, passing a label of "-" that tells Java to make this a separator. The second technique simply uses the method addSeparator() to do the job. Both techniques work equally well. Which you prefer is up to you.

Tip

You can disable a menu item in a menu by using the disable() method contained in the MenuItem class:

```
MenuItem myItem = new MenuItem("Run");
myItem.disable();
```

The last topic to discuss is the creation of a submenu. A submenu is essentially a menu inside of another menu. In Java, you can create a submenu through a very straightforward recursive process of creating a menu and adding a Menu, instead of a menu item, to it. Thus, you are creating a menu in a menu. Consider the following:

```
Menu mySubTestMenu = new Menu("Testing");
MenuItem myFirstItem = new MenuItem("First");
mySubTestMenu.add(myFirstItem);
myMenu.add(mySubTestMenu);
```

Notice that you constructed a Menu mySubTestMenu and added the MenuItem myFirstItem to it. Then, on the last line, you added the Menu mySubTestMenu to the Menu myMenu. Hence, it is a menu in a menu.

Summary

You learned a lot about creating menus in Java, including how to construct menu bars and add them to frames. You also learned how to construct menus and add all sorts of menu items (or even other menus) to it. Take a look at the following code sample:

```
MenuBar myMenubar = new MenuBar();

    myFileMenu = new Menu("File");
    myFileMenu.add(new MenuItem("New"));
    myFileMenu.add(new MenuItem("Open..."));
    myFileMenu.add(new MenuItem("Save"));
    myFileMenu.add(new MenuItem("Save As..."));
    myFileMenu.addSeparator();
    myFileMenu.add(new MenuItem("Exit"));

    myMenubar.add(myFileMenu);

    myExecuteMenu = new Menu("Execute");

    mySubOptionsMenu = new Menu("Options");
    mySubOptionsMenu.add(new CheckboxMenuItem("Debug Mode"));
    mySubOptionsMenu.add(new CheckboxMenuItem("Normal Mode "));
    mySubOptionsMenu.add(new CheckboxMenuItem("Optimized
Mode"));
```

```
myExecuteMenu.add(mySubOptionsMenu);

myMenubar.add(myExecuteMenu);

this.setMenuBar(myMenubar);
```

The first line of code constructs the MenuBar myMenuBar. The second line constructs the Menu myFileMenu. The next six lines use the myFileMenu.add() method to add MenuItems and one separator to myFileMenu.

The following line of code, excerpted from above, uses the myMenuBar.add() method to add the newly populated and constructed myFileMenu Menu to myMenuBar:

```
myMenubar.add(myFileMenu);
```

The next line of code constructs another Menu, myExecute Menu. The line under it constructs the Menu (that will be a subMenu to myExecuteMenu) called mySubOptionsMenu. The next three lines add three CheckboxMenuItems to it. The following line uses myExecuteMenu.add() to add the populated Menu mySubOptionsMenu to the Menu myExecuteMenu. Thus, it becomes a submenu:

```
myExecuteMenu.add(mySubOptionsMenu);
```

The next line of code adds the myExecuteMenu to the MenuBar myMenuBar. Finally, the last line of code uses this to refer to the current Frame and to the setMenuBar() method passing it to myMenuBar. Hence, you constructed a menu bar with two menus populated with menu items, separators, check box menu items, and submenus. Figures 7-16 and 7-17 show the above snippet of code in action.

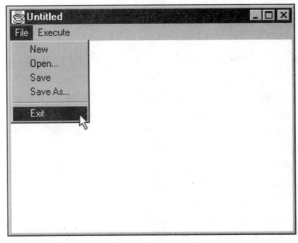

Figure 7-16: Menus example with File expanded.

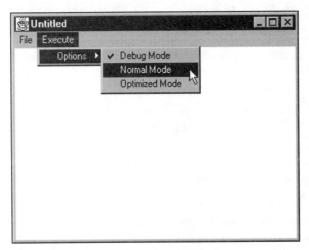

Figure 7-17: Menus example with Options expanded.

Notice that the three choices in Figure 7-17 are all check box menu items, and the item Debug Mode is checked. Creating menus can be a time-consuming process. The next chapter shows you how to use a resource editor in the Developer Studio to actually draw the menus you want. Then, you will learn about the Resource Wizard that converts them directly to 100 percent Java code.

The AWT Layout Managers

By now, you have learned about constructing components and containers. The last topic we'll cover in this chapter is layout mangers, which act as the glue between constructing components and containers. By using layout managers, you can place components relative to other components in an applet or application. This provides more flexibility, especially considering that it is extremely difficult to anticipate all of the screen formats used in the different environments supported by Java.

You can use several types of layouts when developing UIs. When dealing with all of the UI components discussed in the previous sections, you need to form some kind of structure to define how they will be put on the screen. The ideology behind the layout manager is that it handles the components inside of a container.

BorderLayout

Definition
In BorderLayout, UI components are referenced in terms of their geographical locations on the applet (i.e., "North," "South," "East," "West," and "Center").

Syntax
Consider the following

```
setLayout(new BorderLayout());
add("North", new Button("OK"));
show();
```

The default BorderLayout constructor merely adds components with no spaces either above or beside each component. The add() method for BorderLayout is specialized in the sense that you need to specify what region this component belongs to. You can choose "North," "South," "East," "West," and "Center." Consider the following:

```
setLayout(new BorderLayout(10,10));
//Add components here
```

This constructor for BorderLayout specifies 10 points of space between the width and height of each component you add. This happens automatically for the entire layout.

Example

As you can see, the BorderLayout orients UI components on relative geographical locations in the container. The following code shows five command buttons, all created and displayed using the BorderLayout format:

```
setLayout(new BorderLayout(10, 10));
    Button myButton1=new Button("One");
    add("North", myButton1);
    Button myButton2=new Button("Two");
    add("South", myButton2);
    Button myButton3=new Button("Three");
    add("East", button3);
    Button myButton4=new Button("Four");
    add("West", myButton4);
    Button myButton5=new Button("Five");
    add("Center", myButton5);
    show();
```

Figure 7-18 shows several examples of the above snippet of code with various sizes for the Frame.

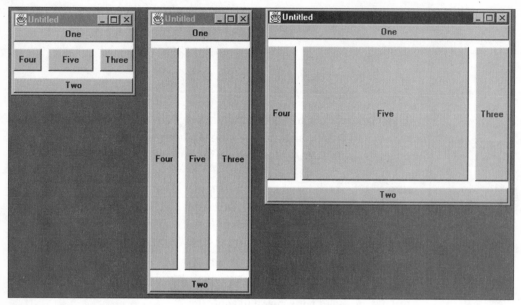

Figure 7-18: Several examples of BorderLayout using the same five button example.

Notice that each item is separated by 10 points on each side as defined in the constructor for BorderLayout in the above code. Secondly, notice that each component maintains its relative position as the frame is set to various sizes from one example to the next.

Note

The five button example shown in Figure 7-18 will be modified and used with all the layout managers in this section. This will give you a better understanding of the similarities and differences between the layout managers.

CardLayout

Definition
CardLayout is unique because it does not show all of the UI components on the screen at any one time. An easy way to under-

stand CardLayout is to think of a stack of cards, where only one is on top at any one time. However, the other components reside underneath and can be brought to the top.

Syntax

The following code shows examples of the two constructors for a CardLayout:

```
setLayout(new CardLayout());
setLayout(new CardLayout(10, 10));
```

The constructors for CardLayout are very similar to those of BorderLayout. The first is obviously the default, and the second takes two ints that represent the space between the components themselves and the borders of the frame.

Example

The following shows the five button example using the CardLayout manger:

```
setLayout(new CardLayout(10, 10));
   Button myButton1=new Button("One");
   add(myButton1);
   Button myButton2=new Button("Two");
   add(myButton2);
   Button myButton3=new Button("Three");
   add(button3);
   Button myButton4=new Button("Four");
   add(myButton4);
   Button myButton5=new Button("Five");
   add(myButton5);
   show();
```

Figure 7-19 shows several examples of the above snippet of code.

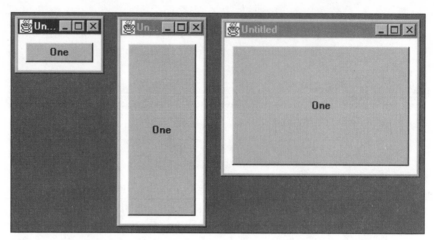

Figure 7-19: Notice that the first button is on the "top of the stack."

Useful Methods

With CardLayout, you can manipulate the components in the CardLayout through several methods that let you determine what and how components are displayed in the container. Table 7-17 shows a list of useful methods for the CardLayout.

Method	Explanation
addLayoutComponent (String txt, Component comp)	Adds the specified comp with the specified txt.
first(Container cont)	Flip to the first card.
last(Container cont)	Flips to the last card of the specified container.
layoutContainer (Container cont)	Performs a layout in the specified panel.
minimumLayoutSize (Container cont)	Calculates the minimum size for the specified panel.
next(Container cont)	Flips to the next card of the specified container.
preferredLayoutSize (Container cont)	Calculates the preferred size for the specified panel.

Method	Explanation
previous(Container cont)	Flips to the previous card of the specified container.
removeLayoutComponent (Component comp)	Removes the specified component from the layout.
show(Container cont, String txt)	Flips to the specified component name in the specified container.
toString()	Returns the String representation of this CardLayout's values.

Table 7-17: java.awt.CardLayout.

Note

CardLayout methods are not usually called directly by your Java program; instead, most often, the container object calls them directly.

FlowLayout

Definition

FlowLayout is one of the easiest containers to use. Its logic is based simply on the fact that, as components are displayed, the container moves in a left to right fashion, laying out UI components until it comes to the border of the container. Then it continues on the next line.

Syntax

Below is an example of how to declare and use FlowLayout:

```
setLayout(new FlowLayout());
setLayout(new FlowLayout(FlowLayout.LEFT));
setLayout(new FlowLayout(FlowLayout.RIGHT, 10, 10));
```

Aside from the default constructor for FlowLayout, you can specify all your components to be right or left justified using the variable FlowLayout.RIGHT and FlowLayout.LEFT. Also, just like all the other layout managers discussed thus far, you can also specify horizontal and vertical gaps (as shown in the third constructor above).

Note

FlowLayout is the default layout manager for Java applets. If you do not explicitly state a layout manger for your UI components, Java uses FlowLayout.

Example

Looking at the following code, notice that it is the five button example used for the previous layout mangers, except that it has been modified to utilize FlowLayout:

```
setLayout(new FlowLayout());
    Button myButton1=new Button("One");
    add(myButton1);
    Button myButton2=new Button("Two");
    add(myButton2);
    Button myButton3=new Button("Three");
    add(button3);
    Button myButton4=new Button("Four");
    add(myButton4);
    Button myButton5=new Button("Five");
    add(myButton5);
    show();
```

Figure 7-20 shows several examples of the above snippet of code.

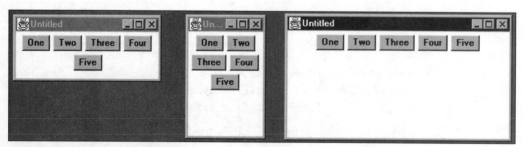

Figure 7-20: Several examples of FlowLayout with a five button example.

Notice in Figure 7-20 that, as the frame is resized from one example to the next, the components dynamically reorient themselves to always be visible.

Useful Methods
Table 7-18 shows a list of the available methods for FlowLayout.

Method	Explanation
layoutContainer (Container cont)	Lays out the specified container
minimumLayoutSize (Container cont)	Returns a Dimension object that contains the minimum dimensions for this container.
preferredLayoutSize (Containercont)	Returns a Dimension object that contains the preferred dimensions for this container.
toString()	Returns a String of this FlowLayout's values.

Table 7-18: java.awt.FlowLayout.

GridLayout

Definition
The container GridLayout gives you one of the most accurate ways to specify a pixel by pixel location for your UI components, hence giving you the most control over where to place your components. When you construct a GridLayout, you specify rows and columns to allocate locations for your UI components. Therefore, you can build a GridLayout that has two components on each row for two rows.

Syntax
Below is an example of one way to construct a GridLayout:

```
setLayout(new GridLayout(4, 2));
//Add Components here
```

Looking at the above constructor, notice that the two int variables specify the number of rows and columns defined for this layout. In this example, there are four rows and two columns. Let's take a look at another example of a GridLayout:

```
setLayout(new GridLayout(2, 2, 10, 10));
//Add Components here
```

This constructor also lets you specify horizontal and vertical gaps between the components in the layout.

With GridLayout, you are constructing a grid. In the above example, for both of these, the layout manager puts two components on the first line and two components on the second line.

Example

Let's take a look at the five button example with several modifications:

```
setLayout(new GridLayout(3,2));
    Button myButton1=new Button("One");
    add(myButton1);
    Button myButton2=new Button("Two");
    add(myButton2);
    Button myButton3=new Button("Three");
    add(button3);
    Button myButton4=new Button("Four");
    add(myButton4);
    Button myButton5=new Button("Five");
    add(myButton5);
    show();
```

Figure 7-21 shows several examples of the above snippet of code.

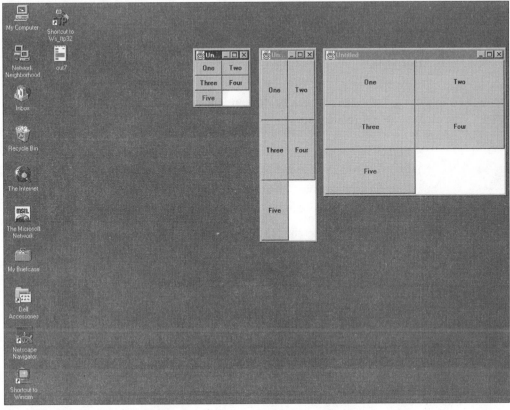

Figure 7-21: Several examples of a GridLayout with three rows and two columns.

You can see that no matter how the frame is resized, the components always reset themselves to a 3, 2 grid format.

GridBagLayout

GridBagLayout is a more versatile and much more complex version of GridLayout. It allows you to allocate several blocks on a grid for a particular component. GridBagLayout is beyond the scope of this chapter; for more information, consult the Java API spec using InfoView in Visual J++.

No Layout Manger

Definition

Alternatively, you do not have to use any layout manager. Basically, you can manually determine how components are going to be laid on the screen.

Syntax

To avoid using a layout manager you need to do several things. First, you tell your container that you do not want to use a layout manager by doing the following:

```
setLayoutManager(null);
```

Secondly, you declare the component and add it to the container using the add() method:

```
TextField myNameField = new TextField(10);
add(myNameField);
```

Finally, you use the reshape() method to specify its location and size:

```
myNameField.reshape(5, 10, 20, 10);
```

Notice that the reshape() method takes ints for the x, y, width, and height of the component.

Example

Consider the following variation to the five button example:

```
setLayout(null);
  Button myButton1=new Button("One");
  add(myButton1);
  myButton1.reshape(30, 30, 50, 25);

  Button myButton2=new Button("Two");
  add(myButton2);
  myButton2.reshape(80, 60, 50, 25);

  Button myButton3=new Button("Three");
  add(myButton3);
```

```
myButton3.reshape(130, 100, 50, 25);

Button myButton4=new Button("Four");
add(myButton4);
myButton4.reshape(180, 140, 50, 25);

Button myButton5=new Button("Five");
add(myButton5);
myButton5.reshape(230, 180, 50, 25);
```

Figure 7-22 shows several examples of the above code in action.

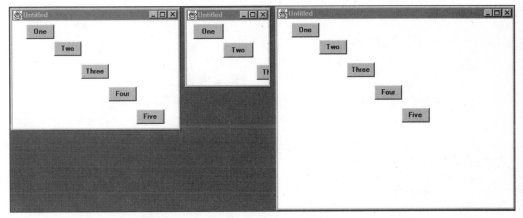

Figure 7-22: The five button example without a layout manager.

Notice that, because you do not have a layout manager to dynamically handle component layout, if the frame changes size in any
way, the components may be cut off. While not using a layout
manger probably gives you the most control over how your components are laid out, it does limit you by not ensuring that your UI
will maintain its integrity between different platforms.

Moving On

In this chapter you learned about the tools needed to construct a UI in Java. This included a description of all of the available components, containers, and layout managers.

While you now know how to layout a user interface, you have not learned how to make it responsive to user input. You'll learn how to do that beginning in Chapter 9. However, in the next chapter, you learn how to use Visual J++ and its resource editors to create user interfaces and how to have Visual J++ automatically generate user interfaces for you.

8

Designing User Interfaces With the Resource Editors

Chapter 7 focused on theoretical Java topics concerning User Interface (UI) design in the Java language using the Abstract Window Toolkit (AWT) package. It gave you a foundation for understanding how to build a UI with Java.

This chapter, however, assumes that you understand everything discussed in the last chapter and focuses on letting Visual J++ build UIs for you. This chapter is loaded with runnable examples.

In this chapter you will learn about the Developer Studio Resource Editors. You will also learn about using Visual J++'s Java Resource Wizard to port the UIs you build in the resource editor to 100 percent Java source code. Probably, the two biggest topics to be discussed include dialogs and menus. Right now, let's become acquainted with the resource editors that are useful for developing Java programs.

Introduction to the Resource Editors

Resources in the Developer Studio are external files, usually related to a UI object or tool. For example, drawings, dialogs (a.k.a. UIs), and menus are all considered resources. No matter what development environment you use in the Microsoft Developer Studio—Visual J++, Visual C++, etc.—the Developer Studio contains a collection of resource editors that let you create and include various resources.

The Developer Studio uses the same resource editors for all its supported environments. This means that you may have a very small learning curve with resource editors. Also, you can reuse resources from other environments like Visual C++. However, you need to know how to best use these editors for the Visual J++ environment. Furthermore, for all the editors (except the Graphic Editor) you will need to use the Java Resource Wizard to port it to Java.

The Graphic Resource Editor

The Graphic Resource Editor is a Bitmap Editor that allows you to create and manipulate graphics to add to your projects in Visual J++. This provides you with a way of editing and manipulating any pictures directly in the Developer Studio. Figure 8-1 shows the Graphic Resource Editor open with an image from the project MyAniApplet that you created in Chapter 6. One of the globe images is in the editor.

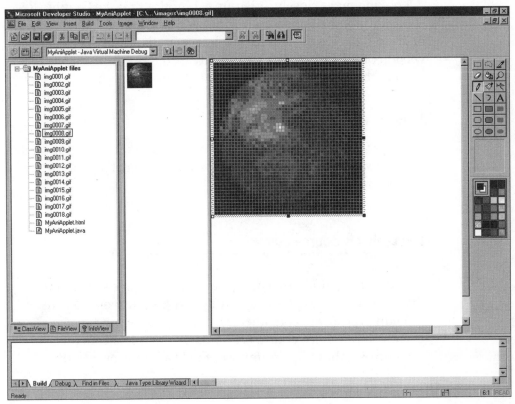

Figure 8-1: The Developer Studio with the Graphic Resource Editor open for one of the globe images for project MyAniApplet.

Looking at the above figure, notice that the Graphic Resource Editor changes the Text Editor window in the Developer Studio into a Bitmap Editor window containing its specific tools. These tools (located on the left of Figure 8-1) give you everything you need to edit and create images.

Looking more closely at Figure 8-1, notice that the Graphic Resource Editor contains a split window of the image. The window on the left shows the image. The image on the right is an enlarged version of the image. The granularity grid lets you work with each pixel of the image.

Note

The Graphic Resource Editor lets you save your images in several formats. However, the only two that are pertinent to Java are the .gif and jpeg (.jpg) formats.

The Dialog Resource Editor

An extremely important editor that you will work with in this chapter is the Dialog Resource Editor. This editor lets you create and edit specialized containers such as windows and dialogs. Then, you can place your UI components within a container.

Figure 8-2 shows an example of the Dialog Resource Editor.

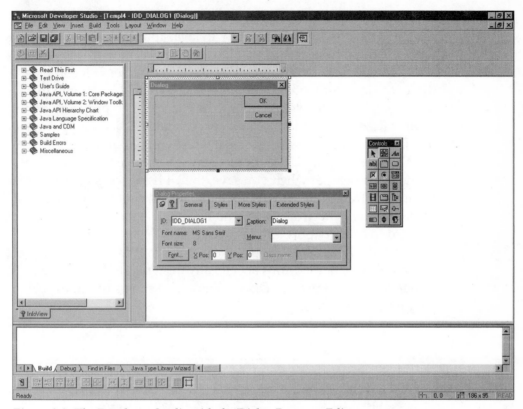

Figure 8-2: The Developer Studio with the Dialog Resource Editor open.

Looking at Figure 8-2, notice that the Dialog Resource Editor window is now open with a Dialog ready for editing.

Tip

Looking at Figure 8-2, notice the toolbox labeled Controls. It is with this Controls toolbox that you can actually drag and drop UI components onto the Dialog pane.

The important thing to note is that not all the components in the Controls toolbox are compatible with Java. Your Java program can only use those components that have a direct relation to one of the AWT components or attributes discussed in Chapter 7. A complete list of the Java-compatible components is provided later on in this chapter. If in the development process you specify a property in the Dialog Resource Editor that does not correlate to a Java property, the Java Resource Wizard ignores it when you port it to Java.

When developing UIs with the Dialog Resource Editor, it is important to note that when you save, the UI is saved as a resource template (.RCT), not a Java source file. Just like all the other resource editors you work with, you need to use the Java Resource Wizard to actually port it to Java code.

Looking at Figure 8-2, notice the status bar at the bottom. It contains command buttons specifically designed to let you manipulate and design your Dialog. Figure 8-3 shows the status bar and what each button does.

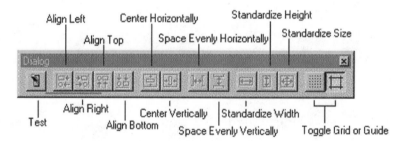

Figure 8-3: The Dialog status bar.

Next, notice the Controls toolbox that we discussed earlier. Figure 8-4 shows a closer view of it, with descriptions of the Java compatible controls.

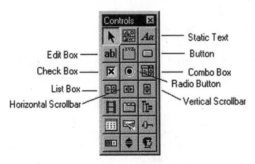

Figure 8-4: The Controls toolbox.

Look at Table 8-1 to see the Java conversions for the Java compatible components labeled in Figure 8-4.

Microsoft Controls	Compatible Java AWT
Static Text	Label
Edit Box	TextField (or TextArea if more than one line)
Button	Button
Check Box	Checkbox
Radio Button	Checkbox linked to a CheckboxGroup
List Box	List
Combo Box	Choice
Horizontal Scrollbar	Scrollbar (with the Scrollbar. HORIZONTAL flag passed)
Vertical Scrollbar	Scrollbar (with the Scrollbar.VERTICAL flag passed)

Table 8-1: Java conversions for the Java compatible components in Figure 8-4.

In Figure 8-2, look at the bottom-right corner and notice the Position Indicator status bar. This status bar gives you two sets of numbers.

The first set of coordinates represents the location of the object in Dialog units (a form of measurement for the Dialog Resource Editor) relative from the origin located at the top-left corner of the Dialog pane.

The second set of coordinates represent the height and width of the object selected.

Menu Resource Editor

The Menu Resource Editor lets you create and edit menus that you can later add to your Java frames. Figure 8-5 shows an example of the Menu Resource Editor in action.

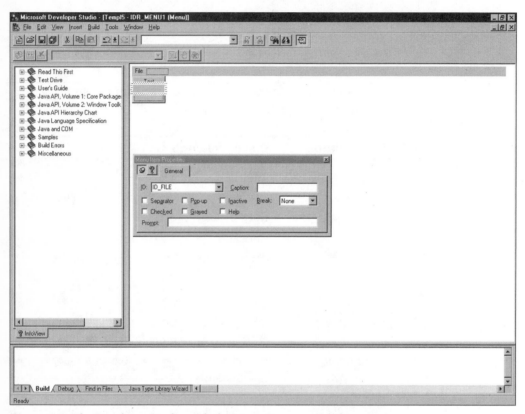

Figure 8-5: The Developer Studio with the Menu Resource Editor open.

Looking at Figure 8-5, notice that you now have the Menu Editor window, showing a Menu being designed.

Just like the Dialog Resource Editor, all menus created in this editor are saved as resource templates—meaning that you have to use the Java Resource Wizard to port them to Java code. Note that whenever you port a Menu Resource Template, the Java Resource Wizard only creates one Java source file for the Menu Resource Template specified.

Introducing the Java Resource Wizard

The Java Resource Wizard is the tool that you use to port Dialog Resources to Java source. A resource file or Binary Resource File (.RES) is created by a Resource Compiler for Windows-based applications with the source Resource Scripts (.RC) lets you port your old Windows based apps that were created in Visual C++ to Java. However, some older resource files (like those created for Windows 3.1) may be incompatible.

You can invoke the Java Resource Wizard by choosing Tools | Java Resource Wizard.

Step 1 of 2

Overall, the Java Resource Wizard is very basic. In the Developer Studio click on Tools | Java Resource Wizard and Step 1 of 2 for the Java Resource Wizard will appear (see Figure 8-6).

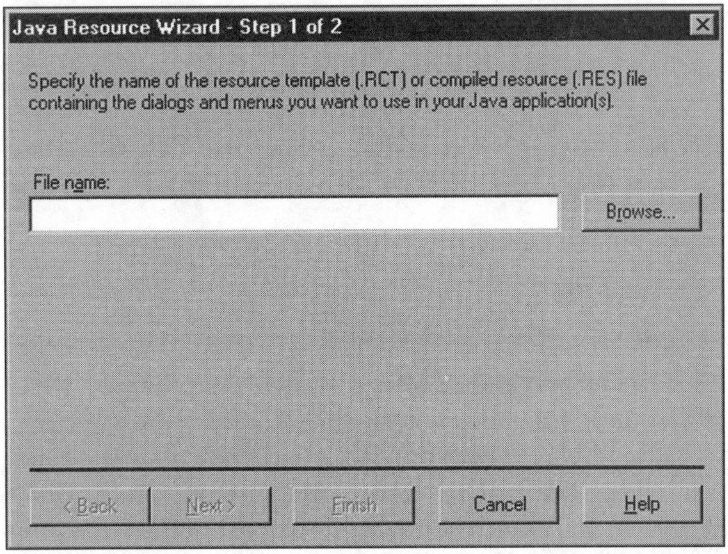

Figure 8-6: The Java Resource Wizard Step 1 of 2.

Looking at Figure 8-6, the Resource Wizard is asking you to specify (or locate using Browse) the location of the resource template (or other file) that you want to port to Java.

Figure 8-7 shows the File name field filled out with the UIApplication example you will be creating later in this chapter. Once you have specified a proper directory (as shown in Figure 8-7), click Next to continue.

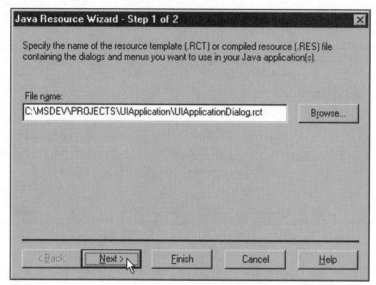

Figure 8-7: The Java Resource Wizard with Step 1 of 2 filled out.

Step 2 of 2

The second and final step shows what the Java Resource Wizard found in the files you specified (see Figure 8-8). In this case it found UIApplicationDialog and will create the class UIApplicationDialog for you to integrate into your UIApplication's source code as part of the UI. At this point, click on Finish to build the Java source files.

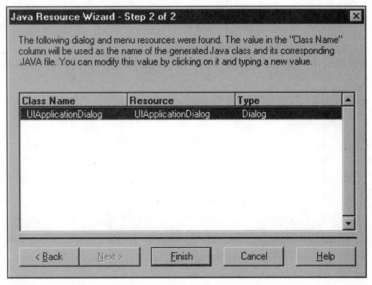

Figure 8-8: The Java Resource Wizard Step 2 of 2.

Tip

*By default the Resource Wizard places the Java source files it con-
structs in the same directory with the original resource template.*

The Confirmation Dialog Box

Once the Java Resource Wizard has finished working, you will see
a dialog box similar to the one in Figure 8-9. This box confirms
what the Java Resource Wizard successfully created.

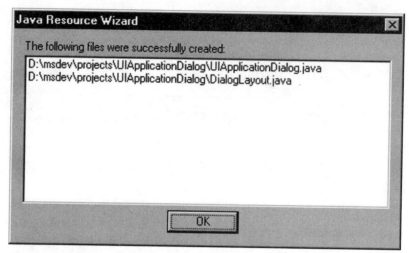

Figure 8-9: The Java Resource Wizard confirmation dialog box.

The Java Resource Wizard created two files (the dialog and a layout manager) that support each other even though you specified only one resource template. Whenever you port a Dialog Resource Template, the Java Resource Wizard always creates a Java source file for the Dialog Resource specified and another Java source file called DialogLayout.

DialogLayout is a layout manager (like those discussed in the last chapter) created by the Resource Wizard to manage components in your Dialog Resource. DialogLayout uses the managing techniques used for Windows-based resources in Visual C++.

Tutorial: Developing a User Interface

This section gives you a complete overview of how to develop a Java application with a UI and menu by using the Developer Studio's resource editors.

Understanding the Process

Anytime you create a Java application that uses a UI, and you want to use the Dialog Resource Editor and Java Resource Wizard, you should follow these global steps:

- Create the project, class, and main() method.
- Create the resource.
- Port the resource to Java using the Java Resource Wizard.
- Add the newly created *.java files to the project.
- Implement the UI in the application's source code.
- Build and execute the project.

At this point, let's begin by creating the project workspace for the Java application in Visual J++.

Creating the Project

In this example you are going to create a very simple Java application and construct its UI using the Dialog Resource Editor and the Resource Wizard.

You need to create a project workspace called UIApplication (see Table 8-2 for instructions).

Step #	Location	Action
1	Developer Studio	Choose File|New.
2	New dialog box	Highlight Project Workspace and click OK.
3	New Project Workspace dialog box	In the Name field, type **UIApplication** and click Create.

Table 8-2: Creating the UIApplication project workspace.

Tip

Remember that you are creating a Java application so do not use the Java AppletWizard.

Go to the main menu and click on Insert | New Java Class. In the Create New Class dialog box that displays, do the following:

1. In the Name field, type **UIApplication**.

2. In the Extends field, type **Frame**.

3. In the Modifiers area, check public.

4. When you finish, click OK.

Let's start by creating a public method called main() (see Table 8-3 for step-by-step instructions) .

Step #	Location	Action
1	Left pane of UIApplication project workspace	On the UIApplication class, right click and choose Add Method from the menu.
2	New Method dialog box	In the Return Type field type **void** and in the Method Declaration field type **main(String argv[ ])**.
3	New Method dialog box	In the Access box, choose public. In the Modifiers area, choose static.
4	New Method dialog box	Verify how the declaration looks, then click OK.

Table 8-3: Creating the main() method.

Now you are ready to move on to the next step: inserting the resource. Inserting the resource can be importing a resource already created or drawing one from scratch. For this example you will be drawing the resource from scratch.

Creating the Resource

Now you are ready to create the Dialog you want to use for your Java application. When you insert a resource, you are technically invoking the Dialog Resource Editor and creating a Resource Template file (.RCT).

Note

In Visual J++ a Dialog Resource Editor creates a Dialog Resource. However, do not confuse a Dialog Resource with the Dialog class you learned about in the last chapter.

To create the resource, in the Developer Studio click on Insert I Resource, which displays the Insert Resource dialog box (see Figure 8-10).

Figure 8-10: The Developer Studio with the Insert Resource dialog box open.

Several different resource editors for the Developer Studio are available in the Insert Resource dialog box. Only three are extremely useful for Visual J++: Bitmap, Dialog, and Menu (Bitmap is the Graphic Resource Editor discussed earlier).

Tip

In the Resource dialog box there is the Custom button, which allows you to add custom resources that may not be listed in the dialog.

In the Insert Resource dialog box, choose Dialog and click OK. The Dialog Resource Editor opens in the Developer Studio (see Figure 8-11) and you are now ready to create your UI as it will appear when you execute your Java application.

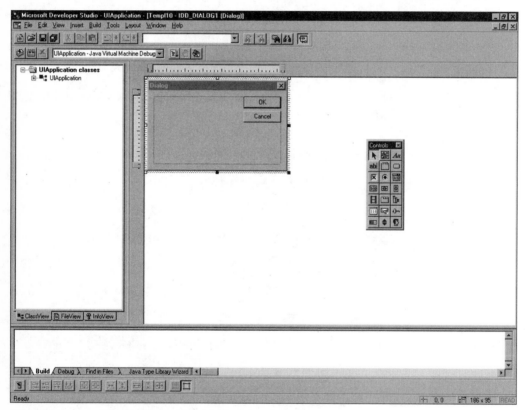

Figure 8-11: The Developer Studio with the Dialog Resource Editor open.

Note

The following section outlines a few techniques that you can use to add and edit controls in the Dialog Resource Editor. For a complete overview, check out InfoView in Visual J++.

To add a control, click on it in the Controls toolbox and then click in the Dialog where you want to add the control (see Figure 8-12). To delete a control, select the control and then press the Delete (Del) key. If you accidentially add or delete a control, select Edit | Undo.

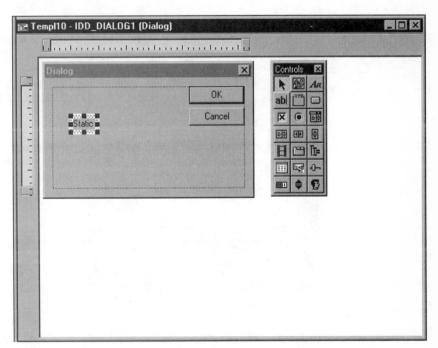

Figure 8-12: Adding static text to the pane in the Dialog Resource Editor.

Let's add static text to the Dialog. Click the Static Text icon in the Controls toolbox, then click in the Dialog pane.

After adding or selecting a control, hash marks appear around the control, meaning that you can size, move, or edit the control. Each control has a set of properties that can be modified. To modify the properties of a control, double-click on the control to open the Properties window.

Double-click on the Static Text field to open its Properties window (see Figure 8-13).

Note

The Dialog pane itself is an object and has a Properties window.

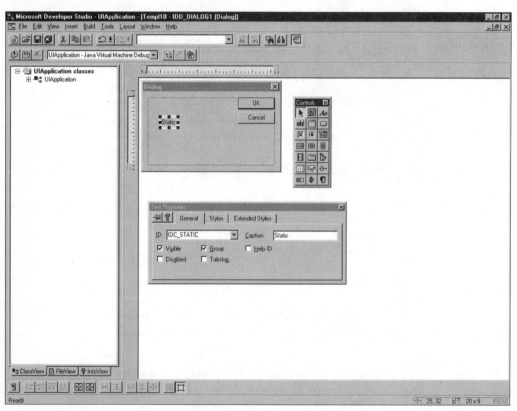

Figure 8-13: Viewing the Properties window for the static test.

In the Properties window, in the General tab, do the following:

1. In the ID field, type the name of the field as it will be known in your Java code. For this example, type **myTitleLabel**. A default value is provided, but you'll want to customize it for your application.

2. In the Caption field, type the label you want displayed in the dialog box for the field. For this example, type **Welcome to my Java Application**. A default value is provided, but you'll want to customize it for your application.

To position the Static Text Control, select the control and then move it to the X,Y coordinates 7,7. To size the Static Text Control, drag the hashed line so that the Height by Width (H x W) ratio is 114 x 8. Use the Position Indicator in the status bar of Developer Studio as a guide for these coordinates.

Tip

Another way to precisely move a control is to select it and use keyboard arrow keys—this moves the control exactly one pixel left, top, etc. You can also resize a control by using the arrow keys with the Shift key pressed.

After sizing and positioning the control, the Dialog Resource Editor looks similar to Figure 8-14.

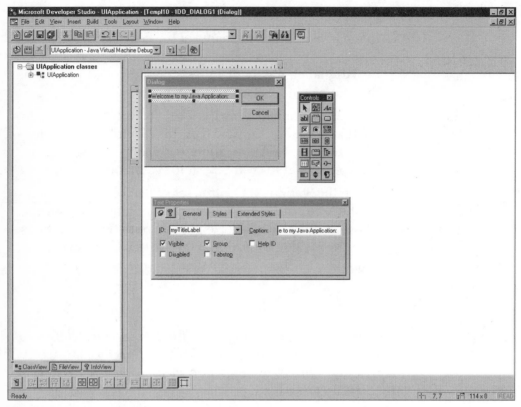

Figure 8-14: The myTitleLabel Static Test Control added to the dialog in the Dialog Resource Editor.

From Now On...

As you can see, creating resources is not very hard. For this easy and repetitive task, a table showing the step-by-step instructions is provided. For example, Table 8-4 shows what you did in the last section when you created the Static Text Control project.

Control	Location	Action
Static Text	Properties dialog box, General Tab	In the ID field, type **myTitleLabel** and in the Caption field, type **Welcome to my Java application**.
Static Text	Dialog Resource Editor, with the aid of the Position Indicators	Move the control to X,Y coordinates 7,7; resize the control to the H x W ratio of 114 x 8.

Table 8-4: Sample Resource Table.

Usually a table like this one will be accompanied by a figure showing what you will see in the Dialog Resource Editor.

Finishing the Dialog Resource for the UIApplication Project

At this point, let's finish adding and editing controls to the UIApplication project to finish building the Dialog you'll use as your UI for the UIApplication project. Use Table 8-5 to add a set of radio buttons to Dialog.

Control	Location	Action
Radio Button #1	Properties dialog box, General Tab	In the ID field, type **myRedCheckGroup** and in the Caption field, type **Red**.
Radio Button #1	Dialog Resource Editor, with the aid of the Position Indicators	Move the control to the X,Y coordinates 7,30; resize the control to the H x W ratio of 35 x 10.
Radio Button #2	Properties dialog box, General Tab	In the ID field, type **myWhiteCheckGroup** and in the Caption field, type **White**.
Radio Button #2	Dialog Resource Editor, with the aid of the Position Indicators	Move the control to the X,Y coordinates 7,40; resize the control to the H x W ratio of 35 x 10.
Radio Button #3	Properties dialog box, General Tab	In the ID field, type **myBlueCheckGroup** and in the Caption field, type **Blue**.
Radio Button #3	Dialog Editor, with the aid of the Position Indicators	Move the control to the X,Y coordinates 7,50; resize the control to the H x W ratio of 35 x 10.

Table 8-5: Remaining controls for the UIApplication.

Figure 8-15 shows what the radio buttons should look like in the Dialog Resource Editor.

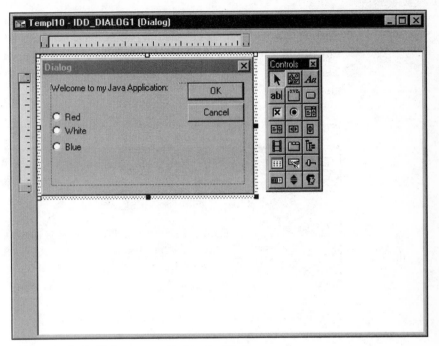

Figure 8-15: Radio buttons added to the Dialog.

Note

The controls (a.k.a. components) you add to the UIApplication are arbitrary to give you a chance to work with the controls contained in the Controls toolbox. Remember that the Resource Editor only does the design of the components, saving you time writing routine code. You still need to write code on the back end to give your components functionality. Chapter 9, on event handling, gives you a chance to work functionality into your UI and its components.

In the Dialog Resource Editor, the main Dialog that you've been adding components to is also an object with a Properties window. Highlight the entire Dialog and double-click it to open the Properties window for the Dialog. Use Table 8-6 to make the following changes to it.

Control	Location	Action
Dialog	Properties dialog box, General Tab	In the ID field, type **UIApplicationDialog** and in the Caption field, type **UIApplicationFrame**.
Dialog	Dialog Resource Editor, with the aid of the Position Indicators	Move the control to the X,Y coordinates 0,0; resize the control to the H x W ratio of 200 x 130.

Table 8-6: Editing properties for the Dialog.

Figure 8-16 shows what the Dialog Resource Editor looks like with the Properties window open.

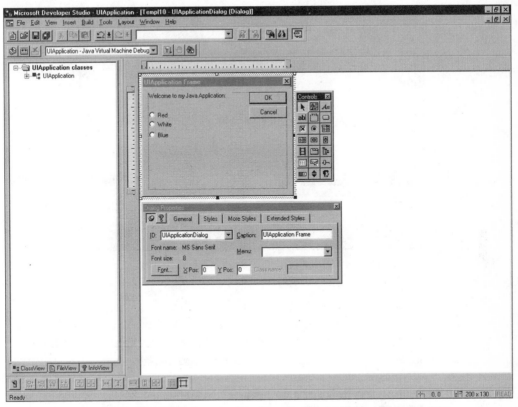

Figure 8-16: The Dialog with its Properties window open in the Dialog Resource Editor.

At this point you have finished building the Dialog, so your next step is to close the Dialog Resource Editor by clicking File | Close. A dialog box asks you if you want to save changes; click Yes and a Save As dialog box opens. Save your file as a resource template (*.rct) in the same directory that you put the UIApplication project in. For this example, the directory is ..\msdev\projects\UIApplication. Save the file as UIApplicationDialog.rct (see Figure 8-17).

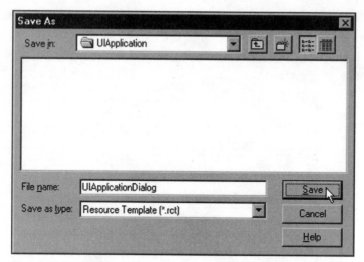

Figure 8-17: Saving the Dialog Resource Template.

After you save the template UIApplicationDialog, the Developer Studio closes the Dialog Resource Editor. You are now ready to move to the next step and port the resource template to Java source code using the Java Resource Wizard.

Porting the Resource to Java

In the last step, you created a resource template for the project UIApplication. However, a resource template is a proprietary format that you will need to port to Java. That is where the Java Resource Wizard comes in. However, Table 8-7 shows the steps you need to follow to use the Java Resource Wizard.

Tip

The Java Resource Wizard can port Resource Template files (.RCT) you create in a resource editor and Binary Resource files (.RES) to Java.

Step #	Location	Action
1	Developer Studio	Choose Tools|Java Resource Wizard.
2	Resource Wizard, step 1	File name field: C:\msdev\projects\UIApplication\ UIApplicationDialog.rct. Or use Browse. Then click Next.
3	Resource Wizard, step 2	Verify that the class name and resource name are correct. Then click Finish.
4	Confirmation dialog box	Verify the Java classes and locations are correct. Then click OK.

Table 8-7: Using the Java Resource Wizard.

Click OK on the Dialog and proceed to the next step in the process.

Adding the Files to the Project

At this point you need to add the newly created source files to the project UIApplication.

Note

When you ran the Java Resource Wizard, you constructed Java source files, not compiled Java classes.

Make sure the UIApplication project is open, then click on Insert | Files into Project. The Insert Files into Project dialog box opens (see Figure 8-18).

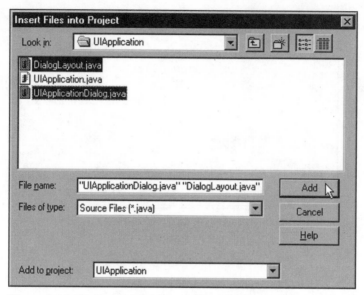

Figure 8-18: The Insert Files into Project dialog box.

Be sure to highlight both the UIApplicationDialog.java file and the DialogLayout.java file so that both files are added, and then click Add. The files are now part of the UIApplication project.

Tip

You can check to see what files belong to a project by going to File | View and expanding the folder at the top.

Implementing the UI in the Application's Source Code

It is at this stage of the process that you are ready to hunker down and edit your application's source code to integrate the UI you created and ported it to Java. You are essentially going to use a specific technique in the main() method of the application that will do the job.

Basically, there are two key points that deal specifically with how the Java Resource Wizard constructs your UI classes.

First, there is a UI constructor that takes any Container object (e.g., Frame, Dialog, Panel, etc.). Remember, just because the Developer Studio calls it a Dialog does not mean that you can only create Dialogs based on the java.awt.Dialog class.

Second, once you have constructed an instance of the UI class created by the Java Resource Wizard, you need to call the CreateControls() method. CreateControls() is responsible for using the DialogLayout layout manager and displaying the components.

Once you have completed these two tasks, you have successfully implemented the UI for any Java application.

In this example the UIApplication class contains the main() method. So, in the Developer Studio open the UIApplication class in the Text Editor window and make the changes that appear in bold:

```java
import java.awt.Frame;

//My code starts here
import UIApplicationDialog;
//My code ends here

/*
 *
 * UIApplication
 *
 */
public class UIApplication extends Frame
{

    public static void main(String args[])
    {

    //My code starts here
    UIApplication myUIApplication = new UIApplication();

    myUIApplication.show();
    myUIApplication.hide();

    UIApplicationDialog theUI = new
UIApplicationDialog(myUIApplication);
```

```
theUI.CreateControls();

myUIApplication.show();
//My code ends here


      }



    }
```

Looking at this code you can see that it is not a very big Java application.

Starting from the top notice that you are *import*ing the resource generated UIApplicationDialog to this class. Moving down to the main() method, you see that you are instancing the application UIApplication:

```
UIApplication myUIApplication = new UIApplication();
```

The following two lines of code may seem odd as to their purpose at this point:

```
myUIApplication.show();
myUIApplication.hide();
```

Basically you are displaying the frame and then immediately hiding it. The reason for this is that when you do this Java gathers information about the user's screen environment. This information is used by the resource generated UI class (i.e., UIApplicationDialog) and resource generated DialogLayout.

Tip

> *If you don't use the show()-hide() technique just mentioned, then the CreateControls() method will be unable to retrieve all the information about the user's screen and will cause a run-time error in your application.*

Following the show()-hide() method technique is the constructor for the resource generated UI class UIApplicationDialog:

```
UIApplicationDialog theUI = new
UIApplicationDialog(myUIApplication);
```

Notice that in the above line of code you are passing the instance of UIApplication called myUIApplication that lets you link the application with the resource generated UI. Remember, you can only pass a Java application that has relation to the Container class. In UIApplication's case, it extends the Frame class.

The next line of code calls the CreateControls() method, which takes care of all the displaying and viewing of the UI components for the Java application:

```
theUI.CreateControls();
```

Underneath the CreateControls() call is the show() method, which displays the application with its newly integrated UI.

The programming technique just discussed in the main() method is one that you can use over and over again to implement a resource generated UI into your Java application with minimal coding.

Tip

> *The programming technique described here can be used for the application half of a Java appletcation.*

Once you have made changes, click File | Save to save the source file; you are now ready to proceed to the last step of the process.

Can I Edit the Resource Wizard Generated Files?

Technically speaking yes; any files created by the Resource Wizard are 100 percent Java source. However, typically you do not edit resource generated files for two reasons.

First, any changes that you make directly to the resource generated Java source files will be overwritten if you run the Resource Wizard again.

Second, practically anything that you need to do can be done using the project's main class, leaving the automatically generated code virtually untouched. It is a good programming practice to have customizations in as few areas as possible.

Building & Executing the Project

At this point nothing should be new to you. All you need to do is build and execute the project.

To build the code, click on Build | Build UIApplication. Then, to execute the code, click on Build | Execute.

Since you are executing this project for the first time in the Developer Studio, a dialog box displays for you to specify the class filename (see Figure 8-19). On this dialog box, in the Class name field, type UIApplication. Also, underneath that you have a choice of using either the jview interpreter or Internet Explorer to view the results. For this example, choose Stand-alone interpreter. Then click OK.

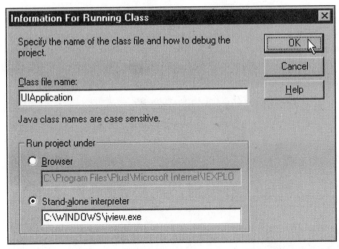

Figure 8-19: Information for Running Class dialog box filled out.

Once UIApplication executes you will see something similar to Figure 8-20.

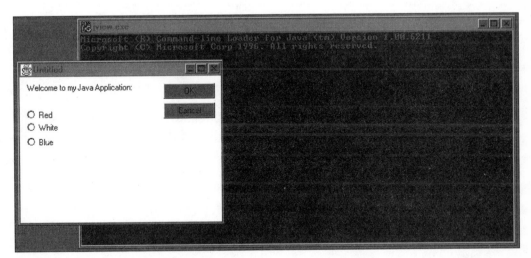

Figure 8-20: Executing UIApplication.

Looking at Figure 8-20 you can see that a DOS box opened with jview executing, and another frame opened with the UI you created—all without writing one line of code!

Note

If you click on the frame you may notice that nothing happens. This is because you do not have any code to handle the events. The next chapter covers event handling. For now, if you want to close the frame, give the DOS box focus and press Ctrl-C. JVIEW to stop execution.

Tutorial: Adding a Menu to Your Java Applications

In the last section you created a Java application and used the Dialog Resource Editor to design your UI. This section builds upon the last section, discussing how to use the Menu Resource Editor in the Developer Studio to visually design a menu for your Java applications. For this example, you are going to use the project UIApplication that you just created. The process for creating and adding a menu to your Java application follows the same steps you used to create and add a UI. Because we are reusing the UIApplication project, we can skip that step in the process.

Creating the Resource

Menu resources are just like Dialog resources—you can create them using the Menu Resource Editor and port them using the Java Resource Wizard or you can use existing menus that you may have lying around. In this example you will be creating a menu from scratch using the Menu Resource Editor.

To create the resource, click on Insert | Resource in the Developer Studio and the Insert Resource dialog box appears (see Figure 8-21).

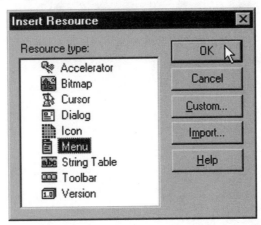

Figure 8-21: The Developer Studio with the Insert dialog box open.

In the Insert Resource dialog box, choose Menu and click OK. The Menu Resource Editor opens (see Figure 8-22), and you are now ready to create your menu as it will appear when you execute your Java application.

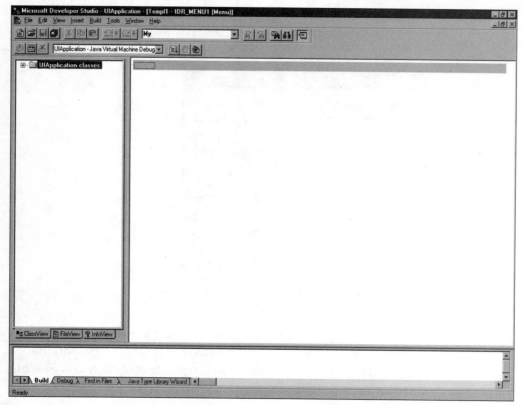

Figure 8-22: The Developer Studio with the Menu Resource Editor open.

Unlike the Dialog Resource Editor, the Menu Resource Editor does not have any toolboxes or status bars that make it hard to understand where to start. However, the first thing to recognize is the gray line in the Menu Resource Editor window on the right. This line actually represents the main menu bar where you can edit and add menus.

Taking a closer look at the menu bar you see a hashed gray square on the left-hand corner. Just like in the Dialog Resource Editor, this represents the object that currently has focus.

To add a menu to the menu bar, double click on that hashed gray square and display the Properties window. In the Caption field, type **File**. Now, notice what happens to the Developer Studio (see Figure 8-23).

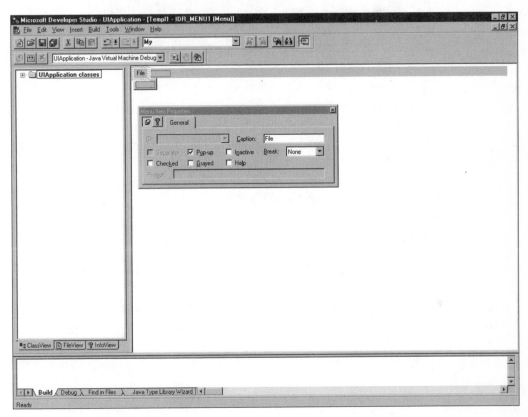

Figure 8-23: Adding the File menu.

As you can see, the File menu opened options for you to create menu items to populate the File menu and an outlined area to the right of File to create another menu.

To add a menu item, double-click on the File menu to display its Properties window. This automatically creates a menu item under the File menu (see Figure 8-24).

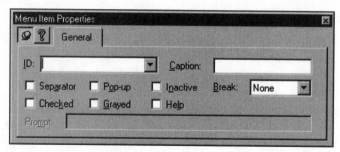

Figure 8-24: Properties window for menu items.

In the ID field, type **mySaveItem** and in the Caption field, type **Save**. Now, Save appears under the File menu.

If you want to add a separator to the menu, double-click on the File menu and check the Separator box. If you want to add a Checked menu, double-click on the File menu and select Checked. You'll create both of these shortly.

Note

Not all the functionality or properties available in the Menu Resource Editor will be available in Java. Like the dialog example described earlier, if the Resource Wizard does find a compatible Java implementation for a specified menu, that functionality will be ignored. For more information on Java supported menu functionality see Chapter 7.

Once you have made the above changes, the Developer Studio should look like Figure 8-25.

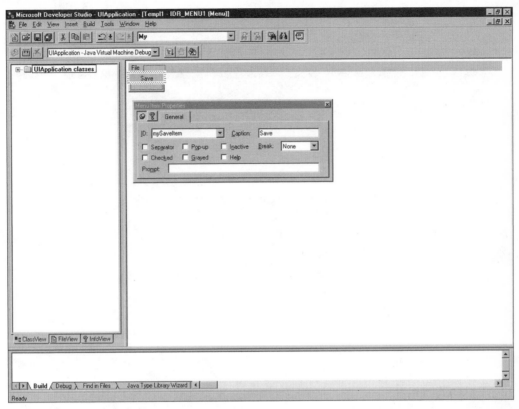

Figure 8-25: Adding the Save item to the File menu.

You have now added a menu item to the File menu. Use Table 8-8 to create the remaining menu items for the the File menu.

Control	Location	Action
File Menu	Properties dialog box (double-click to open)	In the ID field, type **mySaveAsItem** and in the Caption field, type **Save As**.
File Menu	Properties dialog box (double-click to open)	Check the Separator check box.
File Menu	Properties dialog box (double-click to open)	In the ID field, type **myRunItem** and in the Caption field, type **Run**.

Table 8-8: Menus for the File menu.

Figure 8-26 shows what your completely filled out File menu should look like.

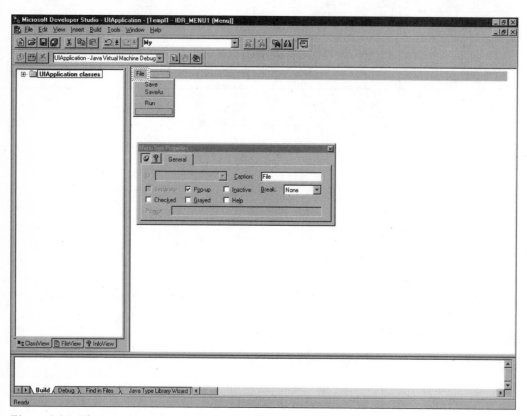

Figure 8-26: The complete File menu.

Note

You may have noticed that every time you add a menu or menu item, the Menu Resource Editor adds another blank outlined box to the end of the menu on the left of the menu bar. This is a design time feature that lets you automatically add items that will not show up outside of the Menu Resource Editor.

Use Table 8-9 to create the Edit menu on the right of the File menu you just built.

Control	Location	Action
Blank box on menu bar	Properties dialog box (double-click to open)	In the Caption field, type **Edit**.
Edit menu	Properties dialog box (double-click to open)	In the ID field, type **myFindItem** and in the Caption field, type **Find**.
Edit menu	Properties dialog box (double-click to open)	In the ID field, type **myReplaceItem** and in the Caption field, type **Replace**.
Edit menu	Properties dialog box (double-click to open)	Check the Separator check box.

Table 8-9: Menus for the Edit menu.

Figure 8-27 shows what your Edit menu should look like in the Developer Studio.

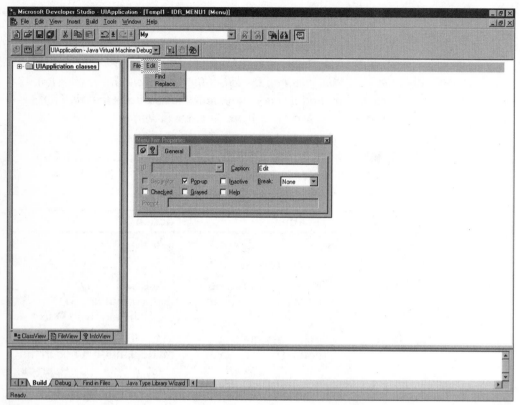

Figure 8-27: The complete Edit menu.

Finally, the last menu that you are going to add is the Options menu. However, you are going to create it as a submenu (or cascading menu as termed in the Menu Resource Editor) to the Edit menu. You do this by simply creating the menu as if it were a completely separate menu item like File and Edit. Then you drag and drop it to the menu you want to it become a submenu to (see Table 8-10).

Control	Location	Action
Blank box on menu bar	Properties dialog box (double-click to open)	In the Caption field, type **Options**.
Options menu	Properties dialog box (double-click to open)	In the ID field, type **myUndoItem** and in the Caption field, type **Undo**.
Options menu	Properties dialog box (double-click to open)	In the ID field, type **myRedoItem** and in the Caption field, type **Redo**.

Table 8-10: Menus for the Options menu.

Figure 8-28 shows what the Options menu should look like in the Developer Studio.

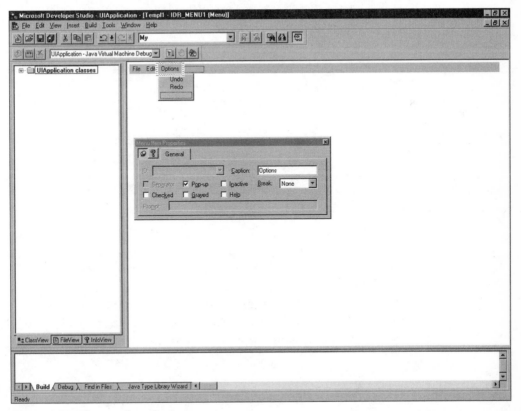

Figure 8-28: The complete Options menu.

Now drag the Options menu over to the end of the Edit menu (underneath the separator) and it will become a submenu to the Edit menu (see Figure 8-29).

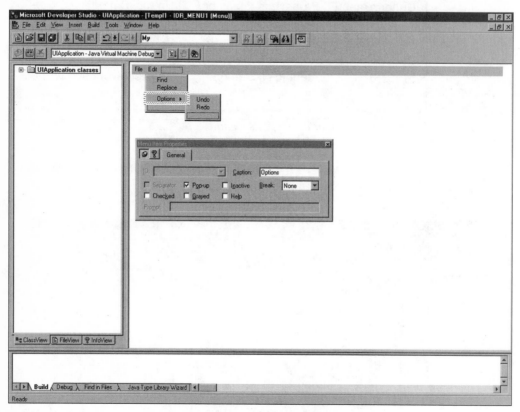

Figure 8-29: Creating a submenu (cascading) out of Options.

Finally, the last thing is to edit the actual menu bar. So, double-click somewhere on the menu bar to open its Properties window. In the ID field, type **UIApplicationMenu**.

At this point you have finished building the menu, so your next step is to close the Dialog Resource Editor by clicking File | Close. A dialog box opens asking if you want to save changes; click Yes and a Save As dialog box opens. Save the resource template you just created in the same directory that you put the UIApplication project. For this example that is the ..\msdev\projects\UIApplication directory, and save the file as UIApplicationMenu.rct (see Figure 8-30).

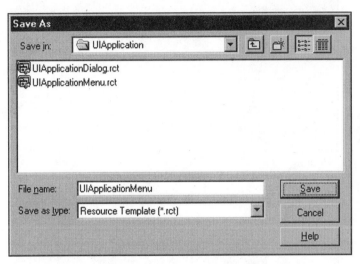

Figure 8-30: Saving the Dialog Resource Template.

Once you've saved the template UIApplicationMenu, the Developer Studio closes the Dialog Resource Editor. You are now ready to move to the next step and port the resource template to Java source code, using the Java Resource Wizard.

Note

For more information on using the Menu Resource Editor, check InfoView in the Developer Studio.

Porting the Resource to Java

In the last section, you created a Menu Resource Template for the project UIApplication. Now you are ready to port it to Java. Use Table 8-11 to port UIApplicationMenu to Java source.

Step #	Location	Action
1	Developer Studio	Choose Tools|Java Resource Wizard.
2	Resource Wizard, step 1	File name field: C:\msdev\projects\ UIApplication\UIApplica- tionMenu.rct. Or use Browse. Then click Next (see Figure 8-31).
3	Resource Wizard, step 2	Verify that the class name and resource name are correct. Then click Finish (see Figure 8-32).
4	Confirmation dialog box	Verify the Java classes and locations are correct. Then click OK (see Figure 8-33).

Table 8-11: Using the Java Resource Wizard.

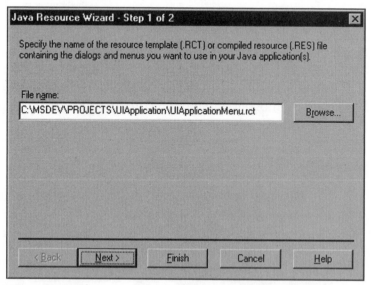

Figure 8-31: The Java Resource Wizard Step 1 of 2.

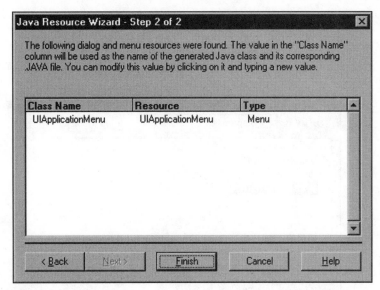

Figure 8-32: The Java Resource Wizard Step 2 of 2.

Figure 8-33: The Java Resource Wizard Confirmation dialog box.

Adding the Files to the Project

At this point you need to add the newly created source files to the project UIApplication.

Make sure the UIApplication project is open, then click on Insert I Files into Project. The Files into Project dialog box opens (see Figure 8-34).

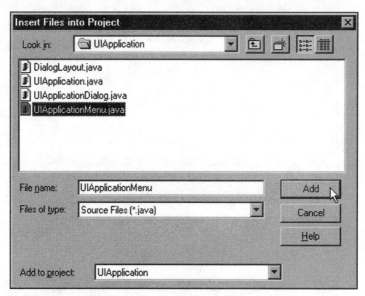

Figure 8-34: The Files into Project dialog box.

In the Files into Project dialog box, highlight UIApplicationMenu.java and click Add to continue. The file is added to the project.

Implementing the Menu in the Application's Source Code

The final step before building and executing the project UIApplication with its newly created menu is to edit the source code in the main() method of the project.

Integrating the Resource Generated Menu

Resource generated menus are very similar to those of dialogs. There are two key points that deal specifically with how the Java Resource Wizard constructs menus.

First, there is a menu constructor that takes any frame object. By passing to it the current frame for the application, the menu is automatically linked to that frame.

Second, once you have constructed an instance of the Menu class created by the Java Resource Wizard, you then need to call the CreateMenu() method. The CreateMenu() method is responsible for actually constructing your menu.

Once you have completed these two tasks, you have successfully implemented the menu for any specified frame in your Java application.

With the Developer Studio open for editing, reopen the UIApplication class and add the bolded code:

```java
import java.awt.Frame;

//My code starts here
import UIApplicationDialog;
//My code ends here

//My secondary code starts here
import UIApplicationMenu;
//My secondary code ends here
/*
 *
 * UIApplication
 *
 */
public class UIApplication extends Frame
{

    public static void main(String args[])
```

```
{

    //My code starts here
    UIApplication myUIApplication = new UIApplication();

    myUIApplication.show();
    myUIApplication.hide();

    UIApplicationDialog theUI = new
UIApplicationDialog(myUIApplication);
    theUI.CreateControls();

    //My secondary code starts here
    UIApplicationMenu theMenu = new
UIApplicationMenu(myUIApplication);
    theMenu.CreateMenu();
    //My secondary code ends here

    myUIApplication.show();
    //My code ends here


}

}
```

Let's take a closer look at the code you added.

There were only three lines of code that you added to integrate a resource generated menu into the Java application UIApplication.

First, you imported the Menu class UIApplication Menu to the UIApplication class:

```
import UIApplicationMenu;
```

Then you instanced the Menu class, passing myUIApplication:

```
    UIApplicationMenu theMenu = new
UIApplicationMenu(myUIApplication);
```

You can pass an instance of UIApplication to UIApplicationMenu because it extends from the Frame class. Finally, you call the CreateMenu() method:

```
theMenu.CreateMenu();
```

You have just been introduced to a programming technique that you can use over and over again to implement a Menu resource into your Java application with minimal coding.

Once you have made changes, click File I Save to save the source file; you are now ready to proceed to the last step of the process.

Building & Executing the Project

At this point you are ready to build the UIApplication project again, this time it will contain a UI and a menu.

To build the code, click on Build I Build UIApplication. Then, to execute the code, click on Build I Execute.

Because you have already executed this project, it automatically displays the results using the Stand-alone interpreter that you specified initially. Once executed, you should see something similar to Figure 8-35.

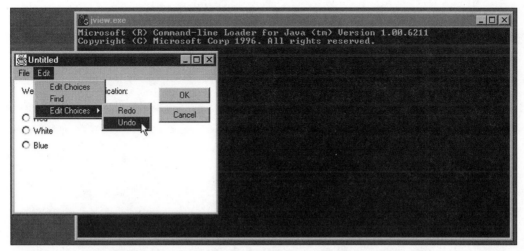

Figure 8-35: Executing UIApplication with a UI and newly created menu.

Looking at Figure 8-35 you can see that a DOS box opened and jview is executing. Another frame opened with the menu you added to the UI—both of which were created without writing one line of code!

Tutorial: Developing a UI for a Java Applet

At this juncture you are going to learn one more Visual J++ programming technique that will let you use the AppletWizard and Resource Wizard together to create one project with the least amount of coding. When you create the project, you use the AppletWizard, which is the only change to the process we have followed to create UIs for Java applications.

Creating the Project Using the AppletWizard

Go to the Developer Studio and use the following table to create the project UIApplet (see Table 8-12 for step-by-step instructions).

Step #	Location	Action
1	Developer Studio	Choose File|New.
2	New dialog box	Highlight Project Workspace and click OK.
3	New Project Work-space dialog box	Highlight JavaAppletWizard. Then, in the Name field, type **UIApplet** and click Create.
4	AppletWizard, step 1	Click Next.
5	AppletWizard, step 2	Click Next.
6	AppletWizard, step 3	For the "Would you like your applet to be multi-threaded?" question, click No, thank you. Then, click Next.
7	AppletWizard, step 4	Click Next.
8	AppletWizard, step 5	Type applet information, then click Finish.
9	New Project Information dialog box	Verify the information is correct (see Figure 8-36), then click OK.

Table 8-12: Creating a UIApplet using the AppletWizard.

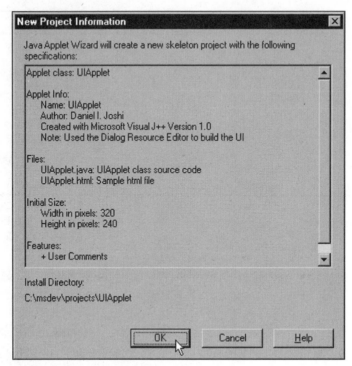

Figure 8-36: The New Project Information dialog box for project UIApplet.

Once the project UIApplet is created with the UIApplet source, you can create and insert the resources to the applet.

Creating the Resource

Now you are ready to create the Dialog you want to use for your Java applet. To create the resource, in the Developer Studio, click on Insert | Resource and the Insert Resource dialog box displays (see Figure 8-37).

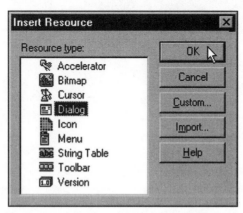

Figure 8-37: The Insert Resource dialog box.

Choose the item Dialog and click OK. The Dialog Resource Editor opens and you are now ready to create your UI as it will appear when you execute your Java application (see Figure 8-38).

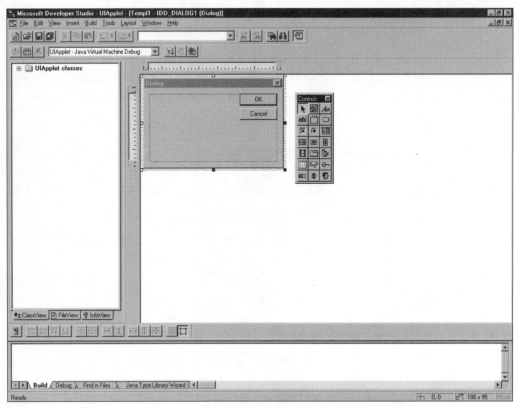

Figure 8-38: The Developer Studio with the Dialog Resource Editor open.

At this point let's finish adding and editing controls to the UIApplet project to complete the Dialog that you are going to use as your UI for the UIApplet project. Use Table 8-13 to add a Static Text Control to this Dialog.

Control	Location	Action
Static Text	Properties dialog box, General Tab	In the ID field, type **myTitleLabel** and in the Caption field, type **Welcome to my Applet**.
Static Text	Dialog Resource Editor, with the aid of the Position Indicators	Move the control to the X,Y coordinates 7,7; resize the control to the H x W ratio of 112 x 13.

Table 8-13: Adding a Static Text Control to UIApplet Dialog.

Figure 8-39 shows the static text drawn on the Dialog.

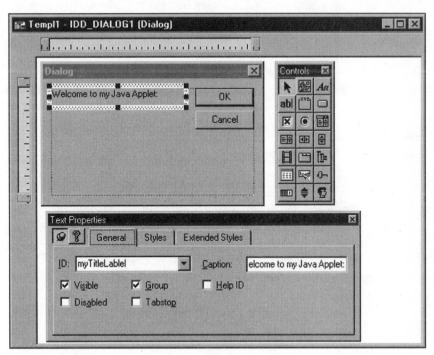

Figure 8-39: Static text added to the Dialog.

Now use Table 8-14 to add a set of check boxes to this dialog .

Control	Location	Action
Check Box #1	Properties dialog box, General Tab	In the ID field, type **myFirstCheck** and in the Caption field, type **One**.
Check Box #1	Dialog Resource Editor, with the aid of the Position Indicators	Move the control to the X,Y coordinates 7,30; resize the control to the H x W ratio of 35 x 10.
Check Box #2	Properties dialog box, General Tab	In the ID field, type **mySecondCheck** and in the Caption field, type **Two**.
Check Box #2	Dialog Resource Editor, with the aid of the Position Indicators	Move the control to the X,Y coordinates 7,40; resize the control to the H x W ratio of 35 x 10.
Check Box #3	Properties dialog, General Tab	In the ID field, type **myThirdCheck** and in the Caption field, type **Three**.
Check Box #3	Dialog Resource Editor, with the aid of the Position Indicators	Move the control to the X,Y coordinates 7,50; resize the control to the H x W ratio of 35 x 10.

Table 8-14: Adding Check Box Controls for UIApplet.

Figure 8-40 shows what the above Check Box Buttons should look like in the Dialog Resource Editor.

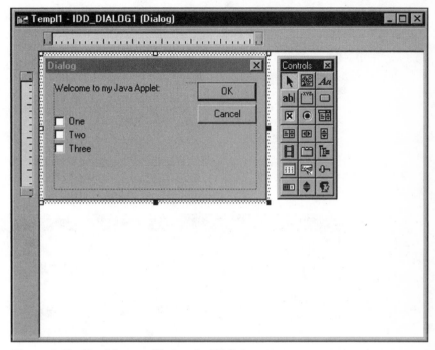

Figure 8-40: Check boxes added to the Dialog.

The last control (a.k.a. component) you are going to add is a Combo box. Use Table 8-15 to add this final control.

Control	Location	Action
Combo box	Properties dialog box, General Tab	In the ID field, type **myNumbersChoice**.
Combo box	Properties dialog box, General Tab	In the Enter listbox, add the items: One, Two, and Three.
Combo box	Dialog Resource Editor, with the aid of the Position Indicators	Move the control to the X,Y coordinates 55,35; Resize the control to the H x W ratio of 60 x 10.

Table 8-15: Adding static text to UIApplet Dialog.

Figure 8-41 shows what the Dialog should look like after adding the Combo box.

Tip

If you are having trouble putting items on their own line in the Enter listbox items text area, press Ctrl+Enter to move to the next line.

Table 8-16 shows the changes you need to make to the properties for the Dialog.

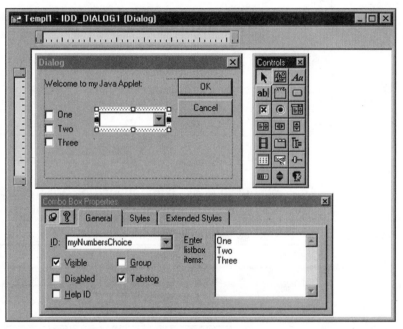

Figure 8-41: Combo box added to the Dialog.

Control	Location	Action
Dialog	Properties dialog box, General Tab	In the ID field, type **UIAppletDialog** and in the Caption field, type **UIAppletPane**.
Dialog	Dialog Resource Editor, with the aid of the Position Indicators	Move the control to the X,Y coordinates 0,0; resize the control to the H x W ratio of 200 x 130.

Table 8-16: Editing properties for the Dialog.

Figure 8-42 shows what the Dialog Resource Editor looks like with the Properties window open.

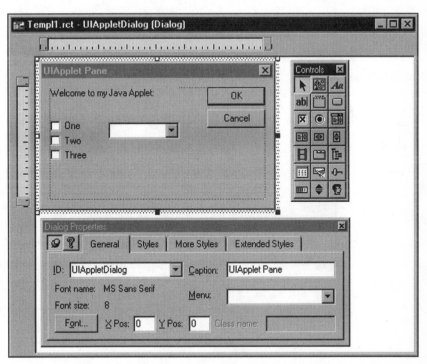

Figure 8-42: The Dialog with its Properties window open in the Dialog Resource Editor.

At this point you are finished building the Dialog step so your next is to close the Dialog Resource Editor by clicking File | Close. A dialog box asks if you want to save changes; click Yes and a Save As dialog box opens. Save the resource template you just created in the same directory that you put the UIApplet project. For this example that is the ..\msdev\projects\UIApplet directory, and the file should be saved as UIAppletDialog.rct.

Porting the Resource to Java

In the last step you created a resource template for the project UIApplet. Now you need to port the resource template to Java using the Java Resource Wizard. Use Table 8-17 to port UIAppletDialog to Java source.

Control	Location	Action
1	Developer Studio	Choose Tools|Java Resource Wizard.
2	Resource Wizard, step 1	File name field: 'C:\msdev\projects\ UIApplication\UIAppletDialog.rct'. Or use Browse. Then click Next. (see Figure 8-43).
3	Resource Wizard, step 2	Verify that the class name and resource name are correct. Then click Finish (see Figure 8-44).
4	Confirmation dialog box	Verify the Java classes and locations are correct. Then click OK (see Figure 8-45).

Table 8-17: Using the Java Resource Wizard.

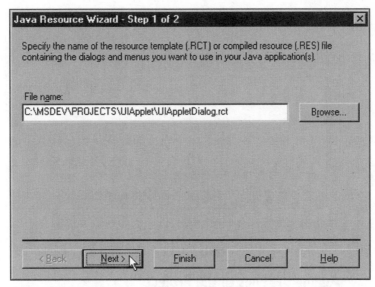

Figure 8-43: The Java Resource Wizard Step 1 of 2.

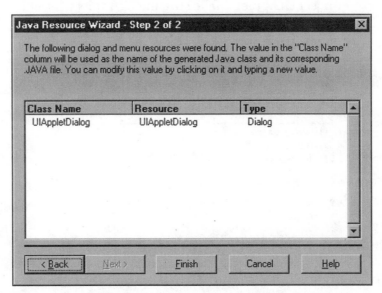

Figure 8-44: The Java Resource Wizard Step 2 of 2.

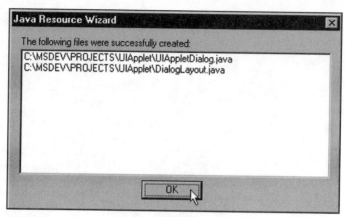

Figure 8-45: The Java Resource Wizard confirmation dialog box.

Adding the Files to the Project

At this point, you need to add the newly created source files to the project UIApplet. Make sure the UIApplet project is open, then click on Insert I Files into Project. The Files into Project dialog box opens (see Figure 8-46).

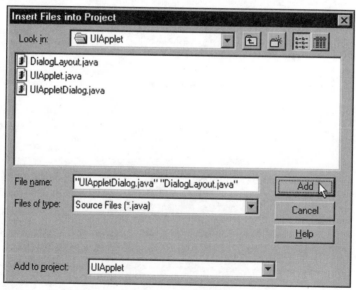

Figure 8-46: The Files into Project dialog box.

In the Files into Project dialog box, highlight UIAppletDialog.java and DialogLayout.java files and click Add to continue. The files are added to the project.

Tip

You can check the files that belong to a project by going to File | View and expanding the folder at the top.

Implementing the UI in the Applet's Source Code

It is at this stage of the process that you are ready to edit your applet's source code to integrate the UI you created and ported to Java. Now, because applets use life-cycle methods as opposed to one main() method, this step is different from what you learned when you tried this example for applications. Essentially you are going to use a specific technique to the init() method of the applet that will do the whole job.

Integrating a resource generated UI to a Java applet is very similar to the method discussed for Java applications.

The two important things to note are that all your UI integration code goes in the init() method of the applet. Secondly, you pass a *this* reference for the constructor of the resource generated UI class to link the UI to the applet. This is possible because all applets extend the Applet class which has roots to the Container object.

With the Developer Studio open for editing, reopen the UIApplet class and add the bolded code:

```
//
*********************************************************************************
// UIApplet.java:   Applet
//
//
*********************************************************************************
import java.applet.*;
import java.awt.*;
```

```
//My code starts here
import UIAppletDialog;
//My code ends here


//==========================================================
// Main Class for applet UIApplet
//
//==========================================================
public class UIApplet extends Applet
{

    //My code starts here
    UIAppletDialog theUI;
    //My code ends here

    // UIApplet Class Constructor
    //----------------------------------------------------------
    public UIApplet()
    {
        // TODO: Add constructor code here
    }


    // APPLET INFO SUPPORT:
    //    The getAppletInfo() method returns a string describing
the applet's
    // author, copyright date, or miscellaneous information.
      //----------------------------------------------------------
    public String getAppletInfo()
    {
        return "Name: UIApplet\r\n" +
               "Author: Daniel I. Joshi\r\n" +
               "Created with Microsoft Visual J++ Version
1.0\r\n" +
               "Note: Used the Dialog Resource Editor to build
the UI";
    }
```

```
    // The init() method is called by the AWT when an applet is
first loaded or
    // reloaded.  Override this method to perform whatever
initialization your
    // applet needs, such as initializing data structures,
loading images or
    // fonts, creating frame windows, setting the layout
manager, or adding UI
    // components.
    //---------------------------------------------------------
    public void init()
    {
        // If you use a ResourceWizard-generated "control
creator" class to
        // arrange controls in your applet, you may want to
call its
        // CreateControls() method from within this method.
Remove the following
        // call to resize() before adding the call to
CreateControls();
        // CreateControls() does its own resizing.
        //-----------------------------------------------------

    //My code starts here
    theUI = new UIAppletDialog(this);
    theUI.CreateControls();

    //resize(320, 240);
    //My code ends here

        // TODO: Place additional initialization code here
    }

    // Place additional applet clean up code here.  destroy()
is called when
    // when you applet is terminating and being unloaded.
    //---------------------------------------------------------
    public void destroy()
    {
```

```
    // TODO: Place applet cleanup code here
}


// UIApplet Paint Handler
//------------------------------------------------------------
public void paint(Graphics g)
{

    //My code starts here
    //g.drawString("Created with Microsoft Visual J++
Version 1.0", 10, 20);
    //My code ends here


}


//   The start() method is called when the page containing
the applet
// first appears on the screen. The AppletWizard's initial
implementation
// of this method starts execution of the applet's thread.
//------------------------------------------------------------
public void start()
{
    // TODO: Place additional applet start code here
}


//   The stop() method is called when the page containing
the applet is
// no longer on the screen. The AppletWizard's initial
implementation of
// this method stops execution of the applet's thread.
//------------------------------------------------------------
public void stop()
{
}


    // TODO: Place additional applet code here


}
```

Looking at the above code, notice that this analysis only focuses on the code you added or edited.

The first snippet of code you added imports the resource generated UI class UIAppletDialog you created using the Java Resource Wizard:

```
import UIAppletDialog;
```

Then under the class declaration for the applet, declare theUI as follows:

```
UIAppletDialog theUI;
```

By doing the above, you are making theUI available to the entire applet—this comes in handy for event handling, which we'll discuss in the next chapter. Then go down to the init() method, instance the resource generated class UIAppletDialog by passing a *this* reference; underneath that is a call to the CreateControls() method:

```
theUI = new UIAppletDialog(this);
theUI.CreateControls();
```

The line of code following the CreateControls() method call is to comment out the resize() call as the CreateControls() method handles any reissuing for the applet :

```
//resize(320, 240);
```

Finally, the last addition you need to make is to comment out the drawString() call in the paint() method:

```
//g.drawString("Created with Microsoft Visual J++
Version 1.0", 10, 20);
```

Not commenting out the above code will cause the statement "Created with Microsoft Visual J++ Version 1.0" to appear in the middle of your UI.

The above analysis is a programming technique that you can use over and over again to implement a resource generated UI into your Java application with minimal coding.

Once you have made changes, click File I Save to save the source file and you are ready to proceed to the last step of the process.

Building & Executing the Project

At this point nothing should be new to you—all that you need to do is build and execute the project.

To build the code, click on Build | Build UIApplication. Then, to execute the code, click on Build | Execute.

Since this is an Applet created by the AppletWizard, Internet Explorer automatically opens a test HTML file and loads the applet UIApplet (see Figure 8-47).

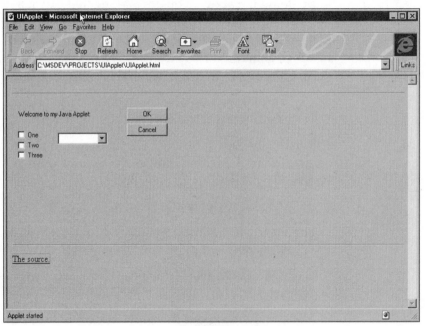

Figure 8-47: Internet Explorer with UIApplet.

Looking at Figure 8-47 you will see the UI you created in the Dialog Resource Editor embedded into your applet.

Tip

If you have not already noticed, the link at the bottom of the page labeled "The source" is a link that you can use to access the source code of the applet being displayed

Tip

The Combo box may not be functional at this point because it may have lost some functionality through the Java Resource Wizard. Always test your UIs to make sure they ported properly with the Java Resource Wizard.

Moving On

In the last chapter you learned how to create user interfaces using the AWT package in the Java class library. In this chapter you learned how to take advantage of Visual J++, resource editors, and the Java Resource Wizard to automatically generate a Java UI. You also learned about several important techniques that you can employ over and over again to efficiently integrate a resource into your Java programs.

However, a topic that has only been mentioned in the last two chapters is the idea of event handling. As you may have noticed in the examples included in this chapter, if you click on a button, nothing happens. That is because you need to add event handling code on the back end to capture those button clicks. Chapter 9 introduces event handling and shows it in several real-world examples.

9

Event Handling

For the last two chapters you have spent a great deal of time learning the Java and Visual J++ aspects of how to create a Java User Interface (UI). However, without inherent functionality on the back end, a UI is worthless. That is why there is event handling. In this chapter, you learn how to use event handling to have a user's mouse click fire code in your Java program, for instance.

You can use several different programming techniques to handle events. Java is an event-driven programming language, meaning that it is reactionary in respect to its environment. Thus, when a user presses a key on the keyboard, an action is processed by the operating system (OS) and sent to the program that currently has focus. Then, based on the programming of that application (or applet), it responds accordingly.

How Java Handles Events

Event driven programming means that your Java program remains idle until an "outside source" sends it a message as an event. This event is then passed to your program where it is processed.

Defining Outside Source

Obviously, the most common outside source responsible for events is based on user input via a keyboard or mouse. However, in the event-driven programming model, your programs can be responsive to other types of events, such as those generated by the system kernel or by another Java program.

Specifically, Java handles events using the Abstract Window Toolkit (AWT). The AWT receives an event, passes it into an instance of the java.awt.Event class and the AWT gives it a specific id (using the variable Event.id which is discussed in more detail later in the chapter). This id helps distinguish this event from other events in the AWT. It also describes the type of event.

Thus, the AWT turns an event into an object in Java. Now that the passed event is an object, it is passed around to various components in the UI until it finds the responsible UI component.

Figure 9-1 shows a simple diagram of how this works.

Note

Events in Java are similar to messages in Windows and other OSes.

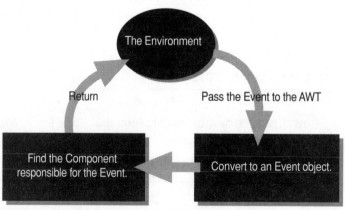

Figure 9-1: Diagram of event handling.

How the AWT Handles Events

java.awt.Component is the class that contains practically all of the methods used by the AWT. Remember, this abstract class is the superclass to every single AWT component and container (excluding the Menu-related classes that use a MenuComponent abstract class similar to the Component class). Thus, containers or the components contained in containers have the inherited functionality to handle events. How does this work? Let's take a more detailed look at how event handling works.

So far, you know that when an event is passed to Java it goes to the AWT and is converted into an instance of the java.awt.Event. At this point, it is up to the AWT containers and components to pass this event to the proper component. The component responsible can either handle the event or pass it to another component object that will. All event management is done using the following three methods, all of which are part of the java.awt.Component class:

- **deliverEvent()**   Passes an event to a component or a sub-component.

- **postEvent()**   Calls handleEvent() for the component. If handleEvent() returns false, the event is passed to the component's parent, and the parent's postEvent() is called. This cycle of postEvent()-handleEvent() continues until the event is handled.

- **handleEvent()**   This method is responsible for handling an event that belongs to a particular component. It can either handle it and tell the AWT that no further action is necessary (by returning true), or it can return false and pass the event on to its parent.

The handleEvent() Method

Based on the id of the event passed to handleEvent(), the handleEvent() method may call one of the following supporting methods that the Event class derived from the Component class: action(), gotFocus(), lostFocus(), keyDown(), keyUp(), mouseEnter(), mouseExit(), mouseMove(), mouseDrag(), mouseDown(), and mouseUp(). You will learn more about these methods later in the chapter.

The diagram in Figure 9-2 shows an example of a hierarchy of components.

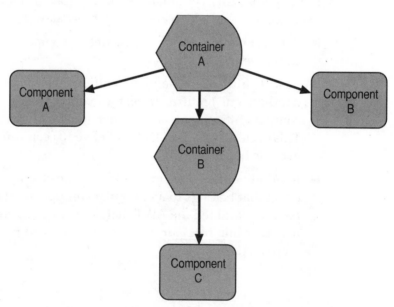

Figure 9-2: Diagram of a component hierarchy for a UI.

Notice that the containers could represent a Frame, Panel, or any other class extending from the java.awt.Container. Components can be anything from a button to a text area. Now imagine that a user clicks on component C, thus causing an event to be passed to it. Figure 9-3 shows a diagram of the event being passed to component C.

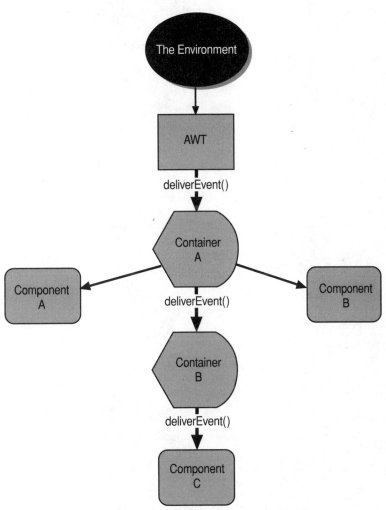

Figure 9-3: Passing the event to the corresponding component.

However, for this type of event, you want container B to handle it. So, you have component C's handleEvent() return a false, and thus pass the event up to its parent. Figure 9-4 shows a diagram of the event now traversing back up to container B.

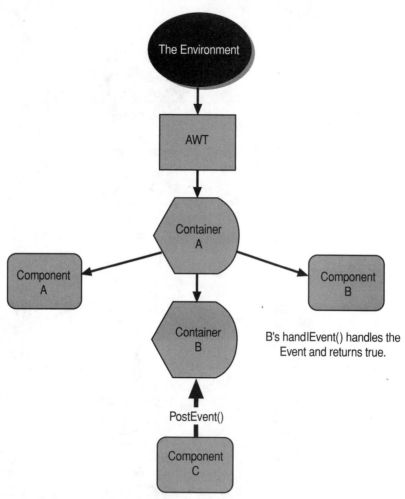

B's handlEvent() handles the Event and returns true.

Figure 9-4: The event being passed back up to container B where it gets handled.

It is not until container B's handleEvent() returns true that the event actually gets handled. At this point, the event has been handled. Thus, you have seen the process that AWT uses to handle events.

Event Handling Techniques

The core level of event handling involves overriding methods from the Component class. You can override the handleEvent() directly or you can override the methods that handleEvent() calls.

Tip

Both of these techniques are useful. However, overriding handleEvent() does have more versatility because it is able to test for a broader spectrum of events. In the end, however, deciding what technique to use depends on the type of event handling you want to do.

The handleEvent() Technique

Overriding the handleEvent() in your Java programs is simple. Consider the following:

```
class Test extends Component{
  //Body of Class
  public boolean handleEvent(Event evt) {
    switch (evt.id)
    {
  case evevt1:
    // handle event1
    return true;
  case evevt2:
    // handle event2
    return true;
  default:
    return super.handleEvent(evt);
    }
  }
}
```

Do the following things inside your overridden handleEvent():

1. Remember that an Event instance contains an id about the event. Technically speaking, id is an integer variable of the Event class. This id contains what type of event it is. In your handleEvent(), the first thing that you need to do is check to see what type of event is using the id.

2. Once you determine if this event is the right one, you can include code that actually performs the event handling. Alternatively, you can create a separate method and only include a call to that method inside your overridden handleEvent().

3. The last step is to call the method handleEvent() of base class, which returns a boolean value. If the handleEvent() finds an event and handles it, then let the AWT know that the event has been handled. However, if the event passed to your handleEvent() is not handled—because it is not the event you or your based class are looking for—then you want to return false. The reason there are quotation marks around false is because in your overridden handleEvent(), you usually do not want to return false. Instead, you want to use a reference to the parent class's handleEvent().

Tutorial: Overriding the handleEvent() Method

As you may have noticed in working with frames earlier, you can not close a frame by traditional windows methods. This example shows you how to write event handling code so that you can close your frames by traditional Windows means.

First, create a project workspace called EventTest (see Table 9-1 for the procedure).

Step #	Location	Action
1	Developer Studio	Choose File|New.
2	New dialog box	Highlight Project Workspace and click OK.
3	New Project Workspace dialog box	In the Name field, type **EventTest** and click Create.

Table 9-1: Creating the EventTest Project Workspace.

Tip

Remember that you are creating a Java application, so do not use the Java AppletWizard.

Now, you need to create a new Java class called EventTest. In the Developer Studio, click Insert | New Java Class. On the Create New Class dialog box, do the following:

1. In the Name field, type **EventTest**.

2. In the Extends field, type **Frame**.

3. In the Modifiers area, choose Public.

Then, click OK (see Figure 9-5).

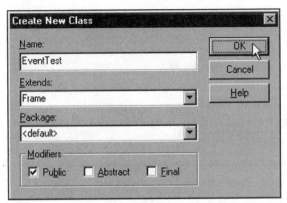

Figure 9-5: The Create New Class dialog box filled in.

Let's start by creating our first public method called main() (see Table 9-2 for step-by-step instructions).

Step #	Location	Action
1	Left pane of EventTest Project Workspace	On the EventTest class, right-click and choose Add Method from the menu.
2	New Method dialog box	In the Return type field type **void** and in the Method declaration field type **main(String argv[])**.
3	New Method dialog box	In the Access box, choose Public. In the Modifiers area, choose Static.
4	New Method dialog box	Verify how the declaration looks then click OK.

Table 9-2: Creating the main() method.

Now you need to add the method handleEvent() to the project. See Table 9-3 for step-by-step instructions.

Step #	Location	Action
1	Left pane of EventTest Project Workspace	On the EventTest class, right-click and choose Add Method from the menu.
2	New Method dialog box	In the Return type field, type **boolean**. In the Method declaration field, type **handleEvent(Event evt)**.
3	New Method dialog box	In the Access box, choose Public.
4	New Method dialog box	Verify how the declaration looks, then click OK.

Table 9-3: Creating the handleEvent() method.

At this point, the Developer Studio automatically opens the class EventTest for editing. Edit it so that it looks like the following. Remember that the bolded code is material you need to add and the regular code listed below is code automatically generated by Visual J++:

```
import java.awt.Frame;

//My code starts here
import java.awt.*;
//My code ends here

/*
 *
 * EventTest
 *
 */
public class EventTest extends Frame
{

    public boolean handleEvent(Event evt)
    {
        //My code starts here
        if (evt.id == Event.WINDOW_DESTROY) {
            System.exit(0);
            return true;
        }

         return super.handleEvent(evt);
        //My code ends here

    }


    public static void main(String args[])
    {

        //My code starts here
        Frame myEventTest = new EventTest();
        myEventTest.resize(300, 300);
```

```
myEventTest.show();
//My code ends here


    }


}
```

Let's start from the top. First, you have Visual J++ importing java.awt.Frame. However, you need to access other AWT classes, including java.awt.Event, so you add the code to import the entire AWT package.

Notice that in the class declaration you are extending from class Frame. Underneath the declaration is the actual handleEvent() method.

Tip

Notice in the above code that handleEvent() is a public boolean method that takes the java.awt.Event class as a parameter. Remember that based on the rules of method overriding, if you do not override it exactly as shown, then you are not actually overriding the handleEvent() method.

Let's take a closer look at the handleEvent() method. Starting with the if statement:

```
if (evt.id == Event.WINDOW_DESTROY) {
    System.exit(0);
    return true;
}
```

The above snippet tests the evt.id (i.e., the event passed to the handleEvent() method) to see if its id is Event.WINDOW_DESTROY. This means that the user, or the system kernel, has created an event to close down the window. Later in the chapter you will be introduced to all of the major Event constants. If this if statement is true, then you call the method exit() from the System class passing 0 (meaning the program has finished executing without any errors). Then you leave the handleEvent() method returning true, letting the AWT know that this event has been handled. On the other hand, if the if statement is not true, then you return a super reference to the handleEvent() of base class.

```
return super.handleEvent(evt);
```

What you are doing is calling the handleEvent() of EventTest's base class Frame, which is passing it the event. This is better than just returning false because it gives the base class' handleEvent() a chance to handle the event.

Finally, the last part of the Java application contains a main() method instancing EventTest and displaying it on the screen.

Now you are ready to save and build your code. To build the code, click on Build | Build EventTest. Then, to execute the code, click on Build | Execute.

Since you are executing this project for the first time in the Developer Studio, a dialog box displays for you to specify the class filename (see Figure 9-6). On this dialog box, in the Class name field, type **EventTest**. Also, underneath that you have a choice of using either the jview interpreter or Internet Explorer to view the results. For this example, choose Stand-alone interpreter. Then, click OK.

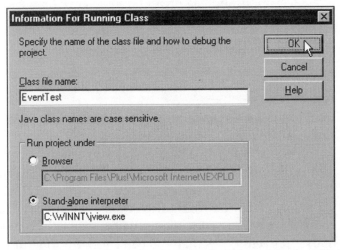

Figure 9-6: The Information For Running Class dialog box filled out.

Once the project is executed, you should see something similar to Figure 9-7.

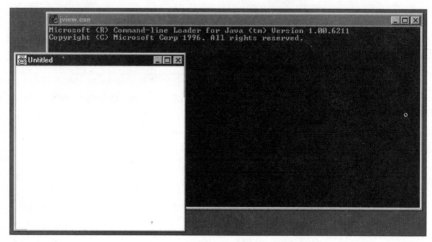

Figure 9-7: Executing EventTest.

While the above EventTest frame has focus, press Alt-F4 as you would with any other window, and the Java application closes. Reload the application and this time click on the X icon on the upper right corner of the frame to close the application. Finally, reload the EventTest application again and double-click on the system menu icon (appearing as a coffee cup for Java applets in Windows 95) on the upper right corner of the frame, and the application closes.

Event Types

Each of the above procedures were passed to the AWT, which is eventually passed to your overridden handleEvent() with the id Event.WINDOW_DESTROY. So, as you can see, even though you may only be testing for one type of event, several forms of user input can be handled. Furthermore, if you tried to close any of the frames in the earlier examples, nothing would have happened, because there was no code to handle the event. Table 9-4 shows a list of useful Event types that you can check for in your overridden handleEvent().

Event.WINDOW_DESTORY	Event.KEY_ACTION
Event.WINDOW_EXPOSE	Event.KEY_ACTION_RELEASE
Event.WINDOW_ICONIFY	Sub-Title: Action Events
Event.WINDOW_DEICONIFY	Event.ACTION_EVENT
Event.WINDOW_MOVED	Event.LOAD_FILE
Sub-Title: Mouse Events	Event.SAVE_FILE
Event.MOUSE_DOWN	Event.GOT_FOCUS
Event.MOUSE_UP	Event.LOST_FOCUS
Event.MOUSE_MOVE	Sub-Title: Scrollbar Events
Event.MOUSE_ENTER	Event.SCROLL_LINE_UP
Event.MOUSE_EXIT	Event.SCROLL_LINE_DOWN
Event.MOUSE_DRAG	Event.SCROLL_PAGE_UP
Sub-Title: Keyboard Events	Event.SCROLL_PAGE_DOWN
Event.KEY_PRESS	Event.SCROLL_ABSOLUTE
Event.KEY_RELEASE	

Table 9-4: Event types, Window events (partial list).

If you have not processed the event in your id handleEvent() method, instead passing it to super.handleEvent(), it will automatically call an appropriate supporting method (e.g., Event.GOT_FOCUS would automatically invoke the gotFocus() supporting method). This brings us to the second technique that in essence, lets you leave handleEvent() alone and override the supporting method instead.

The Supporting Method Technique

Overriding the supporting methods of the handleEvent() method is also very easy. Furthermore, these methods are automatically called when an appropriate event is passed.

You need to override the methods for mouse interactions, keyboard interactions, and other user interface actions, such as clicking a button or checking a check box.

Mouse Interaction

With the graphical user interfaces of today, handling mouse interactions is a big part of programming. Table 9-5 shows the mouse interaction methods that you need to override.

Note

All supporting methods return a boolean to tell the AWT if the event has been handled successfully. Secondly, the x- and y- integers are coordinates representing the current location of the mouse pointer.

mouseUp(Event evt, int x, int y)

mouseDown(Event evt, int x, int y)

mouseDrag(Event evt, int x, int y)

mouseMove(Event evt, int x, int y)

mouseEnter(Event evt, int x, int y)

mouseExit(Event evt, int x, int y)

Table 9-5: Supporting mouse-related methods.

Detecting Mouse Buttons in Java

No matter what operating system (OS) you are using, Java can only detect a mouse click as a mouse click (not distinguishing between a left, middle, or right mouse click), because not all OSs support multiple mouse buttons. More than likely, the next version of Java will make improvements to this.

Inside the mouse-related methods you can use the integer evt.clickCount member, indicating the number of consecutive clicks (1 for single-clicks, 2 for double-clicks, and so on).

Tutorial: Overriding Mouse Events

One of the features of the AppletWizard is that you can have it generate the framework code to override supporting mouse events. Essentially, you create an applet that changes its background color from white to green and vice versa. This color change takes place whenever you click on the applet pane. Let's create the real-world applet MouseTest.

Use the Applet Wizard to create a JavaApplet called MouseTest (see Table 9-6 for step-by-step instructions).

Step #	Location	Action
1	Developer Studio	Choose File|New.
2	New dialog box	Highlight Project Workspace and click OK.
3	New Project Workspace dialog box	Highlight JavaAppletWizard. Then, in the Name field, type **MouseTest** and click Create.
4	AppletWizard, step 1	Click Next.
5	AppletWizard, step 2	Click Next.
6	AppletWizard, step 3	For the "Would you like your applet to be multi-threaded?" question, click No, thank you. For the "Which mouse event handlers would you like added?" question, select mouseDown(), mouseUp(). Then, click Next.
7	AppletWizard, step 4	Click Next.
8	AppletWizard, step 5	Type **applet information**, then click Finish.
9	New Project Information dialog box	Verify the information is correct (see Figure 9-8), then click OK.

Table 9-6: Creating the MouseTest using the AppletWizard.

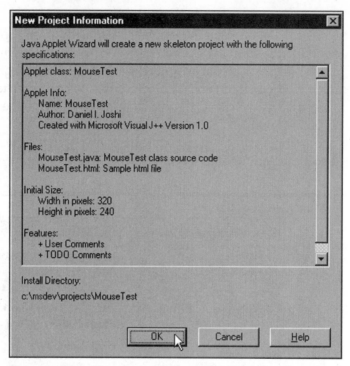

Figure 9-8: The New Project Information dialog box for project MouseTest.

Now, edit the code as shown in the MouseTest class code. Remember that the bolded code is material that you need to add and the regular code listed below is code automatically generated by the AppletWizard of Visual J++:

```
//***********************************************************
// MouseTest.java:  Applet
//
//***********************************************************
import java.applet.*;
import java.awt.*;


//===========================================================
// Main Class for applet MouseTest
//
```

```
//===========================================================
public class MouseTest extends Applet
{

  // MouseTest Class Constructor
  //----------------------------------------------------------
  public MouseTest()
  {
    // TODO: Add constructor code here
  }


  // APPLET INFO SUPPORT:
  //   The getAppletInfo() method returns a string describing
the applet's
  // author, copyright date, or miscellaneous information.
   //----------------------------------------------------------
  public String getAppletInfo()
  {
    return "Name: MouseTest\r\n" +
           "Author: Daniel I. Joshi\r\n" +
           "Created with Microsoft Visual J++ Version 1.0";
  }



  // The init() method is called by the AWT when an applet is
first loaded or
  // reloaded.  Override this method to perform whatever ini-
tialization your
  // applet needs, such as initializing data structures,
loading images or
  // fonts, creating frame windows, setting the layout man-
ager, or adding UI
  // components.
   //----------------------------------------------------------
```

```
public void init()
{
    // If you use a ResourceWizard-generated "control
creator" class to
    // arrange controls in your applet, you may want to
call its
    // CreateControls() method from within this method.
Remove the following
    // call to resize() before adding the call to
CreateControls();
    // CreateControls() does its own resizing.
    //-----------------------------------------------------
    resize(320, 240);

    // TODO: Place additional initialization code here
}


// Place additional applet clean up code here.  destroy()
is called
// when your applet is terminating and being unloaded.
//-----------------------------------------------------
public void destroy()
{
    // TODO: Place applet cleanup code here
}


// MouseTest Paint Handler
//-----------------------------------------------------
public void paint(Graphics g)
{
    g.drawString("Created with Microsoft Visual J++ Version
1.0", 10, 20);
```

```
    //My code starts here
    if (getBackground() == Color.white) {
       setBackground(Color.green);
    } else setBackground(Color.white);
    //My code ends here
}


//    The start() method is called when the page containing
the applet
//  first appears on the screen. The AppletWizard's initial
implementation
//  of this method starts execution of the applet's thread.
//----------------------------------------------------------
public void start()
{
    // TODO: Place additional applet start code here
}


//    The stop() method is called when the page containing
the applet is
//  no longer on the screen. The AppletWizard's initial
implementation of
//  this method stops execution of the applet's thread.
//----------------------------------------------------------
public void stop()
{
}



// MOUSE SUPPORT:
//    The mouseDown() method is called if the mouse button
is pressed
//  while the mouse cursor is over the applet's portion of
the screen.
```

```
//-------------------------------------------------------------
public boolean mouseDown(Event evt, int x, int y)
{

    // TODO: Place applet mouseDown code here

    //My code starts here
    repaint();
    //My code ends here

    return true;
}


// MOUSE SUPPORT:
//    The mouseUp() method is called if the mouse button is
released
// while the mouse cursor is over the applet's portion of
the screen.
//-------------------------------------------------------------
public boolean mouseUp(Event evt, int x, int y)
{

    // TODO: Place applet mouseUp code here

    return true;
}



    // TODO: Place additional applet code here

}
```

Looking at the above code, there are two spots to focus on. The first is the code you added in the paint() method:

```
if (getBackground() == Color.white) {
    setBackground(Color.green);
} else setBackground(Color.white);
```

In the above snippet of code, you are using two methods from the Graphics class: getBackground(), to return the Color for the background color of the applet's pane; and setBackground(), to set the applet's pane to the specified color. With this combination, you can toggle between a background color of green and white.

The second spot to focus on in the previous applet is the mouseDown() method. Here is the crucial link in making the applet MouseTest responsive to a user's mouse clicks:

```
public boolean mouseDown(Event evt, int x, int y)
{

    // TODO: Place applet mouseDown code here

    //My code starts here
    repaint();
    //My code ends here

    return true;
}
```

Looking at the method mouseDown(), remember that this method is automatically invoked by the AWT if it detects that a mouse button has been depressed (i.e., clicked) over the applet's pane. If this happens, mouseDown() uses the repaint() method to call paint() and redraw the applet's graphics. That also causes MouseTest to toggle its background color. Then, MouseTest returns true, telling the AWT that the event has been successfully handled.

Tip

The MouseTest only concerns itself with single-clicks on the applet pane. However, the Event class contains the field clickCount where you can test to determine how many clicks have been passed in rapid succession.

Now you are ready to save and build your code. To build the code, click on Build | Build MouseTest. Then to execute the code, click on Build | Execute.

Since this is an applet and you had the AppletWizard automatically generate the HTML file, Visual J++ invokes Internet Explorer, which invokes and loads the applet (see Figure 9-9).

Initially, the applet loads with a background of gray—the same as the background for the rest of the browser. However, click anywhere on the MouseTest's applet pane and the background turns white. Click again and it turns green.

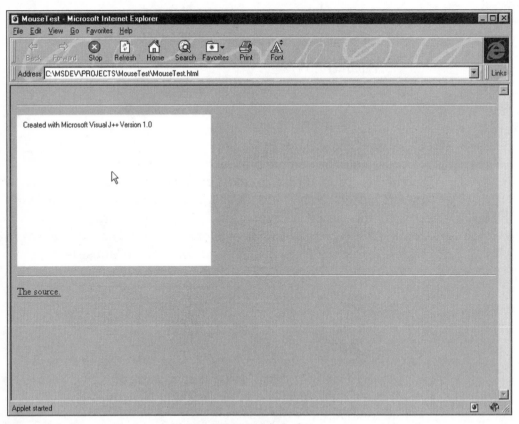

Figure 9-9: Internet Explorer with MouseTest toggled white.

As you can see, the MouseTest will toggle its background between white and green, depending on your mouse clicks. Try using both mouse buttons (left and right) and you should see that Java responds to each button the same way. Finally, try clicking anywhere outside the MouseTest applet pane. You will see that nothing happens, because the applet only accepts mouse clicks as events to be passed to the AWT if they are over the pane.

Other Interactions

The code that toggles the colors for the MouseTest's applet pane is in the paint() method. If you maximize or resize the browser, the AWT passes an event to your applet that calls the paint() method—thus it will toggle the background color. This gives you a chance to see some of the built-in event handling.

Keyboard Interaction

Despite the popularity of the mouse, the keyboard is still a staple for user input. With the keyboard supporting event handling methods, you can retrieve how the key is being pressed and exactly what key is being pressed. Table 9-7 outlines the two available keyboard-related methods.

```
keyUp(Event evt, int key)
keyDown(Event evt, int x, int key)
```

Table 9-7: Supporting keyboard-related methods.

Note

Unlike Windows, Java does not combine keyUp() and keyDown() into a single WM_CHAR message. Also, the repeat counter is not supported in Java.

The following is a pseudo-example of overriding the keyDown() method:

```
public boolean keyDown(Event evt, int key) {
    switch (key)
    {
    case (int)'a':
    case (int)'A':
      //Process 'a' keystroke
      break;
    case Event.HOME:
      //Process "home" keystroke
      break;
    default:
      //Process all other characters
      break;



    }
    return true;
}
```

Looking at the above code, you can see that the keyDown() method has a switch-case flow control statement. When a key is pressed, the AWT passes the Event to this method, which first checks to see if the key was a lowercase or uppercase. This is a technique that can be used to test whether a particular key is pressed.

The switch-case statement underneath the key test checks to see if the Home key has been pressed by comparing the value passed from key with static members contained in the java.awt.Event class. Table 9-8 is a list of available related noncharacter-based constants.

Constant	Corresponding Key
Event.DOWN	Down arrow key
Event.END	End key
Event.F1	F1 key
Event.F2	F2 key
Event.F3	F3 key
Event.F4	F4 key
Event.F5	F5 key
Event.F6	F6 key
Event.F7	F7 key
Event.F8	F8 key
Event.F9	F9 key
Event.F10	F10 key
Event.F11	F11 key
Event.F12	F12 key
Event.HOME	Home key
Event.LEFT	Left arrow key
Event.PGDN	PageDown key
Event.PGUP	PageUp key
Event.RIGHT	Right arrow key
Event.UP	Up arrow key

Table 9-8: List of noncharacter constants.

The last part of the above keyDown() method to discuss is the else statement containing the following line of code:

```
myChar = (char)key;
```

myChar is a character data type that was declared earlier in the Java program. This line of code casts the integer key to its corresponding character value. Thus, this line of code lets you retrieve the alphanumeric (i.e., character-based) key currently being pressed.

Tip

There are also three supporting methods available if a modifier key is being pressed: controlDown(), metaDown(), shiftDown(). These enable you to see if a user is holding down a modifier button (i.e., Control) while simultaneously pressing another key.

Tutorial: Overriding Keyboard Methods

Use the AppletWizard to create a JavaApplet called KeyTest (see Table 9-9 for step-by-step instructions).

Step #	Location	Action
1	Developer Studio	Choose File|New.
2	New dialog box	Highlight Project Workspace and click OK.
3	New Project Workspace dialog box	Highlight JavaAppletWizard. Then, in the Name field, type **KeyTest** and click Create.
4	AppletWizard, step 1	Click Next.
5	AppletWizard, step 2	Click Next.
6	AppletWizard, step 3	For the "Would you like your applet to be multi-threaded?" question, click No, thank you. Then, click Next.
7	AppletWizard, step 4	Click Next.
8	AppletWizard, step 5	Type applet information, then click Finish.
9	New Project Information dialog box	Verify the information is correct (see Figure 9-10), then click OK.

Table 9-9: Creating the KeyTest using the AppletWizard.

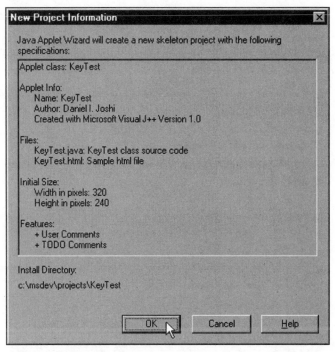

Figure 9-10: The New Project Information dialog box for project KeyTest.

Now let's look at the keyDown() method to the same class using Table 9-10 for step-by-step instruction.

Step#	Location	Action
1	Left pane of KeyTest Project Workspace	On the KeyTest class, right-click and choose Add Method from the menu.
2	New Method dialog box	In the Return type field, type **boolean**, and in the Method declaration field type **keyDown(Event evt, int key).**
3	New Method dialog box	In the Access box, choose Public.
4	New Method dialog box	Verify how the declaration looks, then click OK.

Table 9-10: Creating the keyDown() method.

Now, edit the code as shown in the KeyTest class code. Remember that the bolded code is material you need to add, and the regular code listed below is code automatically generated by the AppletWizard of Visual J++:

```
//********************************************************
// KeyTest.java:    Applet
//
//********************************************************
import java.applet.*;
import java.awt.*;


//========================================================
// Main Class for applet KeyTest
//
//========================================================
public class KeyTest extends Applet
{

    //My code starts here
    int x;
    int y;
    //My code ends here

    public boolean keyDown(Event evt, int key)
    {

        //My code starts here
        switch (key) {
        case Event.UP:
            y -= 5;
            break;
        case Event.DOWN:
            y += 5;
            break;
        case Event.LEFT:
            x -= 5;
            break;
```

```
        case Event.RIGHT:
            x += 5;
            break;
    }
    repaint();
    return true;
    //My code ends here


}


// KeyTest Class Constructor
//----------------------------------------------------------
public KeyTest()
{
    // TODO: Add constructor code here
    //My code starts here
    x = 0;
    y = 0;
    //My code ends here
}


// APPLET INFO SUPPORT:
//   The getAppletInfo() method returns a string describing the applet's
// author, copyright date, or miscellaneous information.
  //----------------------------------------------------------
public String getAppletInfo()
{
    return "Name: KeyTest\r\n" +
           "Author: Daniel I. Joshi\r\n" +
           "Created with Microsoft Visual J++ Version 1.0";
}
```

```
    // The init() method is called by the AWT when an applet is
first loaded or
    // reloaded.  Override this method to perform whatever ini-
tialization your
    // applet needs, such as initializing data structures,
loading images or
    // fonts, creating frame windows, setting the layout man-
ager, or adding UI
    // components.
    //---------------------------------------------------------
    public void init()
    {
        // If you use a ResourceWizard-generated "control
creator" class to
        // arrange controls in your applet, you may want to
call its
        // CreateControls() method from within this method.
Remove the following
        // call to resize() before adding the call to
CreateControls();
        // CreateControls() does its own resizing.
        //-------------------------------------------------
    resize(320, 240);

        // TODO: Place additional initialization code here

    //My code starts here
    requestFocus();
    //My code ends here


    }

    // Place additional applet clean up code here.  destroy()
is called
    // when your applet is terminating and being unloaded.
    //---------------------------------------------------------
```

```java
public void destroy()
{
    // TODO: Place applet cleanup code here
}


// KeyTest Paint Handler
//--------------------------------------------------------
public void paint(Graphics g)
{
    g.drawString("Created with Microsoft Visual J++ Version
1.0", 10, 20);

    //My code starts here
    setBackground(Color.white);
    g.fillOval(x, y, 20, 20);
    //My code ends here


}


//   The start() method is called when the page containing
the applet
// first appears on the screen. The AppletWizard's initial
implementation
// of this method starts execution of the applet's thread.
//--------------------------------------------------------
public void start()
{
    // TODO: Place additional applet start code here
}


//   The stop() method is called when the page containing
the applet is
// no longer on the screen. The AppletWizard's initial
implementation of
// this method stops execution of the applet's thread.
//--------------------------------------------------------
```

```
public void stop()
{
}


// TODO: Place additional applet code here

}
```

The Java applet KeyTest draws a filled-in circle on the applet pane that you can move using the arrow keys on your keyboard. Looking at the above code, notice there are four items to discuss.

First, let's take a look at the following declaration inside the Applet KeyTest:

```
int x;
int y;
```

The coordinates x and y represent where you want to draw the circle on the applet pane. They are specifically declared inside the KeyTest class so that they will be available to all of the other members of the KeyTest class.

Secondly, let's take a closer look at the keyDown() method. The method contains a switch control flow statement that determines which key was pressed. If any of the arrow keys (up, down, left, or right) were pressed, then either the x or y values change to cause the circle to be located at a corresponding location. For example, if the user pushes the left key, then the x value will be reduced by five, causing the new location of the circle to be five points to the left of its original location. Underneath the switch statement is a call to repaint() the method which updates the applet pane and returns true, letting the AWT event handler know that the event has been handled.

Next, notice that you added the following line of code to the init() method:

```
requestFocus();
```

requestFocus() is a method that comes from the java.awt.Component class and causes the applet to get focus. (If you need to do some special action when your applet gets focus, you can do it by overriding the gotFocus() method.) Only one component at any time has focus and receives keyboard input. Without this statement being started, your applet window will not have focus, but you can give it focus by clicking the mouse in its area.

Focus is needed because without it (as in the MouseTest example), when you click outside the applet pane, nothing happens. You also need to give the KeyTest applet focus so it can receive key-based events.

Finally, the last snippet of code to discuss is inside the paint() method:

```
setBackground(Color.white);
g.fillOval(x, y, 20, 20);
```

The first statement sets the background to white. The second uses the variables you declared earlier (x and y) as the coordinates for the fillOval() method from the Graphics class.

Now you are ready to save and build your code. To build the code, click on Build I Build KeyTest. Then, to execute the code, click on Build I Execute.

Since this is an applet, and you had the AppletWizard automatically generate the HTML file, Visual J++ invokes Internet Explorer, which invokes and loads the applet.

Initially the applet loads with a background of gray—the same as the background for the rest of the browser. However, press any of the four arrow keys on your keyboard, and the background changes to white while the circle moves in the corresponding direction (see Figure 9-11).

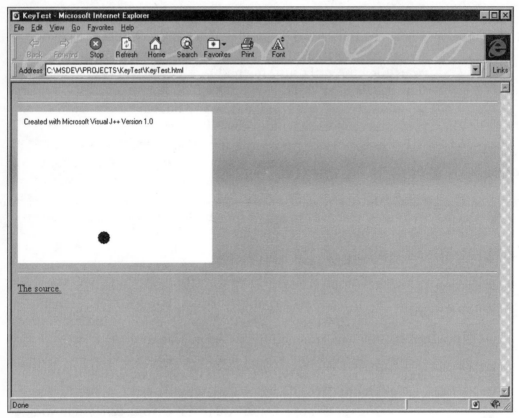

Figure 9-11: Internet Explorer with KeyTest.

Now, try moving the circle off of the applet pane using the arrow keys. Also, click on something else in the browser (or on your desktop) and try pressing the arrow keys. Notice that, because your applet no longer has focus, it no longer receives those events. Finally, use your mouse to click anywhere on the applet pane to give focus back to KeyTest. Then, press an arrow key and notice that the applet now has focus, the circle is responsive to the arrow keys.

You can also recognize if the Shift and/or Control keys were pressed with the given key by processing the modifiers property of the event. Java provides four constants: Event.ALT_MASK,

Event.CTRL_MASK, Event._MASK, and Event.META_MASK. The last constant is not supported by Windows and is reserved for other OSes. Pressing the Alt key activates the browser's menu, so you can't actually see ALT_MASK for applets. You can use bitwise AND operator & (not logical &&) to see if the modifiers member of your Event contains a corresponding flag.

Modify keyDown() and paint() methods in the above example to see how it works:

```
String str;
public boolean keyDown(Event evt, int key)
  {
  boolean alt   = (evt.modifiers & Event.ALT_MASK) != 0;
  boolean ctrl  = (evt.modifiers & Event.CTRL_MASK) != 0;
  boolean shift = (evt.modifiers & Event.SHIFT_MASK) != 0;
  str = "Key="+(char)key+"  Alt="+alt+"  Ctrl="+ctrl+"
Shift="+shift;
  repaint();
  return true;
  }
  public void paint(Graphics g)
  {.
    g.drawString(str, 10, 20);
  }
```

User Interface Interactions

The last topic that we are going to look at is the action-based event handling. Thus far, you have been introduced to handling a variety of events from mouse clicks to keyboard input. However, in the last chapter, you learned how to design a front end. How would you handle it if a user were to click a button or uncheck a check box? This section describes how the AWT accomplishes this using the action() method.

Do I Need to Override handleEvent() to Use the action() Method?

No. In most cases you do not need to override the handleEvent() method to use the action() method. Both of them are present in the UIEventTest example, but they both have different jobs. The handleEvent() method is responsible for exiting the application after the appropriate event is passed, and the action() method is responsible for event handling when the user clicks on the myClickMeButton.

To implement action-based event handling you need to do two things. First, you override the action() method contained in the component. Then, you need to figure out what UI component is the target of the event being passed. Usually, the UI components involved with the action() event are Button, Checkbox, Choice, and TextField. Once you have determined which component is involved, you can put any event handling code you want. Consider the following:

```
public boolean action(Event evt, Object arg) {
  if (evt.target == myFirstButton) {
    //Put some Event Handling code here
  }
}
```

The above pseudo-example assumes you created a UI that contains an instance of a Button called myFirstButton. Then, if the user clicks that button, the action() method is automatically called by handleEvent().

The second input for the action() method means different things to different UI components that are passed. A Button arg contains a String with the label of the Button. If the event belongs to a Checkbox, then arg is a boolean value representing the current state of the Checkbox. Choice arg is a String containing the item(s) selected. Finally, TextField arg is also a String containing the text entered in the field.

Tip

You can use the handleEvent() approach as opposed to the interception approach described here. To use the handleEvent() approach, you would override handleEvent() and check for the ACTION_EVENT constant.

Tutorial: Handling Actions from UIs

At this point, let's create a simple example using all the Visual J++ tools that you have learned about thus far. This will be a Java application with a UI created in the resource editor, and it will contain a very simple UI that includes code to handle various events from user and system input.

First, create a project workspace called UIEventTest (see Table 9-11 for the procedure).

Step #	Location	Action
1	Developer Studio	Choose File|New.
2	New dialog box	Highlight Project Workspace, and click OK.
3	New Project Workspace dialog box	In the Name field, type **UIEventTest**, and click Create.

Table 9-11: Creating the UIEventTest Project Workspace.

Tip

Remember that you are creating a Java application, so do not use the Java AppletWizard.

Now you need to create a new Java class called UIEventTest. In the Developer Studio, click Insert | New Java Class. On the Create New Class dialog box, do the following:

1. In the Name field, type **UIEventTest**.

2. In the Extends field, type **Frame.**

3. In the Modifiers area, choose Public.

Then, click OK (see Figure 9-12).

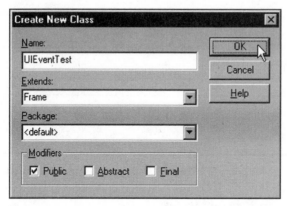

Figure 9-12: The Create New Class dialog box filled in.

Let's start by creating our first public method called main() (see Table 9-12 for step-by-step instructions).

Step #	Location	Action
1	Left pane of Workspace	On the UIEventTest class, right-UIEventTest Project click and choose Add Method from the menu.
2	New Method dialog box	In the Return type field, type **void**, and in the Method declaration field type **main(String argv[ ])**.
3	New Method dialog box	In the Access box, choose Public. In the Modifiers area, choose Static.
4	New Method dialog box	Verify how the declaration looks, then click OK.

Table 9-12: Creating the main() method.

Next, you need to add the action() method to the UIEventTest class (see Table 9-13 for step-by-step instructions).

Step #	Location	Action
1	Left pane of UIEventTest Project Workspace	On the UIEventTest class, right-click and choose Add Method from the menu.
2	New Method dialog box	In the Return type field type **boolean** and in the Method declaration field type **action(Event evt, Object arg).**
3	New Method dialog box	In the Access box, choose Public. In the Modifiers area, choose Static.
4	New Method dialog box	Verify how the declaration looks, then click OK**.**

Table 9-13: Creating the action() method.

Finally, let's add the handleEvent() method to the UIEventTest class (see Table 9-14 for step-by-step instructions).

Step #	Location	Action
1	Left pane of UIEventTest Project Workspace	On the UIEventTest class, right-click and choose Add Method from the menu.
2	New Method dialog box	In the Return type field type **boolean** and in the Method declaration field type **handleEvent(Event evt).**
3	New Method dialog box	In the Access box, choose Public.
4	New Method dialog box	Verify how the declaration looks, then click OK.

Table 9-14: Creating the handleEvent() method.

At this point, your Developer Studio should look similar to Figure 9-13.

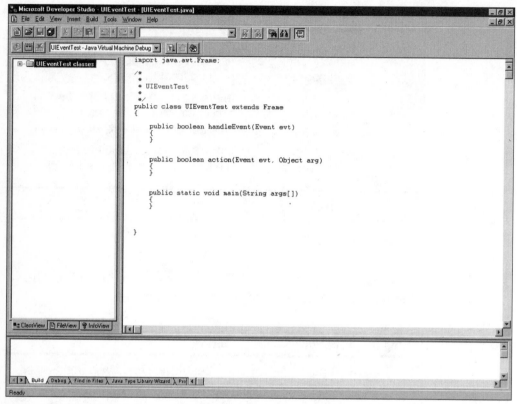

Figure 9-13: The Developer Studio with the UIEventTest project open.

Now let's create the Dialog resource in the resource editor that you will use for the UI in UIEventTest. In the Developer Studio, click on Insert.Resource and the Insert Resource dialog box displays.

Choose Dialog and click OK. The Dialog Resource Editor opens, and you are ready to create your UI as it will appear when you execute your Java application (see Figure 9-15).

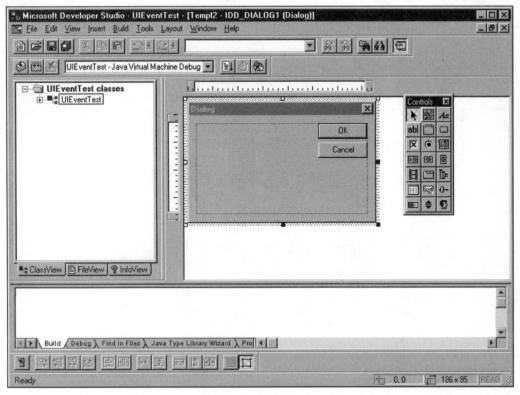

Figure 9-14: The Developer Studio with the Dialog Resource Editor open.

The first thing to do is delete the two buttons on the left corner of the Dialog. You can do that by highlighting them and pressing the Delete (Del) key. Once those two buttons have been deleted, you need to add a button to the Dialog by following the steps in Table 9-15.

Step #	Location	Action
Button	Properties dialog box, General tab	In the ID field, type **myClickMeButton,** and in the Caption field, type **Click Me!**
Button	Dialog Editor, with the aid of the Position Indicators	Move the control to the X-,Y- coordinates of (70,40); resize the control to the H x W ratio of (50 x 14).

Table 9-15: Adding a button to UIEventTest.

Once you are finished, the Dialog Resource Editor should look similar to Figure 9-15.

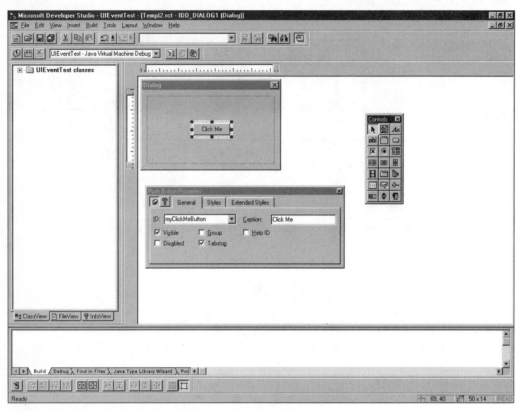

Figure 9-15: Developer Studio with the Dialog Resource Editor.

Now, highlight the entire Dialog and double-click it to open the Properties window for the Dialog. Then use Table 9-16 and make the following changes to it.

Control	Location	Action
Dialog	Properties dialog box, General tab	In the ID field, type **UIEventTestDialog**, and in the Caption field, type **UIEventTest**.
Dialog	Dialog Editor, with the aid of the Position Indicators	Move the control to the X-,Y- coordinates of (0,0); resize the control to the H x W ratio of (200 x 130).

Table 9-16: Editing properties for the Dialog.

At this point you have finished building the Dialog, so your next step is to close the Dialog Resource Editor by clicking File | Close. A dialog box opens asking if you want to save changes; click Yes, and a Save As dialog box opens. Save the resource template you just created in the same directory that you put the UIEventTest project. For this example, that is ..\msdev\projects\UIEventTest, the file should be saved as UIEventTestDialog.rct (see Figure 9-16).

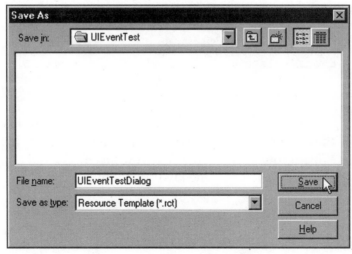

Figure 9-16 Saving the Dialog Resource Template.

Once you save the template UIEventDialog, the Developer Studio closes the Dialog Resource Editor. Now, ready port the resource template to Java source code using the Java Resource Wizard.

In the Developer Studio, click on Tools | Java Resource Wizard. For step 1, in the File name field, type **C:\MSDEV\PROJECTS\UIEventTest\UIEventTestDialog.rct** (see Figure 9-17) and then click Next to continue. You can also use the Browse button to locate the file.

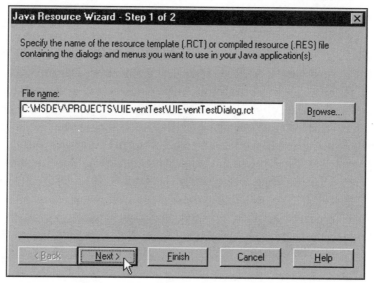

Figure 9-17: The Java Resource Wizard Step 1 of 2 filled out.

For step 2, verify that the correct class and resource appear in the list. The second and final step shows what the Java Resource Wizard found in the files that you specified (see Figure 9-18). Then click Finish to build the Java source files.

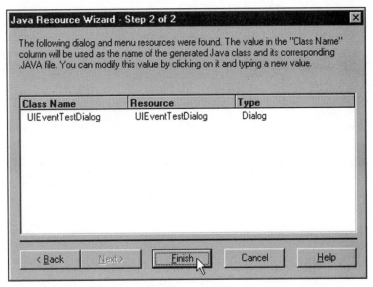

Figure 9-18: The Java Resource Wizard Step 2 of 2.

In the Confirmation dialog box for the Java Resource Wizard, verify what has been created (see Figure 9-19), and click OK to continue.

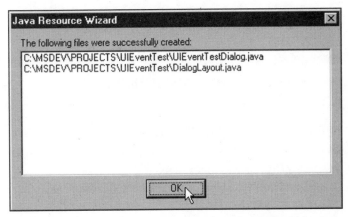

Figure 9-19: The Java Resource Wizard confirmation dialog box.

At this point you need to add the newly created source files to the project UIEventTest. Make sure the UIEventTest project is open, then click on Insert | Files into Project. In the Files into Project dialog box, highlight both the UIEventTestDialog.java and the DialogLayout.java files so that both files are added. Click Add to continue, and you have added the files to the project.

Finally, your last step before building and executing the project is to implement the UI you created in the resource editor (UIEventTestDialog) to the class UIEventTest. In the Developer Studio, with the class UIEventTest open, add the bolded code:

```java
import java.awt.Frame;

//My code starts here
import java.awt.*;
import UIEventTestDialog;
//My code ends here

/*
 *
 * UIEventTest
 *
 */
public class UIEventTest extends Frame
{

    //My code starts here
    static UIEventTestDialog theUI;
    //My code ends here

    public boolean handleEvent(Event evt) {

        //My code starts here
        if( evt.id == Event.WINDOW_DESTROY) {
            System.exit(0);
            return true;
        }
```

```java
        return super.handleEvent(evt);
          //My code ends here


    }

    public boolean action(Event evt, Object arg)
    {

        //My code starts here
        if (evt.target == theUI.myClickMeButton) {
          theUI.myClickMeButton.setLabel("Ouch!");
        }

        return true;
        //My code ends here


    }

    public static void main(String args[])
    {

        //My code starts here
        UIEventTest myUIEventTest = new UIEventTest();

        myUIEventTest.show();
        myUIEventTest.hide();

        theUI = new UIEventTestDialog(myUIEventTest);
        theUI.CreateControls();

        myUIEventTest.show();
        //My code ends here


    }


}
```

Looking at the above code, first notice that you import the AWT package and the UIEventTestDialog class to this class. Then, underneath the class declaration for UIEventTest, you declare the variable theUI as follows:

```
static UIEventTestDialog theUI;
```

Basically, you are declaring the UI to be static. It is not required until the main() method where you will instantiate it. However, you also need to work with the UI in the action() method. So, by declaring it static, you are making it available to the entire class, including the static main() method.

Static & the main() Method

Anytime you want to use a variable both inside and outside of the main() method, you must declare it static because the main() method is static. Effectively, static tells Java that there can only be one of that method of variable in the entire class.

Using static variables is not always the best solution. Instead, it is better to initialize and use any other necessary variables in the class's constructor.

The next block of code to look at is the handleEvent() method. This method and its contents should not be new to you. It is only responsible for closing the UIEventTest window.

The next method to look at is the action() method. It is in this method that you will determine which UI component was the target of an event, and then perform the appropriate action. Let's take a closer look at the contents of the action() method:

```
if (evt.target == theUI.myClickMeButton) {
   the UI.myClickMeButton.setLabel("Ouch!");
}

return true;
```

The first thing you are doing is using the target field of the Event class to see if the myClickMeButton is the focus of the event.

Determining Event Targets Using UI Component Labels

Another common programming technique for finding out which UI component is responsible for an event is to perform a check based on the label on the given component. For example:

```
if (arg.equals("Click Me")) {
//Rest of the Method
```

This line of code has the same functionality as the target technique used in UIEventTest. This is not usually a recommended technique.

If the myClickMeButton is responsible for this event, then the following line of code using setLabel() from the button class causes it to change its label from "Click Me" to "Ouch!" Finally, you return true for the method. Note that you can only do it once.

The last method contained in the UIEventTest class is the main() method. It uses the programming techniques described in Chapter 8. The main() method starts by instancing UIEventTest as myUIEventTest. Secondly, the main() method uses the show()-hide() technique to retrieve information about the users' environment. Finally, the main() method instances the UI for UIEventTest called as theUI and calls CreateControls() to actually build the UI. The last line of code is the show() method that displays the UIEventTest window with the integrated UI.

Build UIEventTest by clicking on Build | Build UIEventTest. Once it is finished, you are ready to execute it by clicking on Build | Execute. Since you are executing this project for the first time, the Developer Studio asks you to enter a class filename. In this case, type **UIEventTest**. Also, underneath that you have a choice of using either jview or Internet Explorer. For this example, choose Stand-alone interpreter (see Figure 9-20).

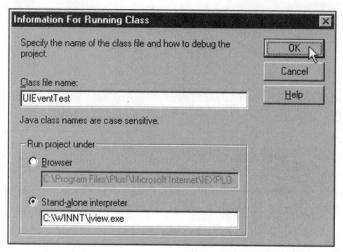

Figure 9-20: The Information For Running Class dialog box filled out.

Once you have filled out the Information For Running Class dialog box, and it looks like the above figure, click OK to execute. Once executed, you should see something similar to Figure 9-21.

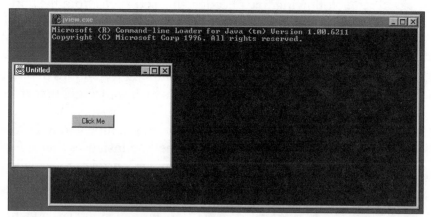

Figure 9-21: Executing UIEventTest.

Now click on the button and you will see the label of the button change to Ouch! (as shown in Figure 9-22).

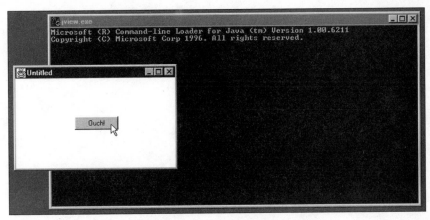

Figure 9-22: Executing UIEventTest with the button clicked.

Moving On

In this chapter, you learned how Java uses the AWT to handle events. You also learned several techniques that you can use in your Java programs to perform event handling. Finally, you had a chance to create a simple UI and use event handling to make it responsive.

This chapter covered many aspects of Java event handling. It gave you a chance to learn several techniques and examples to reinforce the material.

The next chapter moves forward by focusing on the debugging aspect of Java and the tools available in Visual J++. You will have a chance to debug a real-life Java program and to follow the logic that a typical programmer would use to fix a program.

Debugging in Visual J++

Debugging in general is a fairly advanced topic. That is why it was not discussed in more depth in Chapter 5. The bugs planted in Chapter 5's tutorial are easy to spot. However, bugs come in all shapes and sizes. Some are easy to spot and others may not show up for months. Furthermore, fixing one bug may cause another one to appear. In essence, programmers spend a good part of their development time debugging. Moreover, it takes more than just reading this chapter to become proficient in removing bugs. Debugging is truly an art, and the best way to master it is through experience. This chapter introduces you to a debugging session in Visual J++.

Debugging Sessions in Visual J++

Technically speaking, in Chapter 5 you dealt with a form of bugs called compile-time bugs. However, there are other more complex (and more difficult to debug) errors that can arise. These usually fall into the category of *run-time* bugs.

Run-time bugs are difficult to detect because they do not show up at compile time. Meaning that your project compiles without a problem. However, attempting to execute the Java program throws an exception or the program simply does not work right.

Removing these "hidden errors" is not easy because they simply may not show up in your program right away. In fact, they may not show up for months or until the conditions are right! This can be a hard concept for nonprogrammers and programmers alike to understand. However, the larger and more complex your programs, the greater the likelihood there is for these implicit run-time errors to appear. It is in removing these bugs that Visual J++ really shines.

Using the debugging tools in Visual J++, you can start a program and while it is executing, pry into the program. This gives you the ability to look at (or manipulate) individual threads, values belonging to variables, and much more. Not, only does this help you remove bugs, but it also facilitates a way for you to test your programs more vigorously than simply executing it.

Note

Throughout these sections, you'll see that the project MyAniApplet created in Chapter 6, demonstrates Visual J++'s debugging tools.

The following sections introduce you to an assortment of Visual J++ debugging tools that are at your disposal.

Starting a Debugging Session

To debug your Java programs you need to do two things. First, you must make sure that the project configuration is set to "Java Virtual Machine Debug." With the project open, click Build I Set Default Configuration. A dialog box appears as shown in Figure 10-1.

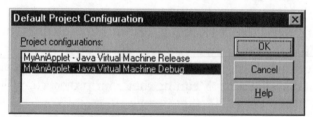

Figure 10-1: Setting the default project configuration.

In Figure 10-1, the unhighlighted configuration is the default. If you want to have debugging turned on, you need to select "Java Virtual Machine Debug." This option sets the project configuration to Debug mode. It is important that you do this because it adds special debugging-based components to the compiled class, making the compiled file larger. Furthermore, it is not optimized to the fullest extent.

The second thing that you need to do is to start a debugging session in Visual J++. Take note that debugging is in essence executing your project. However, it is a very special form of execution. Thus, starting a debugging session is different than simply executing a project by using the Build I Execute procedure.

In the Developer Studio, go to Build I Debug and you see a cascading submenu (for instance) showing you various debug options (see Figure 10-2).

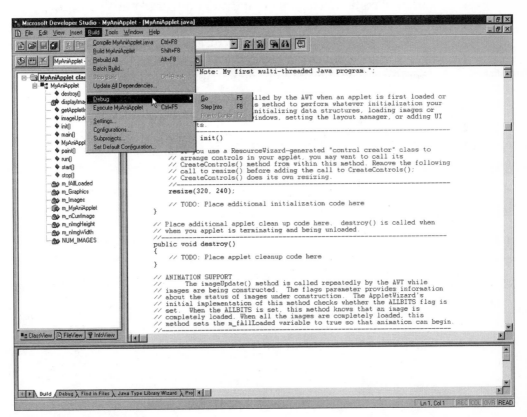

Figure 10-2: The Debug menu.

The Build | Debug submenu contains three menu items:

- **Build | Debug | Go** starts execution in a debugging session and continues until it hits a breakpoint.

- **Build | Debug | Step Into** steps you through every instructional line of code and call each methods.

- **Build | Debug | Run to Cursor** starts the debugger and lets it execute until it reaches the line in the source code where the cursor is positioned. If there is no cursor in the source code, this option is disabled.

Breakpoints

For a debugging session to be successful, you may need to set *breakpoints* within your code. Breakpoints are placed at specific lines of code where you want the debugger to pause execution. Breakpoints give you the ability to pry into your program in the middle of its execution and look inside the program. Without breakpoints, your project would start a debugging session, execute, and exit without giving you a chance to look inside it. You can set breakpoints within a debugging session or outside of a debugging session.

Specifying a breakpoint is extremely simple. In the source code of your project, right click on the line of code where you want to halt the program's execution and a pop-up menu opens (see Figure 10-3).

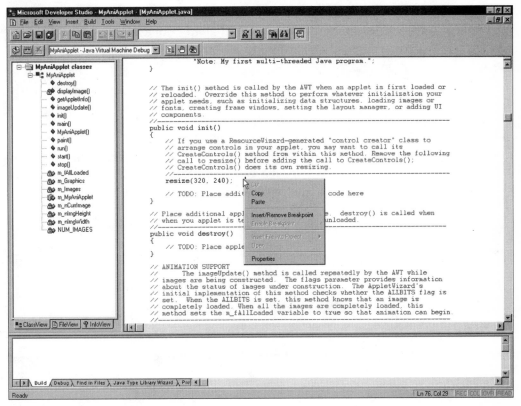

Figure 10-3: Specifying a breakpoint.

Looking at the pop-up menu in figure 10-3, choose Insert/ Remove Breakpoint. This option places filled-in a in red dot on the left. Now, when you start your debugging session, the program will halt at that line of code.

Tip

Breakpoints need to be specified on an instructional line of code, not a blank line or comment line in the source code.

In addition, notice that Insert/Remove Breakpoint gives you the ability to toggle a breakpoint at any one given line of code. Thus, you use this command to remove the breakpoint you just created.

Tip

Aside from inserting and removing a breakpoint, you can use the item Disable Breakpoint to have the debugger temporarily skip it. You can tell when a breakpoint has been disabled because the red dot on the left will not be filled in.

To view and edit a list of all the breakpoints in your program, choose Edit | Breakpoints to use the Breakpoints dialog box (see Figure 10-4).

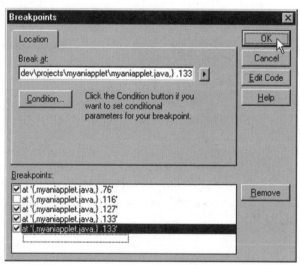

Figure 10-4: The Breakpoints dialog box.

Tip

The Breakpoints dialog box also gives you the ability to create what are known as advanced breakpoints. Advanced breakpoints are breakpoints that are enabled only if a certain condition is met in your program. You can do this by clicking the Condition button in the Breakpoints dialog box for the highlighted breakpoint.

At this point, let's specify a breakpoint and start a debugging session in the project MyAniApplet. Set a breakpoint on line 219, which says:

```
m_Images[i-1] = getImage(getDocumentBase(), strImage);
```

To start the debugging session, click Build | Debug | Go. This puts your project in a debugging session and the Developer Studio in a debugging mode. The sections that follow describe the variables and expressions (tools) that you can use to view information in the debugger and to present the Call Stack, Disassembly, Exceptions, and Thread windows that are available during your debugging session.

Viewing Information About Variables & Expressions

Notice that several windows close and others open in the Developer Studio. Secondly, Internet Explorer invokes while the program is debugged.

Tip

Looking at the main menu of the Developer Studio notice that a Debug menu replaced the Build menu. This Debug menu contains all of the tools available to you. In this menu you have options to step in, over, and out of the lines of code in your program called Debug | Step Into, Debug | Step Over, Debug | Step Out, and Debug | Run to Cursor.

Once the program breaks at the location you specified, you will see a yellow arrow showing you exactly where the program halted execution (see Figure 10-5).

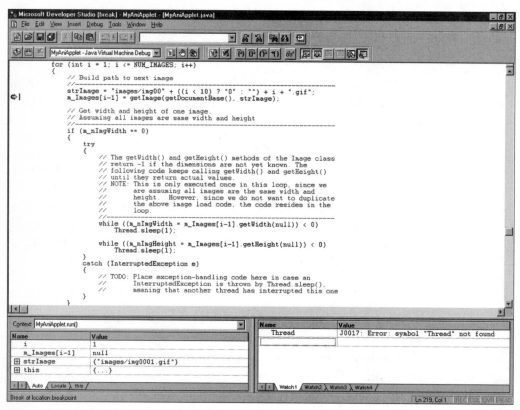

Figure 10-5: Debugging MyAniApplet.

It is here that you have paused the program in the middle of its execution. You can now retrieve information and/or manipulate it in real execution time.

DataTips

Using your mouse, rest the cursor over the variable "strImage" located just above the specified breakpoint. A DataTip box displays (see Figure 10-6).

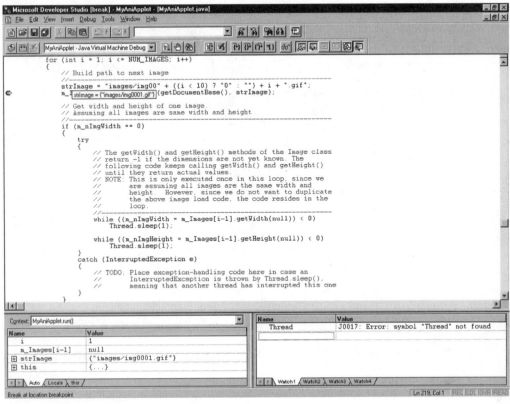

Figure 10-6: Using DataTips while debugging.

Looking at Figure 10-6, you can see that the DataTip box displays the current value for the variable "strImage." DataTips provide you with a fast and easy way to query information about variables contained in your program.

QuickWatch

Another tool you can use to not only query information about variables in your program but to also change variable data is QuickWatch. For example, in the line of code five lines above the breakpoint is a statement that uses the "NUM_IMAGES" variable. Highlight this statement and click Debug | QuickWatch. The QuickWatch dialog box appears as shown in Figure 10-7.

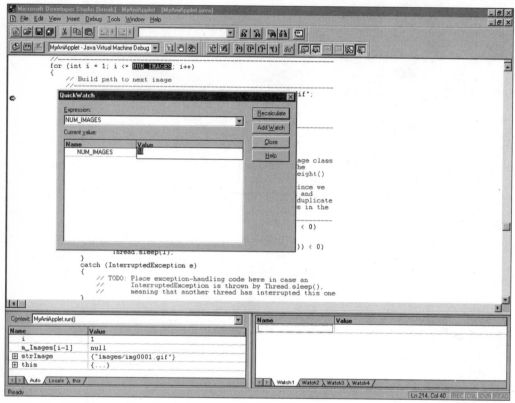

Figure 10-7: Using QuickWatch while debugging.

Tip

You can also view and manipulate the values of expressions using QuickWatch.

QuickWatch not only gives you the ability to view the value of a variable, but it also lets you change the value of a variable. For example, if you want to see how the program responds to values other than 18 for the variable "NUM_IMAGES," you can change the value in QuickWatch.

The Watch Window

Before closing the QuickWatch dialog box there is one other thing
to point out. You already know you can use DataTips to query
information quickly and QuickWatch to manipulate it. However,
what if you want to constantly watch the value of a variable or
expression throughout the debugging session (assuming the
variable is in scope)? You can do this using the Watch window
located on the lower right corner of the Developer Studio.

Tip

*Just like in QuickWatch, you can manipulate the values of variables
or expressions in the Watch window.*

One way you can add variables is by using the Add Watch
button. This adds the variable or expression to the Watch window
in the lower right corner of the Developer Studio. To try this, click
Add Watch. NUM_IMAGES is added to the Watch window and
the QuickWatch dialog box closes (see Figure 10-8).

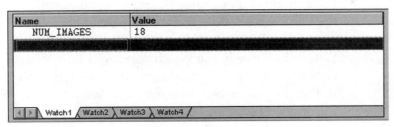

Figure 10-8: The Watch window with a variable added.

The Variables Window

The Visual J++ debugger also provides you with one easy way to
access all the variables in your program—the Variables window. It
is located on the lower left corner, adjacent to the Watch window.
Figure 10-9 shows a closer look at the Variables window.

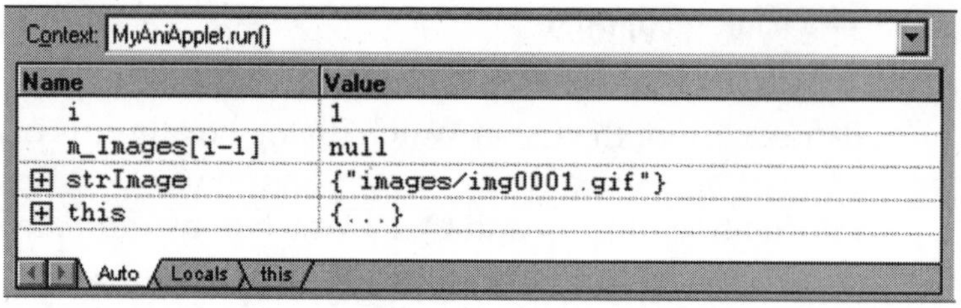

Figure 10-9: The Variables window.

Look at the Variables window and notice that the Context text field shows your program scope (i.e., method). Also, notice that there are three tabs at the bottom. The Auto tab displays the variables used in, at, or near your program's execution point. The Locals tab displays all the variables that belong to the current method in the Context field. Finally, the This tab represents all the variables that belong to object, as defined by "this."

Dragging & Dropping Information Between Windows

During a debugging session in Visual J++, you can drag and drop information (such as a variable) from one window to another. This is useful if you find something in one window that you want to use in another. For example, let's drag and drop a variable from the Variables window and put it in the Watch window—that way even when it is no longer in scope in the Variables window you can see its value in the Watch window. In the Variables window, click the variable "i" and drag it to the Watch window on the left so that the mouse button is over the Watch window. Then let go of the mouse button and the variable "i" is added to the Watch window (see Figure 10-10).

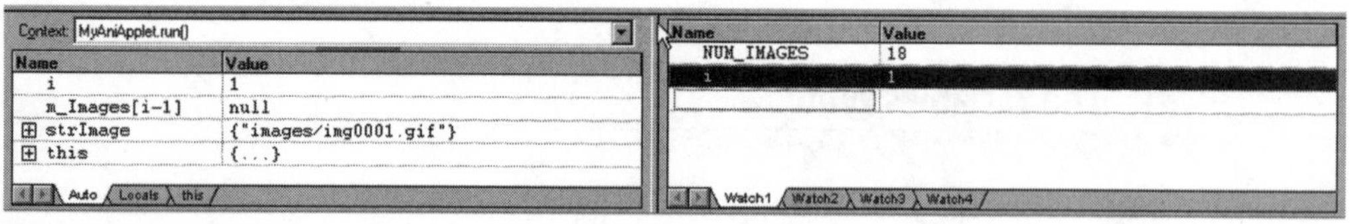

Figure 10-10: Dragging and Dropping "i" from the Variables window to the Watch window.

The Call Stack Window

The Call Stack window provides a Stack based view of all the method calls currently active in your program. Call Stack windows display a Last In First Out (LIFO) list of methods currently running in your program at any given time of execution. Secondly, each entry in the Call Stack window shows the line number from which the methods are called. To access the Call Stack window, click View | Call Stack in the Developer Studio's main menu (see Figure 10-11).

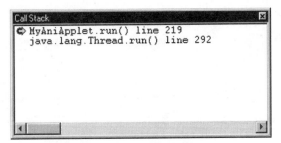

Figure 10-11: The Call Stack window.

In the Call Stack window you can go to the line of source by double-clicking on an entry. For example, in the Call Stack window listed above, double click on the second item called "java.lang.Thread.run()." You will see the Developer Studio jump to the line of source code in the java.lang.Thread class from the Java class library (see Figure 10-12).

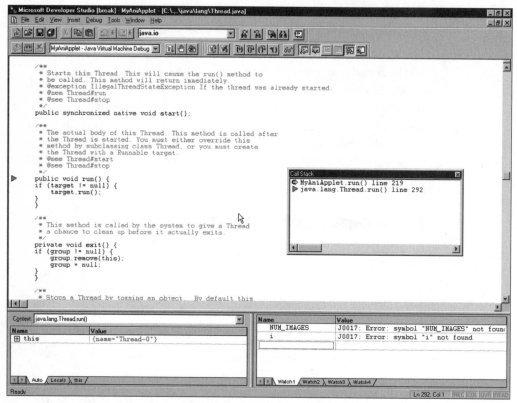

Figure 10-12: Going to the source from the Call Stack window.

Looking at Figure 10-12, notice the arrow that shows the correspondence between the entry in the Call Stack window and the line of source code.

Tip

> *To access the source code for the Java class libraries as shown above, you need to make sure that during the installation of Visual J++ you select to have the source code available for the Java class libraries.*

The Disassembly Window

One of the more advanced windows that you can open to help you debug your Java program is the Disassembly window. Basically, the Disassembly window displays your program on a bytecode level. Thus, you step through each bytecode instruction as you did in your source code earlier in the chapter.

Disassembling your source code to individual bytecode instructions is only useful in the most advanced debugging situations. Furthermore, it requires an understanding of bytecodes in the first place. For more information on bytecodes, see Chapter 14. To open the Disassembly window, click View | Disassembly (see Figure 10-13).

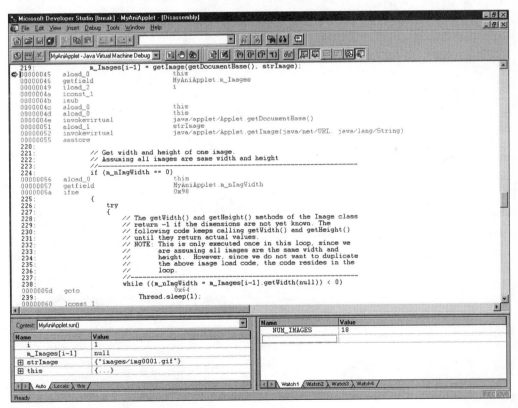

Figure 10-13: The Disassembly window.

Looking at the Disassembly window, you can see that it lists MyAniApplet, giving a line for each bytecode instruction on the left. On the right is the bytecode and corresponding source code instruction. Line 219 in your source code contains 11 bytecode instructions before moving to line 220.

One of the confusing parts of using the Disassembly window is all the Hexadecimal addressing. For example, all of the bytecode instructions are listed with corresponding Octal addresses. Use your mouse to move the cursor over to 00000045 address. A Data-Tips box pops up displaying the Octal's decimal value (see Figure 10-14). This is also true for any Hexadecimal numbers as well.

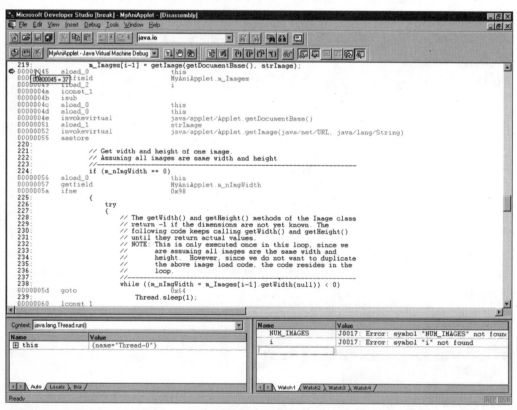

Figure 10-14: Using ToolTips in the Disassembly window.

The Exceptions Window

You learned that certain operations (such as using the sleep( ) method in the Thread class) can throw an exception. In your Java programs, you can code your program to catch and handle the exception. However, sometimes an exception can be thrown and there is no code to handle it. Thus, your exception is thrown causing your program to error out.

While you are debugging a Java program, there is a way for you to tell Visual J++ what you want to do in the event an exception is thrown. You can specifically decide what you want the debugger to do for a particular exception by using the Exceptions window. Basically, you have two options with the Exceptions window. First, you can specify the debugger to stop only on exceptions that are not handled. Or, you can specify it to stop anytime an exception is raised. For more information on exception handling see Chapter 14.

The Exceptions window can be accessed via Debug | Exceptions (see Figure 10-15).

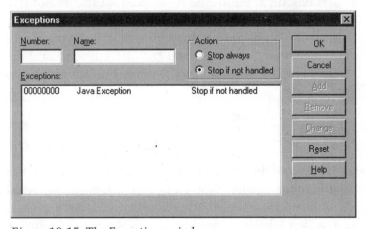

Figure 10-15: The Exceptions window.

The Thread Window

Accessible from Debug | Thread, the Thread window gives you the ability to debug all the threads executing in your project on an individual basis (see Figure 10-16).

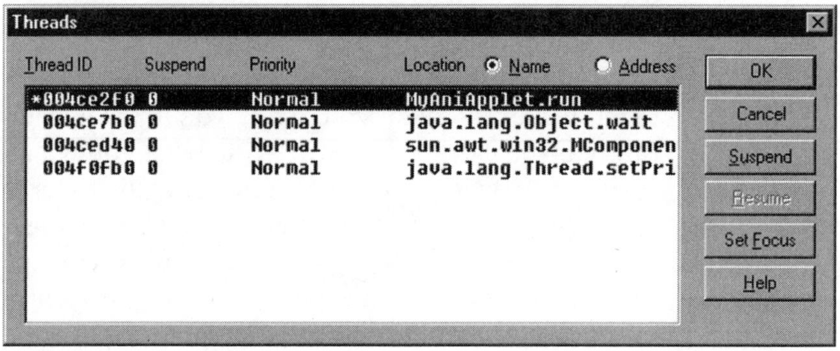

Figure 10-16: The Thread window.

Looking at Figure 10-16, notice that the thread with the asterisk is the thread that currently has focus. You can give another thread focus by highlighting the new thread that you want to have focus and clicking Set Focus. You can also suspend and resume a thread by using the Suspend and Resume buttons respectively.

Closing a Debugging Session

This section ends our discussion on debugging in Visual J++. When you wish to close a debugging session, all that you need to do is click Debug | Stop Debugging. Essentially, what happens when you stop debugging is that the Developer Studio returns to the Text Editor mode. Any changes you made during the debugging session carry over and are viewable using the Text Editor; upon exiting the Text Editor, you can choose whether or not to save your changes to disk.

Moving On

In this short chapter you had a chance to debug a real Java program that contained "jury rigged" errors. You also had a chance to take an extensive look at the capabilities and overall limitations of the debugger in Visual J++. Generally, it is extremely sophisticated and a valuable part of Visual J++.

Debugging in any language is an advanced topic, and this chapter only introduced you to the possibilities of debugging with Visual J++. Probably, the best way to gain more expertise in debugging is through experimentation and experience. You can also reference InfoView to help you.

The next chapter turns to a more advanced topic in Java known as *streams*. Streams are the backbone behind your Java program code structure that allows you to communicate with other entities such as files, databases, and other Java programs.

Using Streams to Handle I/O

J ava uses streams to perform input and output processing to standard I/O devices, files, and buffers. It includes the java.io package that provides all the classes for performing stream-based I/O. The java.io hierarchy classes include InputStream, OutputStream, File, RandomAccessFile, FileDescriptor, and StreamTokenizer. The InputStream and OutputStream are the two major Java classes for stream-based I/O. They are further subclassed to provide a variety of I/O capabilities.

In this chapter you'll learn about streams and how Java performs stream-based I/O. You'll learn about the java.io class hierarchy and the extensive set of classes it provides for handling I/O to and from various devices. This chapter provides an indepth look into the java.io classes and their member variables and methods. This chapter also includes three Visual J++ tutorials that utilize Java I/O classes and methods.

Understanding Streams

The definition of a stream in the Oxford dictionary is "a flowing body of water, brook or small river." In the computer world a stream is analogous to a flowing body of bytes. A stream represents a sequence of bytes. The sequence of bytes travels from one endpoint (source) to another endpoint (destination). Java supports streams-based I/O. A Java application reads bytes from an input stream and writes bytes to an output stream. I/O streams include (but are not limited to) local or network files, memory buffers, or separate input or output devices. Other types of I/O include:

- Console and port I/O
- Low-level I/O

You can read and write data to a console (e.g., a terminal) or an I/O port (e.g., a printer port) using console and port I/O. Data is read and written in bytes. In a way, you can consider console and port I/O an extension of streams.

Streams could be buffered or unbuffered. In the first case, application uses a part of memory as a buffer between data source and program, although in your program it looks like you read/write data directly. Since each call to an I/O device (hard drive, for instance) takes considerable time, it can give you a big advantage in speed. For instance, instead of reading 1000 times per 1 byte from a file, you will actually read 1 time per 1000 bytes, but in your program code it will look like you are reading and processing only 1 byte at a time. Unbuffered operations read/write directly to/from data source and require more programmer's responsibility.

The low-level I/O uses the operating system's I/O capabilities. It does not support buffered data.

Java defines two main classes of streams: InputStream and OutputStream. The java.io package includes several classes and methods to handle these streams:

- The BufferedInputStream and BufferedOutputStream classes handle memory buffer streams.

- The FileInputStream and FileOutputStream handle file I/O streams.

- The StringBufferInputStream handles string buffer I/O streams.

- The ByteArrayInputStream and ByteArrayOutputStream classes handle byte array I/O streams.

- The PipedInputStream and PipedOutputStream classes handle piped I/O communication between Java threads.

- The RandomAccessFile class handles random access file I/O.

Java also supports markable streams. In a markable stream you can mark a position in the stream and later reset the stream so that you can reread the stream from the marked position.

The java.io package includes a rich set of classes for performing stream-based I/O. Figure 11-1 shows the java.io class hierarchy.

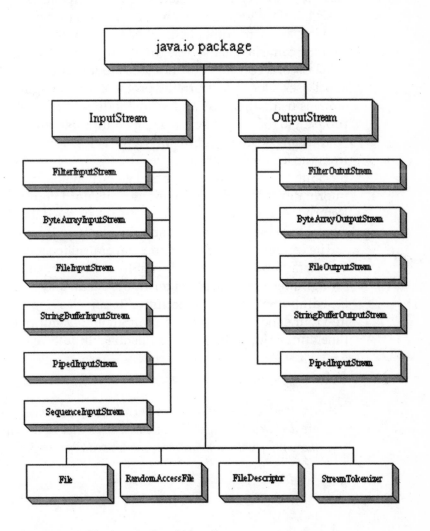

Figure 11-1: The java.io class hierarchy.

This chapter describes each of the java.io classes—their subclasses and methods—in detail. It also covers three separate Visual J++ tutorials that utilize these I/O classes and methods.

The InputStream Class

The InputStream class is an abstract class. Since it is an abstract class, it cannot be instantiated. The InputStream class defines a basic interface for reading streams. It is one of the two important java.io classes, the other being the OutputStream class. The InputStream class is the base for all other InputStream classes subclasses; accordingly its methods are inherited by all of its subclasses. Once you learn the protocol for managing input streams using this class and its methods, you can apply similar protocol to different devices using an InputStream derived class.

You can use an InputStream derived class to read information from the keyboard, for example. The InputStream class uses a blocking technique to wait until data is available. When you input information using the keyboard, it waits until you press the Return key. Once you press the Return key, the data becomes available in the input stream and the blocking is removed.

The InputStream class includes several subclasses: ByteArrayInputStream, FileInputStream, SequenceInputStream, StringBufferInputStream, FilterInputStream, and PipedInputStream. The FilterInputStream class is further classified into four subclasses: BufferedInputStream, DataInputStream, LineNumberInputStream, and PushBackInputStream.

Note

An abstract class is a class that contains one or more methods that are declared abstract. Abstract classes cannot be instantiated. For more information on abstract classes see Chapter 3.

Methods of the InputStream Class

A rich set of methods is included in the InputStream class. It includes three different types of read() methods. The read() methods read data from the input stream. Each variation includes a different set of parameters to read data from the input stream. Each variation also includes a close() method that lets you close the input stream explicitly. We recommend you use this method even though streams are automatically closed when they are destroyed. This class also includes methods to mark and reset streams.

Different applications may have different ways of handling the input stream. For example, you can use the available() method to determine the number of bytes available in the input stream before you start reading data from the input stream. In some other applications you may need to skip a certain number of bytes in the input stream. Use the skip() method to accomplish this.

The read() Methods

Use the read() methods to read data from the input stream. The InputStream class includes three overloaded read() methods. They read the input data in different ways.

The first read method, abstract int read(), is an abstract method. Abstract int read() takes no parameters, reads the input data, and returns the byte read as an integer. A return value of -1 indicates the end of the input stream (no bytes have been read).

The second read method, int read(byte b[]), reads an array of bytes and returns the number of bytes read. A return value of -1 indicates the end of input stream.

The third read method, int read(byte b[], int off, int len), takes three parameters: an array of bytes, an integer offset, and an integer length. The length parameter specifies the maximum number of bytes to read. The offset parameter indicates the offset into the byte array where you want the new data placed.

The available() Method

Use the available() method to determine the number of bytes that are available to read without blocking. It takes no parameters and returns the number of available bytes.

The close() Method

Use the close() method to close the input data stream. Closing the input stream releases all resources associated with the stream. Although streams automatically close when they are destroyed, it is a good programming practice to call this method when you are finished processing the input stream.

The skip() Method

Use the skip() method to skip a specified number of bytes in the input stream of data. The skip() method takes a long value as its only parameter—the number of bytes you want to skip. This method returns the actual number of bytes skipped. A return value of -1 indicates that you have reached the end of the input stream.

The mark() & reset() Methods

Use the mark() method to mark a position in the input stream. The mark() method takes an integer parameter that specifies the number of bytes you want to read before the mark becomes invalid. Use the reset() method to return to the marked position in the input stream.

The markSupported() Method

Use the markSupported() method to identify if a stream supports mark and reset capabilities. The return value is boolean—true if the stream supports it and false if it does not. Console and port I/O is an example of a stream that does not support marks.

The ByteArrayInputStream Class

This class uses an array of bytes as the input stream. Reading from arrays of bytes is faster than reading from input devices. You buffer data to provide faster access. You read more data than required so that subsequent reads are from the buffer and not from the device The ByteArrayInputStream class inherits its methods from the InputStream class which you can override. You can use the available() method to determine the number of bytes available in the array before you start reading it. If your application needs to skip a certain number of bytes, you can use the skip()

method. For example if the input stream consists of special charac-ters before the names and addresses of customers, use the skip() method to skip the special characters before you start reading the names and addresses. This class includes two constructors:

- **ByteArrayInputStream(byte() buf)** creates ByteArrayInputStream from the specified array of bytes. Below is an example of instantiating the ByteArrayInputStream class using this constructor:

```
        ByteArrayInputStream
  myByteArrayInputStream = new
  ByteArrayInputStream (byte() buf) ;
buf is the byte array buffer.
```

- **ByteArrayInputStream (byte () buf, int offset, int length)** creates a ByteArrayInputStream from the specified array of bytes. Below is an example of instantiating the ByteArrayInputStream class using the second constructor:

```
        ByteArrayInputStream
  myByteArrayInputStream = new
  ByteArrayInputStream (byte () buf, int offset,
  int length) ;
```

buf is the byte array buffer, *offset* is the offset into the buffer, and *length* is the length of the buffer.

Both constructors use a single parameter—a byte array—to create the input stream. The difference is in how the stream is converted. Use the toByteArray() method to convert the stream to an array of bytes. Use the toString() method to convert the stream to a String object. Assume outStream represents an instance of the ByteArrayOutputStream class in the above example constructors.

The FileInputStream Class

The FileInputStream class reads input from a file. A file may reside on the local or network drive. This class can be instantiated using any one of the following three constructors:

- FileInputStream(String name)
- FileInputStream(File file)
- FileInputStream(FileDescriptor fd)

The first constructor, FileInputStream(String name), takes a single parameter as a string—the name of a file you want to use as input. Below is an example of instantiating the FileInputStream class using the first constructor:

```
FileInputSream myFileInputStream = new
FileInputStream ("fileio.txt") ;
The string "Fileio.txt" denotes a file used as the input
stream.
```

The second constructor, FileInputStream(File file), is similar to the first constructor; it takes a single parameter—a File object—to use as input. Class File represents a filename of the host file system. The filename can be relative or absolute. It must use the filenaming conventions of the host platform (see class description below). Below is an example of instantiating the FileInputStream class using the second constructor:

```
FileInputStram myFileInputStream = new
FileInputStream (File myfile) ;
```

myfile is an instance of type File. It represents the file used as the input stream.

The third constructor, FileInputStream(FileDescriptor fd), also takes a single parameter—a FileDescriptor object—to use as input. Class FileDescriptor represents a system-dependent value that describes an open file. (See class description below.) Below is an example of instantiating the FileInputStream class using the third constructor:

```
FileInputStream myFileInputStream = new
FileInputStream (FileDescriptor fd) ;
```

fd is an instance of type FileDescriptor. It represents the file used as the input stream.

The following are two new methods associated with the FieldInputStream class. These methods are in addition to the methods inherited from the InputStream class that you can override:

- **finalize()** performs garbage collection when the input stream is closed. The finalize() method is available for any Java object. It plays the role of destructor.

- **getFD()** retrieves the FileDescriptor object that is used as the input file stream.

The SequenceInputStream Class

As the name suggests, the SequenceInputStream class combines a sequence of two or more input streams into a single input stream. It includes two constructors:

- SequenceInputStream(InputStream in1, InputStream in2)

- SequenceInputStream(Enumeration in)

The first constructor, SequenceInputStream(InputStream in1, InputStream in2), takes two parameters—both input streams— and combines them into a single, logical input stream. Below is an example of instantiating the SequenceaInputStream class using the first constructor:

```
SequenceInputStream mySequenceInputStream = new
SequenceInputStream (InputStreaminStream, InputStream
inStream 2) ;
```

The second constructor, SequenceInputStream(Enumeration in), takes an enumeration of input streams. The Enumeration interface is defined in the java.util package. Below is an example of instantiating the SequenceInputStream class using the second constructor:

```
SequenceInputStream mySequenceInputStream = new
SequenceInputStream (Enumeration in ) ;
```

The StringBufferInputStream Class

A string is the source of the input stream in the StringBufferInputStream class. The string operates as a buffer from where the data is read. This class is very useful in applications that require string processing, for example, a natural language parser. The StringBufferInputStream class inherits all its methods from the InputStream class. It does not define any new methods. However, it does include three member variables that are useful for string processing. The variable buffer stores the string data. Use this variable to obtain the current string. Another useful variable is pos; it identifies the current position in the string buffer.

Use the following constructor to instantiate the StringBufferInputStream class:

■ **StringBufferInputStream(String s)** takes one parameter—a String object—that is the source of the input stream. Below is an example of instantiating the StringBufferInputStream class using this constructor:

```
StringBufferInputStream myStringBufferInputStream =
new StringBufferInputStream (String s) ;
```

Table 11-1 lists the member variables with their descriptions.

Type	Variable	Description
String	buffer	Stores the string data.
int	count	Specifies the number of characters to use in the buffer.
int	pos	Specifies the current position in the buffer.

Table 11-1: Member variables of the StringBufferInputStream class.

The FilterInputStream Class

The FilterInputStream class is a subclass of the InputStream class. As the name suggests it represents a class that you can use to process and filter the input stream in different ways. It is further subclassed into four classes: BufferedInputStream, DataInputStream, LineNumberInputStream, and PushBackInputStream. Each subclass provides a different way to process and filter the input stream.

The BufferedInputStream class provides a buffered stream of input. This class provides faster read access since it can read more data into the buffered stream than requested. This means subsequent reads are from the buffer rather than the input device. The DataInputStream class is useful for reading primitive Java data types in a portable fashion. If you want to keep track of the line numbers in the input stream, use the LineNumberInputStream class. If you need to push the bytes that have already been read back into the input stream class, use the PushBackInputStream class.

The BufferedInputStream Class

The BufferedInputStream class reads data from a buffer. The buffer is the input data stream. This type of input method provides speed and efficiency since the input operation takes place in memory. This class can read more data into the buffered stream than requested. This makes subsequent reads faster, as they come directly from memory.

The BufferedInputStream class inherits its methods from the InputStream class. You can instantiate this class using either one of the following two constructors:

- BufferedInputStream(InputStream in)

- BufferedInputStream(InputStream in, int size)

Both constructors take InputStream (described above) as their first parameter. The first constructor uses the default buffer size. Below is an example of instantiating the BufferedInputStream class using the first constructor:

```
BufferedInputStream myBufferedInputStream = new
BufferedInputStream (InputStream in, int bufSize) ;
```

bufSize is a variable representing the size of the buffer.

Table 11-2 lists the member variables with their descriptions.

Type	Variable	Description
byte	buf[]	The buffer where the data is stored.
int	count	Indicates the number of bytes in the buffer.
int	pos	Indicates the current position in the input buffer.
int	markpos	Specifies the current mark position in the input buffer.
int	marklimit	Specifies the maximum number of bytes that can be read before the mark is no longer valid.

Table 11-2: Member variables of the BufferedInputStream class.

The DataInputStream Class

This class reads Java data types from an input stream. You can instantiate this class using the only constructor it includes:

- **DataInputStream(InputStream in)** takes an InputStream object as its only parameter. Below is an example of instantiating the DataInputStream class using this constructor:

```
DataInputStream myDataInputStream = new DataInputStream
(InputStream in) ;
```

The DataInputStream read() methods have different variations. Each version of the readType() method takes a different data type that is read as input. For example the readChar() method takes a char data type as input. The readFloat() method takes a float data type as input. The readDouble() method takes a double data type as input. The readBoolean() method takes a boolean data type as input. The readInt() method takes an integer data type as input. The readLong() method takes a long data type as input. There are several other readType() methods included in this class. All of those methods are declared as final, so they can't be overridden. The Data I/O tutorial in the tutorials section of this chapter demonstrates the use of DataInputStream class and its read and write methods.

The DataInputStream class also includes another method, the skipBytes() method. Use it to skip *n* number of bytes where *n* is an integer parameter to the method. This method blocks until all specified number of bytes have been skipped. No other activity can take place until the specified number of bytes has been skipped.

The PushBackInputStream Class

The PushBackInputStream class implements an input stream that has a 1-byte push back buffer, so you have an ability to push a previously read byte back into the input stream. You can push back only a single byte at a time. Once it is pushed back into the input stream you can reread it. This class inherits its methods from the InputStream class.

The unread() Method

The unread() method is the only new method introduced in this class. It is used to push a byte back into the input stream.

The LineNumberInputStream Class

The LineNumberInputStream class keeps track of input line numbers. It inherits its methods from the InputStream class. The following new methods are introduced in this class:

- **setLineNumber()** sets the current line number to a particular value.

- **getLineNumber()** gets the value of the current line number.

The PipedInputStream Class

Threads communicate via streams using piped I/O. The PipedInputStream class is used for piped I/O between threads. It overrides the methods provided by the InputStream class.

The OutputStream Class

The OutputStream class is the logical counterpart to the InputStream class. Just like InputStream is an abstract class, OutputStream is also an abstract class. It cannot be instantiated. The OutputStream class defines a basic interface for writing streams. It is one of the two important java.io classes, the other being the InputStream class. It is the base for all other OutputStream classes that are derived from it. Its methods are inherited by all of its subclasses. Therefore once you learn the protocol for managing output streams using this class and its methods, you can apply it to different devices using an OutputStream derived class. You can use an OutputStream derived class to write information to a display device, for example.

The OutputStream class includes several subclasses: ByteArrayOutputStream, FileOutputStream, FilterOutputStream, and PipedOutputStream. The FilterOutputStream class is further classified into three subclasses: BufferedOutputStream, DataOutputStream, and PrintStream.

Methods of the OutputStream Class

A rich set of methods is included in this class. The OutputStream class includes three different types of write() methods. The write() methods write data to the output stream. Each variation includes a different set of parameters. The OutputStream class also includes a close() method that lets you close the output stream explicitly. We recommend that you use this method even though streams automatically close when they are destroyed.

The write() Methods

Use the write() methods to write data to the output stream. The OutputStream class includes three overloaded write() methods. These methods are similar to the three overloaded read() methods for the InputStream class. Each method writes data in a different way.

The first write method, abstract void write(int b), is an abstract method. It takes a single byte as its only parameter and writes it to the output data stream.

The second write method, void write(byte b[]), writes an array of bytes to the output data stream.

The third write method, void write(byte b[], int off, int len), writes a segment of an array to the output data stream. This method takes three parameters: an array of bytes, an integer offset and an integer length. The length parameter specifies the maximum number of bytes you want to write. The offset parameter indicates the offset into the byte array from where you want the data written.

The close() Method

Use the close() method to close the output data stream and release all resources associated with the stream. Although streams are automatically closed when they are destroyed, it is a good programming practice to call this method when you are finished writing to the output stream.

The flush() Method

Use the flush() method to flush the output stream. This method empties the buffers of any data. Invoke this method to make sure that your data is actually written to the output stream.

The ByteArrayOutputStream Class

This class uses an array of bytes as the output stream. Writing to an array of bytes is faster than writing to an output device because you are writing directly to memory. Use this class to write data to an array of bytes. Once the array is full, you can flush out the stream to an output device. The ByteArrayOutputStream class includes these two constructors:

- ByteArrayOutputStream(int size)
- ByteArrayOutputStream()

The first constructor, ByteArrayOutputStream(int size), takes an integer parameter that specifies the initial size of the byte array. Below is an example of instantiating the ByteArrayOutputStream class using this first constructor:

```
ByteArrayOutputStream myByteArrayOutputStream = new
ByteArrayOutPutSTream (int bufSize) ;
```

bufSize is the size of the buffer.

The second constructor, ByteArrayOutputStream(), takes no parameters and sets the output buffer to the default size. Below is an example of instantiating the ByteArrayOutputStream class using the second constructor:

```
ByteArrayOUtputStream myByteArrayOUtputStream = new
ByteARrayOUtputStream () ;
```

The ByteArrayOutputStream class includes two new methods:

- **toByteArray()** converts the input data to an array of bytes.
- **toString()** converts the input data to a String object.

The FileOutputStream Class

The FileOutputStream class is similar to FileInputStream in a lot of ways. It writes output to a file. A file may reside on the local or network drive. Similar to FileInputStream, it includes three constructors:

- FileOutputStream(String name)
- FileOutputStream(File file)
- FileOutputStream(FileDescriptor fd)

The first constructor, FileOutputStream(String name), takes a single parameter—a string—which is the name of a file you want to use as output. Below is an example of instantiating the FileOutputStream class using the first constructor:

```
FileOutputStream myFileOutputStream = new FileOUtputStream
("fileio.txt") ;
```

The string *"fileio.txt"* denotes a file used as the output stream.

The second constructor, FileOutputStream(File file), is similar to the first constructor; it takes a single parameter—a File object—which represents a filename of the host file system. Below is an example of instantiating the FileOutputStream class using the second constructor:

```
FileOuputStream myFileOutputStream = new FileOutputStream
(File file) ;
```

file is an instance of type File. It represents the file used as the output stream.

The third constructor, FileOutputStream(FileDescriptor fd), also takes a single parameter—a FileDescriptor object—which is the file you want to use as output. Below is an example of instantiating the FileOutputStream class using the third constructor:

```
FileOutputStream myfileOutputStream = new FileOUtputStream
(FileDescriptor fd );
```

fd is of type FileDescriptor. It represents the file used as the output stream.

The following are two methods associated with this class. The FileOutputStream class, in addition to the methods inherited from the OutputStream class which you can override. They are:

- **finalize()** works the same for output stream as it does for the input stream.
- **getFD()** retrieves the FileDescriptor object that is used as the output file stream.

The FilterOutputStream Class

The FilterOutputStream class is a subclass of the OutputStream class. As the name suggests it represents a class you can use to process and filter the output stream in different ways. It is further subclassed into three different classes: BufferedOutputStream, DataOutputStream, and PrintStream. Each subclass provides a different way to process and filter the output stream. The BufferedOutputStream class provides a buffered stream of output. It provides faster write access since data is first written to memory before being flushed out to the output device. The DataOutputStream class is useful for writing primitive Java data types in a portable fashion to an output stream. The PrintStream class prints output data in the form of text.

The BufferedOutputStream Class

Use the BufferedOutputStream class to write data to a buffer. The buffer is the output data stream. If the buffer is full or flushed, this class can write the data stream to an output device. This type of output method provides speed and efficiency since most of the operation takes place in memory before it is written to an output device.

The BufferedOutputStream class inherits its methods from the OutputStream class. You can instantiate this class using either one of the following two constructors:

- BufferedOutputStream(OutputStream out)
- BufferedOutputStream(OutputStream out, int size)

Both constructors take OutputStream as a parameter. The first constructor uses the default buffer size. Below is an example of instantiating the BufferedOutputStream class using the first constructor:

```
BufferedOutputStream myBufferedOutputStream = new
BufferedOUtputStream (OutputStream out ) ;
```

You specify the size as the second parameter in the second constructor. Below is an example of instantiating the BufferedInputStream class using the second constructor:

```
BufferedOutputStream my BufferedOutputStream = new
BufferedOUtputStream (OUtputStream out, int bufSize) :
```

bufSize is a variable that represents the size of the buffer.

In addition to the two constructors, this class includes the following two member variables:

- **byte buf[]** is the buffer where the data is stored.

- **int count** indicates the number of bytes in the buffer.

The DataOutputStream Class

Use this class to write Java data types to an output stream. You can instantiate this class using its only constructor:

- DataOutputStream(OutputStream out)

The constructor takes an OutputStream object as its only parameter. Below is an example of instantiating the DataOutputStream class suing this constructor:

```
DataOutputStream myDataOutputStream = new DataOutputStream
(OutputStream out) ;
```

The DataOutputStream write() methods have different variations. Each version of the writeType() method takes a different data type that is written as output. For example, the void writeChar(int v) method writes to a char data type. The void writeFloat(float v) method writes to a float data type. The void writeDouble(double v) method writes to a double data type.

Use the size() method to determine the number of bytes that have been written to the output stream.

The PrintStream Class

Use the PrintStream class to print output data in the form of text. This class includes the following two constructors:

- PrintStream(OutputStream out)

- PrintStream(OutputStream out, boolean autoflush)

The first constructor, PrintStream(OutputStream out), takes one parameter—the OutputStream object. Below is an example of instantiating the PrintStream class using the first constructor:

```
PrintStream myPrintStream = new PrintStream (OUtputStream
out) ;
```

The second constructor, PrintStream(OutputStream out, boolean autoflush), takes two parameters—the OutputStream object and an autoflush parameter. The autoflush parameter indicates that you want the stream flushed every time it encounters a newline character. Below is an example of instantiating the PrintStream class using the second constructor:

```
PrintStram myPrintStream = new PrintStream (OutputStream out,
true) ;
```

The PrintStream class includes a variety of methods to print data of different types. For example the Print(int i) method prints data of type integer. The Print(float f) method prints data of type float. The Print(double d) method prints data of type double. The number of methods are used to print a value as a single line. In particular, the println(String s) have been used throughout the book to print some text lines on the screen.

The checkError() method returns true if an error occurs when the stream is flushed.

The PipedOutputStream Class

Use the PipedOutputStream class for piped I/O between threads. This class overrides the methods provided by the OutputStream class.

The File Class

The File class includes methods that provide attribute information about a file including its name, path, length, and so on. The purpose of this class is to deal with most of the system-dependent filename features such as the separator character, root, device name, etc. It also includes methods for creating, deleting and renaming files and directories. The File class includes three constructors; you can instantiate this class using any one of them:

- File(String path)
- File(String path, String name)
- File(File dir, String name)

The first constructor, File(String path), takes a single parameter—the fully qualified path name of the file. Below is an example of instantiating the File class using the first constructor:

```
File myFile = new File("c:/myfiles/fileio.txt") ;
```

The string *"fileio.txt"* represents a file. You specify the fully qualified path along with the filename as the parameter.

The second constructor, File(String path, String name), takes two parameters—the first parameter is the directory path of the file, and the second parameter is the name of the file. Below is an example of instantiating the File class using the second constructor:

```
File myFile = new File("c:/myfiles/",'fileio.txt");
```

The string *"c:/myfiles/"* represents the path of the file. The string *"fileio.txt"* represents the file.

The third constructor, File(File dir, String name), also takes two parameters—the first parameter is a File object that specifies the directory path of the file, and the second parameter is the name of the file. Below is an example of instantiating the File class using the third constructor:

```
File myfile = new File(File dirpath,"fileio.txt");
```

dirpath is a File object that specifies the path of the file. The string *"fileio.txt"* is name of the file.

The File class includes several methods that you can use to obtain important information about a specified file. We can divide these methods into the following two categories: GetInfo and GetStatus.

GetInfo Methods

You can get important information about a file such as its name, path, absolute path, parent, and so on, using these methods:

- **getName()** returns the name of a file as a string.
- **getAbsolutePath()** returns the absolute path of a file.
- **getPath()** returns the path of a file.
- **getParent()** returns the parent directory of a file.

■ **lastModified()** returns a long value that indicates the time when the file was last modified.

■ **length()** returns a long value that specifies the length of the file.

GetStatus Methods

You can use these methods to see if a specified file exists and if it can be read from or written to, for example.

■ **exists()** returns true if a file exists. It returns false if it does not exist.

■ **canRead()** returns true if the file can be accessed to read.

■ **canWrite()** returns true if the file can be accessed to write.

■ **isFile()** returns true if this object represents a normal file (not directory).

■ **isDirectory()** returns true if this object represents the directory.

■ **isAbsolute()** returns true if a filename is absolute.

■ **delete()** deletes the specified file and returns true if the file delete was successful.

The RandomAccessFile Class

Using the RandomAccessFile class methods, you can write or read data from random locations within a file. It does not need to be a continuous stream. It uses the seek() method to achieve this functionality. You can instantiate the RandomAccessFile class using either one of the following two constructors:

■ RandomAccessFile(String name, String mode)

■ RandomAccessFile(File file, String mode)

The difference between the two constructors is in the first parameter it takes. The first constructor takes a String parameter which specifies the name of the file to access. Below is an example of instantiating the RandomAccessFile class using the first constructor:

```
RandomAccessFile myRandomAccessfile = new
RandomAccessFile("fileio.txt", "r") ;
```

The second constructor takes a File object as the first parameter. Below is an example of instantiating the RandomAccessFile class using the second constructor:

```
RandomAccessFile myRandomAccessFile = new
RandomAccessFile(File file, "rw") :
```

file is an instance of type File. It represents the file to be opened in random access read and write modes.

The second parameter in both the constructors defines the type of mode for the file you want to access—*"r"* for read and *"rw"* for read/write mode. Any other mode throws an IOException.

The RandomAccessFile class includes several read and write I/O methods.

The read() Methods

There are different variations on the read() methods depending on the type of data being read and the manner in which it is read. For example the int read(byte b[]) method reads an array of bytes and returns the number of bytes read. The char readChar() method reads data of type char. The int readInt() method reads integer data. The long readLong() method reads data of type long. The boolean readBoolean() method reads data of type boolean. Choose the right read() method depending on the type of data being read.

The write() Methods

Similar to the read() methods, there are different variations on the write() methods depending on the type of data being written and how it is being written. For example, the void write(byte b[]) method writes an array of bytes. The void writeChar(int v) method writes data of type char. The void writeInt(int v) method writes an integer data. The void writeLong(int v) method writes data of type long. The void writeBoolean(boolean v) method writes data of type boolean. Choose the correct write() method depending on the type of data being written.

In addition to the different variations on write() methods, the OutputStream class also includes the following two methods. They are similar to the methods discussed in the InputStream class.

- int skipBytes(int n)
- void close()

Unique Methods: seek(), getFilePointer() & length()

The RandomAccessFile class includes three unique methods. The seek() method is probably the most important method in this class. It makes random file I/O possible. To read or write data to random locations in a file, you need the ability to jump directly to such random locations. The seek() method provides this ability. It sets the file pointer to a particular location within the file. Once this position is set, you can use the appropriate read() or write() method to perform the I/O. The next unique method is the getFilePointer() method. Use it to determine the current location of the file pointer within the file. To determine the length of a file in bytes, use the length() method—the third unique method in this class.

Use the seek() method to set the file pointer to a specified absolute position within the file. This position is specified as a long parameter to the method. Once the file pointer is set to a particular location within the file, you can perform read or write operations. This is the most important method in this class. Using the seek() method, you can perform random input and output operations.

Use the getFilePointer() method to retrieve the current position of the file pointer within the file. The return value is of type long.

The third unique method in this class is the length() method. Use the length() method to determine the length of the file in bytes. The return value is of type long.

The FileDescriptor Class

Using the FileDescriptor class, you can obtain information about the file descriptors maintained by the operating system when someone accesses the directories and files. This class includes only one method: valid(). This class indicates if the FileDescriptor object is valid.

The StreamTokenizer Class

Using the StreamTokenizer class, you can parse an input stream into a stream of tokens. You can specify the type of input token you want to consider when parsing the input stream. You can instantiate the StreamTokenizer class using its only constructor:

- **StreamTokenizer(InputStream in)** takes an InputStream object as a parameter and generates a StreamTokenizer object.

Some of the most useful methods are:

- **nextToken()** gets the next token from the input stream.
- **pushBack()** pushes the current token back into the input stream.
- **lineno()** retrieves the current line number in the input stream.
- **commentChar()** defines the comment characters.
- **lowerCaseMode()** converts the input stream words into lowercase.

java.io Exceptions

Java includes built-in exception handling. It lets you handle errors easily without having to write any special code. There are two types of errors: errors that are bugs and errors that occur due to certain situations (e.g., file does not exist, invalid path, low memory, etc.). You need to fix errors that are bugs. Once fixed they will not occur again (hopefully!). Errors that occur due to certain situations are called *exceptions*. Refer to the section "Exception Handling" in Chapter 13 for a detailed discussion on exception handling.

Java uses class objects to handle exceptions. They may contain both data and methods. You can easily add Java exceptions to existing methods. So far we have reviewed the different java.io classes, their member variables, and methods. Let's now look at the exceptions thrown by these classes. Figure 11-2 shows the java.io exception hierarchy.

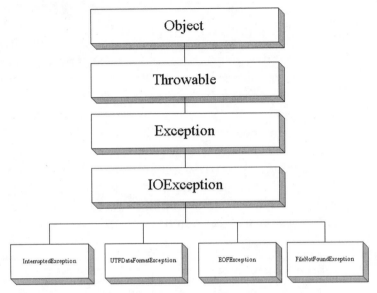

Figure 11-2: The java.io exception hierarchy.

Tutorial: File I/O

In this tutorial you will create the application *fileio* that creates a file, writes some text to it, and reads the data from the same file along with the number of bytes in the file. To begin, create a new project workspace called fileio (see Table 11-3 for the step-by-step instructions).

Step #	Location	Action
1	Developer Studio	Choose File|New.
2	New dialog box	Highlight Project Workspace, then click OK.
3	New Project Workspace dialog box	In the Name field, type **fileio**; then click Create.

Table 11-3: Creating the fileio Project Workspace.

First, you need to create a class. In the Developer Studio, click Insert | New Java Class. Using the Create New Class dialog box that appears, type **fileio** in the Name field, then click OK.

Next add the main() method to the same class. Again, you'll define access and class modifiers, which we'll discuss later. Use Table 11-4 to add this main() method.

Step #	Location	Action
1	Left pane of fileio Project Workspace	On the fileio class, right-click and choose Add Method from the menu.
2	New Method dialog box	In the Return type field type **void** and in the Method declaration field type **main(String argv[]) throws Exception**.
3	New Method dialog box	In the Access box, choose public and in the Modifiers box, check static.
4	New Method dialog box	Verify how the declaration looks, then click OK.

Table 11-4: Creating the main() method.

In the following lines of code, the bolded lines are those that you need to add to the source file in the text file displayed in the right pane of the Developer Studio:

```java
import java.io.File;
import java.io.IOException;
import java.io.FileInputStream;
import java.io.FileOutputStream;
import java.lang.System;

/* This is a fileio Java example application written using
Visual J++ 1.0. The fileio application creates a file, writes
some text to it and reads data from the same file
alongwith the number of bytes in the file.
*/

/*
 *
 * fileio
 *
 */
class fileio
{

    public static void main(String argv[]) throws Exception
    {

    //My code starts here

        FileOutputStream outStream = new
FileOutputStream("fileio.txt");

        // Set up the string
        String s = "This is a sample Visual J++ application that
demonstrates the use of java.io classes and methods.";

        // Write to the output stream
        for (int i=0; i<s.length(); ++i)
          outStream.write(s.charAt(i));

        // Close the output stream
        outStream.close();

        // Now let us open the file we just created and read
data from it
```

```
      // We use the FileInputStream class to do this
      FileInputStream inStream = new
FileInputStream("fileio.txt");

      // Read the available bytes
      int inBytes = inStream.available();

                  // Print the number of available bytes in the
input stream
      System.out.println("inStream has " +inBytes+" available
bytes");

      // Read the bytes
      byte inBuf[] = new byte[inBytes];
      int bytesRead = inStream.read(inBuf, 0, inBytes);

      // Indicate how many bytes were read
      System.out.println(bytesRead + " bytes were read from
the file.");

      // Indicate what the bytes are
      System.out.println("The bytes read are: " + new
String(inBuf, 0));

      // Close the input stream
      inStream.close();

   //My code ends here


   }


}
```

Let's analyze the above code. The following lines indicate inclusion of the java.io.File, java.io.IOException, java.io.FileInputStream, java.io.FileOutputStream, and java.lang.System classes. By including these classes you are making all the methods and member variables of these classes available to you. Consider these classes as the building blocks that you are using to build your own Java application.

In the following line you are using the FileOutputStream() constructor to instantiate the FileOutputStream class. The instance is called outStream. The output file is fileio.txt:

```
FileOutputStream outStream = new
FileOutputStream("fileio.txt");
```

Next, set up the string you want written to the file. In the following line a String object *s* is created and the text "This is a sample Visual J++ application that demonstrates the use of java.io classes and methods." is assigned to it:

```
String s = "This is a sample Visual J++ application that
demonstrates the use of java.io classes and methods.";
```

Now write the string to the output stream. Loop through the string character by character and write one character at a time to the output stream. Loop through the string until the end of string is reached:

```
for (int i = 0; i < s.length(); ++i)
    outStream.write(s.charAt(i));
```

Close the output stream using the close() method. Although streams automatically close when they are destroyed, it is a good programming practice to call the close() method when you are finished writing to the output stream:

```
outStream.close();
```

Now use the FileInputStream(String name) constructor to create an instance of the input stream called inStream. Of course, the file you are going to read from is fileio.txt:

```
FileInputStream inStream = new
FileInputStream("fileio.txt");
```

Use the available() method to get the number of available bytes in the input stream:

```
int inBytes = inStream.available();
```

Print the available bytes in the input stream:

```
System.out.println("inStream has " + inBytes + "
available bytes");
```

Now let's read the bytes from the input stream. Create an instance of byte array using the byte() constructor. This instance is the buffer to hold the bytes read from the input stream:

```
byte inBuf[] = new byte[inBytes];
```

Use the read() method to read the bytes into the input buffer. The read() method returns the number of bytes successfully read:

```
int bytesRead = inStream.read(inBuf, 0, inBytes);
```

Now that you have the information available—the number of bytes successfully read from the file and what the bytes are—print them. This will verify if the bytes written are the same as the bytes read:

```
System.out.println(bytesRead + " bytes were read from
the file.");
```

```
System.out.println("The bytes read are: " + new
String(inBuf, 0));
```

You are finished. Close the input stream. This releases all resources associated with it. You have already closed the output stream:

```
inStream.close();
```

Once you finish typing the above code, you are ready to build the Java application. To build the code, click Build | fileio. Then, to execute the code, click Build | Execute.

Since you are executing this project for the first time the Developer Studio, a dialog box displays for you to specify the class file name (see Figure 11-3). Using this dialog box, type **fileio** in the Class filename field. Also, underneath that you have a choice of using either the jview interpreter or Internet Explorer to view the results. For this example, choose Stand-alone interpreter (which already has the jview program specified). Then, click OK.

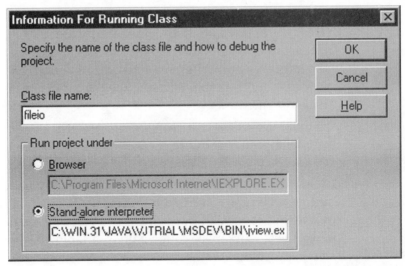

Figure 11-3 : The Information For Running Class dialog box filled out.

Once the Java program executes, you should see something similar to Figure 11-4.

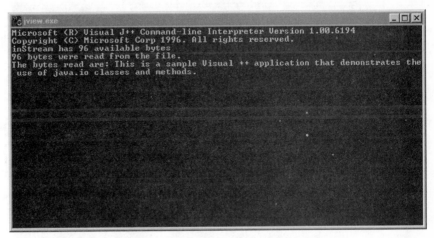

Figure 11-4: Executing the fileio application.

As you can see in Figure 11-4, the text string "This is a sample Visual J++ application that demonstrates the use of java.io classes and methods" was written to the file fileio.txt using the FileOutputStream write() method. It is read back along with the number of bytes in the file using the FileInputStream read() and available() methods.

Tutorial: ByteArray I/O

In this tutorial you will create the application *baio* that creates a byte array, writes some text to it, and reads the data from the same byte array along with the number of bytes in it. To begin, create a new project workspace called baio (see Table 11-5 for the step-by-step instructions).

Step #	Location	Action
1	Developer Studio	Choose File|New.
2	New dialog box	Highlight Project Workspace, then click OK.
3	New Project Workspace dialog box	In the Name field, type **baio**; then click Create.

Table 11-5: Creating the baio Project Workspace.

First, you need to create a class. In the Developer Studio, click Insert \| New Java Class. Using the Create New Class dialog box that appears, type **baio** in the Name field, then click OK.

Next add the main() method to the same class. Again, you'll define access and class modifiers, which we'll discuss later. Use Table 11-6 to add this main() method.

Step #	Location	Action
1	Left pane of baio Project Workspace	On the baio class, right-click and choose Add Method from the menu.
2	New Method dialog box	In the Return type field type **void** and in the Method declaration field type **main(String argv[]) throws Exception.**
3	New Method dialog box	In the Access box, choose public and in the Modifiers box, check static.
4	New Method dialog box	Verify how the declaration looks, then click OK.

Table 11-6: Creating the main() method.

In the following lines of code, the bolded lines are those that you need to add to the source file in the text file displayed in the right pane of the Developer Studio:

```
import java.io.IOException;
import java.io.ByteArrayInputStream;
import java.io.ByteArrayOutputStream;
import java.lang.System;


/* This is a ByteArrayIO Java example application written
using Visual J++ 1.0
The BAIO creates a byte array as an output stream, writes
some text to it and reads data from the same array along with
the number of bytes in it.
*/

/*
 *
 * baio
 *
 */
class baio
{
```

```
public static void main(String argv[]) throws Exception
{

//My code starts here

    // First let us create a byte array and write some text
to it
    // We use the ByteArrayOutputStream class to do this
    ByteArrayOutputStream outStream = new
ByteArrayOutputStream();

    // Set up the string
    String s = "This is a sample Visual J++ application that
demonstrates the use of java.io classes and methods.";

    // Write to the output stream
    for (int i = 0; i < s.length(); ++i)
       outStream.write(s.charAt(i));

    // Now let us open the byte array we just created and
read data from it
    // We use the ByteArrayInputStream class to do this
    ByteArrayInputStream inStream = new
ByteArrayInputStream(outStream.toByteArray());

    // Get the available bytes in the input stream
    int inBytes = inStream.available();

    // Print the number of available bytes in the input
stream
    System.out.println("inStream has " + inBytes + "
available bytes");

    // Read the bytes
    byte inBuf[] = new byte[inBytes];
    int bytesRead = inStream.read(inBuf, 0, inBytes);

    // Indicate how many bytes were read
    System.out.println(bytesRead + " bytes were read from
the byte array.");
```

```
        // Indicate what the bytes are
        System.out.println("The bytes read are: " + new
    String(inBuf, 0));

        // Close the input stream
        inStream.close();

        // Close the output stream
        outStream.close();

    //My code ends here


    }


}
```

Let's analyze the above code. The following lines indicate inclusion of the java.io.IOException, java.io.ByteArrayInputStream, java.io.ByteArrayOutputStream, and java.lang.System classes. By including these classes you are making all the methods and member variables of these classes available to you. Consider these classes as the building blocks that you are using to build your own Java application.

In the following line you are using the ByteArrayOutputStream() constructor to instantiate the ByteArrayOutputStream class. The instance is called outStream:

```
        ByteArrayOutputStream outStream = new
    ByteArrayOutputStream();
```

Next, set up the string that you want written to the array. In the following line a String object s is created and the text "This is a sample Visual J++ application that demonstrates the use of java.io classes and methods." is assigned to it:

```
        String s = "This is a sample Visual J++ application that
    demonstrates the use of java.io classes and methods.";
```

Now write the string to the output stream. Loop through the string character by character and write one character at a time to the output stream. Loop through the string until the end of string is reached:

```
for (int i = 0; i < s.length(); ++i)
   outStream.write(s.charAt(i));
```

Now use the toByteArray() to convert the output stream into a byte array. This byte array creates an instance of the input stream using the ByteArrayInputStream class constructor:

```
ByteArrayInputStream inStream = new
ByteArrayInputStream(outStream.toByteArray());
```

Use the available() method to get the number of available bytes in the input stream:

```
int inBytes = inStream.available();
```

Print the available bytes in the input stream:

```
System.out.println("inStream has " + inBytes + "
available bytes");
```

Now let's read the bytes from the input stream. Create an instance of byte array using the byte() constructor. This instance is the buffer to hold the bytes read from the input stream:

```
byte inBuf[] = new byte[inBytes];
```

Use the read() method to read the bytes into the input buffer. The read() method returns the number of bytes successfully read:

```
int bytesRead = inStream.read(inBuf, 0, inBytes);
```

Now that you have the information available—the number of bytes successfully read from the byte array and what the bytes are—print them. Use this information to verify if the bytes written are the same as the bytes read:

```
System.out.println(bytesRead + " bytes were read from
the byte array.");
```

```
System.out.println("The bytes read are: " + new
String(inBuf, 0));
```

You are finished. Close the input and output streams. This releases all resources associated with the streams. Although streams automatically close when they are destroyed, it is a good programming practice to call the close() method when you are finished writing to the output stream and reading from the input stream:

```
inStream.close();
outStream.close();
```

Once you finish typing the above code, you are ready to build the Java application. To build the code, click Build I baio. Then, to execute the code, click Build I Execute.

Since you are executing this project for the first time the Developer Studio, a dialog box displays for you to specify the class file name (see Figure 11-5). Using this dialog box, type **baio** in the Class filename field. Also, underneath that you have a choice of using either the jview interpreter or Internet Explorer to view the results. For this example, choose Stand-alone interpreter (which already has the jview program specified). Then, click OK.

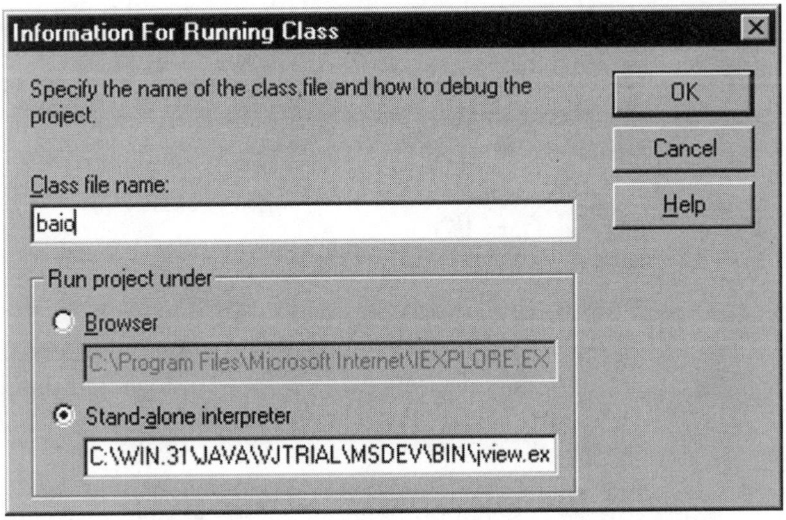

Figure 11-5: The Information For Running Class dialog box filled out.

Once the Java program executes, you should see something similar to Figure 11-6.

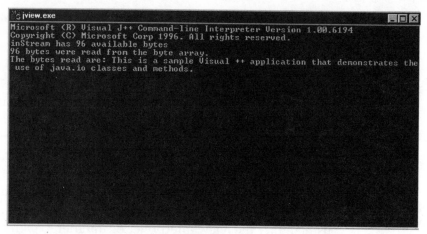

Figure 11-6: Executing the baio application.

As you can see in Figure 11-6, the text string "This is a sample Visual J++ application that demonstrates the use of java.io classes and methods" was written to the byte array using the ByteArrayOutputStream write() method. It is read back along with the number of bytes in the file using the ByteArrayInputStream read() and available() methods.

Tutorial: Data I/O

In this tutorial, you will create the application *dataio* that creates a file, writes some data to it, and reads the data from the same file. To begin, create a new project workspace called dataio (see Table 11-7 for the step-by-step instructions).

Step #	Location	Action
1	Developer Studio	Choose File|New.
2	New dialog box	Highlight Project Workspace, then click OK.
3	New Project Workspace dialog box	In the Name field, type **dataio**, then click Create.

Table 11-7: Creating the dataio Project Workspace.

First, you need to create a class. In the Developer Studio, click Insert | New Java Class. Using the Create New Class dialog box that appears, type **dataio** in the Name field, then click OK.

Next, add the main() method to the same class. Again, you'll define access and class modifiers, which we'll discuss later. Use Table 11-8 to add this main() method.

Step #	Location	Action
1	Left pane of dataio Project Workspace	On the dataio class, right-click and choose Add Method from the menu.
2	New Method dialog box	In the Return type field type **void** and in the Method declaration field type **main(String argv[]) throws Exception**.
3	New Method dialog box	In the Access box, choose public and in the Modifiers box, check static.
4	New Method dialog box	Verify how the declaration looks, then click OK.

Table 11-8: Creating the main() method.

In the following lines of code, the bolded lines are those that you need to add to the source file in the text file displayed in the right pane of the Developer Studio:

```
import java.io.IOException;
import java.io.FileInputStream;
import java.io.FileOutputStream;
import java.io.DataInputStream;
import java.io.DataOutputStream;
import java.io.File;
import java.lang.System;
```

```
/* This is a dataio Java example application written using
Visual J++ 1.0. The dataio creates a sample file as an output
stream, writes some data to it and reads data from the same
file.
*/

/*
 *
 * dataio
 *
 */
class dataio
{

    public static void main(String argv[]) throws Exception
    {

    //My code starts here

        // First let us create a file and write some text to it
        // We use the FileOutput and DataOutputStream classes to
do this
        File file = new File("dataio.txt");
        FileOutputStream outFile = new FileOutputStream(file);
        DataOutputStream outStream = new
DataOutputStream(outFile);

        // Write to the output stream
        outStream.writeChar('R');
        outStream.writeInt(567);

        // close the output stream
        outStream.close();

        // close the file
        outFile.close();

        // Now let us open the file we just created and read
data from it
        // We use the FileInputStream and DataInputStream
classes to do this
```

```
FileInputStream inFile = new FileInputStream(file);
DataInputStream inStream = new DataInputStream(inFile);

// Read the data and print it
System.out.println(inStream.readChar());
System.out.println(inStream.readInt());

// Close the input stream
inStream.close();

// Close the file
inFile.close();

//My code ends here

    }

}
```

Let's analyze the above code. The following lines indicate inclusion of the java.io.IOException, java.io.FileInputStream, java.io.FileOutputStream, java.io.DataInputStream, java.io.DataOutputStream, java.io.File, and java.lang.System classes. By including these classes you are making all the methods and member variables of these classes available to you. Consider these classes as the building blocks and you are using them to build your own Java application.

In the following line you are using the File() constructor to create a file dataio.txt:

```
File file = new File("dataio.txt");
```

Next, create an instance of output stream using the file created in the above line of code. Use the FileOutputStream(File file) to create the instance of output stream:

```
FileOutputStream outFile = new FileOutputStream(file);
```

In the following line, you use the DataOutputStream(OutputStream outStream) to create an instance of the data output stream called outStream:

```
DataOutputStream outStream = new
DataOutputStream(outFile);
```

Now write two types of data—a character and an integer—to the data output stream. Use the writeChar() and writeInt() methods to do this:

```
outStream.writeChar('R');
outStream.writeInt(567);
```

Close both the output stream and file. You are finished writing data to them:

```
outStream.close();
outFile.close();
```

Now let's open the file and read the data back. Use the FileInputStream(File file) constructor to create an instance of the FileInputStream class. This instance is called inFile. Use the DataInputStream(InputStream instream) constructor to create the data input stream:

```
FileInputStream inFile = new FileInputStream(file);
DataInputStream inStream = new DataInputStream(inFile);
```

Now read the data and print it. Use the readChar() method to read the character. Use the readInt() method to read the integer:

```
System.out.println(inStream.readChar());
System.out.println(inStream.readInt());
```

Close both the input stream and file. You are finished reading from them:

```
inStream.close();
inFile.close();
```

Once you finish typing the above code, you are ready to build the Java application. To build the code, click Build | dataio. Then, to execute the code, click Build | Execute.

Since you are executing this project for the first time the Developer Studio, a dialog box displays for you to specify the class file name (see Figure 11-7). On this dialog box, in the Class filename field, type **dataio**. Also, underneath that you have a choice of using either the jview interpreter or the Internet Explorer to view the results. For this example, choose Stand-alone interpreter (which already has the jview program specified). Then, click OK.

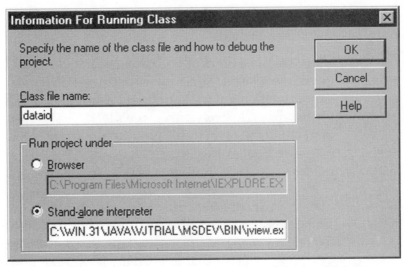

Figure 11-7: The Information For Running Class dialog box filled out.

Once the Java program executes, you should see something similar to Figure 11-8.

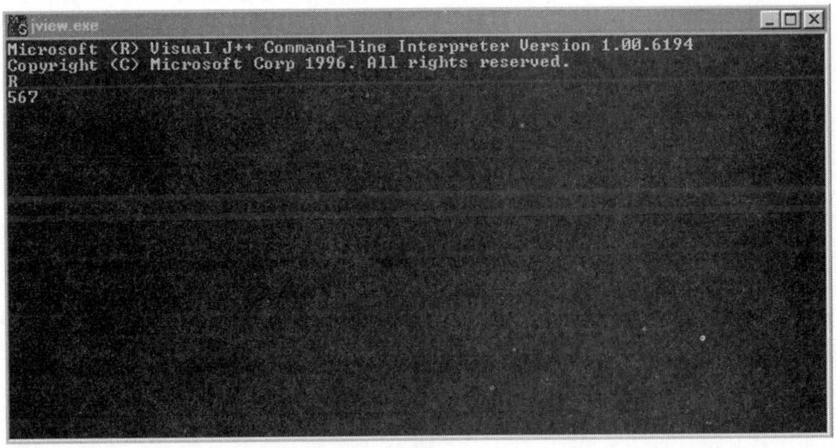

Figure 11-8: Executing the dataio application.

As you can see in Figure 11-8, the data—character R and integer 567—that was written to the file dataio.txt using the FileOutputStream and DataOutputStream methods, is read back using the FileInputStream and DataInputStream methods.

Moving On

There are three types of I/O: streams, low-level, and console and port. Low-level I/O does not support buffered data. Streams support buffered data. You should use either low-level functions or streams exclusively on a given file. Streams represent sequences of bytes. They travel from one endpoint (source) to another endpoint (destination).

Java supports stream-based I/O. The java.io package includes a rich set of predefined classes that you can use in your Java programs. This chapter provided an indepth look at these classes. Of all the classes, the InputStream and OutputStream are probably the two most important classes. This chapter also included three Visual J++ tutorials that utilized the Java I/O classes and methods.

Chapter 12 discusses the Java networking classes and how you can use them to develop network-enabled Java applications. Chapter 13 takes a closer look at the Java Database Connectivity (JDBC) API. The JDBC API provides transparent and seamless access to a variety of popular databases for your Java applications.

12

Network Programming

Network programming in Java is not hard to understand. There are a few classes and procedures in the java.net package that you need to follow. The tricky part is in understanding exactly how communication works on the Net in the first place. Once you have an understanding of communication and you know how to use the java.net package, you should be able to develop network enabled Java programs with very little difficulty. This chapter introduces you to a very high-level understanding of how communication takes place on the Net and in Java. Then, you will also learn what you need to know to effectively design a Java program to connect to the Internet, a server, or even another applet.

Introduction to Networking

When communication takes place you need to have a protocol so each side of the communicating party can understand each other. Data communication protocols are responsible for managing and implementing the data exchange between all the available participants in a given application or, more generally, a network. There are several protocols available for just about every different environment. A few of the major protocols are IPX/SPX (which allows communication on Novell networks), AppleTalk (which lets Apple computers communicate), and NetBIOS (a protocol for IBM and compatibles).

All the services or protocols just mentioned are not very practical for applications based on Java's heterogeneous design, because each one is specific to one or two platforms. As a result, you need a way to have all environments communicate regardless of the platform constraints. That is where TCP/IP comes in. TCP/IP is the protocol of the Net that lets communication take place with all kinds of computers and in all sorts of ways.

In the real world, you follow various protocols every time you communicate with someone or even with things. For example, when you decide to write a document on your computer, you turn on the computer, load the word processor, and start working. That is the essence of what a protocol does for the Net. Without it you might start working before you turn on the computer. The TCP/IP protocol defines what two programs need to do to ensure that there is proper communication taking place, and everyone is not trying to talk at the same time.

TCP/IP Basics

TCP/IP stands for Transmission Control Protocol/Internet Protocol. The TCP/IP protocol actually refers to several protocols. TCP/IP is a topic that can and has been discussed at length. To use TCP/IP effectively for network programming, you'll only need to know the basics of an otherwise complex communication protocol.

Starting from the beginning, TCP/IP was created by the Department of Defense (the creator of the Internet) as a way of distributing information to all the participating computers on any given network. In this distributed environment, if part of the network becomes dysfunctional (something that could happen in a time of war), the rest of the network could remain functional. This was a major step forward in fault tolerance from older networking models, where if one member of the network went down, it would take the whole network with it. TCP/IP has since facilitated the infrastructure for the Internet. Simply stated, without TCP/IP there would be no Internet. More precisely, there would be an Internet with no way to communicate.

The TCP & IP Protocols

Two protocols make up TCP/IP: TCP and IP. Together, they make a reliable and useful protocol for a network environment.

The IP protocol chops up a data stream into byte (no pun intended) size packets, labeling each packet with its contents and destination. Then, these packets attempt to choose the quickest path to their destination. Sometimes the shortest route is not always the fastest. External factors like network load or partial network failure may cause packets to choose a physically longer route.

The TCP protocol sorts the packets of data into the correct order and, if a packet is missing, requests that packet again. So, the IP protocol makes data transfer efficient, and the TCP protocol makes it reliable. Figure 12-1 shows a diagram of a typical day on the Internet, where a server is sending information to a client or vice versa.

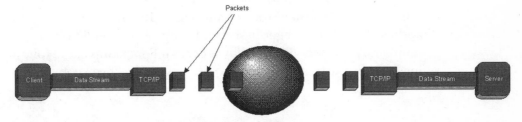

Figure 12-1: Visual view of TCP/IP connecting a client with a server. The sphere represents any potential environment (i.e., Internet, intranet, LAN, etc.).

The Datagram Protocol

Another protocol that is at the same level as the TCP of TCP/IP is User Datagram Protocol (UDP). This protocol, UDP/IP, is basically a connection-less version of TCP/IP. This means that each packet is sent as a single entity as opposed to TCP/IP which sends a group of related packets. The advantage of this is that you are able to have multiple servers communicating with one client at the same time. Also, if the data you plan to send across the wire is extremely small, you can send it in one self-contained packet, making the communication potentially faster than TCP/IP.

The disadvantage of having a UDP connection is that unlike TCP it does not verify that all the packets have been received, nor does it determine the proper order for each packet.

You can use the UDP/IP protocol in your Java programs by using the DatagramSocket and related classes that are part of the java.net package (reference the Java API specifications in InfoView for more information).

IP Addressing

To be a participant on any network (Internet, intranet, LAN, or WAN), you need to have a unique name. This gives you an unambiguous reference or address on the network. With TCP/IP this is done through Internet Protocol addresses (IP addresses). An IP address is a 32-bit integer based on four groups of eight binary numbers, each one separated by a period. For example, the following is an IP address where each of the values has been converted to a decimal:

```
234.122.23.33
```

Note

Another name for IP address is a dotted octet. Dotted octet comes from the fact that each decimal number above represents an 8-bit binary number (separated by dots).

IP Addressing on the Internet

On the Internet, notice that you do not have to run around inputting IP addresses to connect to your favorite sites. You simply enter the URL (Uniform Resource Locator)—for example: **http://home.netscape.com**.

This is because there are Domain Name Services (DNSs) on the Net that figure out what you have inputted and will convert your input back to an IP address. So when you enter something like the above into your browser, it goes to a DNS server, and the server retrieves that actual dotted octet.

Several DNS servers can work together to resolve an IP address from a name. Also, through the use of a DNS you can have aliases created so that you can have several different addresses pointing to the same server. To illustrate, http://www.myGreatServer.com, http://www.mySuperServer.com, and http://www.myPowerServer.com could all be pointing to one physical server called http://www.myServer.com.

If you are connected to the Net, you have a unique IP address assigned to you. The first thing to look at is how you can retrieve your IP address in Java and on your system.

As mentioned earlier, the package that you will use extensively is the java.net package. In this package are the tools necessary to do just about everything in Java. You can use the class java.net.InetAddress tool to retrieve information about your IP address and hostname. Consider the following:

```
try {

  //Returns your IP address
  InetAddress myAddress = InetAddress.getLocalHost();

  } catch(Exception e) {
}
```

Since *InetAddress* throws an exception and does not have a constructor, you need to use exception handling and use the method getLocalHost(), passing it to the instance variable *myAddress*.

Dynamic Addressing

Depending on your setup of TCP/IP you may not have a static address hard-coded in your configuration. So every time you log on to the network, you get assigned a different IP address.

This form of IP addressing is called Dynamic Host Configuration Protocol (DHCP). DHCP is a dynamic way to receive an IP address every time you log on to a network. DHCP is a more efficient way of managing IP addresses across a network. It is also a very effective way of not needing to hard code an IP address to each of the participants of the network.

Another utility that is available for Windows NT is a command-line executable called ipconfig.exe, or, in Windows 95, winipcfg.exe. Either one tells you information about your IP address and other TCP/IP related things.

Tip

The one that interests you the most is the dotted octet on the IP address line. Your numbers will vary, but, if you received a message that TCP/IP is not configured, then you will need to have TCP/IP reconfigured or installed or you may experience difficulties with examples in this chapter. Secondly, if you receive all zeros (0.0.0.0), then your setup of TCP/IP is configured, but you are not connected to your network.

Ports

IP addresses help identify everyone on the Net, and *ports* help you connect to other participants of the Net. Looking at the Internet, you will notice that there are many different ways to access information besides the World Wide Web. These include protocols like FTP and Telnet, to name two. Not only do ports give servers the ability to facilitate all the protocols on the Net, ports also let several clients access these different protocols at the same time. Ports connect the server to the client and to where information is transferred, based on the designated port. Technically speaking, a port is an integer (16 bits) TCP uses to listen for incoming information. Then, when a request for connection is sent from a client to that port, TCP verifies and manages the connection. You do not need to worry about how to request a connection or handle requests for connections.

There are predefined port numbers used on the Internet to distinguish between the various major protocols for the Net. The Internet Assigned Numbers Authority (IANA) is in charge of maintaining a list of protocols and the port numbers with which they should work. For example, port 21 is usually reserved for FTP (File Transfer Protocol). Port 23 is used for Telnet, and 80 is for HTTP (HyperText Transfer Protocol). Since a port represents a 16-bit integer, you could potentially have over sixteen thousand protocols listening in their respective ports. Fortunately, there are way fewer standard protocols than available ports. In fact, it is a safe bet to say that any ports above 1024 are probably not used.

As mentioned earlier, there are many ports for many different protocols. However, what if two clients both want to access the HTTP port of a given client? This is done through the use of *sockets*.

Sockets

Sockets are effectively the endpoints in communication that takes place between two entities. With a socket, you have a source IP address and source port and a destination IP address and a destination port. You can have more than one socket connected to a single port, thus you can have multiple connections to a single port. In Java you will be able to work with a number of classes that let you deal directly with a socket.

Network Programming in Java

So far, everything you have read has been on communication in general. However, this section specifically discusses how the above information ties into Java, and how you can take advantage of it.

Network programming in Java deals with the implementation of what you learned in the last section, all of it relating to the java.net package. There are classes and levels at which you can make your Java programs network-aware. Using TCP/IP, java.net, and Visual J++ you can create Java programs to communicate with browsers, servers, and other Java programs. You will also learn about special programming techniques that allow multiple applets to communicate on the same HTML page.

Communicating With Internet Protocols

In Java, the *URL class* represents a URL that you use on the Internet. Remember that a URL can use the HTTP protocol for hyperText documents, FTP for transferring files, or many other Internet-supported protocols (Gopher, for example). In your Java programs, you can use URL to connect to a specific resource on the Net, allowing you to create Network-aware Java programs.

The following is an example of creating a new URL pointing to the Web site http://www.microsoft.com.

```
try {
    URL myMsURL= new URL("http://www.microsoft.com ");
    URL myMsURL2 = new URL("http", "www.microsoft.com", 80,
"index.html")
} catch(MalformedURLException e) {}
```

Looking at the above example, notice that the URL class throws the Exception MalformedURLException class and needs to be caught. There are two URL constructor examples, both connecting to the same site (http://www.microsoft.com). The first sample takes the string "http://www.microsoft.com." The second constructor has four input parameters starting with the protocol, followed by the site, port, and file to load. (There are other combinations that you can use to construct URLs. See the Java API specifications in InfoView for more information.)

Note

You can use both relative and absolute URLs in the java.net.URL class.

However, constructing a URL is only half of the puzzle because all it does is represent a real URL. Now, you need to implement a way to retrieve that information from the site. That can be done one of several ways. One way is to use the URLConnection class and the openConnection() method. The next section introduces URLConnection and contains a tutorial to actually retrieve information from Microsoft's site.

It is possible to retrieve data directly from the URL class using streams or by using the getContent() method that belongs to URL. But the most versatile way to connect is to use the URLConnection class because it allows you to retrieve and send data.

URLConnection represents the actual network connection to a specified URL on the Internet. Using URLConnection in conjunction with URL gives you the ability to retrieve and send information. The following is an example for creating a URLConnection called myMsConnection:

```
try {
    URL myMsURL = new URL("http://www.microsoft.com ");

    URLConnection myMsConnection = myMsURL.openConnection();
} catch(MalrformedURLException e) {}
```

Looking at the above examples you can see that you are instancing myMsURL to point to http://www.microsoft.com. Then you pass the URL connection for myMsURL to myMsConnection, using the openConnection() method in the URL class. Once this is done, you can retrieve data from the specified location.

Tutorial: Using URLConnection

In this tutorial you will create a Java application that connects to Microsoft's home page and retrieves information from it. Create a new project workspace called URLConnectionTest (see Table 12-1 for the step-by-step instructions).

Step #	Location	Action
1	Developer Studio	Choose File|New.
2	New dialog box	Highlight Project Workspace, then click OK.
3	New Project Workspace dialog box	In the Name field, type **URLConnectionTest**, then click Create.

Table 12-1: Creating the URLConnectionTest Project Workspace.

First, you need to create a class. In the Developer Studio, click Insert | New Java Class. Using the Create New Class dialog box that appears, type **URLConnectionTest** in the Name field, type **Frame** in the Extends field, and click OK.

Now, add a handleEvent() method to the same class. See Table 12-2 for step-by-step instructions.

Step #	Location	Action
1	Left pane of URLConnectionTest Project Workspace	On the URLConnectionTest class, right-click and choose Add Method from the menu.
2	New Method dialog box	In the Return type field, type **boolean** and in the Method declaration field, type **handleEvent(Event evt)**.
3	New Method dialog box	In the Access box, choose public.
4	New Method dialog box	Verify how the declaration looks, then click OK.

Table 12-2: Creating the handleEvent() method.

Next add the clickedmyMsButton() method. See Table 12-3 for step-by-step instructions.

Step #	Location	Action
1	Left pane of URLConnectionTest Project Workspace	On the URLConnectionTest class, right-click and choose Add Method from the menu.
2	New Method dialog box	In the Return type field type **void**, and in the Method declaration field type **clickedmyMsButton( )**.
3	New Method dialog box	In the Access box, choose public.
4	New Method dialog box	Verify how the declaration looks, then click OK.

Table 12-3: Creating the clickedmyMsButton() method.

Next add the URLConnectionTest() method. See Table 12-4 for step-by-step instructions.

Step #	Location	Action
1	Left pane of URLConnectionTest Project Workspace	On the URLConnectionTest class, right-click and choose Add Method from the menu.
2	New Method dialog box	In the Method declaration field type **URLConnectionTest( )**.
3	New Method dialog box	In the Access box, choose public.
4	New Method dialog box	Verify how the declaration looks, then click OK.

Table 12-4: Creating the URLConnectionTest() constructor.

Finally, use Table 12-5 to create the main() method for this application.

Step #	Location	Action
1	Left pane of URLConnectionTest Project Workspace	On the URLConnectionTest class, right-click and choose Add Method from the menu.
2	New Method dialog box	In the Return type field type **void**, and in the Method declaration field type **main(String args[ ])**.
3	New Method dialog box	In the Access box, choose public, and in the Modifiers box, check static.
4	New Method dialog box	Verify how the declaration looks, then click OK.

Table 12-5: Creating the main() method.

In the following lines of code, the bolded lines are those that you need to add to the source file in the text file displayed in the right pane of the Developer Studio:

```
import java.awt.Frame;

//My code starts here
import java.net.*;
import java.awt.*;
import java.io.*;
//My code ends here

/*
 *
 * URLConnectionTest
 *
 */
class URLConnectionTest extends Frame
{

    //My code starts here
    Button myMsButton;
```

```
    TextArea myTextPane;
    static URL myURL;

    static URLConnection myURLConnection;
    InputStream myInStream;
//My code ends here

public static void main(String args[])
{

   //My code starts here
   new URLConnectionTest();
   //My code ends here

}



public URLConnectionTest()
{

   //My code starts here
   setLayout(new FlowLayout());
   myMsButton = new Button("WWW.MICROSOFT.COM");
   add(myMsButton);
   myTextPane = new TextArea(20,70);
   add(myTextPane);
   resize(600, 400);
   show();
   //My code ends here

}



public void clickedmyMsButton()
{

   //My code starts here
           //Construct the URL
```

```
        try {
            myURL  = new URL("http://www.microsoft.com");
        } catch(MalformedURLException e) {
            System.out.println("Unable to retieve URL. Error:
" + e);
        }

        //Retrieve the Data
        try {
            myURLConnection = myURL.openConnection();
            myInStream = myURLConnection.getInputStream();
            DataInputStream myDataInStream = new
DataInputStream(myInStream);

            //Read the first 20 lines of the site
            for (int i = 1; i < 20; i++) {

            String temp = myDataInStream.readLine();
            myTextPane.appendText(temp + "\n");
            }
        } catch(IOException e) {
            System.out.println("An IO error occured. Error: "
+ e);
        }
    //My code ends here

    }


    public boolean handleEvent(Event evt)
    {

    //My code starts here
    if (evt.id == evt.ACTION_EVENT && evt.target ==
myMsButton) {
            clickedmyMsButton();
            return true;
        } else if (evt.id == evt.WINDOW_DESTROY) {
            System.exit(0);
```

```
            return true;
        }
        return super.handleEvent(evt);
    //My code ends here


    }


}
```

Look at the above code and focus on the area that contains the line clickedmyMsButton(). The first line of code under the try statement is as follows:

```
myURL   = new URL("http://www.microsoft.com");
```

Here you instance the URL *myURL* to point to http://www. microsoft.com. The next line of code to look at is the instances myURLConnection using openConnection() from the URLConnection class to represent the connection that myURL has with http://www.microsoft.com:

```
myURLConnection = myURL.openConnection();
```

From here things start to look extremely similar to the last chapter that discussed streams, because at this point you are simply reading data from a stream.

```
myInStream = myURLConnection.getInputStream();
            DataInputStream myDataInStream = new
DataInputStream(myInStream);
```

The first line of code directs the input stream for the connection myURLConnection to myInStream (an instance of the InputStream). The second line instances myDataInStream, passing it myInStream, allowing you to retrieve information from the stream. The next line is the for loop that cycles twenty times, calling the following two lines of code:

```
String temp = myDataInStream.readLine();
            myTextPane.appendText(temp + "\n");
```

The first line of code uses the readLine() method to read a line of code from the stream and put in a temporary String variable called temp. The second line of code uses the appendText() method to add the line of code to the text area myTextPane. Once that is done you have effectively connected, retrieved, and displayed information from the http://www.microsoft.com site.

Now you are ready to build your code. To build the code, click Build | Build URLConnectionTest. Then, to execute the code, click Build | Execute.

Since you are executing this project for the first time, the Developer Studio displays a dialog box for you to specify the class file name (see Figure 12-2). On this dialog box, in the Class name field, type **URLConnectionTest**. Also, underneath that you have a choice of using either the jview interpreter or the Internet Explorer to view the results. For this example, choose Stand-alone interpreter (which already has the jview program specified). Then, click OK.

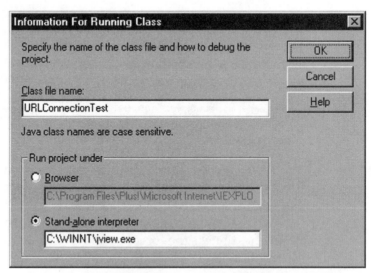

Figure 12-2: Information for Running Class dialog box filled out.

Once the Java application executes you should see something similar to Figure 12-3.

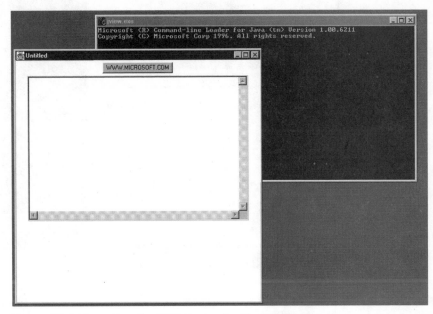

Figure 12-3: Executing the URLConnectionTest application.

Now, make sure you are connected to the Net and click the WWW.MICROSOFT.COM button. The HTML code for the site loads into the text area, as shown in Figure 12-4.

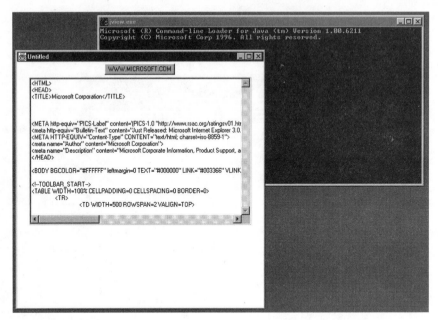

Figure 12-4: URLConnectionTest application with www.microsoft.com retrieved.

Communicating With the Browser

Another programming technique that is extremely useful for applets is the ability to communicate with the browser. Giving the browser the ability to be responsive to an applet opens the door to many solutions where you can enhance your Web site using Java.

This section shows you how you can use your applet to open a site on the Net. Implementing this is extremely simple because Java has a method that takes care of this for you. That method is the showDocument() method, which comes from the interface AppletContext and is part of the Applet class. The following shows an example:

```
getAppletContext().showDocument(myMsURL);
```

Looking at the above example, notice that you need to call the method getAppletContext() that retrieves a handle for the browser; then call the showDocument() method and pass it a URL.

There is another showDocument() method that takes two input parameters. The first parameter is a URL and the second is a string that specifies whether you want to load the URL in a new browser window or a specific frame in the browser. Consider the following:

```
getAppletContext().showDocument(myMsURL, "_blank");
```

The above example instructs the browser to load the URL myMsURL in a new window. You use this second variable to specify the name of the frame and other generic locations into which you want the document to load. Table 12-6 shows a list of items strings that you can use.

String Parameter	Meaning
_self	Specifies the document you want to load in the current frame or location of the applet. This is the default if you do not use the second parameter.
_parent	Specifies the document you want to load in the parent frame.
_top	Specifies the document you want to load in the topmost frame.
_blank	Specifies the document you want to load in a new window.
FrameName	Specifies the document you want to load in the frame labeled FrameName.

Table 12-6: Options for using the second input parameter in the showDocument() method.

Communicating Between Applets

Network programming can also take place between applets. Java has no limit to the number of applets that you can load on an HTML page. On sites that use multiple applets, the need may arise to somehow have the applets communicate. There is nothing inherently complex about this. You simply need to make sure that you have covered the following three key points:

- Both applets must be referenced on the same HTML page and have a unique NAME attribute in the <APPLET> tag.

- Use the getAppletContext() to retrieve a handle on the browser and environment. Once you have this handle use getApplet(), passing it the name of the other applet to which you wish to connect. This enables your applet to retrieve a handle to another applet.

- Implement event handling so that an event can be "sent" from one applet to the other applet.

At the very core level, the actual communication taking place is one applet transporting an event to another. Thus, almost all the connecting is accomplished using the handleEvent() methods for each applet involved.

Let's take a look at a pseudo example. You have applet myXApplet and applet myYApplet. Essentially, you want applet Y to handle events triggered in applet X. Figure 12-5 shows a diagram of this scenario.

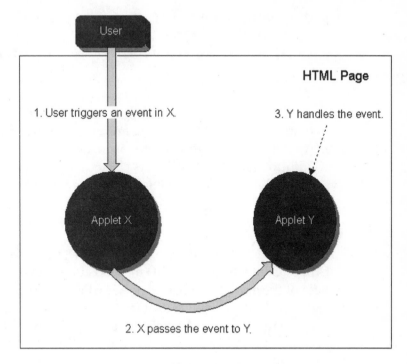

Figure 12-5: Schema of how Applet X communicates with Applet Y.

The first place to look is the HTML page that references the applets. In the <APPLET> tag you need to have the attribute NAME. This NAME must be unique, and can be different from the class name of the applet. Consider the following:

```
<APPLET CODE=myYApplet.class NAME=theYApplet WIDTH=100
HEIGHT=100> </APPLET>
```

To communicate with applet *myYApplet* you must reference its NAME, which in the above example is *theYApplet*. In this example, communication goes from my*XApplet* to *myYApplet* and not both ways—you do not need to have the NAME attribute in the myXApplet <APPLET> tag reference. However, you do need to have some special code in its handleEvent() method.

```
public boolean handleEvent(Event evt) {
   if (evt.target == myOKButton) {
   Applet Y  = getAppletContext().getApplet("theYApplet");
return Y.handleEvent(evt); }
return super.handleEvent(evt);
}
```

Looking at the above code, you are assuming that in the myXApplet a myOKButton button is instaniated. When myOKButton (labeled "OK") gets clicked, myXApplet passes the event to myYApplet using the following two lines of code:

```
   Applet Y  = getAppletContext().getApplet("theYApplet");
return Y.handleEvent(evt);
```

The first line of code declares the variable Y and uses the getAppletContext().getApplet() methods to retrieve a reference handle of the applet that has been NAMEd theYApplet. Thus, it retrieves myYApplet and puts it in Y instance. In essence, Y is a *pointer* reference to myYApplet. The second line of code calls myYApplet's handleEvent() method passing it the current event.

Tip

Another method you can use is the getApplets() that returns an enumeration of all the reachable applets it finds. A reachable applet is one that has its NAME attribute defined in its <APPLET> tag.

At this point, you know how to send an event to another applet (i.e., myYApplet). However, you now need to program myYApplet's handleEvent() to effectively catch and handle the event. Let's take a look at what myYApplet's handleEvent() might look like.

```
public boolean handleEvent(Event evt) {
    if (event.arg.equals("OK")) {
    if ("One".equals(event.arg)) {
    //Put Event Handling Code Here
    return true; }

    return super.handleEvent(evt);
    }
```

Looking at the above code, notice that you handle the event as if myOKButton (labeled with OK) belongs to myYApplet and not myXApplet. The only thing that you may not have seen before is having to check the label of the event evt to see if it is OK. This lets you determine if this is the event you wish to handle.

Communicating With Servers

The last topic we'll discuss in this chapter is developing lines of communication for client/server programs in the Java language using sockets. Client/server programming is very useful because it gives you the ability to create a distributed program that can be used by many people. All of these people (i.e., clients) are able to work with a uniform front end and communicate to one central part of the program known as the server.

In Java you effectively have three parts: a server program, a client program, and a Socket connection between the two.

Another way to think of client/server architecture is that a client is a taker, and the server is a giver. That is the easy part. The tough part is understanding how exactly the client communicates with the server. There are many ways that clients communicate with a server (and vice versa). Figure 12-6 shows a very simple client/server model with the client on top; the communication section represented by the line, and the server is on the bottom.

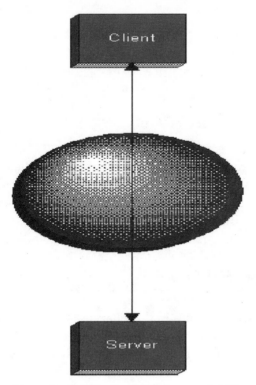

Figure 12-6: A simple client/server model. The sphere represents any environment (i.e., Internet, intranet, LAN, etc.) that can distance the client from the server.

Programming the Server

Specifically, the server in Java is designed to do the following:

- Using the ServerSocket class in the java.net package, the server listens to a designated port by constructing an instance of the ServerSocket class.

- The server listens for activity on the designated port using the accept() method in ServerSocket. In particular, the server is listening for a client attempting to establish a connection with it.

- An instance of the Socket class represents a successful connection between the client and the server. Note that you can program more than one client to communicate with a server through the same port. Each is an instance of the Socket class.

■ At this point you can begin sending and receiving data using getInputStream() and getOutputStream() (both are members of the Socket class), respectively. From here your program looks like the stream examples discussed in the last chapter.

Consider the following:

```
try {

    //Designate port 1234
        ServerSocket myServerSocket = new ServerSocket( 1234
);

        //Listen to the port
        Socket my1234Socket = mySocketServer.accept();

    //Use Streams to send and retrieve data from the client
        }
catch(Exception e) { }
```

Looking at the above code, the first thing that you do is construct an instance of the ServerSocket class passing an integer (1234 in this case). This specifies the designated port for the server to use as shown below:

```
ServerSocket myServerSocket = new ServerSocket( 1234 );
```

If in your Java programs you keep getting exceptions raised every time your program tries to construct the ServerSocket, you are most likely specifying a port that is already in use. Try connecting to another port. The next line of code uses the accept() method to listen for activity:

```
Socket my1234Socket = mySocketServer.accept();
```

Note that accept() halts program execution until a client requests a connection. That is why it is usually good programming practice to put the above code in its own thread, allowing your program to do other things. Once a client has successfully requested a connection, then my1234Socket represents this new connection and you can now begin sending and retrieving data.

This represents only a simple server networking technique. Many more complex techniques include the use of multi-threading techniques that were discussed in Chapter 6.

Programming the Client

The role of the client is quite simple. Request a connection to a given port on a specified server. You can do this by constructing an instance of the Socket class. Then, once a connection has successfully been established, use the getInputStream() and getOutputStream() methods to communicate with the server.

The following shows an example of how we connect to a fictitious server www.AnyServer.com at port 1234:

```
try {
    Socket mySocket1 = new Socket("www.AnyServer.com", 1234);
    //Use streams to send and retrieve data.
catch(Exception e) {}
```

Looking at the above code, you can see the constructor for Socket.

Note

There are several other constructors you can use to pass InetAddresses, and specify if this connection is a datagram connection (i.e., meaning you want to use the UDP/IP protocol discussed earlier). If the connection is successfully made to the server, this is all that is necessary.

Moving On

In this chapter you had a chance to learn a little more about how TCP/IP works. We also introduced you to several network programming techniques that you can use to communicate with a browser, applet, or server.

Network programming is an extremely large concept. And, as you will learn in the next chapter, you can use network programming techniques discussed here along with Java Database Connectivity (JDBC) to connect a client to a SQL database.

13

Java Database Connectivity (JDBC)

Open Database Connectivity (ODBC) has emerged as the de facto standard for communicating with a variety of databases on the Windows and Macintosh platforms. The concept and purpose of Java Database Connectivity (JDBC) is the same as ODBC—to provide transparent and seamless access to a variety of popular databases. What ODBC does for your desktop and network applications JDBC does for your Web and Internet applications. The ODBC architecture has gained wide acceptance and is probably the most popular method used by developers and programmers around the world for communicating with a variety of databases. Such databases include Sybase SQL Server, Microsoft SQL Server, Microsoft Access, Paradox, Oracle, xBase, and many more. You can even set up ASCII text and Excel files as ODBC data sources.

ODBC is the communication layer between the Graphical User Interface (GUI) front end and the database back end of your application. It makes the data source specific functions and commands transparent to your application. You use the standard Structured Query Language (SQL) commands to access your database and need not worry about the specific database commands. ODBC makes your code portable. You can port your application from an Access database to an SQL Server database with little or no modifications as long as your database schema does not change.

Because of the similarity between JDBC and ODBC, this chapter briefly discusses ODBC and its architecture. We describe the JDBC Application Programming Interface (API) and its architecture. We also present the advantages and disadvantages of using JDBC. This chapter then provides a closer look at the java.sql package, its interfaces, classes, and exceptions. This chapter focuses on some of the important methods of the java.sql package. Next, it outlines the basic steps involved in implementing database access using the JDBC interface. A real-world JDBC program that queries information from a SQL database is also included in this chapter.

If you have already used ODBC and are familiar with it, you'll find JDBC easy to learn and understand. If you are not familiar with ODBC, please read through the sections on ODBC in this chapter.

Open Database Connectivity (ODBC)

A client-server architecture consists of three main components: client, network, and database. The database component is usually a relational database such as Sybase SQL Server, Microsoft SQL Server, or Oracle. The client could be a Windows, Macintosh, or PowerPC application, or simply a utility such as ISQL or Windows ISQL (WISQL). ISQL (Interactive SQL) is a utility you can use to execute SQL commands and review results on an ad hoc basis. WISQL is the Windows version of ISQL. The client application can be written using any of the GUI tools such as Visual Basic, PowerBuilder, Optima++, Clarion, and Delphi.

The client-server architecture is an open system—you can write the GUI front end in whatever tool you choose and you can choose your favorite relational database as the back end—as long as there is a common protocol established and both client and database adhere to this protocol, you have a client-server architecture that is interoperable, scaleable, and networkable. One of the proposed protocol of communication between the client and the server is Open Database Connectivity (ODBC) from Microsoft.

JDBC is Open Database Connectivity for Java applications. You can use the JDBC API to connect your Java applications to a variety of relational databases. This lets you build client-server applications using Java as the programming language and the Internet or an intranet as the network backbone.

The Architecture of ODBC

Figure 13-1 shows the ODBC architecture. At the top is the application followed by the ODBC driver manager. Underneath the ODBC driver manager are as many drivers as there are data sources. These drivers communicate directly with the data sources. Figure 13-1 shows five data sources: Oracle, SQL Server, xBase, Paradox, and Access.

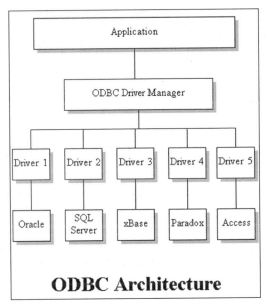

Figure 13-1: ODBC architecture.

The top-level application can be a GUI front end written with PowerBuilder, Visual Basic, or Delphi, or it could be a simple WISQL utility. The application communicates with the ODBC driver manager. On the Windows platform, the ODBC driver manager consists of dynamic link libraries (DLLs). Two important DLLs are the ODBC driver manager odbc.dll and the ODBC installation file odbcinst.dll. These DLLs are usually installed in your \windows\system directory. The initialization file odbc.ini is located in your \windows directory.

The ODBC driver manager communicates with the different drivers. Each data source requires a different set of drivers, and the ODBC driver manager makes the task of communicating with the data source easy by making the database access transparent to the application. On the other hand, the data source does not even know the calls are coming from the ODBC driver manager. The data source itself communicates only with the drivers.

ODBC makes your job as a programmer easy. It lets you focus on your application requirements instead of wondering about all the specific calls you need to make to the data source. It lets you focus on the data itself instead of wondering about where the data is located and how to access it. ODBC also makes your application portable. You can switch from an Access to an SQL Server database with very little or no modifications to the database calls at the application level.

A common complaint with the ODBC architecture has been the slow data retrievals and updates. This is because the ODBC driver manager adds an additional layer of processing. The application does not directly communicate with the drivers. However, you can use the sql_passthrough option to bypass ODBC and make your application communicate directly with the drivers. Microsoft claims that the delay caused by the ODBC driver manager doesn't matter because the database specific drivers are so efficient. There are a number of third party vendors that provide drivers for a variety of databases. According to Microsoft, selecting the right driver is the key to getting the best performance from your ODBC architecture-based application.

ODBC Pros & Cons

Without the ODBC driver manager, an application communicates directly with each database driver. With such a setup you'll need to understand the nature of each driver and its set of function calls. This will make your task of setting up lines of communication tedious and time consuming. On the other hand, since there is no additional layer of processing between your application and the database specific drivers, you may find that data access and update are quicker compared to the ODBC architecture.

ODBC API Conformance Levels

Microsoft has specified three different ODBC API conformance levels: Core, Level 1, and Level 2 APIs. These three conformance levels indicate the degree of ODBC API support. The conformance levels establish a standard of communication with the database using the ODBC drivers. Microsoft has enforced these standards for programming ODBC drivers. The Core API is the lowest level to which a driver must conform. Level 2 API is the highest conformance level that also includes conformance to the Core and Level 1 API levels. It is recommended that a driver should conform to at least Level 1 API.

Core API

Core API level includes the following database functions:

- Allocate and free handles for environment, connections, and statements.

- Establish connections to data sources.

- Use multiple statements on a connection.

- Prepare and execute SQL statements over an established connection.

- Commit or roll back transactions over an established connection.
- Retrieve error information returned by the data source.
- Assign storage variables to hold parameters in SQL statements and column data in result sets.
- Retrieve result set data.
- Retrieve information about a result set.

Level I API

Level 1 API includes all the Core API functions as well as the following functions:

- Connect to data sources using driver-specific dialog boxes.
- Retrieve catalog information about database items.
- Inquire about current option settings.
- Retrieve information about drivers.
- Retrieve information about data sources.
- Send part or all of a result column value.
- Send part or all of a parameter value.
- Set options for statements and connections.

Level 2 API

Level 2 API is the highest and most advanced conformance level. It includes the following functions in addition to all the Core and Level 1 API functions:

- Browse connection information to list all available data sources.
- Retrieve native SQL statements generated.
- Define and use scrollable cursors.
- Retrieve catalog information stored in system tables.

- Retrieve information on stored procedures parameters.
- Call DLLs.
- Assign parameter values to arrays.
- Send arrays for use with stored procedures.
- Retrieve result column values into arrays.

The JDBC Architecture

With the popularity of ODBC and its architecture, it is only natural to expect a similar architecture that enables Java applications to access a variety of databases over the Net. JavaSoft has developed the JDBC API. The JDBC API is a standard uniform SQL database access interface. JDBC does for the Net what ODBC does for the desktop. It provides Java programmers with a uniform, seamless interface to a wide variety of relational and nonrelational databases. Yes, you can interface your Java application with nonrelational databases as long as you have the correct set of drivers installed on your system.

The JDBC architecture is similar to the ODBC architecture (see Figure 13-2). The ODBC driver manager is replaced by the JDBC driver manager. The client at the top of the diagram in Figure 13-2 is a Java application. It interfaces with the JDBC driver manager. The JDBC driver manager translates the SQL calls into the appropriate native SQL using the driver based on the data source to which you are connected. The JDBC API lets your Java application connect with a variety of SQL databases including Oracle, Sybase SQL Server, MS SQL Server, Microsoft Access, xBase, Paradox, and many more.

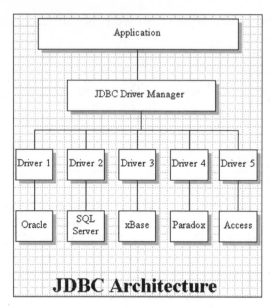

Figure 13-2: The JDBC architecture.

If the JDBC drivers are written entirely in Java, you can download the drivers as an applet. Note that JDBC drivers can also be written using native methods(i.e., in C).

The JDBC API comprises Java classes. These classes represent database connections, SQL statements, result sets, and so on. They let your Java application issue SQL statements to the database back end and receive and process the result sets. The HTML file tree.htm on the Companion CD-ROM shows the Java class hierarchy of which the java.sql package is a part. Use your favorite browser to view this file. Figure 13-3 shows the hierarchy for the java.sql package.

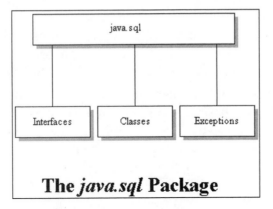

Figure 13-3: The java.sql package hierarchy.

The java.sql Package

The java.sql package includes a number of classes, interfaces, and exceptions. This section discusses some of the important and commonly used classes and interfaces. For a complete list of all classes, interfaces, and exceptions download the JDBC API from JavaSoft's Web site: http://www.javasoft.com/.

The java.sql Interfaces

The java.sql package includes several interfaces. The Connection interface represents a database session. You must open a Connection interface before you execute any SQL statements. It must be closed when it is no longer needed. The Statement interface executes a single SQL statement. The PreparedStatement interface can be used to prepare a batch of SQL statements that can be executed multiple times. The Callable Statement interface can be used to execute stored procedures. Each database driver you use must supply a class to implement the Driver interface. The DatabaseMetaData interface provides additional information about the database. The ResultSet interface represents the data returned as a result of execution of the SQL query. Each of these interfaces is discussed in further detail in the next few pages. For more information on classes and interfaces reference Chapter 3.

■ **Connection**   A connection represents a session with a specific database. You can open and close a connection with a database. You can execute SQL statements while a connection is open. If no connection is open, and you try to execute a SQL statement, an error occurs.

By default all SQL statements submitted are automatically committed.

Use the commit() method to issue an explicit commit. The commit() method makes all changes since the last commit/rollback. It also releases all locks held by the database connection. It is important to understand the effect of locking on your database and application. When you submit a SQL statement to the database it should be committed as soon as possible if no errors occur else it should be rolled back immediately. This helps avoiding any locking contention and improves the response time of your system.

Use the rollback() method to issue an explicit rollback. The rollback() method discards all changes since the last commit/rollback. Similar to the commit() method, rollback() also releases all locks held by the database connection.

Tip

Avoid long-running transactions. Commit or roll back immediately!

Use the method close() to close a database connection. When a database connection is closed, all the JDBC resources are immediately released.

Use the setTransactionIsolation() method to set the isolation level of a newly opened database connection. You can pass any of the transaction variables such as TRANSACTION_NONE, TRANSACTION_READ_COMMITTED,

TRANSACTION_READ_UNCOMMITTED and so on as a parameter to this method.

■ **Statement**   The Statement interface executes a single SQL statement and obtains results produced by it.

Use the method executeQuery() to execute a SQL statement that returns a single ResultSet_object.

Use the method executeUpdate() to execute an insert, update, or delete statement. This method returns the row count or zero if the SQL returns nothing.

Use the method setMaxRows() to set the maximum number of rows that any ResultSet can contain. If max rows limit is set to zero, it means the ResultSet can contain an unlimited number of rows.

Use the method setQueryTimeout() to set the number of seconds the driver should wait for the SQL statement to execute.

■ **PreparedStatement**   It extends the Statement interface. It stores a precompiled SQL statement and executes it multiple times, as needed.

Use the method executeQuery() to execute the prepared SQL query and process the ResultSet.

■ **CallableStatement**   It extends the PreparedStatement interface. It executes stored procedures and processes single or multiple ResultSets as the case may be. Multiple ResultSets are handled using methods inherited from Statement. A stored procedure is a batch of SQL statements residing on the server.

■ **Driver**   Each driver should supply a driver class that implements the Driver interface.

Use the method connect() to get a connection to the specified URL.

Use the method acceptsURL() to check if the driver can open a connection to the specified URL.

Use the method getPropertyInfo() to prompt the user for database information.

Use the method jdbcCompliant() to find out whether the

driver is JDBC compliant. A driver is JDBC compliant if it includes full support for the JDBC API and SQL 92 Entry Level.

- **DatabaseMetaData** An interface that provides information about the database such as URL for the database, selectable tables, callable procedures, name and version numbers of the driver, and so on.

- **ResultSet** A ResultSet is the data returned as a result of execution of SQL query.

    A ResultSet maintains a cursor pointing to its current row of data. Initially the cursor is positioned before the first row. Use the next() method to move the cursor to the next row.

    Use the method getCursortName() to get the name of the SQL cursor used by the ResultSet.

- **ResultSetMetaData** An interface that provides information about the ResultSet such as name of the ResultSet, number, types and properties of a ResultSet's columns, and so on.

The java.sql Classes

There are several java.sql classes. The Date and Time classes are subsets of java.util.date. You use them for date and time manipulation in your Java applications. You use the DriverManager to load the driver classes. You use the DriverPropertyInfo to set and retrieve the driver properties. You represent the different SQL types using the Type class. You represent SQL timestamps using the Timestamp class.

The java.sql classes include the following:

- **Date** A subset of java.util.date. It deals only with days and ignores hours, minutes, and seconds.

- **DriverManager** This class uses the system property jdbc.drivers to load all the driver classes. When a database connection is opened, the DriverManager class attempts to load the appropriate driver from the set of registered drivers.

    Use the registerDriver() method to register a new driver with the DriverManager class. Use the deregisterDriver() method to drop a driver from the DriverManager's list.

Use the method setLoginTimeout() to set the maximum time in seconds the drivers waits when trying to log into a database.

Use the method getLoginTimeout() to get the current setting in seconds the drivers waits when trying to log into a database.

■ **DriverPropertyInfo**   This class gets and sets properties on the different drivers such as name of the driver, major and minor version numbers of the driver, and so on.

■ **Numeric**   This performs fixed point integer arithmetic.

■ **Time**   A subset of java.util.date. It deals only with hours, minutes, and seconds.

■ **Timestamp**   Extends the sun.util.date class. It represents SQL timestamps.

■ **Types**   Defines the constants that represent SQL types such as integer, double, float, and so on. The type Other is mapped to a Java object. It is database specific.

There are two types of application errors: errors that are bugs and errors that occur due to special circumstances. The second type of errors are called exceptions. They represent certain exceptional situations (for example, a specified file does not exist, invalid file format, low memory, insufficient space, and so on). Java includes support to handle such exceptions. java.sql includes exception handling for SQL errors. It includes the SQLException class that provides information on database access errors and the SQLWarning class that provides information on database access warnings.

■ **SQLException** provides information on database access errors. It extends the java.lang.exception class. There are four different methods that you can use to construct different types of SQL exception errors.

Use the method SQLException(String reason, String SQLState, int vendorCode) to construct a fully specified SQL exception.

Use the method SQLException(String reason, String SQLState) to construct a SQL exception without the vendor code.

Use the method SQLException(String reason) to construct a SQL exception with only a reason.

Use the method SQLException() to construct a SQL exception with no description.

- **SQLWarning** provides information on database access warnings. Similar to the SQLException class, there are four different methods you can use to construct different types of SQL warnings.

  Use the method SQLWarning(String reason, String SQLstate, int vendorCode) to construct a fully specified SQL warning.

  Use the method SQLWarning(String reason, String SQLstate) to construct a SQL warning without the vendor code.

  Use the method SQLWarning(String reason) to construct a SQL warning with only a reason.

  Use the method SQLWarning() to construct a SQL warning with no description.

- **DataTruncation** extends the SQLWarning class. If JDBC truncates a data value, it indicates a DataTruncation warning on reads and throws a DataTruncation exception on writes.

JDBC Implementation

The JDBC specification states that any JDBC implementation must support at least the ANSI SQL-2 Entry Level standard. If database independence is a requirement for your application, it must be written to JDBC specification, make no database specific calls, and strictly conform to the ANSI SQL-2 standard. Any JDBC implementation requires that you implement all of the interfaces previously described.

The following eight steps implement a database access using the JDBC interface:

1. **Get a Connection interface through the DriverManager.** The DriverManager handles all communication with the drivers and provides the application with a Connection reference to the specified database.

2. **Ask the Connection for a Statement or subclass of Statement.** You can now use the Connection to ask for a Statement. A Statement is an unbound SQL call to the database. Statement has the subclass PreparedStatement. PreparedStatement has a subclass CallableStatement. A PreparedStatement is a precompiled database call. It requires parameters to be bound. Use the CallableStatement interface for stored procedures with OUT parameters.

3. **Bind any parameters for subclasses of Statement.** As discussed above, the PreparedStatement requires parameters to be bound.

4. **Execute the Statement.** Use the appropriate execute methods to execute the Statement.

5. **Check the number of rows returned.** Check for multiple result sets by calling Statement.getResultSet().

6. **Close the Statement.** Close the current Statement.

7. **Process any other Statements.** Are there any other Statements to be executed and their result sets processed?

8. **Close the Connection.** If you are finished processing all the Statements, close the database Connection. This releases all JDBC resources.

Client-server Computing Using JDBC

Client-server computing using JDBC includes a front end Java application and a back end database. The back end database is usually a relational database such as SQL Server, Informix, or Oracle. The front end handles the presentation and user interface. The back end handles execution of SQL statements submitted by the front end and returns the result sets. A JDBC implementation requires the use of appropriate database drivers. The driver manager handles the communication between the Java application and data source. Client-server computing using JDBC includes four main components: the Java application, JDBC driver manager, drivers, and data source.

- **Java Application** addresses the business problem. The JDBC function calls allow it to use SQL against one or more JDBC-compliant data sources.

- **JDBC** loads the specific data source driver requested by the JDBC function call.

- **Drivers** are supplied by both Microsoft and various third party vendors. In most cases these are in the form of DLLs—each specific to a data source and platform. The drivers perform the processing of JDBC function call submitted by the application. Such processing includes establishing connection with the data source, executing SQL statements, processing result sets, and returning codes obtained from the data source. Sometimes the drivers have to translate the JDBC calls and modify them to suit the specific requirements of certain data sources. The drivers also manage transactions and cursors.

  There are two types of drivers: single- and multiple-tier. Single-tier drivers process the SQL statements themselves. They are used with some of the old database systems (e.g., xBase, Paradox, etc.). Such database systems do not natively support SQL. They are also very limited in functionality. In the case of multiple-tier drivers, the processing is handled by the RDBMS.

A number of vendors provide drivers for different database systems. Microsoft provides a set of drivers for Microsoft Access, Microsoft Excel, Btrieve, Paradox, Microsoft FoxPro, and ASCII text files. Intersolv is another popular vendor that provides an extensive set of drivers. Some of the other vendors provide very specific drivers (e.g., drivers that connect to MDI Gateway, AS/400, etc.).

■ **Data source** in a client-server architecture is usually a RDBMS such as Microsoft Access, Microsoft SQL Server, Sybase SQL Server, Oracle, and so on. The data source is the destination of all SQL statements. They are processed by the data source, and the return codes and result sets are sent back to the client via the drivers and JDBC driver manager.

Advantages & Disadvantages of Using JDBC

The JDBC API helps you connect your Java applications to a variety of relational databases. This lets you build client-server applications using Java as the programming language, any of the popular browsers as the user-friendly interface for your application, the Internet or an intranet as the network backbone, and your favorite relational database as the database back end. Some of the advantages and disadvantages of using JDBC are listed below:

Advantages

■ The JDBC API follows the popular ODBC path. Therefore, it is easy to learn and understand.

■ The JDBC API is freely distributed by JavaSoft. A number of third party vendors have endorsed JDBC and are working on JDBC-enabled products.

■ JDBC does for the Net what ODBC does for the desktop. It frees you, the programmer, from the hassles of learning each specific driver's commands and function calls. It lets you focus on your application and the business requirements it must meet.

- JDBC makes the database transition portable. If you want to move your Java applications from Oracle to Sybase SQL Server, the JDBC API makes your transition as smooth as possible, if your database schema has not changed.

- The JDBC API lets you leverage your investment in database technology. You can retain your database and change the GUI front end from a PowerBuilder application (for example) to a Java-enabled Netscape Navigator or Microsoft Internet Explorer browser interface.

- The JDBC API is object oriented. It consists of classes that let you define database connections, issue SQL statements, process result sets, and much more. It meshes well with Java as it is also an object-oriented programming language.

- You can use the JDBC-ODBC bridge driver for converting JDBC function calls to ODBC. You can download this bridge driver from JavaSoft's Web site (http://splash.javasoft.com/jdbc/).

Disadvantages

- The JDBC driver manager adds an additional layer of processing. It may slow down the response time of your system, especially the time it takes to receive the result sets from the database.

- The Statement class includes two methods:

    Use the setQueryTimeout() method to set the amount of time your application waits for the results of a query submitted to the database before a timeout event occurs.

    Use the getQueryTimeout() method to retrieve the current timeout value.

- You could face driver incompatibility problems. Since the drivers are database specific and are manufactured by several different vendors (including different groups of Microsoft), you are likely to run into driver incompatibility problems at the time of upgrade or switching or adding database sources. Although these problems cannot be directly attributed to JDBC, you may end up spending a lot of time and effort on resolving software incompatibility issues instead of designing business solutions for your customers.

■ Products from several different vendors are involved in the JDBC architecture. If you add a new data source or replace an existing one, you need the database-specific driver. Such a driver is likely to be available from several different vendors. Choosing the right driver and vendor is important and should not be taken lightly. However, it does add to the list of different vendors you have to deal with should you encounter any problems.

■ Another concern with the JDBC architecture is its longevity. Although Microsoft has openly promoted the ODBC standard in the past, recently it has also been discussing using OLE for database links. It remains to be seen how effective and successful the OLE solution for database links is and the kind of effect it may have on ODBC and JDBC.

Overview of Structure Query Language (SQL)

This section provides a quick overview of the SQL data modification (DML) statements including insert, update, and delete. The select statement is used for querying purposes. The tutorial included in this chapter uses the select SQL command. Table 13-2 shows samples of the DML statements.

Command	Example
select	select pub_id, total = sum(total_sales) from titles where advance < 10000 and total_sales !=0 group by pub_id having count(*) > 1
insert	insert publishers values ("1234", "Ventana Publishing", "Richmond", "VA")
delete	delete authors where state != "TX"
update	update titles set price = price * 1.5 where titles.pub_id = publishers.pub_id and publishers.state = "VA"

Table 13-1: DML statement overview.

Tutorial: Creating a JDBC Program

In this tutorial, you create the applet checkBal that queries checking account balance information from a SQL manager . This tutorial uses JDBC function calls to query the SQL database, mSQL. mSQL is a Microsoft SQL database engine that you can download from its home page.

Create a table called Accounts with the following fields:

Name	Type	Attribute
userid	char(100)	primary_key
password	char(8)	
checking	double	
savings	double	

Table 13-2: Fields for the table Accounts.

The mSQL script for the above table definition looks as follows:

```
DROP TABLE accounts\p\g

CREATE TABLE accounts {
    userid    CHAR(100)    PRIMARY_KEY,
    password  CHAR(8),
    checking  DOUBLE
}\p\g
```

Populate the Accounts table with some sample data. All figures are in U.S. dollars.

userid	password	checking	savings
usr110	boston	5000	10000
usr210	sanjose	6500	20000
usr310	maine	7500	30000
usr410	tokyo	8500	40000

Table 13-3: Data for the table Accounts.

Create a new project workspace called checkBal, and use the AppletWizard to create an applet called checkBal (see Table 13-1 for the step-by-step instructions). Also refer to Figures 13-4 through 13-10 that follow Table 13-4.

Step #	Location	Action
1	Developer Studio	Choose File|New.
2	New dialog box	Highlight Project Workspace, then click OK.
3	New Project Workspace dialog box	Highlight JavaAppletWizard. In the Name field, type **checkBal**, and then click Create.
4	Applet Wizard, step 1	For the "How would you like to be able to run your program?" question, select As an applet only. For the "What would you like to name your class?" question, type **checkBal**. For the "Would you like to generate source file comments?" question, select Yes, please. Then, click Next.
5	Applet Wizard, step 2	For the "Would you like a sample HTML file?" question, select Yes, please. Then, click Next.
6	Applet Wizard, step 3	For the "Would you like your applet to be multi-threaded?" question, select No, thank you. Then, click Next.
7	Applet Wizard, step 4	Enter the first parameter, driver. Enter the second parameter, url. Enter the third parameter, user. Enter the fourth parameter, password. Enter the fifth parameter, balance. Then, click Next.
8	Applet Wizard, step 5	Type applet information, then click Finish.
9	New Project Information dialog box	Verify the information is correct (see Figure 13-11), then click OK.

Table 13-4: Creating the checkBal Project Workspace.

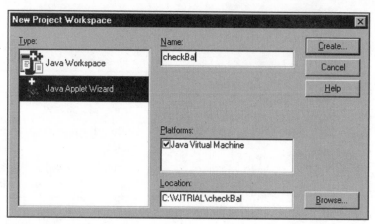

Figure 13-4: The New Project Workspace dialog box.

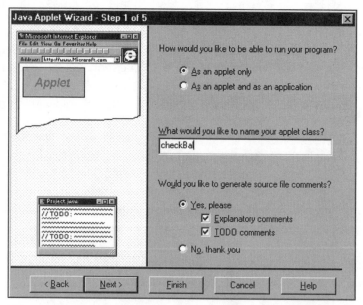

Figure 13-5: Step 1, naming the applet using the Java AppletWizard.

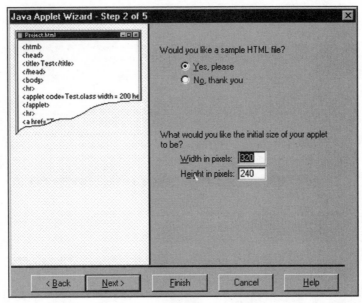

Figure 13-6: Step 2, selecting a sample HTML file using the Java AppletWizard.

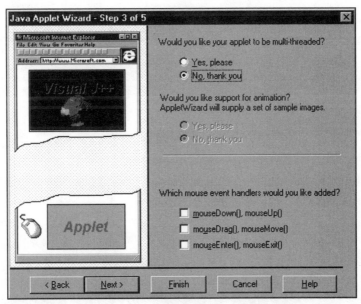

Figure 13-7: Step 3, making this applet not multithreaded using the Java AppletWizard.

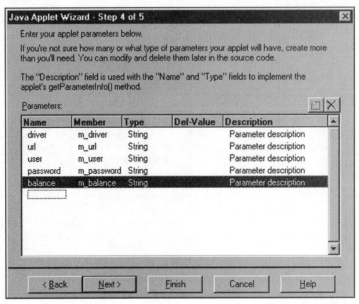

Figure 13-8: Step 4, entering the applet parameters using the Java AppletWizard.

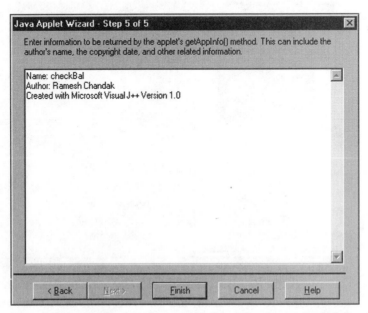

Figure 13-9: Step 5, entering return information for getAppInfo() using the Java AppletWizard.

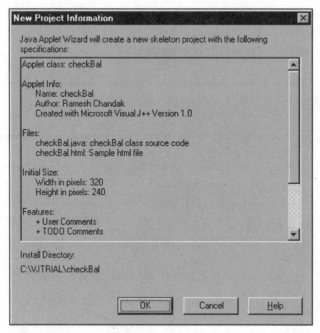

Figure 13-10: The applet's specifications appear in the New Project Information window.

In the following lines of code, the bolded lines are those that you need to add to the source file in the text file displayed in the right pane of the Developer Studio:

```
/* This is a checkBal Java applet written using Visual J++
1.0. The checkBal applet queries information from a SQL
database (mSQL) using the JDBC function calls.
*/

//*********************************************************
// checkBal.java:   Applet
//
//*********************************************************
import java.applet.*;
import java.awt.*;
import java.sql.Connection;
```

```
import java.sql.Statement;
import java.sql.ResultSet;
import java.sql.DriverManager;

//============================================================
// Main Class for applet checkBal
//
//============================================================
public class checkBal extends Applet
{
    // PARAMETER SUPPORT:
    //   Parameters allow an HTML author to pass information to
the applet;
    // the HTML author specifies them using the <PARAM> tag
within the <APPLET>
    // tag.  The following variables are used to store the
values of the
    // parameters.
      //-------------------------------------------------------

    // Members for applet parameters
    // <type>        <MemberVar>    = <Default Value>
      //-------------------------------------------------------
    private String m_driver = "";
    private String m_url = "";
    private String m_user = "";
    private String m_password = "";
    private String m_balance = "";

    //My code starts here

    Database db;

    //My code ends here
```

```
     // Parameter names.  To change a name of a parameter, you
need only make
     // a single change.  Simply modify the value of the
parameter string below.
     //-------------------------------------------------------
   private final String PARAM_driver = "driver";
   private final String PARAM_url = "url";
   private final String PARAM_user = "user";
   private final String PARAM_password = "password";
   private final String PARAM_balance = "balance";

   // checkBal Class Constructor
   //---------------------------------------------------------
   public checkBal()
   {
      // TODO: Add constructor code here.
   }

   // APPLET INFO SUPPORT:
   //    The getAppletInfo() method returns a string describing
the applet's
   // author, copyright date, or miscellaneous information.
   //---------------------------------------------------------
   public String getAppletInfo()
   {
      return "Name: checkBal\r\n" +
             "Author: Ramesh Chandak\r\n" +
             "Created with Microsoft Visual J++ Version 1.0";
   }

   // PARAMETER SUPPORT
   //    The getParameterInfo() method returns an array of
strings describing
   // the parameters understood by this applet.
   //
      // checkBal Parameter Information:
```

```
      //  { "Name", "Type", "Description" },
      //-------------------------------------------------------
   public String[][] getParameterInfo()
   {
      String[][] info =
      {
         { PARAM_driver, "String", "Parameter description" },
         { PARAM_url, "String", "Parameter description" },
         { PARAM_user, "String", "Parameter description" },
         { PARAM_password, "String", "Parameter description" },
         { PARAM_balance, "String", "Parameter description" },
      };
      return info;
   }


   // The init() method is called by the AWT when an applet is
first loaded or
   // reloaded.  Override this method to perform whatever
initialization your
   // applet needs, such as initializing data structures,
loading images or
   // fonts, creating frame windows, setting the layout
manager, or adding UI
   // components.
      //-------------------------------------------------------
   public void init()
   {
      // PARAMETER SUPPORT
      //   The following code retrieves the value of each
parameter
      // specified with the <PARAM> tag and stores it in a
member
      // variable.
      //-------------------------------------------------------
      String param;
```

```
// driver: Parameter description
//----------------------------------------------------
param = getParameter(PARAM_driver);
if (param != null)
  m_driver = param;

// url: Parameter description
//----------------------------------------------------
param = getParameter(PARAM_url);
if (param != null)
  m_url = param;

// user: Parameter description
//----------------------------------------------------
param = getParameter(PARAM_user);
if (param != null)
  m_user = param;

// password: Parameter description
//----------------------------------------------------
param = getParameter(PARAM_password);
if (param != null)
  m_password = param;

// balance: Parameter description
//----------------------------------------------------
param = getParameter(PARAM_balance);
if (param != null)
  m_balance = param;

    // If you use a ResourceWizard-generated "control
creator" class to
    // arrange controls in your applet, you may want to
call its
```

```
        // CreateControls() method from within this method.
Remove the following
        // call to resize() before adding the call to
CreateControls();
        // CreateControls() does its own resizing.
        //---------------------------------------------------
    resize(320, 240);

    // TODO: Place additional initialization code here.

  //My code starts here

    try {

        Class driverClass =
Class.forName(m_driver);                    db = new
Database(m_url, m_user, m_password);
        m_balance = db.getCheckingBalance( m_user);
    repaint();
    db.close();
    }
    catch (java.sql.SQLException e) {
      e.printStackTrace();
      m_balance = "Database exception";
    }
    catch (Exception e) {
      e.printStackTrace();
      m_Balance = "Driver could not be loaded";
    }

  //My code ends here

    }

    // Place additional applet clean up code here.  destroy()
is called when
    // when your applet is terminating and being unloaded.
    //---------------------------------------------------------
```

```java
public void destroy()
{
   // TODO: Place applet cleanup code here.
}

// checkBal Paint Handler
//------------------------------------------------------------
public void paint(Graphics g)
{

//My code starts here

   g.drawString("Your checking balance is"+m_Balance, 10,
20);

//My code ends here


}

//   The start() method is called when the page containing
the applet
// first appears on the screen. The AppletWizard's initial
implementation
// of this method starts execution of the applet's thread.
//------------------------------------------------------------
public void start()
{
   // TODO: Place additional applet start code here.
}

//   The stop() method is called when the page containing
the applet is
// no longer on the screen. The AppletWizard's initial
implementation of
// this method stops execution of the applet's thread.
//------------------------------------------------------------
```

```java
    public void stop()
    {
    }


    // TODO: Place additional applet code here.
}

    //My code starts here

public class Database {
    private Connection connection;


    public Database(String url, String userid, String pass)
throws java.sql.sqlException {
        connection = DriverManager.getConnection(url, userid,
pass);
    }

    public String getCheckingBalance(String userid) {
        double  balance = 0.0;
        try {
            java.sql.Statement statement =
connection.CreateStatement();
            java.sql.ResultSet result_set;
            String sql;

            sql = "SELECT checking_balance FROM accounts " +
                "WHERE user_id = ' " + user_id + "'";
            result_set = statement.executeQuery(sql);
            if (!result_set.next()) balance = 0.0;
            else balance = result_set.getDouble(1);
            statement.close();
        }
        catch (java.sql.SQLException e) {
            e.printStackTrace();
        }
        return (" " + balance);
```

```
    }
// It's better to move this outside, otherwise you'll always
use this connection only once.
public void close() {        connection.close();
    }

    //My code ends here


}
```

Let's analyze the above code. The analysis is done only for the bolded lines.

The following lines indicate inclusion of the java.sql.Connection, java.sql.Statement, java.sql.ResultSet, and java.lang.DriverManager classes. By including these classes, you are making all the methods and member variables of these classes available to you. Consider these classes as building blocks that you are using to build your own Java application:

```
import java.sql.Connection;
import java.sql.Statement;
import java.sql.ResultSet;
import java.sql.DriverManager;
```

In the following line, *db* is declared of type Database. It is used later to create an instance of the Database class.

```
    Database db;
```

In the following lines, a try-catch block is used. In the try block, first the driver is loaded. Next, an instance db of the Database class is created. The URL, userid, and password are passed as the parameters. The balance in checking account is obtained by calling the Database method getCheckingBalance.

There are two types of exceptions that are handled. The first is the SQLException. If a SQLException is trapped, the string "Database exception" displays. All other exceptions are handled by the second catch block in which case the string "Driver could not be loaded" displays:

```
try {

    Class driverClass =
Class.forName(m_driver);                        db = new
Database(m_url, m_user, m_password);
        m_balance = db.getCheckingBalance(
repaint();
    db.close();
        db = New Database(m_url, m_user, m_pass);
        balance = db.getCheckingBalance(m_balance);
    }
    catch (java.sql.SQLException e) {
      e.printStackTrace();
      m_balance = "Database exception";
    }
    catch (Exception e) {
      e.printStackTrace();
      m_Balance = "Driver could not be loaded";
    }
```

In the following lines, the String m_balance displays.
m_balance may contain the balance figure or the appropriate error
message as the case may be:

```
g.drawString(("Your checking balance is"+m_Balance, 10,
20);
```

In the following lines, a class Database is implemented. It uses a
Connection object established using the getConnection method in
the DriverManager class. The URL, userid, and password are
passed as the parameters.

Next, a method getCheckingBalance is declared. It takes the
userid as its only parameter. The variable balance of type double
is set to 0.0.

A try-catch block is set up to prepare the SQL statement and
execute it. The method CreateStatement of the Connection class
creates the necessary SQL statement. This SQL statement is a select statement that queries against the database to retrieve the current value of the checking field from the Accounts table for the
given userid. The SQL statement is executed using the method

ExecuteQuery of the Statement class. Executing the SQL statement returns a ResultSet. If the ResultSet is not empty, its value will be retrieved in the variable balance else the variable balance is set to 0.0.

At this point the Statement is closed. The catch block is used to catch any SQL exceptions that might occur. Then, when you are finished with db object, use db.close() to close Connection.

If there are no exceptions, the value of the variable balance is returned:

```java
Public class Database {
   private Connection connection;

   public Database(String url, String userid, String pass)
throws java.sql.sqlException {
      connection = DriverManager.getConnection(url, userid,
pass);
   }

   public String getCheckingBalance(String userid) {
      double  balance = 0.0;
      try {
         java.sql.Statement statement =
connection.CreateStatement();
         java.sql.ResultSet result_set;
         String sql;

         sql = "SELECT checking FROM accounts " +
            "WHERE userid = ' " + userid + "'";
         result_set = statement.executeQuery(sql);
         if (!result_set.next()) balance = 0.0;
         else balance = result_set.getDouble(1);
         statement.close();
      }
      catch (java.sql.SQLException e) {
         e.printStackTrace();
      }
      return (" " + balance);
   }

// It's better to move this outside, otherwise you'll always
```

```
use this connection only once.
public close() {
  connection.close();
  }
```

Once you finish typing this code, you are ready build the Java application. To build the code, click Build | checkBal. Then, to execute the code, click Execute | checkBal. Figure 13-11 shows the results if you execute the Java applet with the following parameters:

```
driver=mSQL
url=<Enter your web site URL here>
user= usr410,
password=tokyo
userid usr410.
```

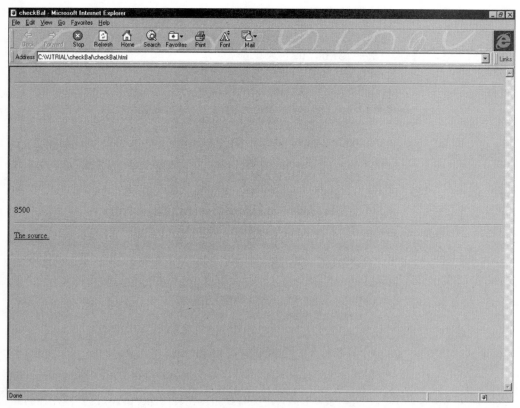

Figure 13-11: Executing the checkBal application.

In this tutorial you created a Java applet checkBal that queries the table accounts stored in a SQL database and retrieves the checking account balance.

Moving On

JDBC provides seamless and transparent access to a number of popular databases. Any JDBC implementation requiring database independence must conform to the ANSI SQL 2 standards. The JDBC API is object oriented. It includes a rich set of classes, interfaces, and exceptions.

In Chapter 14 you'll learn that the Java Virtual Machine (JVM) is the core of the Java runtime system. We'll discuss bytecodes—their structure and verification process. We'll tell you how to create native methods in C and call them in your Java code. We'll also describe how you implement error-handling capabilities in your Java programs.

14

Advanced Java Computing

This chapter discusses four important advanced Java topics: the Java Virtual Machine (JVM), the structure and verification of bytecodes, native method access in your Java programs, and exception handling.

One of the reasons for Java's popularity is its ability to generate platform independent portable code. Java executables run on the Java Virtual Machine (JVM). JVM is the core of the Java runtime system. It translates Java executables into platform specific instructions. The JVM is a software-based microprocessor. Therefore, although Java code itself is platform independent, JVM is not. JVM is platform specific. This chapter provides an overview of JVM and its structure. It explains the process of creating and executing Java applications and why and how Java code is portable.

In addition to JVM, this chapter discusses bytecodes—their structure and verification process. You compile your Java program into compiled bytecodes using the Java compiler. Bytecode is a form that you can execute on the Java Virtual Machine. Java bytecode is interpreted, because the Java Virtual Machine is not a real microprocessor. Recently, with the introduction of Just-In-Time (JIT) compilers, you can translate Java bytecode into machine code on-the-fly.

Furthermore, this chapter discusses native methods—how you can create native methods in C and in your Java code. Native methods are platform specific and therefore limit your Java application. You should avoid using native methods as much as possible if one of the primary goals of your Java application is to be platform independent. However, there are certain situations where it becomes necessary to access the raw speed or other platform specific features. Java provides a way to create and call such native methods.

Later in this chapter, you'll learn about exception handling and how to implement error handling capabilities in your Java programs. You learn how to declare exceptions and identify methods that use them. You learn how to throw exceptions in your Java code in response to error conditions and how to catch and process them.

The Java Virtual Machine (JVM)

The JVM microprocessing layer that you use to run Java class files is platform specific, even though the Java language is not. Traditional executables run directly on the target machine without a JVM layer. Such executables communicate directly with the target machine, using the machine specific instruction set. Figure 14-1 shows the communication layer between the traditional executables and the target machine instruction set.

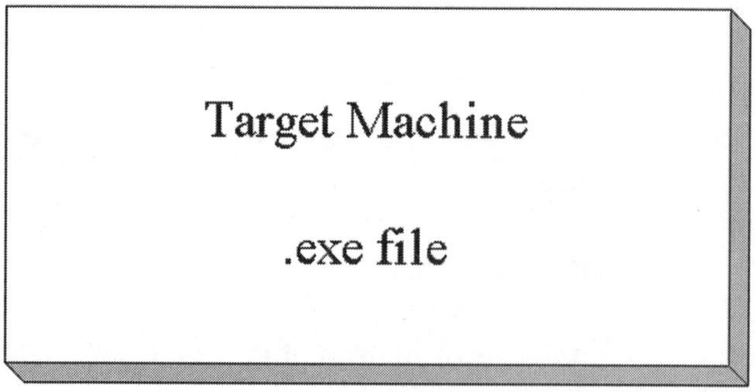

> ## Target Machine
>
> ## .exe file

Figure 14-1: Traditional executables run directly on the target machine.

Unlike traditional executables, Java executables do not run directly on the target machine. They run on the Java Virtual Machine—an intermediate layer between the Java executables and the target machine (see Figure 14-2).

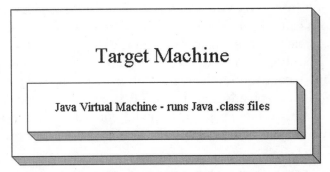

Figure 14-2: Java executables run on the Java Virtual Machine.

The JVM runtime translates Java executables into platform specific instructions by using a microprocessing layer that resides between the Java executables and the operating system platform. The extra layer of JVM makes Java programs sluggish compared to native programs written in C, C++, or Pascal. Native programs execute faster on their target platforms, but they lack portability.

Netscape Navigator 3.0 and Microsoft Internet Explorer 3.0 support Java. The Java Virtual Machine is built into these browsers. When the browser comes across a Java applet, it is downloaded and executed by the browser's built-in runtime interpreter. This is how you get portability with Java programs.

A Java-enabled browser implies the Java runtime interpreter—the JVM—is built into it. If you are using a browser on the Windows platform, the browser itself is Windows specific and has a Windows specific implementation of the JVM built into it. Similarly, if you are using a browser on the Macintosh platform, the browser itself is Macintosh specific and has a Macintosh specific implementation of the JVM built into it. As you can see, instead of the target application being platform specific, it is the intermediate layer—the JVM—that is platform specific.

This implementation is unique in a way because the JVM is a microprocessor by functionality, but it is implemented completely as a software construct. You can even run Java programs on consumer appliances such as televisions and microprocessors as long as the appliance supports the runtime interpreter. This gives the opportunity to create some very innovative applications and solutions using Java. It is advantageous for the JVM to be as lean as possible because a compact JVM is easier and faster to download.

The sluggishness of Java programs has been a major concern. Only recently, with the release of Just-In-Time (JIT) compilers, has this issue been addressed. The JIT compilers compile the bytecodes into native code on-the-fly. The JIT compiler is the intermediate layer between the JVM and the target machine (see Figure 14-3).

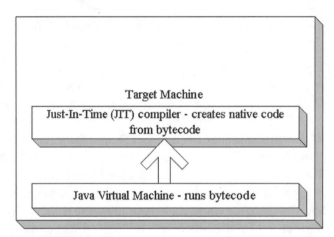

Figure 14-3: The JIT compiler converts bytecode into native code.

The beauty of such a compiler is that it is transparent to everything (including your Java application) except the JVM. It is sort of a plug-and-play module. The JIT compiler creates compiled code that is faster than the interpreted mode of the JVM. Instead of the JVM manually making the calls to the underlying platform, it is the JIT compiler that performs this function. Thus, the JIT compiler changes the role of the JVM in the Java framework.

The JVM calls the JIT compiler. The JIT compiler generates the compiled native code. This code is passed to the native operating system. The speed of JIT compiled Java programs is comparable to the native C and C++ programs.

Understanding Bytecodes

The Java Virtual Machine understands compiled *bytecodes*. Bytecodes are nothing but .class files (object modules) created by the Java compiler from the .java source files (see Figure 14-4). The .class files are basically Java object modules. If you have used a C++ or Pascal compiler, you'll notice that the compiler first creates an .obj module from the source-code files. The Java .class files are the equivalent of such .obj modules. In traditional programs, multiple .obj modules are combined together to create an executable. In Java, the .class files represent the object modules and the Java Virtual Machine represents the executable. The JVM acts on the .class files.

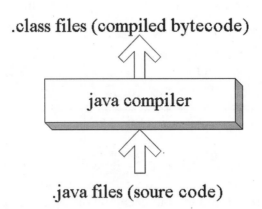

.class files (compiled bytecode)

java compiler

.java files (soure code)

Figure 14-4: The Java compiler converts .java files to .class files.

The .class File

To understand bytecodes, it is necessary to understand the structure of a .class file. Table 14-1 lists the elements of a .class file.

Name	Type
magic	unsigned 4-byte
major_version	unsigned 2-byte
minor_version	unsigned 2-byte
access_flags	unsigned 2-byte
this_class	unsigned 2-byte
super_class	unsigned 2-byte
interfaces_count	unsigned 2-byte
interfaces[interface_count]	unsigned 2-byte
fields_count	unsigned 2-byte
fields[fields_count]	fields_info
methods_count	unsigned 2-byte
methods[methods_count]	method_info
attributes_count	unsigned 2-byte
attributes[attribute_count]	attribute_info
constant_pool_count	unsigned 2-byte
constant_pool[constant_pool_count - 1]	cp_info

Table 14-1: The elements of a .class file.

A bytecode is comprised of 8-bit values. The cp_info, fields_info, method_info, and attribute_info are substructures. Let's take an indepth look at each one of these elements.

■ The **magic** number of a class is 0xcafebabe. This unsigned 4-byte number must appear in the class file. If it does not appear, the class file is assumed to be invalid and the program is not executed.

- **major_version and minor_version** numbers in a class file denote the version number of the compiler used to create it. The version number is represented as M.m, where M is the major version and m is the minor version. For example if the version number is 47.3, 47 is the major version number, and 3 is the minor version number. Both major and minor versions are unsigned 2-byte numbers.

- **access_flag** is also an unsigned 2-byte number. This represents the access characteristics of the first class in the package. This field can be a combination of values shown in Table 14-2.

Access Flag	Value
ACC_PUBLIC	0x0001
ACC_PRIVATE	0x0002
ACC_PROTECTED	0x0003
ACC_STATIC	0x0008
ACC_FINAL	0x0010
ACC_SYNCHRONIZED	0x0020
ACC_THREADSAFE	0x0040
ACC_TRANSIENT	0x0080
ACC_NATIVE	0x0100
ACC_INTERFACE	0x0200
ACC_ABSTRACT	0x0400

Table 14-2: The valid access_flags.

- **this_class** is an unsigned 2-byte index into constant_pool indicating ID of the current class.

- **super_class** is also an unsigned 2-byte index indicating ID of the parent class.

- **interfaces_count** is an unsigned 2-byte number. It denotes the number of interfaces implemented in the class.

- **interfaces[interface_count]** is an array that contains information about the interfaces of a class.

- **fields_count** is an unsigned 2-byte number. It represents the number of fields (class variables) in the class.

- **fields[fields_count]** is an array that contains information about the fields of a class.

- **methods_count** is an unsigned 2-byte number. It denotes the number of methods implemented in this class.

- **methods[methods_count]** is an array that contains information about the methods of a class.

- **attributes_count** is an unsigned 2-byte number. It denotes the number of applet's attributes (parameters in HTML file, including code name).

- **attributes[attributes_count]** is an array that contains information about the attributes of a class.

- **constant_pool_count** is an unsigned 2-byte number. It indicates the number of constants (final static variables) implemented in this class.

- **constant_pool[constant_pool_count - 1]** is an array that stores class names, field names, string constants, and all constants referenced in the body of the code.

Understanding the Bytecode Verifier

One of the major goals of the designers of Java was to create an environment that lets you create secure applications easily. The Java Virtual Machine is stack based. It includes a bytecode verifier that checks the internal consistency of the class and validates the code.

When a class is loaded, the verifier checks it before it is executed. This is the same verifier that performs security checks on Java applets when you browse a Java-enabled Web site using a

Java-enabled browser such as Microsoft Internet Explorer 3.0 or Netscape Navigator. When your browser comes across a Java applet, it downloads and runs it through the bytecode verifier.

There are advantages and disadvantages to having the bytecodes verified. The advantage is increased security. Verifying the bytecodes makes your application and environment more secure. Having a secure application and environment is extremely important in these Internet and intranet days. The disadvantage is some degradation in execution performance. Due to the extra steps of verification and security checks, Java applications and applets are slow to execute. Until the verification process is complete, the bytecodes are not executed.

You can force or skip the verification process programmatically if you need to. Use the available compiler options to force an explicit verification or skip it. Use the -verify option to make the interpreter verify all the local classes it loads:

```
java -verify test.class
```

The above command forces the Java interpreter to perform security checks on test.class before it loads.

Use the -noverify option to make the interpreter skip verification of all local classes:

```
java -noverify test.class
```

The above command forces the Java interpreter to skip all security checks on test.class before it loads.

Use the -verifyremote option to make the interpreter verify all the classes that are remotely loaded. In other words, it verifies all the classes the classloader loads:

```
java -verifyremote test.class
```

The default option for the interpreter is -verifyremote.

The bytecode verifier uses a four pass verification algorithm to check the applet before it is executed. What does the verifier check? It verifies that:

- All register operations are legal.
- Method parameter calls are legal.

■ There is no stack overflow.

■ Type conversion is okay.

■ No illegal pointers are used.

The bytecode verifier is a useful tool included in the JVM.

Native Methods

A native method is an interface between Java and C++ programs. Some applications may need to interface with existing C++ libraries. This may be for speed or to reuse an existing library of code. Integrating native method calls into your Java code makes it nonportable, since the C++ libraries are native to the target platform. For example, if you integrate calls to DLLs in your Java application, it limits your application to the Windows platform. This is because only the Windows platform supports the dynamic link library (DLL) structure.

The section on the Java Virtual Machine in this chapter offered a closer look at the Java architecture and why it helps you create portable applications. Java, unlike C++, does not support pointers and structures. This makes it easy to write and understand Java code. One of the major complaints with the C++ programming language has been its use of pointers and the varied number of problems if they are not used correctly. Understanding and implementing pointers and pointer arithmetic correctly has been a challenge for even the most experienced C++ programmers. Java eliminates such problems by not supporting its use at all. In addition, Java forces you to think in terms of classes, objects, attributes, and methods. Since Java does not support the use of structures, a C++ structure is implemented as a Java class. All of this and the JVM architecture helps you create robust, object-oriented, and portable Java applications.

On one hand, integrating native C++ libraries with your Java code makes it nonportable to other platforms. On the other hand, your application gains speed and efficiency by their use. Native C++ code is faster than comparable Java code. Basically it is a tradeoff. The decision to use native method access depends on the goals of your application. If portability is of paramount importance, you should avoid the use of native methods. If portability is not a primary concern, but speed and efficiency is and you have an existing library of native C++ code that you could easily reuse, integrating such a library with your Java code makes sense.

What Is a Dynamic Link Library ?

Understanding DLLs will help you better understand native method access. A *dynamic link library* is defined as a set of functions that are linked dynamically with your executable. In other words, they are linked at runtime. Using DLLs with your application reduces the size of your executable. They make the calling application modular in nature. You can reuse the same DLLs across several different applications, provided they are loaded into the memory, thus saving you valuable time and memory space.

Note

Usually DLL files have the .DLL extension. Some of Windows system DLLs have the .EXE extension. They are still DLLs.

Windows DLLs

Windows 95 is comprised of three main DLLs: gdi32.exe, user32.exe, and kernel32.exe. Windows 3.1 is comprised of the same three DLLs but only their 16-bit versions: gdi.exe, user.exe, and kernel.exe.

The default location for DLLs is the system subdirectory of your Windows directory (i.e., c:\windows\system).

Accessing Windows Native Methods

Let's consider accessing native methods from your Java application on the Windows platform. On the Windows platform native methods or functions are usually available in dynamic link library (DLL) form. The steps involved in accessing DLL native methods are:

1. Load the dynamic link library.
2. Declare the method.
3. Call the method.

Load the Dynamic Link Library

The class java.lang.Runtime includes the methods to load a DLL and dynamically link to it. The following example demonstrates the use of the loadLibrary() method:

```java
import java.lang.Runtime;
public class dllExample
          // sample example to
   // demonstrate the use of
          // loadLibrary method
{
   static
   {
     try
     {
        loadLibrary("sampleDLL");
        //load the example DLL - sampleDLL
     }
     catch Exception(e)
     {
        // catch the exception
        // print appropriate message
     }
     public native int exampleMethod(int x);
}
```

The above example class, dllExample, demonstrates the use of the loadLibrary() method. If the method fails, it throws an exception which is caught by the catch expression.

Declare the Native Method

A native method must be declared before it can be used. In the declaration you must include the name of the method, its parameters, the type of parameters, and the return type. A native method is always declared as public:

```
public native int exampleMethod(int x);
```

This code demonstrates how to declare a native method. The directive *native* indicates to the Java compiler that the method is a natively implemented method. It is not implemented in Java. If you declare a Java method, you associate the code with the method itself. If you declare a native method, you do not need to include the code with it. This is because the code is already implemented in the native language such as C++.

Call the Native Method

Once you declare the native method, you can call it just like any other Java method. This process of loading the library and declaring the methods is similar to the process of declaring a reference to the library and defining the library functions using a tool such as PowerBuilder or Visual Basic. For example, in Visual Basic you declare the DLL functions in the declaration section of the code, usually a .BAS file. You do not need a specific loadLibrary function call since the Visual Basic compiler takes care of it. Once the library functions are declared, you can use them just like any other Visual Basic function. The same concept applies to integrating native methods in a DLL with your Java application code.

Creating Native Methods

To develop any standard Java application, you compile your source code into a .class file. To develop Java applications that support native method access, you require three more files: the class header file, the stub C file, and the stubspreamble.h file. The Java Development Kit includes a utility called *javah* that you can use to create the native method interface for your Java programs. The process of creating native methods includes the following three steps:

1. Create the header file using the javah utility.

2. Create the stub C file using the javah utility.

3. Create your C source file and compile altogether into a DLL.

Create the Header File Using Javah

A header file indicates the data layout within your Java class to the native C code. It also includes prototype declarations of the native methods. Execute the following command to create the header file:

```
javah dllExample
```

This command creates a header file, dllExample.h, in the CClassHeaders directory. The file includes the following header information:

```
/* Header for class dllExample */
/* Do NOT edit this file */
/* It is machine generated */
#ifndef _Include_dllExample
#define _Include_dllExample
typedef struct ClassdllExample{
    int number;
} dllExample;
HandleTo(dllExample);
#ifdef _cplusplus
extern "C" _declspec(dllexport)
#endif
int exampleMethod(struct dllExample, int x);
#endif;
```

Create the Stub C File Using Javah

The stubs file translates parameters for the native C methods. The Java interpreter calls this stub, which in turn, calls the native method within the DLL that you loaded with the loadLibrary() function. Execute the following command to create the stub C file:

```
javah -stubs dllExample
```

This command creates the dllExample.stubs file in the stubs subdirectory. The stub C file dllExample.stubs includes the following information:

```
/* DO NOT EDIT THIS FILE */
/* It is machine generated */
#include <StubPreamble.h>


/* Stubs for class DLLExample */
/* SYMBOL: "DLLExample/exampleMethod(I)I",
__declspec(dllexport) stack_item
*dllExample_exampleMethod_stub(stack_item *_P_,struct execenv
*_EE_) {
    extern int dllExample_exampleMethod(void *, int);
    _P_[0].i = dllExample_exampleMethod(_P_[0].p,
((_P_[1].i)));
    return _P_ + 1;
}
```

Create the Source File & Compile It Into a DLL

Now that the header and stubs files are created, you are ready to create the DLL. For native method implementation you need the stubspreamble.h, dllExample.h, and dllExample.stubs files. The file dllExample.stubs is located in the ./hotjava/include subdirectory.

To create the native method DLL, include both the header files, dllExample.h, and stubspreamble.h. Next, include the contents of the stub file (using cut and paste) and the native method prototype definition. The code for the dllExample native DLL is as follows:

```
#include dllExample.h
#include stubsPreamble.h
```

```
/* paste the contents of the stub file */
/* Stubs for class DLLExample */
/* SYMBOL: "DLLExample/exampleMethod(I)I",
__declspec(dllexport) stack_item
*dllExample_exampleMethod_stub(stack_item *_P_,struct execenv
*_EE_) {
    extern int dllExample_exampleMethod(void *, int);
    _P_[0].i = dllExample_exampleMethod(_P_[0].p,
((_P_[1].i)));
    return _P_ + 1;
}


/* include the native method prototype definition */
int dllExample_exampleMethod(struct HdllExample *this, int
number)
{
   return ~number;
}
```

Now compile this file into a DLL. Name the DLL file the same as the one specified in the loadLibrary() function. In this case, name the DLL sampleDLL. The above example calculates the two's complement of a given number.

Exception Handling

Java's exception handling lets you handle errors easily without having to write any special code. You can fix errors that are bugs programmatically. You cannot really fix errors that occur due to certain situations. They are handled by your program. Such errors are called *exceptions*. Examples are low memory, file does not exist, invalid path, and so on. Java provides a class java.lang.Throwable that includes methods to handle such exceptions.

Java handles errors and exceptions using class objects, since Java exceptions are class objects they may contain both data and methods. You can easily add Java exceptions to existing methods.

Throwing Java Exceptions

Java supports two types of exceptions: runtime exception and program exception. A runtime exception is detected when classes are loaded and their methods are executed. A runtime exception is thrown by the Java runtime system—the JVM. Runtime exceptions are objects of the class java.lang.RuntimeException or of its subclasses. A program exception is thrown by your Java code. It is usually thrown when your Java code detects a program malfunction. When an exception is thrown, it must be caught or the current thread of execution terminates and an error displays.

Use the throw statement to throw an exception. The syntax for the throw statement is:

```
throw Expression;
```

Expression represents an object that is an instance of a subclass of the java.lang.Exception class. The Exception class is included in the Java API.

Any new or existing methods can be written to throw exceptions. For example, the following method, computeSum, throws the sampleException exception:

```
static boolean computeSum( int x, int y) throws
sampleException {


}
```

You can throw multiple exceptions associated with the same method. The multiple exceptions are separated by commas in the definition of the method. For example, the following computeSum method throws two exceptions: sampleException1 and sampleException2:

```
static boolean computeSum( int x, int y) throws
sampleException1, sampleException2 {


}
```

Catching Java Exceptions

The try & catch Blocks

Use the try and catch blocks to catch exceptions thrown by your Java methods. Every try block is associated with one or more catch blocks.

To catch an exception thrown by a method, place the method in a try block. The syntax for a try block is:

```
try
   {
      //call the method here
   }
```

The catch block catches the exception thrown by the method in the try block. The syntax for catch block is:

```
catch { Exception e }
   {
      //exception is caught
      //handle it
      //display appropriate error message
   }
```

When any method in the try block throws an exception, execution of the try block stops. The control of the program is passed immediately to the appropriate catch block if it exists. If it does not exist, the exception is not caught and the current thread of program execution terminates. An error message and stack trace displays.

A try block may have multiple catch blocks. Each catch block is for a different exception. The following is the syntax for a try block with multiple catch blocks:

```
try
   {
      //call the method here
   }
catch ( Exception e1 )
   {
```

```
        //exception e1 is caught
        //handle it
        //display appropriate error message
    }
catch ( Exception e2 )
    {
        //exception e2 is caught
        //handle it
        //display appropriate error message
    }
catch ( Exception e3 )
    {
        //exception e3 is caught
        //handle it
        //display appropriate error message
    }
```

The above syntax indicates three catch blocks associated with a try block. Each catch block is for a different exception. If the type of exception occurred is assignable to exception e1, the program control is passed to the first catch block. If the type of exception occurred is assignable to exception e2, the program control is passed to the second catch block. Lastly, if the type of exception occurred is assignable to exception e3, the program control is passed to the last catch block.

The finally() Block

You can add another block to your try-catch block of code, called the finally block. The block of code in the finally clause is always executed irrespective of whether an exception is caught or no exception at all occurred. The following example demonstrates the use of the finally clause:

```
try
    {
        //call the method here
    }
catch ( Exception e1 )
    {
        // exception e1 is caught
```

```
        // handle it
        // display appropriate error message
      }
    finally()
      {
      //this block of code is always executed
      }
```

In this example, if an exception is thrown it is caught and the block of code in the catch expression is executed. This is followed by execution of code in the finally clause.

If an exception is thrown but not caught, the block of code in the finally clause is still executed. If an exception is not thrown, the block of code in the finally clause is executed immediately after the try block is executed.

Nested try Blocks

You can implement nested exception handling by using nesting try blocks. Each try block has a corresponding catch block. If an exception is generated, it is passed to the first catch block. If it is not handled by the first catch block, it is passed to the catch block at the next level. If it is still not handled, it is passed further up the exception handling hierarchy.

The following example shows the syntax for nested exception handling having two levels of try-catch blocks:

```
    try
      {
        try
          {
            //call the method here in
      //the inner level try
    //block
          }
        catch ( Exception e1 )
          {
            //exception e1 is caught
            //handle it
            //display appropriate
    //error message
```

```
        }
       //call the method here in the outer
//level try block
     }
   catch ( Exception e2 )
     {
       //exception e2 is caught
       //handle it
       //display appropriate error message
     }
```

Exceptions Thrown by Different Java Classes

Java includes a rich set of classes. Each class includes several methods you can use to implement different functionality in your Java programs. These methods throw exceptions that Java can catch and handle. The Java classes that throw exceptions include:

- java.io
- java.util
- java.lang
- java.awt
- java.net

Rethrowing Java Exceptions

If the catch block catches a thrown exception, the catch block may rethrow it. If an exception is rethrown, the catch clause of the higher level try statement can catch and process the exception. The following shows the syntax for an example where the Java exception is rethrown:

```
    try
      {
        try
          {
            //call the inner level
```

```
//method here
    }
  catch ( Exception e1 )
    {
        //exception e1 is caught
        //handle it
        //display appropriate
//error message

        throw e1
    //throw exception e1
//again!
    }
    //call the outer level method here
  }
catch( Exception e1 )
  {
  }
```

Moving On

In this chapter you learned about JVM (Java Virtual Machine), a software based microprocessor that translates Java executables into platform-specific instructions. You also learned about the structure of bytecodes, creating native methods in C++ and integrating them with your Java code, and handling exceptions in your Java programs.

The next chapter introduces Microsoft's new ActiveX technology, discussing what ActiveX is and where it is going. We'll also compare it to Java. Finally, the next chapter briefly discusses how to use Visual J++ to create Web-based solutions using the best of both worlds (ActiveX and Java).

Using ActiveX With Java

Among all the Internet buzzwords you hear today I am sure one of them is ActiveX. What is ActiveX? Why is it so hot and what makes it "active?" The computing industry has undergone significant transformation in a very short time. First the Internet, then the World Wide Web, followed by Netscape Navigator, Java, Microsoft Internet Explorer, and now ActiveX. The Internet has significantly transformed the development and distribution paradigm. For some it has even changed the way they interact and communicate.

With the advent of browsers and Web authoring tools, creating and navigating Web pages has become very easy. But these pages are mostly static with very little or no interactivity—as if they have no life of their own. They are straight renderings of text and graphics. Static pages generate very little interest for the surfer. Thus, the introduction of tools capable of livening up the experience of surfing the Internet—Java, JavaScript, VBScript, and now ActiveX.

ActiveX is a Microsoft technology that has multiple purposes for networked environments. You can do several things using ActiveX. If you are a Visual Basic programmer, you can create and embed ActiveX controls within your Visual Basic applications. If you design and develop Web sites, you can make your sites active. You can integrate ActiveX controls and scripts with your Web pages (see Figure 15-1). You can embed an ActiveX component in your Web page for end users to download. This is similar to creating a Java applet and embedding it within your Web page. Users can also download Java applets. If you are a corporate developer, you can create active documents for your intranet using ActiveX. ActiveX also includes support for Java.

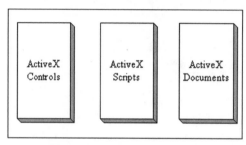

Figure 15-1: The ActiveX components.

This chapter introduces ActiveX—its features and the technology behind it. This chapter provides a brief historical perspective discussing data transfer technologies including clipboard, dynamic data exchange (DDE), and object linking and embedding (OLE). It discusses the ActiveX Component Object Model (COM) and the advantages and disadvantages of using it. You'll learn how to seamlessly integrate ActiveX COM objects into your Java programs. You'll learn how to create ActiveX COM objects using Java. Finally, you'll see some real-world examples of ActiveX on the Web today.

What is ActiveX?

ActiveX is a technology with multiple purposes for networked environments. It is based on COM. It includes ActiveX controls, ActiveX documents, and ActiveX scripting. *ActiveX controls* are objects with specific functionality, such as spell checking, that can be integrated into your Web and other client/server applications. *ActiveX documents* are controls that represent Office documents such as Word, Excel, and PowerPoint, in Web applications. *ActiveX scripting* is Web scripting using a scripting language such as VBScript or JavaScript and ActiveX controls.

ActiveX is presently supported on the Windows platform. Microsoft anticipates support for the Macintosh and UNIX platforms by the end of 1996. Microsoft is working with Metrowerks for including ActiveX support on the Macintosh. And they are working with Bristol and Mainsoft to include ActiveX support on the UNIX platform. Microsoft Internet Explorer 3.0 is the only browser in the market today that includes full support for ActiveX technology. You can use ActiveX controls with Netscape Navigator 3.0 if you use the ActiveX plug-in from NCompassLabs (http://www.ncompasslabs.com)—a third-party software vendor. ActiveX is the new kid on the technology block; it is expected to undergo revisions and enhancements over time.

Tip

To keep abreast of the latest on ActiveX technology, visit Microsoft's Web site (http://www.microsoft.com/activex) regularly.

The ActiveX Internet Model

The Internet computing model has evolved over time. Figure 15-2 shows the traditional HTTP/HTML (HyperText Markup Language/HyperText Transfer Protocol) model. The HTML client interacts with the HTTP server. The server stores all the Web pages and serves them upon client request. There is no interactivity, and the model is inactive.

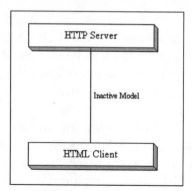

Figure 15-2: The inactive model.

Next came the Common Gateway Interface (CGI); it can be used to extend HTML and add server side processing for Web applications. For example, you can use CGI scripts on the server to parse the form filled out by users and to mail it to the intended recipients. Still, this model is limited in functionality. Figure 15-3 shows the CGI model.

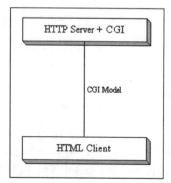

Figure 15-3: The CGI model.

Microsoft's proposed Internet model includes using ActiveX controls on both the client and the server. You use a scripting language such as VBScript on the client side to handle tasks such as processing mouse clicks, validating user response, and so on. Use the Internet Information Server (IIS) as the server for your Web applications. Use dbWeb as the database back end for deploying relational data based applications over the Web. You use Internet Server Application Programming (ISAPI) interface to handle server-side processing. ISAPI replaces the CGI interface in Microsoft's Internet model. Figure 15-4 shows the Microsoft ActiveX based Internet model.

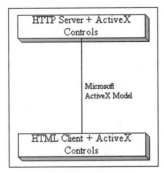

Figure 15-4: Microsoft ActiveX model.

ActiveX Controls

An ActiveX control is a control that you can easily integrate with a Web or client/server application, a Java applet, a Web browser, and so on. You can download a control over the Net. Controls can be a part of your corporate intranet. You can load an ActiveX control into your Visual Basic application for example. It is a control in binary form that provides certain functionality. You can download a library of ActiveX controls from Microsoft's ActiveX Web site (http://www.microsoft.com/activex). One such control is the stock ticker control. It continuously displays changing data. The control downloads the URL specified at regular intervals and displays that data. The data can be in text or XRT format. You can integrate such a control with your Java, Visual Basic, or Web application. One control serves multiple purposes.

Microsoft has developed an application called the ActiveX Control Pad that you can use to design and develop your active Web pages visually. Figure 15-5 shows the ActiveX Control Pad.

Figure 15-5: The ActiveX Control Pad provides a visual way to integrate ActiveX controls into your Web pages.

When programming with tools such as Visual Basic, Power-Builder, and Delphi, you can visually integrate a number of user interface controls such as buttons, labels, text, list boxes, and so on. The Control Pad provides a similar way of accomplishing ActiveX scripting. Using ActiveX Control Pad you can visually insert an ActiveX control into a Web page. You can set the properties of the control using its property sheet. Once all the properties are set, the Control Pad inserts the appropriate <OBJECT> tag declaration for the control into your HTML code.

Tip

You can download the Control Pad from Microsoft's home page (http://www.microsoft.com).

At the time of this writing, Microsoft is giving away a suite of ActiveX controls for the Internet. It is called the Internet Control Pack and is available for download at http://www.microsoft.com/icp/us/icpdown/icpdown.htm. Using such controls, developers can construct powerful Internet applications quickly, easily, and efficiently.

Microsoft Internet Control Pack

The control pack consists of the following controls:

- FTP
- HTML
- HTTP
- NNTP
- POP
- SMTP
- Winsock TCP
- Winsock UDP

ActiveX Scripting

ActiveX scripting is scripting using VBScript or JavaScript and ActiveX controls. VBScript is a lightweight, portable subset of Visual Basic, the language; Visual Basic for Applications is the scripting language used in Microsoft Office applications such as Word and Excel. It is a scripting language that you can use to extend your HTML code for designing and modifying Web pages. You can change the appearance and behavior of your Web pages dynamically by using VBScript. You can process mouse events such as a mouse click or a mouse moving over a certain part of the Web page, and initiate certain actions on such events. You can also use VBScript as part of other applications that use ActiveX controls, OLE Automation servers, and Java applets.

Using ActiveX scripting with your HTML code reduces Internet traffic. You can perform data validation on the client side instead of sending the data over to the server for CGI scripts to process. Only valid data is transmitted over the Net. This is similar to a client/server environment using PowerBuilder or Visual Basic and Sybase where the GUI front end performs data validation and Sybase receives only validated data with which to work.

How does VBScript compare to JavaScript? VBScript is a competitor of JavaScript. Both languages have their advantages and disadvantages. Visual Basic has been around for quite some time. Java is relatively new. The introduction of VBScript is clearly a welcome sign for all the Visual Basic programmers. A lot of them may find it easier to use VBScript with their HTML code than to learn a new language like JavaScript. Neither JavaScript nor VBScript can produce stand-alone applets. However, you can use them to add intelligence and interactivity to HTML documents.

Presently, VBScript is available for Windows 95, Windows NT, Windows 3.1, and Power Macintosh platforms. UNIX versions of VBScript for Sun, HP, Digital, and IBM platforms are under development. You can use VBScript with HTML code and with or without ActiveX controls.

Note

As of this writing, VBScript is available only as part of Microsoft Internet Explorer 3.0.

ActiveX Objects in HTML

The new HTML object extension lets you incorporate any type of object, including ActiveX objects, into your Web pages. The HTML object extension lets you reuse an object control. You can create such an object control yourself or you can use a third party control. Objects are the building blocks of today's object-oriented applications. They help you develop your applications easily and rapidly. If you have programmed using Visual Basic, you have probably used Visual Basic Controls (VBX) and OLE Controls (OCX). VBXs and OCXs are nothing but objects that plug-and-play with your Visual Basic application. You simply insert a component into your application that adds the required function. You can programmatically drive the component to work with your application. For example, you can integrate a spell-checker object into your application. Similarly, ActiveX controls are objects that plug-and-play with your Web and other client/server applications.

The tag you use to indicate an object in HTML is <OBJECT>. Its syntax is:

```
<OBJECT
classid="clsid:XYZ"

    id=NNN
    width=NNN
    height=NNN
    align=NNN
    hspace=NNN
    vspace=NNN
>
<param name 1 = <name of parameter> value = <value of
parameter>>
<param name 2 = <name of parameter> value = <value of
parameter>>
<param name 3 = <name of parameter> value = <value of
parameter>>

...

...

...
<param name n = <name of parameter> value = <value of
parameter>>
</OBJECT>
```

Table 15-1 describes the tag attributes used in the above syntax example.

Attribute	Description
classid	Class identifier for the object.
id	A documentwide identifier.
width	Width of the object.
height	Height of the object.
align	Alignment of the object (center, left, right).
hspace	Horizontal margin.
vspace	Vertical margin.
param name 1...n	parameters 1 through n.

Table 15-1: <Object> tag attributes.

The <OBJECT> tag includes more attributes than shown above. Refer to your HTML documentation for detailed information on all the <OBJECT> tag attributes.

The following example shows the object declaration for an ActiveX stock ticker control (you can download this control from Microsoft's ActiveX Web site):

```
<OBJECT
        id=iexr2
        type="application/x-oleobject"
        classid="clsid:0CA4A620-8E3D-11CF-A3A9-
00A0C9034920"
        width=300
        height=50
>
<param name="DataObjectName" value="http://www.mycompany.com/
iexrt.xrt">
<param name="DataObjectActive" value="1">
<param name="scrollwidth" value="5">
<param name="forecolor" value="#ff0000">
<param name="backcolor" value="#0000ff">
<param name="ReloadInterval" value="5000">
</OBJECT>

<OBJECT
id=iexr1
```

```
          type="application/x-oleobject"
          classid="clsid:0CA4A620-8E3D-11CF-A3A9-
00A0C9034920"
          width=300
          height=50
    >
    <param name="DataObjectName" value="http://www.mycompany.com/
    iexrt.dat">
    <param name="DataObjectActive" value="1">
    <param name="scrollwidth" value="5">
    <param name="ReloadInterval" value="5000">
    </OBJECT>
```

From ActiveX to BrandX

On July 26, 1996, Microsoft announced in a press release its decision to transfer ActiveX and COM technologies to an independent standards group. Microsoft decided to do so to fulfill its vision of making ActiveX an open technology. By transitioning it to an independent standards group, Microsoft has announced its willingness and desire to further its goal of the Component Object Model—developing reusable objects that plug-and-play in a heterogeneous environment of different operating systems and networks. It also indicates that Microsoft would like to make ActiveX technology as open and cross-platform as possible—hence, BrandX.

A group of independent software vendors, corporations, and platform vendors will convene to determine the process for transitioning ActiveX technology to an independent organization. The group is a customer-driven organization. Microsoft is one of its decision-making members. Included in the technology transfer is Microsoft's Distributed Computing Model (DCOM) specification for linking objects across heterogeneous operating systems and networks. The standards group is responsible for management of all ActiveX, COM, and DCOM technologies. It is charged with soliciting and reviewing ActiveX and COM specifications, ensuring interoperatibility with other object specifications on Windows, Macintosh, UNIX, and other operating systems, as well as administering reference implementations.

ActiveX & OLE

Apple Computer initially included a simple concept called the clipboard in their operating system for the Macintosh. Using the clipboard, you can transfer data between documents of the same application and documents of different applications. Later, the clipboard concept was adopted in Windows. It became the foundation for OLE (Object Linking & Embedding). Data transfer using the clipboard is driven through the operating system. A document that supports OLE is called a *compound document*. A compound document is a heterogeneous document that contains a variety of documents embedded or linked with it. For example a word processing document can contain a chart, a graph, and a spreadsheet. Using OLE, applications can import information without understanding the format or origin of the data being imported.

Note

To support OLE, a Windows application must be OLE-aware.

The true strength of OLE lies in its ability to improve an application user's productivity. The advantages of using OLE are as follows:

- Simple and consistent data handling controls.
- Automatic update of object data is possible.
- Document space is conserved in object linking.
- Increase in user's productivity. Users can focus on their task at hand and not worry about the data origin, format, and location.

Microsoft renamed OLE controls as ActiveX controls in an effort to push their Internet technology and standards aggressively.

A frequently asked question is: Isn't ActiveX nothing but a new name for OLE? The answer is: yes, but it is much more. ActiveX is OLE redefined for the Internet. The different VBXs and OCXs that have been developed over the years by several software vendors were not compatible for integration with the Web and the Internet. Moreover, these VBXs and OCXs have been traditionally large files, not suitable for download over the Net. Microsoft introduced the ActiveX technology—the level next to OLE, but redefined for the Internet. ActiveX controls are OLE controls with specific and limited functionality. This makes the controls smaller in size, thus they are easier to download over the Net.

ActiveX Versus Java

Are ActiveX and Java the same? Or are they different? If they are different, how is one different from the other?

Java is an object-oriented programming language. It includes a runtime interpreter, an application programming interface (API), and a set of development tools. It is distributed as the Java Development Kit (JDK). As of this writing the latest version of JDK is 1.1. You can download JDK from the JavaSoft Web site (http://java.sun.com).

A Java-enabled browser is one that has the Java runtime interpreter—Java Virtual Machine—integrated with it. Applets are Java programs linked to the browser. You can use an applet to enhance a Web document so that it can display animation or play sound. The Java runtime interpreter executes the applet.

JavaScript

Java and JavaScript are not the same. Nor are they competitors of each other. While Java is an object-oriented *programming* language, JavaScript is a *scripting* language. JavaScript is an extension to your HTML code. If you download and install Netscape Navigator, Microsoft Internet Explorer, or HotJava, you have basically everything you need to use JavaScript.

ActiveX is *not* a programming language. It is a language-independent technology that encompasses ActiveX controls, ActiveX client- and server-side scripting, and ActiveX documents.

You can use Visual Basic, Visual C++, Borland C++, and other programming tools to create ActiveX controls. The fact of the matter is, you can even use Java to create ActiveX controls. This is where you see these two technologies merging. You can integrate ActiveX controls with your Web and other client/server applications.

You can access ActiveX controls from Java applets. And you can access Java applets from ActiveX controls. What does this mean? It means two totally different objects—coming from two totally different technologies—can interact with each other and, therefore, can be integrated into your application. For example, if you have a Java applet that performs certain mathematical calculations and an ActiveX animation control, you can use both if your application demands this. You don't need to write a new Java applet that achieves the same animation that the ActiveX control does. And you don't need to write a new ActiveX control that performs the same mathematical calculations that the Java applet does. By reusing and plugging together existing objects, you can develop your application faster, better, and cheaper.

Java applets and ActiveX controls are similar, but not the same. An ActiveX control has wider scope than a Java applet. It is a superset to Java applets. You can use an applet only with a browser or an applet viewer. You can use an ActiveX control with a browser or you can integrate the control with an application. (Sun is developing Java Beans—presumably its answer to ActiveX controls.)

There is no technology in Java that compares to ActiveX documents. ActiveX documents are ActiveX controls that deal specifically with the representation of documents created using Microsoft Office applications such as Word, Excel, and PowerPoint.

You can use the ISAPI (Internet Server Application Programming Interface) scripting language to write ActiveX scripts on the server side. ISAPI replaces CGI scripting. (Java servlets are Sun's response to ISAPI.)

Java is supported by all three industry standard browsers—Netscape Navigator, Microsoft Internet Explorer, and HotJava. There are several applications that have been written using Java. HotJava is written completely using Java.

Microsoft Internet Explorer 3.0 is written entirely using the ActiveX software development kit (SDK). It is the only browser on the market today that includes full support for ActiveX technology. You can use ActiveX controls with Netscape Navigator 3.0 if you use the ActiveX plug-in from NCompassLabs (http://www.ncompasslabs.com)—a third-party software vendor.

Table 15-2 summarizes the features and capabilities of ActiveX and Java.

ActiveX	Java
Language independent technology.	Object-oriented programming language.
All encompassing technology: includes ActiveX controls, ActiveX scripts, and ActiveX documents.	Distributed as JDK: includes compiler, debugger, runtime interpreter, and so on.
You can integrate ActiveX controls with Web and other client/server applications.	Applets work with browsers or applet viewers only.
You can access Java applets from ActiveX controls.	You can access ActiveX controls from Java applets.
ActiveX scripting is easy to learn and use.	Java programming is based on C++; it may include a steep learning curve.
ActiveX documents are controls with specific representation for documents created using Office applications.	No comparable equivalent yet.
Uses digital signature to implement security.	Uses bytecode verifier to implement security; applets cannot access user's hard drive.
You can use ActiveX Control Pad to develop active Web pages.	You can use Visual J++, a visual Integrated Development Environment, to develop your Java applications and applets.

Table 15-2: ActiveX versus Java.

ActiveX & COM

ActiveX is modeled after the Component Object Model (COM) specification. To understand ActiveX a little better, let's take a look at this specification.

The COM (Component Object Model) specification was first proposed by Microsoft Corporation and Digital Equipment Corporation. The draft version 0.9 was released on October 24, 1995. The model specification is being constantly revised and enhanced.

The COM model specifies an architecture to support the building and reusing of component objects. You can write such objects in completely different languages, on completely different platforms, and have them reside on completely different networks. Yet they can communicate and integrate with each other with plug-and-play ease. This is the basic goal of COM—the ability to create reusable components that can interact with each other easily, irrespective of their language or location of origin. The COM specification includes the following:

- Standard APIs.

- Standard suites of interfaces or used by software written in a COM environment.

- Network protocols used by COM in support of distributed computing.

COM defines a binary interoperatibility standard (which to some is a disadvantage because you cannot access the source code and tweak it to fit your needs). In network computing, COM defines a standard architecture-independent wire format and protocol for interaction between objects on heterogeneous platforms.

Why COM?

Writing software is an intensive task. It requires good concentration, time, and effort. But it could get really frustrating if you have to rewrite certain pieces of code for one application that you have already written for another application. Building applications using existing pieces of code is a lot easier and quicker than writing each and every application from scratch every time. User demand makes it even more important to facilitate code reusability. Thus we have objects; an object represents a certain piece of *encapsulated* code. Encapsulation means both data and functions are embedded within the object. External objects are not particularly interested in the object's architecture. They are more interested in the object's behavior, and its interaction with the other objects.

The growing demand and use of objects has created a whole new industry—the component industry. A large number of independent software vendors are now developing reusable objects for a variety of applications. Visual Basic has a large following of third-party vendors writing DLLs, VBXs, and OCXs that integrate with Visual Basic applications. Similarly PowerBuilder and Delphi have a large following of third-party vendors that write reusable objects that integrate with their respective applications.

A solution to a problem creates an opportunity. Let's pretend you bought a spell-checker object that you want to integrate into your Visual Basic application. Since Visual Basic is Windows-based, obviously you bought a Windows-based spell checker. A few months later, let's assume you need a spell checker for one of your Macintosh applications. The question is: Can you reuse the spell checker you bought, and integrate it into your Macintosh application? In all likelihood you would not be able to reuse it. Now you would have to buy another spell-checker object—this time for the Macintosh platform. There you go! You spend double the money for the same functionality, and double the time and effort to learn the object, its attributes, and methods so that you can integrate it effectively with the host application. The question is: why isn't there a one-for-all general purpose spell-checker object that you can plug into any application on any platform? This is what the COM specification tries to address—creating reusable components that you can use across a wide array of applications deployed on a heterogeneous network of operating systems.

The COM specification defines a component as a reusable piece of software, in binary form, that you can plug into components from other vendors with relatively little effort. For example, a component might be a spell checker designed and developed by one vendor, but you can plug the spell checker into several different word processing applications from different vendors. This component would be in binary form. Its behavior and interaction with external objects is important. What language the component is written in or what platform it supports is of little or no consequence. You may write the component using a procedural language. It does not matter. You want an object to have a certain functionality. You search for it in the component marketplace. If you find such an object, you plug it into your application. You are ready to start your application!

The COM specification defines and implements a mechanism for components to connect and communicate with each other. COM is a system service API. It provides operations through which a client of some service can connect to multiple providers of that service in a polymorphic fashion. Once the connection is established, COM drops out of the picture. The client and object communicate directly through the communication channel established with the assistance of COM.

A Distributed COM (DCOM) model extends the theory of the COM model to a distributed environment—a COM object on one network can communicate with a COM object on another network in a distributed environment (see Figure 15-6).

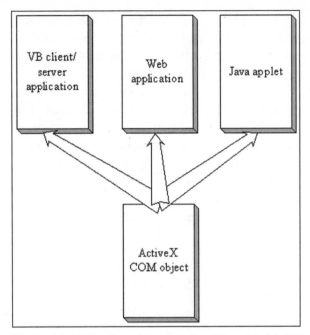

Figure 15-6: Distributed Component Object Model (DCOM).

Both COM and DCOM integrate well with Java. Because Visual J++ includes a reference implementation to the Java Virtual Machine, ActiveX controls are seen as just another set of Java classes. Java includes RMI (Remote Method Invocation) support for Java classes in a distributed environment. The RMI interface works with remote classes as if they are local classes. As a Java programmer, you do not notice any difference. You can use the same RMI interface to access DCOM ActiveX controls as if they were local COM controls.

ActiveX technology is modeled after the COM specification. You can access ActiveX controls from Java applets, and you can access Java applets from ActiveX controls. Two totally different objects coming from two totally different technologies can interact with each other. You can integrate them with your application. This is the core theory of the COM model—software components written in totally different languages able to communicate and integrate with each other. If you have a Java applet that performs certain fractal calculations and an ActiveX user interface control you can use both if your application demands this. You can develop your applications better, faster, and cheaper by reusing existing software components.

COM establishes a connection between the software component (object) and the client that requests the services of the object. A client can never access an ActiveX COM object directly. It has access only to the object's interface. An ActiveX COM object may have multiple interfaces, just like a Java class can have multiple interfaces (see Figure 15-7).

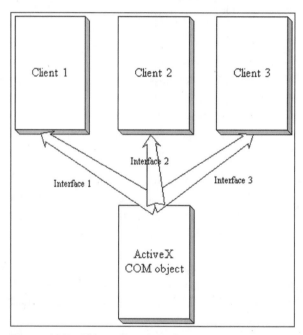

Figure 15-7: Object-client interface.

Why You Should Consider Using ActiveX COM Objects

There are a number of reasons why you should consider using ActiveX COM objects. ActiveX COM object is based on the concept of object-oriented technology and reusable software objects.

To be able to reuse software objects offers significant time and cost savings. Some of the other reasons for considering ActiveX COM objects are:

- It is a Microsoft technology.

- It has been transferred to an independent standards group. Microsoft is one of its decision-making members.

- Thousands of independent software vendors have endorsed and embraced this technology, and are developing a variety of innovative and useful ActiveX controls ready to plug into your applications.

- It promotes the concept of reusable software components across a distributed network of heterogeneous systems.

- It has evolved through DDE (Dynamic Data Exchange) to OLE (Object Linking & Embedding) to ActiveX, and it continues to evolve.

- ActiveX COM objects are all encompassing—you can integrate them with your Internet, intranet, and other client/server applications. You can download ActiveX controls over the Net.

- It is multithreaded, object oriented, and platform independent.

- Visual J++ includes support for integrating ActiveX COM objects with your Java applications.

- Java and ActiveX COM objects mesh well together.

Table 15-3 compares and contrasts Java with COM. Features such as multithreading, object oriented, and platform independence are common to both technologies. They enable these two technologies to mesh well with each other. There is also a significant difference between them. While Java is a programming language, COM is language independent.

Java	COM
Programming language	Language independent component architecture
Object oriented	Object oriented
Platform independent	Platform independent
Multithreaded	Multithreaded and distributed
Supports single inheritance	Supports multiple aggregates
Includes virtual machine	Does not include virtual machine

Table 15-3: Compare and contrast of Java and COM.

ActiveX COM Objects & Java

Microsoft has endeavored to make the integration of ActiveX COM objects and Java seamless for the developer with its reference implementation of the Java Virtual Machine for the Windows platform in Visual J++.

Note

For a detailed discussion on JVM refer to Chapter 14.

Calling an ActiveX COM object from Java is the same as calling a Java class from Java. There is no difference. An ActiveX COM object is the same as a Java class. This simple and seamless integration makes it very easy for the developer to integrate ActiveX COM objects with Java (see Figure 15-8).

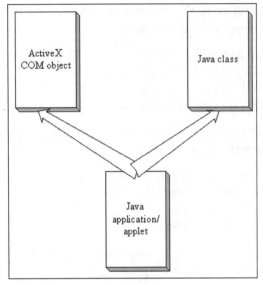

Figure 15-8: COM and Java.

Let's consider an example that presents the general syntax of calling Java and COM objects. Assume JavaClassSample and ComObjectSample are two objects defined in Java and COM, respectively, that perform the same functionality. Assume JavaClassSample has the following methods:

- JavaClassSampleMethod1

- JavaClassSampleMethod2

- JavaClassSampleMethod3

To call JavaClassSample in your Java code, use its constructor to create its instance and call its methods.

Assume ComObjectSample has the following methods:

- ComObjectSampleMethod1

- ComObjectSampleMethod2

- ComObjectSampleMethod3

To call ComObjectSample in your Java code, use its constructor to create its instance and call its methods. This is similar to the approach for calling Java classes. It is possible due to the seamless integration of these two different technologies that Visual J++ provides.

The following code shows how you instantiate the Java class JavaClassSample and call its methods:

```
JavaClassSample JCS = new JavaClassSample();
  JCS.JavaClassSampleMethod1();
  JCS.JavaClassSampleMethod2();
  JCS.JavaClassSampleMethod3();
```

The following code shows how you instantiate the COM object ComObjectSample and call its methods:

```
ComObjectSample CCS = new ComObjectSample();
  CCS.ComObjectSampleMethod1();
  CCS.ComObjectSampleMethod2();
  CCS.ComObjectSampleMethod3();
```

Let's consider a specific example now. SupermanJC is a Java class designed for an exciting game. It has the following methods:

- fly()
- descend()
- shoot()

Use the constructor to instantiate the SupermanJC class:

```
SupermanJC mySupermanJC = new SupermanJC();

  mySupermanJC.fly();
  mySupermanJC.descend();
  mySupermanJC.shoot();
```

SupermanCO is an ActiveX COM object that does the same thing as the SupermanJC class. It has the same methods:

- fly()
- descend()
- shoot()

Use the constructor to instantiate the SupermanCO object:

```
SupermanCO mySupermanCO = new SupermanCO();

  mySupermanCO.fly();
  mySupermanCO.descend();
  mySupermanCO.shoot();
```

Using ActiveX COM Objects With Java Applets

Java is a secure language. One of the major goals of the designers of Java was to create an environment that would let you create secure applications easily. The Java Virtual Machine includes a bytecode verifier that checks the internal consistency of the class and validates the code. When a class is loaded, the verifier checks it before it is executed. This is the same verifier that performs security checks on Java applets when you browse a Java-enabled Web site using a Java-enabled browser such as Microsoft Internet Explorer 3.0, Netscape Navigator, or HotJava. When your browser comes across a Java applet, it downloads and runs it through the bytecode verifier. The bytecode verifier uses a four-pass verification algorithm to check the applet before it is executed. For more on the bytecode verifier refer to the section "Understanding Bytecodes," in Chapter 14.

Java applets running within a Web browser have limited functionality. They are restricted for security reasons:

- Applets cannot call native methods.

- Applets cannot call Java classes that have not been verified by the bytecode verifier.

- Applets cannot read and write to the user's hard drive.

Calling a COM object in Java is similar to making native method calls. Since a Java applet cannot call native methods, it also cannot call COM objects.

A downloaded applet cannot perform file I/O. It also cannot call COM objects. Java applets are therefore limited in functionality. They cannot take advantage of Java/COM integration and the benefits derived from such integration. JavaSoft is presently working on a security implementation based on digital signatures. An applet is digitally signed by its author. Any tampering with the applet invalidates the signature, and then you cannot execute the applet. An applet is considered a "trusted" object if it is digitally signed. A "trusted" applet can make COM calls.

Building ActiveX COM Objects in Java

In Visual J++, ActiveX COM objects and Java classes integrate seamlessly with each other. You can use Java to create ActiveX COM objects. A COM class object is a type library compiled from the Interface Definition Language (IDL). IDL is a language used to define the COM class object and its interfaces. A type library is the runtime form of the COM object. You import the type library into your Java application using the import statement. Parameter passing for COM interface methods is by reference. COM performs garbage collection by using the reference counting technique. This technique is discussed in detail below. When you integrate a COM object with your Java application, the JVM handles the reference counting.

Creating a COM Class Object

To use a COM class object in your Java application, it must be created using certain steps. The import statement in Java can import both Java classes and COM type libraries. To be able to use a COM class object in your Java application, you must create a type library from the COM object's IDL file. Creating a COM class object involves the following steps:

1. Include a coclass statement in the IDL file.
2. Compile the IDL file into a type library.
3. Use the import statement to import the type library just like you import a Java class.
4. Use the coclass name as the name of the Java class.

Implementing COM Interfaces

To implement an interface in Java you either declare it within the source-code module (the .java file) or in a .class file which is imported using the import statement.

The same rule applies to COM interfaces. However, a COM interface is never defined via Java. It is defined in IDL and compiled into a type library. The type library is imported into Java in the same manner as a standard Java .class file.

For example, if an IDL file is compiled into superman/supermanCO.tlb type library containing COM interfaces, you use the following statement to import it in your Java code:

```
import superman.supermanCO.*
```

supermanCO is the type library and *superman* is its path.

When importing the type library, you specify the library name along with its path in the above fashion. As you can see, this import statement is similar to the import statement used to import a standard Java class.

Note

Java objects are COM objects.

Passing Parameters

Parameters for COM interface methods can be simple data types such as integers, characters, and floating point values. Parameter passing is by reference. In most cases these parameters are "out" parameters.

The following COM interface function takes parameters by reference and returns HRESULT type:

```
HRESULT SampleCOMInterfaceMethod([out] long a, [out] long b,
[out, retval]
long * retval)
```

When such interface methods are used with Java, the JVM translates parameter references to corresponding Java objects. For each of the intrinsic Java types: boolean, char, byte, int, short, float, long, and double, the JVM uses an equivalent Java object. This is how Java handles COM interface methods that take parameters by reference.

Single Inheritance

Java supports single inheritance only. A Java class can be singly inherited using the extends modifier. On the other hand, COM supports multiple inheritance. If you want to implement COM class inheritance in your Java application, COM classes must be aggregated into a single class because Java does not support multiple inheritance. Such a COM class can then be singly inherited in Java using the extends modifier—just like you inherit a Java class.

Reference Counting

In COM, garbage collection is accomplished using the reference counting technique. Each software component (object) keeps track of the number of references it has. When the reference count decrements to zero the object deletes itself. When an ActiveX control is used in a Java program, the JVM handles the reference counting. Therefore, when implementing ActiveX COM objects in Java, you don't need to worry about reference counting or garbage collection.

Limitations

Although integration of Java and COM has several advantages, there are a couple of limitations you should be aware of. They are:

- Presently Java supports single inheritance and COM supports multiple aggregates. Java classes can aggregate in only one COM class.

- If you cannot compile a COM interface into a type library, you cannot integrate it with Java. Java supports COM interfaces available in the form of type libraries only.

Visual J++ ActiveX Samples

Visual J++ comes with a number of sample examples. Table 15-4 lists three interesting examples. The javabeep example is an important one as it demonstrates a Java application calling a COM object. This example gives you an idea of how calling a COM object is similar to calling a Java class in a Java application. The orgchart example demonstrates the use of an ActiveX control with a Java applet. These two examples, javabeep and orgchart, together demonstrate integration of ActiveX COM objects with both

Java applications and applets. The mmedia example demonstrates use of Java and ActiveX to play AVI files. It gives you an idea of how you can integrate Java with ActiveX to build multimedia Web applications.

Example	Description
javabeep	Demonstrates a Java application calling a COM object.
orgchart	Demonstrates use of ActiveX control within a Java applet.
mmedia	Demonstrates integration of Java and ActiveX to play AVI.

Table 15-4: Sample examples included with Visual J++.

Real-world ActiveX on the Net

ActiveX is the result of Microsoft's five years of investment in the field of developing component technology. A large number of third-party software vendors have endorsed and embraced this technology. They have developed a variety of ActiveX controls that you can integrate into your Web and client/server applications. There are literally thousands of ActiveX controls available today. According to the GIGA Information Group, there will be $240 million worth of components sold in the year 1996. It is expected to rise to $1 billion by the year 2000. You can certainly expect a large number of innovative and useful ActiveX controls in the coming years. There are also a large number of software companies that offer ActiveX consulting and development services.

If you search the Web you will find a plethora of sites related to ActiveX in one form or the other. Figure 15-9 shows a sample of Yahoo! search results on ActiveX.

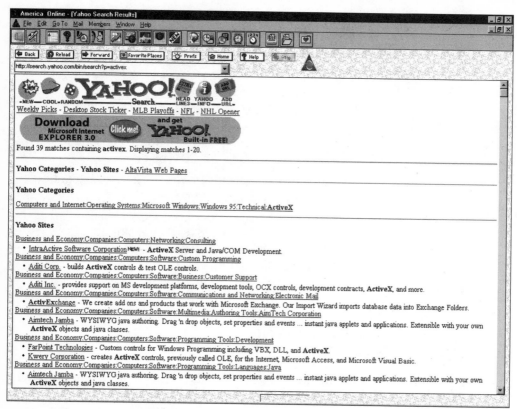

Figure 15-9: A Yahoo! search for ActiveX sites.

This section highlights some of the interesting sites. First and foremost is the Microsoft ActiveX home page (http://www.microsoft.com/activex). It is part of the Microsoft Site Builder Workshop. Figure 15-10 shows the Microsoft ActiveX site.

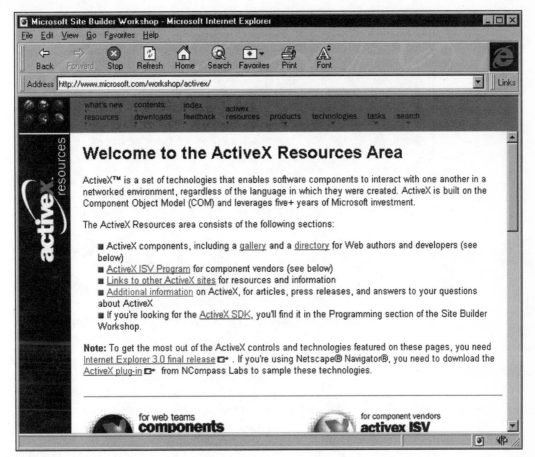

Figure 15-10: Microsoft's ActiveX site.

If you visit this site using Microsoft Internet Explorer 3.0, you can see demonstrations of ActiveX animation controls. This site includes links to a gallery of ActiveX controls and a directory of Web authors and developers. Table 15-5 lists some of the ActiveX controls available from this site.

Name of Control	Description
AnimatedButton	Uses the Windows registry; an animation control to display various frame sequences of an AVI state, depending on the button.
Chart	Enables you to draw various types of charts with different styles.
Gradient	Shades the area with a range of colors, displaying a transition from one specified color to another.
Label	Displays given text at any specified angle. It can also render the text along user-defined curves.
Marquee	Scrolls, slides, and/or bounces URLs within a user-defined window.
Menu	Displays a menu button or a pull-down menu.
Pop-up Menu	Displays a pop-up menu whenever the Pop-Up method is called, and fires a Click event when a menu item is selected.
Pop-Up Window	Displays specified HTML documents in a pop-up window. Use this control to provide tool tips or previews of links.
Preloader	Downloads the specified URL and puts it in the cache. The control is invisible at runtime and starts downloading when enabled.
StockTicker	Continuously displays changing data. The control downloads the URL specified at regular intervals and displays that data. The data can be in text or XRT format.
Timer	Invokes an event periodically. It is invisible at runtime.
ViewTracker	Generates OnShow and OnHide events whenever the control falls within/out of the viewable area.

Table 15-5: Gallery of real-world ActiveX controls at Microsoft's ActiveX page.

The Microsoft ActiveX Web site also includes links to the ActiveX ISV program for Web and ActiveX developers. This is one of the most important sites for keeping up-to-date on ActiveX technology. If you are an active ActiveX developer, mark this site as one of your favorites.

CMP Media, Inc. has created a Web site dedicated to the ActiveX community. This site promises to be the ultimate Web site for the ActiveX community. You can find it all—top stories about ActiveX and related technologies, library of ActiveX controls, list of events, and so on. The URL is http://www.activextra.com/. Mark this site also as one of your favorites. Figure 15-11 shows the ActiveXpress home page.

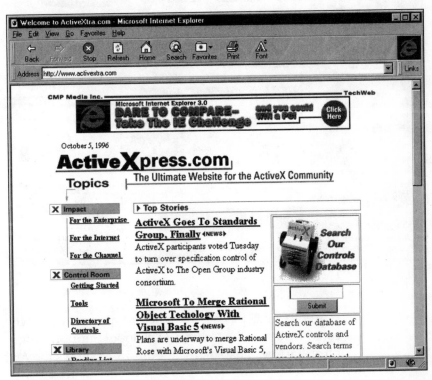

Figure 15-11: The ActiveXpress home page.

ZD Net also has a site devoted to ActiveX (http://www.zdnet.com/activexfiles/). Figure 15-12 shows its home page.

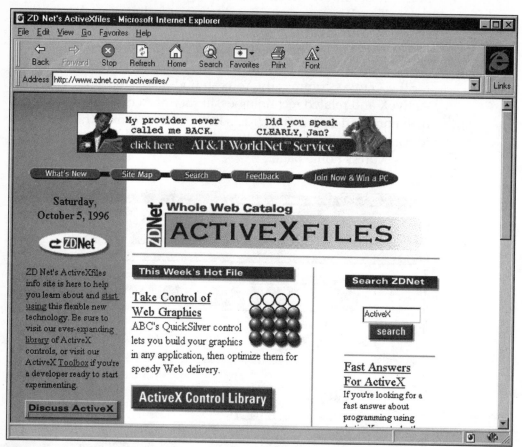

Figure 15-12: ZD Net's ActiveX files.

Another site that seems to be promising, but which is still under construction, is the ActiveX Developer Support Program. Its URL is http://activex.adsp.or.jp/. Figure 15-13 shows the ActiveX DSP site.

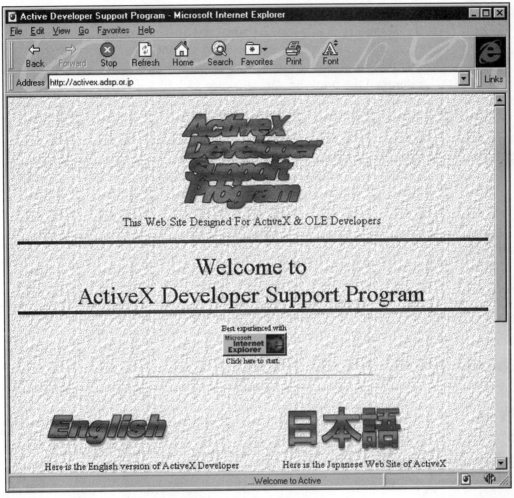

Figure 15-13: The ActiveX Developer Support Program site.

Conclusion

This chapter introduced ActiveX—its features and the technology behind it. It discussed the ActiveX COM model—its advantages and disadvantages. It went into detail about how to call ActiveX

COM objects from Java applications and why you cannot call them from Java applets. It compared and contrasted ActiveX with Java. Some very interesting Web sites related to ActiveX were included in this chapter. For more information on ActiveX, reference the book *Exploring ActiveX* by Shannon Turlington (Ventana).

The goal of this book was to provide you with a complete overview of the Java language, using Visual J++. This book showed you both the Java and Visual J++ way of doing things. Hopefully, you have gained more than familiarity with Visual J++ and expertise in Java.

About the Companion CD-ROM

The Companion CD-ROM consists of 39 source files for projects described in this book. The projects are all located in the [CD-ROM Drive]:\MSDEV\PROJECTS directory, with larger projects each having their own subdirectory. For example, the larger project WordAddition will be located in the [CD-ROM drive]:\MSDEV\PROJECTS\WordAddition directory.

To access the projects, first launch Visual J++ (not included in the Companion CD-ROM), and select Open Project Workspace from the File menu. A standard File Open dialog box appears. Use it to navigate to the CD-ROM (generally the D:\drive), and select one of the project folders. Open the project file (.MDP extension). If you save the project, be sure to save it to your hard drive. When executing a project from the CD-ROM for the first time in Visual J++, an Information for Running dialog box appears. Enter the name of the Java class you wish to execute in the dialog box. Then, choose where you wish to execute the project. Select Browser if you want the project to execute using Internet Explorer, or Stand-alone interpreter if you want to execute it using jview.

Technical Support

Technical support is available for installation-related problems only. The technical support office is open from 8 a.m. to 6 p.m. Monday through Friday and can be reached via the following methods:

Phone: (919) 544-9404 extension 81
Faxback Answer System: (919) 544-9404 extension 85
E-mail: help@vmedia.com
FAX: (919) 544-9472
World Wide Web: http://www.vmedia.com/support
America Online: keyword **Ventana**

Limits of Liability & Disclaimer of Warranty

The authors and publisher of this book have used their best efforts in preparing the CD-ROM and the programs contained in it. These efforts include the development, research, and testing of the theories and programs to determine their effectiveness. The authors and publisher make no warranty of any kind expressed or implied, with regard to these programs or the documentation contained in this book.

The authors and publisher shall not be liable in the event of incidental or consequential damages in connection with, or arising out of, the furnishing, performance, or use of the programs, associated instructions, and/or claims of productivity gains.

Source Code Generated by the AppletWizard

This appendix gives you an analysis of the automatic code generated by the AppletWizard when you create a multithreaded animation. Except for the naming conventions you specify in the AppletWizard, the code and programming techniques remain the same every time you create a multithreaded animation with the AppletWizard.

Let's look at the MyAniApplet project in Chapter 6, where you created your first multithreaded animation with no coding. Let's take a closer look at the code for this applet. Click on File | Open and an Open dialog box opens; choose MyAniApplet.java from the MyAniApplet subdirectory of the directory you placed the project in. For the book example, the file is in the directory ..\MSDEV\PROJECTS\MyAniApplet\MyAniApplet.java. Figure B-1 shows the Developer Studio with MyAniApplet.java opened.

Tip

The Visual J++ AppletWizard generated approximately 300 lines of code. This appendix only covers the highlights and does not go into the details of the techniques or methods used.

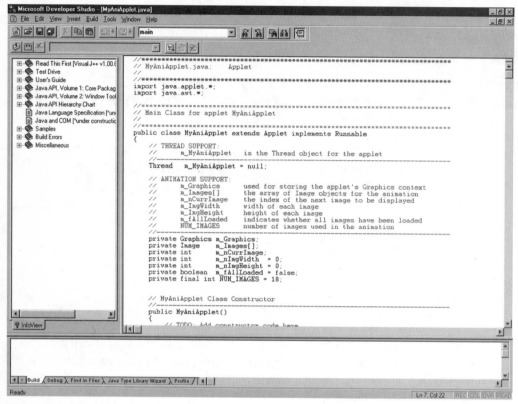

Figure B-1: MyAniApplet open in the Developer Studio.

The following is the code contained in MyAniApplet with numbers placed before each line. The line numbers will be used as reference points for the discussion following the source code:

```
1./*********************************************
2.// MyAniApplet.java:    Applet
3.//
4.//*********************************************
5.import java.applet.*;
6.import java.awt.*;
7.
8./=============================================
9.// Main Class for applet MyAniApplet
10.//
11./=============================================
```

```
12.public class MyAniApplet extends Applet implements
Runnable
13.{
14. // THREAD SUPPORT:
15. //   m_MyAniApplet  is the Thread object for the applet
16. //------------------------------------------------------
17. Thread   m_MyAniApplet = null;
18.
19. // ANIMATION SUPPORT:
20. //   m_Graphics      used for storing the applet's
Graphics context
21. //   m_Images[]      the array of Image objects for the
animation
22. //   m_nCurrImage    the index of the next image to be
displayed
23. //   m_ImgWidth      width of each image
24. //   m_ImgHeight     height of each image
25. //   m_fAllLoaded    indicates whether all images have
been loaded
26. //   NUM_IMAGES      number of images used in the
animation
27. //------------------------------------------------------
28. private Graphics m_Graphics;
29. private Image    m_Images[];
30. private int      m_nCurrImage;
31. private int      m_nImgWidth  = 0;
32. private int      m_nImgHeight = 0;
33. private boolean  m_fAllLoaded = false;
34. private final int NUM_IMAGES = 18;
35.
36.
37. // MyAniApplet Class Constructor
38. //------------------------------------------------------
39. public MyAniApplet()
40. {
41.   // TODO: Add constructor code here.
42. }
43.
44. // APPLET INFO SUPPORT:
45. //   The getAppletInfo() method returns a string
describing the applet's
```

```
46. // author, copyright date, or miscellaneous information.
47.    //---------------------------------------------------
48. public String getAppletInfo()
49. {
50.    return "Name: MyAniApplet\r\n" +
51.            "Author: Daniel I. Joshi\r\n" +
52.            "Created with Microsoft Visual J++ Version
1.0\r\n" +
53.            "Note: My first multithreaded Java program.";
54. }
55.
56.
57. // The init() method is called by the AWT when an applet
is first loaded or
58. // reloaded.  Override this method to perform whatever
initialization your
59. // applet needs, such as initializing data structures,
loading images or
60. // fonts, creating frame windows, setting the layout
manager, or adding UI
61. // components.
62.    //---------------------------------------------------
63. public void init()
64. {
65.        // If you use a ResourceWizard-generated "control
creator" class to
66.        // arrange controls in your applet, you may want
to call its
67.        // CreateControls() method from within this
method. Remove the following
68.        // call to resize() before adding the call to
CreateControls();
69.        // CreateControls() does its own resizing.
70.        //---------------------------------------------------
71.    resize(320, 240);
72.
73.    // TODO: Place additional initialization code here.
74. }
75.
```

```
76. // Place additional applet clean up code here.
destroy() is called
77. // when your applet is terminating and being unloaded.
78. //--------------------------------------------------------
79. public void destroy()
80. {
81.    // TODO: Place applet cleanup code here.
82. }
83.
84. // ANIMATION SUPPORT
85. //    The imageUpdate() method is called repeatedly by the
AWT while
86. // images are being constructed.  The flags parameter
provides information
87. // about the status of images under construction.  The
AppletWizard's
88. // initial implementation of this method checks whether
the ALLBITS flag is
89. // set.  When the ALLBITS is set, this method knows that
an image is
90. // completely loaded. When all the images are completely
loaded, this
91. // method sets the m_fAllLoaded variable to true so that
animation can begin.
92. //--------------------------------------------------------
93. public boolean imageUpdate(Image img, int flags, int x,
int y, int w, int h)
94. {
95.    // Nothing to do if images are all loaded
96.    //---------------------------------------------------
97.    if (m_fAllLoaded)
98.       return false;
99.
100.   // Want all bits to be available before painting
101.   //---------------------------------------------------
102.   if ((flags & ALLBITS) == 0)
103.      return true;
104.
105.   // All bits are available, so increment loaded count
of fully
```

```
106.    // loaded images, starting animation if all images are
loaded
107.    //-----------------------------------------------------
108.    if (++m_nCurrImage == NUM_IMAGES)
109.    {
110.      m_nCurrImage = 0;
111.      m_fAllLoaded = true;
112.    }
113.
114.    return false;
115. }
116.
117.    // ANIMATION SUPPORT:
118.    // Draws the next image, if all images are currently
loaded
119.    //-----------------------------------------------------
120. private void displayImage(Graphics g)
121. {
122.    if (!m_fAllLoaded)
123.      return;
124.
125.    // Draw Image in center of applet
126.    //-----------------------------------------------------
127.    g.drawImage(m_Images[m_nCurrImage],
            (size().width - m_nImgWidth)  / 2,
            (size().height - m_nImgHeight) / 2, null);
128. }
129.
130. // MyAniApplet Paint Handler
131. //-----------------------------------------------------
132. public void paint(Graphics g)
133. {
134.    // ANIMATION SUPPORT:
135.    //   The following code displays a status message
until all the
136.    // images are loaded. Then it calls displayImage to
display the current
137.    // image.
138.    //-----------------------------------------------------
139.    if (m_fAllLoaded)
```

```
140.    {
141.       Rectangle r = g.getClipRect();
142.
143.       g.clearRect(r.x, r.y, r.width, r.height);
144.       displayImage(g);
145.    }
146.    else
147.       g.drawString("Loading images...", 10, 20);
148.
149.    // TODO: Place additional applet Paint code here.
150. }
151.
152. //   The start() method is called when the page
containing the applet
153. // first appears on the screen. The AppletWizard's
initial implementation
154. // of this method starts execution of the applet's
thread.
155. //-----------------------------------------------------
156. public void start()
157. {
        if (m_MyAniApplet == null)
158.    {
159.       m_MyAniApplet = new Thread(this);
160.       Thread x = new Thread("Test");
161.       m_MyAniApplet.start();
162.       x.start();
163.    }
164.    // TODO: Place additional applet start code here.
165. }
166.
167. //   The stop() method is called when the page containing
the applet is
168. // no longer on the screen. The AppletWizard's initial
implementation of
169. // this method stops execution of the applet's thread.
170. //-----------------------------------------------------
171. public void stop()
172. {
173.    if (m_MyAniApplet != null)
```

```
174.    {
175.      m_MyAniApplet.stop();
176.      m_MyAniApplet = null;
177.    }
178.
179.    // TODO: Place additional applet stop code here.
180. }
181.
182. // THREAD SUPPORT
183. //   The run() method is called when the applet's thread
is started. If
184. // your applet performs any ongoing activities without
waiting for user
185. // input, the code for implementing that behavior
typically goes here. For
186. // example, for an applet that performs animation, the
run() method controls
187. // the display of images.
188. //------------------------------------------------------
189. public void run()
190. {
191.    repaint();
192.
193.    m_Graphics = getGraphics();
194.    m_nCurrImage = 0;
195.    m_Images = new Image[NUM_IMAGES];
196.
197.    // Load in all the images
198.    //------------------------------------------------------
199.    String strImage;
200.
201.    // For each image in the animation, this method first
constructs a
202.    // string containing the path to the image file; then
it begins loading
203.    // the image into the m_Images array.  Note that the
call to getImage
204.    // will return before the image is completely loaded.
205.    //------------------------------------------------------
206.    for (int i = 1; i <= NUM_IMAGES; i++)
```

```
207.     {
208.       // Build path to next image
209.       //---------------------------------------------------
210.       strImage = "images/img00" + ((i < 10) ? "0" : "") +
i + ".gif";
211.       m_Images[i-1] = getImage(getDocumentBase(),
strImage);
212.
213.       // Get width and height of one image.
214.       // Assuming all images are same width and height
215.       //---------------------------------------------------
216.       if (m_nImgWidth == 0)
217.       {
218.         try
219.         {
220.             // The getWidth() and getHeight() methods
of the Image class
221.             // return -1 if the dimensions are not yet
known. The
222.             // following code keeps calling getWidth()
and getHeight()
223.             // until they return actual values.
224.             // NOTE: This is only executed once in
this loop, since we
225.             //        are assuming all images are the
same width and
226.             //        height.  However, since we do not
want to duplicate
227.             //        the above image load code, the
code resides in the
228.             //        loop.
229.             //-------------------------------------
230.             while ((m_nImgWidth = m_Images[i-
1].getWidth(null)) < 0)
231.                 Thread.sleep(1);
232.
233.             while ((m_nImgHeight = m_Images[i-
1].getHeight(null)) < 0)
234.                 Thread.sleep(1);
```

```
235.          }
236.          catch (InterruptedException e)
237.          {
238.              // TODO: Place exception-handling code
here in case an
239.              //         InterruptedException is thrown by
Thread.sleep(),
240.              // meaning that another thread has
interrupted this one
241.          }
242.      }
243.
244.      // Force image to fully load
245.      //--------------------------------------------------
246.      m_Graphics.drawImage(m_Images[i-1], -1000, -1000,
this);
247.  }
248.
249.  // Wait until all images are fully loaded
250.  //--------------------------------------------------
251.  while (!m_fAllLoaded)
252.  {
253.    try
254.    {
255.        Thread.sleep(10);
256.    }
257.    catch (InterruptedException e)
258.    {
259.        // TODO: Place exception-handling code here in
case an
260.        //         InterruptedException is thrown by
Thread.sleep(),
261.        //             meaning that another thread has
interrupted this one
262.    }
263.  }
264.
265.  repaint();
```

```
266.
267.    while (true)
268.    {
269.      try
270.      {
271.        // Draw next image in animation
272.        //-------------------------------------------------
273.        displayImage(m_Graphics);
274.        m_nCurrImage++;
275.        if (m_nCurrImage == NUM_IMAGES)
276.            m_nCurrImage = 0;
277.
278.        // TODO: Add additional thread-specific code here
279.        Thread.sleep(50);
280.      }
281.      catch (InterruptedException e)
282.      {
283.        // TODO: Place exception-handling code here in case an
284.        //       InterruptedException is thrown by Thread.sleep(),
285.        //       meaning that another thread has interrupted this one
286.        stop();
287.      }
288.    }
289. }
290.
291.
292.
293. // TODO: Place additional applet code here
294.
295.}
```

You can see that this code contains large blocks of comments. It is important that you read the comments carefully because they will help to complement the analysis.

Imports & Declarations

Starting from the top, lines 5 and 6 import pertinent packages for the class. Notice that line 12 declares the class MyAniApplet and implements the interface Runnable. Line 17 declares m_MyAniApplet, that is an instance of the Thread class. m_MyAniApplet is the thread used throughout the applet. Lines 19 through 27 are comments that describe the member variables for the entire class declared in lines 28 through 34. Lines 28-34 are used do declare the applet's variables.

Constructor for MyAniApplet()

Lines 39 through 42 contain the default constructor for MyAniApplet that is not needed for this example. However, here is where you would place any custome variable initializations.

getAppletInfo()

Lines 48 through 54 contain the overloaded getAppletInfo() with the information entered from step 5 in the AppletWizard.

init()

Weeding out all of the comments leaves only one thing of importance in the init() (lines 63 through 74), and that is the resize() method on line 71 to resize the applet to have a width of 320 and a height of 240.

destroy()

After init() is the life-cycle method destroy() (lines 79 through 82), which is not implemented in this animation.

imageUpdate()

The next method is imageUpdate() (lines 93 through 115), described in the comment in lines 84 through 92. imageUpdate() is called by the AWT package while the images needing the animation are loaded and constructed. However, if the flag m_fAllLoaded is true (lines 97 and 98), meaning all the images have been loaded, then there is nothing for it to do, so it returns false. Lines 102 and 103 are an if statement, checking to see if the flag ALLBITS is set to flags parameter. If ALLBITS is set, it tells the method that an image has completely loaded and the method then returns true (line 103).

Lines 108 through 112 use an if conditional to determine what location the applet is at in loading, and, if it has reached the end of the figures, then it resets it to start over. Variable m_nCurrImage (a variable that keeps track of the current image) is equal to the variable NUM_IMAGES on line 108. (In this example, the variable's value is 18; see line 34 for the declaration.) If true, then line 110 sets the m_nCurrImage to 0 and line 111 sets the m_fAllLoaded to true. m_FAllLoaded, declared on line 33 with an initial value of false, is used by the rest of the program to determine whether all the images are loaded.

displayImage()

The next method, displayImage() (lines 120 through 128) is responsible for the actual drawing of the images on the screen. The method essentially does two things: first, it checks the variable m_fAllLoaded to see if all the images are loaded (line 122), and, if this is not true, then it returns (line 123). On line 127 the method drawImage() is used from the Graphics class to draw the image on the screen. It calculates x and y parameters for drawImage() to place image into the center of applet's space (selected in init() method).

paint()

The next method is paint() (lines 132 through 150), a method used by Java to display text and graphics in the applet pane. The if statement starting on line 139 checks to see if all the images are loaded by checking the boolean m_fAllLoaded. If all the images are loaded, then it clears the applet pane using the clearRect() method (line 143) and passes this method to the dimensions of the applet retrieved using getClipRect() on line 141. It then displays a new image using the method displayImage() on line 144. If not all the images have been loaded, drawString() is used to print out "Loading Images…" (line 147) on the applet pane.

Tip

clearRect clears the applet pane based on the dimensions specified. In this example, it is the entire applet pane. Be aware that this may lead to flickering in the animation.

start()

The applet life-cycle method start() begins on line 156 and ends on line 165. Basically, contained in start() is the code to construct a new thread m_MYAniApplet, passing to it the reference to applet MyAniApplet class (line 159). Once the thread has successfully started on line 161 and is in a Running state, run() is automatically called (see Chapter 6).

stop()

Underneath start() is the other life-cycle method, stop() (lines 171 through 180). stop() checks to see if the thread m_MyAniApplet is dead (line 173), and, if not, then it kills it by invoking stop() to it on line 175 and setting it equal to null on line 176.

run()

The last method, and by far the largest method, to discuss is the run() method (lines 189 through 295).

When Does run() Get Invoked?

Run is automatically invoked when a thread is start()ed. For more information on starting (i.e., invoking the start() method) and running (i.e., invoking the run() method) threads, reference Chapter 6.

The beginning of this method loads the images. Then it contains an infinite while loop that performs the actual animation. Lines 191 and 265 contain the repaint() method. This method lets you manually invoke the paint() method to display (or redisplay) text and graphics on the applet pane. Lines 193 through 195 initialize variables used throughout the method. The variable strImage (line 199) is a string that will contain the location of each image that you are going to load. Three sections describing the run() method follow:

Part I: Loading the Images

Starting on line 206 and going to line 247 is one big for loop that goes through and loads the images. Using strImage as a temporary holding tank, line 210 constructs a string giving the relative path and the name of each image file. On line 211, the getImage() method is invoked, loading the given image using the constructed string strImage to the m_Images array. The if statement following the getImage() method inside the for loop (lines 216 through 242) is responsible for retrieving the width and height of one of the images. The important thing to note here is that this entire if statement is only executed once to retrieve the height and width of the first image.

Note

This applet only retrieves the height and width for a given image once, assuming that all of the images are the same size.

The two foci of this if statement are the two while loops (lines 230 and 233). The first while loop (in line 230) uses the getWidth() method to retrieve the width for the image contained in the Images[] array. If the width of the image is still unknown at this point, then getWidth() will return -1, and the while loop will execute again. The second while loop (line 233) does exactly the same thing, except this time it is retrieving the height of the given image using the getHeight() method. One last thing to note before moving on is that inside both while loops (lines 231 and 234) is a sleep() method that causes the current thread to pause for one millisecond. Because the sleep() method throws an exception, you have exception handling starting on line 218 and on lines 236 through 241. The last line in the for loop (line 246) uses the drawImage() method to force the given image to load completely.

Part II: Pausing the Thread

The next part of the run(), in lines 251 through 263, is a while loop that checks the boolean m_fAllLoaded to see if all the images have loaded. If they have not, then it reloops and causes the thread to sleep() for 100 milliseconds. This effectively forces the thread to loop, sleep(), loop, sleep(), and so forth until all the images have loaded; then, it can proceed to the last section of the run() method.

Part III: The Animation Algorithm

The final section of the run() method (and the applet) is the actual algorithm responsible for performing the animation. Starting on line 267 and continuing to the end of the run() method on line 289, is the body of the while loop. Inside this while loop, on line 273, is a call to the displayImage() method discussed earlier that does the actual drawing of the images on the screen. Line 274 increments the variable m_nCurrImage (responsible for keeping a tally on the current image) so that when the while reloops, the next image is loaded. The if statement on line 275 checks to see whether you have reached the end of the images to load, and, if so, then line

276 resets m_nCurrImage to 0 so the animation can start over. Thus, the animation will continue indefinitely or until the user leaves or unloads the applet. The very last thing to discuss is the reason for the sleep() method on line 279. Its purpose is to pause the thread between each cycle so the images do not update too fast.

Configuring the Speed of the Animation

You can configure how fast the animation will take place by putting different values for the sleep time in milliseconds on line 279 . The larger the value, the longer the thread will rest between each update (resulting in a slower animation) and vice versa.

Conclusion

Appendix B is not designed to give you a complete understanding of all the methods and programming techniques used by the AppletWizard to generate this animation. It is, however, meant to explain what the AppletWizard is doing and why.

Index

A

ABC class   157, 170–171, 297

ABClass.class applet   200

absolute URLs (Uniform Resource Locators)   585

abstract classes   172, 177, 536, 545

abstract int read() method   537

Abstract Window Toolkit   186

accept() method   600–601

acceptsURL() method   613

access modifiers

    final   171

    no modifiers   171

    private   171

    private keyword   170–171

    protected   171

    public   171

    synchronized   171

action() method   462, 495–499, 508

action-based events   495–510

activeCount() method   295

ActiveX   4, 663–665

    ActiveX controls   664–665

    ActiveX documents   665

    ActiveX scripting   665

    animation controls   693, 694

    applets and COM objects   687

    COM (Component Object Model) and   678–683

    COM objects   682–690

    independent standards group for   673

    Internet Explorer   665

    ISV program   695

    Java and COM objects   684–686

    Java vs., 675–677

    OLE (Object linking and Embedding) and   674–675

    Visual J++ and   4

ActiveX Control Pad   667–668

ActiveX controls   664–665, 667–668

    ActiveX Control Pad   667–668

    applets and   676

    Internet   691–696

    Internet Control Pack   669

ActiveX Developer Support Program   696

ActiveX documents   665

ActiveX Internet model

    dbWeb   666–667

    IIS (Internet Information Server)   666

    ISAPI (Internet Server Application Programming) interface   667

    VBScript   666

ActiveX objects   670–673

ActiveX samples   690–691

ActiveX scripting   665

    JavaScript   669–670

    VBScript   669–670

ActiveXpress home page   695

add() method   275, 332, 340, 358, 367–369, 374, 384

addItem() method   340–345

addition (+) arithmetic operator   59

addLayoutComponent() method   331, 378

addNotify() method   356

addSeparator() method   368, 370

advanced breakpoints   519

advanced computing
    bytecodes 641, 645–650
    exception handling 642, 656–662
    JVM (Java Virtual Machine) 641–645
    native methods 642, 650–656
allowsMultipleSelections() method 345
AND (&&) logical operator 64–65
AND (&) bitwise operator 66–67
animation running on own thread 291–293
APIs (Application Programming
    Interfaces) 3
appendText() method 354, 592
Applet class 186, 194, 240, 261, 274, 594
<APPLET>...</APPLET> tag 180, 200–201,
   216, 229, 596, 597
    ALIGN attribute 202–203
    ALT attribute 201
    browsers and 217
    CODEBASE attribute 201–202
    HEIGHT attribute 202, 227
    NAME attribute 250, 596–598
    PARAM attribute 250, 264–265
    VALUE attribute 250
    WIDTH attribute 202, 227
AppletCation appletcation program 267–276
AppletCation class 268, 274–275
AppletCationFrame class 268, 274–275
appletcations 5, 6, 224, 226, 266
    applet with life-cycle methods 267
    AppletWizard 267–276
    boolean flag to determine actions 267
    programming technique 266
    security and 267
applets 3, 5–6, 179–181, 219, 223–232
    ActiveX COM objects 687
    ActiveX controls and 676
    advantages of 180
    alignment 202–203
    alternative text to 201
    automatically loading Internet
      Explorer 195–196

bandwidth 181
basics 181–185
border size 227
browser responding to 594–595
browser support of 3
browser-security for 6
capabilities of 6
classes 182
code to retrieve information 249–252
color 208–209, 261
communicating between 596–599
configurable and reusable 180
constructing 184
customizing animation handling 228
default images 228
default or custom information
    about 231
destroy() method 182, 185
disadvantages of 181
displaying graphics in 195
embedding 200–203
enhancing with graphics 203–214
explanatory comments 226
fonts 207–208
garbage collection 185
HTML files and related attributes for
    testing 226–227
HTML pages 200–203
importing classes and packages 185
information about 230
init() method 182–184
Internet 180
Internet examples 7–10
JIT (Just In Time) compiler 181
lack of versatility 6
life-cycle methods 182–185, 307
limitations of 6
loading for first time 184
malicious code 6
multithreading 308
no source code on server 180

overriding life-cycle methods 186–200
overriding paint() method 203–204
passing arguments in 244–250
passing parameters 252–265
passing parameters from HTML
   pages 229–230
pausing 194–195
platform-independence 215
portability 180
reinitializing items 184
reinstating code 184
responding to mouse events 228–229
Runnable interface 306–308
secure programming model 180
security restrictions 6, 181
self-limiting design 6
slow 181
specifying how displayed 202
specifying location of 201
start() method 182–184
status bar 197
stop() method 182, 185
subclassing Thread class 298
suspending not needed items 185
testing 216
threads spawned in start() method 307
TODO comments 226
Trojan Horse attack 6
UI (User Interface) 438–457
unloading 185
users of 7
verified and interpreted 181
viewing in AppletViewer 216–217
viewing in Netscape Navigator
   215–216
Welcome 233–242
wide audience for 180
working directory of 8
AppletViewer 217
   command-line utility 216

not as effective as regular
   browsers 217
viewing applets in 216–217
AppletWizard 25, 219, 223–225, 227, 233,
   252–265, 277–287, 291–294, 438–439, 475,
   622–623
appletcations 224, 226, 267–276
applets 224, 226
automatically generating HTML
   page 227, 241
border size for applet 227
customizing applet animation
   handling 228
default images for applet 228
default options 233
default or custom information about
   applet 231
default Welcome class constructor 240
Finish command button 225
HTML files and related attributes for
   testing applets 226–227
information about applet 230
multithreaded support 228
naming class created 226
New Project Information dialog
   box 230–233
passing parameters from HTML
   page 229–230
responding to mouse events 228–229
Running Class dialog box 241
source code generated by 701–717
starting 224–225
type of applet 225
   applications 5–6. See also programs
main() method 181–182
process 290
architecture neutral 18
ArgTest applet program 244–249
ArgTest class 245–246
argv[] String array 243–244
arithmetic operators 59,–61
Array class 186

arrays
  assigning values and declaring 148
  declaring 147–148
  index beginning number 147
  instancing 147
  multidimensional 148
assignment operators 62
available() method 537–538, 561, 570
AWT (Abstract Window Toolkit) 204,
  328–385, 460–464
  Color class 208
  components 329–354
  containers 329–330, 355–373
  Font class 207–208
  layout managers 330–331, 374–385
awt package, importing 185

B

baio.java program 564–570
binary numerical system 41, 44
Binary Resource File (RES) 395, 412
Bitmap Editor window 389
bits 44
bitwise assignment operators 74–75
bitwise operators
  AND (&) 66–67
  left shift (<<) 70–73
  NOT (~) 66–69
  operands 66
  OR (|) 66,–68
  right shift (>>) 70,–73
  unsigned right shift (>>>) 72
  XOR (^) 66–68
Book class 129–131, 155–157
boolean data type 50–52
boolean literals 42
boolean operators 64
boolean variables 50–51
BorderLayout class 375–376
BorderLayout layout manager 374–376

break keyword 100
break statement 107–110
  label keyword 111
breakpoints 119, 516,–530
  advanced 519
  temporarily skipping 518
  toggling 518
  viewing and editing 518
  viewing and manipulating
    threads 324
Breakpoints dialog box 518–519
browsers
  applet support 3
  <APPLET>...</APPLET> tag 217
  communicating with 594–595
  interpreting HTML code 215
  Java-compliant 201
  Java-enabled 643
  nonJava-compliant 201
  responding to applet 594–595
buffered input stream 542–543
BufferedInputStream class 534, 536, 542–543
BufferedOutputStream class 534–545,
  549–550
bugs
  compile-time 513
  fixing 556
  run-time 513–514
building projects 31–33
Build | baio command 569
Build | Build ArgTest command 247
Build | Build CarThread command 305
Build | Build CustApplet command 263, 275
Build | Build DebugTest command 282,
  285–287
Build | Build EventTest command 471
Build | Build KeyTest command 493
Build | Build LifeCycle command 195, 241
Build | Build MethodTest command 166
Build | Build MouseTest command 482
Build | Build MyAniApplet command 293
Build | Build myIntegerTest command 48

Build | Build ScopeTest command 153

Build | Build SecondApplet command 213

Build | Build ThreadTest command 319

Build | Build UIApplication command 418, 437, 456

Build | Build UIEventTest command 509

Build | Build URLConnectionTest command 592

Build | Build WordAddition command 145

Build | checkBal command 638

Build | dataio command 574

Build | Debug | Go command 516, 519

Build | Debug | Run to Cursor command 516

Build | Debug | Step Into command 516

Build | Execute command 35, 49, 145, 153, 166, 195, 213, 241, 247, 263, 275, 293, 305, 319, 418, 437, 456, 471, 482, 493, 509, 515, 562, 569, 574, 592

Build | Execute CustApplet command 265

Build | fileio command 562

Build | Set Default Configuration command 514

Build | Settings command 249

built-in classes 186, 194

Button class
    instancing 333
    methods 334

Button component 333–334

buttons 333, 334

byte array I/O streams 534

byte data type 44, 48

ByteArrayInputStream class 534, 536, 538–539, 568, 570

ByteArrayOutputStream class 534, 545, 547, 567, 570

ByteArrayOutputStream() method 567

bytecode verifier 648–650

bytecodes 19, 641, 645–650

bytes 44

byvalue keyword 40

C

C programming language 12–13
    arrays 146–147
    functions 13
    inline, typedef, enum, unions, and structures 13
    linking code to Java 173
    memory management 19, 20
    pointers 12, 13
    preprocessor model 13
    strings 146
    usefulness of 12

C++ 1–2, 12–13
    arrays 146–147
    existing libraries 650–651
    function overloading 133
    functions 13
    inline, typedef, enum, unions, and structures 13
    lack of portability of 2
    linking code to Java 173
    memory management 19–20
    multiple inheritance 13
    overloading operators 134
    pointers 12–13, 650
    preprocessor model 13
    strings 146
    structures 650
    subclasses and superclasses 155
    templates 13–14
    tracking and destroying objects 20
    usefulness of 12

Cafe and AppExpress 223

Call Stack window 525–526

CallableStatement interface 611, 613

canRead() method 553

Canvas class 334
    methods 335

Canvas component 334–335

canvases 334–335

canWrite() method   553
CardLayout class   376–377
    methods   378–379
CardLayout layout manager   376–379
CarThread class   298, 301, 303–304
CarThread.java program   300–306
casting   50, 55,–58, 168–170
    instanceof operator   168
catch block   658,–659
catching exceptions   658–660
CGI (Common Gateway Interface)   66
char data type   52–54
character literals   42
    char data type   52
    collections of   42
    escape characters   42–43
characters, 16-bit   52
checkAccess() method   295
checkBal applet program   622–639
Checkbox class   335–338
    methods   337
Checkbox component   335–337
checkboxes   335–337
    default value   335
CheckboxGroup class   337–339
CheckboxGroup component   337–339
CheckboxMenuItem class   369–370
checkError() method   551
Choice class   340
    methods   341
Choice component   340–341
Circle class   158–159
class files   645–648, 688
    applet attributes   648
    arrays   648
    class attributes   648
    class interface information   648
    class number   646
    compiler version number   647
    current class   647
    elements of   646–648

    first class in   647
    method information   648
    number of constants   648
    number of fields in class   648
    number of interfaces implemented   647
    number of methods in class   648
    parent class ID   647
class header file   654
class libraries   179
class modifiers
    abstract   172
    final   172
    public   172–173
classes   129–146
    abstract   172, 177, 536, 545
    applets   182
    automatic destruction of   130
    built-in   186, 194
    casting between   168
    class modifiers   172–173
    common method definitions   173
    declaration of   129
    defining   129
    displaying organization of   116
    extending subclasses to   155
    final   172
    implementing interfaces   174–175
    implementing objects   129
    importing   185
    inheriting   174
    inheriting multiple frameworks
        175–176
    instance variable   130
    instancing   129–131
    java.util package   219–223
    JDBC (Java Database Connectivity)
        API   610
    methods   132–146
    name of   129
    object instance of another   131

passing reference of current to next   157
public   172–173
referencing variable or method within   157
regulating access to   170–173
related   171
single inheritance   174
syntax for   129
that throw exceptions   661
variables   131–132
ClassView   116
clear() method   345
clickedmyMsButton() method   591
clickmyMsButton() method   586–587
client/server architecture   604
client/server computing   599–602
data source   619
drivers   618–619
Java application   618
JDBC (Java Database Connectivity)   618–619
loading data source driver   618
clients   604
programming   602
Close (Alt+F4) key combination   472
close() method   537–538, 546, 555, 561, 568, 612
closing
frames   466–469, 470–472
projects   46
code
balancing needs in   90
condensing   90
documenting   90
spaces in   93
color
applets   261
comments   32
custom   209
graphics   208–209
keywords   32
RBG format   209
text   208, 209
Text Editor window   32
Color class   208–209
colorFromString() method   254, 261–262
COM (Component Object Model)
ActiveX and   678–683
components   680
reasons to use   679–680
COM class objects   688–690
COM interfaces
implementing   688–689
limitations   690
passing parameters   689
reference counting   690
single inheritance   689–690
COM objects   682,–690
combine() method   134, 136, 138–140
combo boxes   340–341, 445–446
command-line arguments passing to programs   242–244
commentChar() method   556
comments
color   32
multiple-line   48
single-line   48
commit() method   612
ComObjectSample class   686
Companion CD-ROM   699–700
tree.htm file   610
comparison operators   62–64
compile-time bugs   513
compilers
forcing bytecode verification   649
number of errors listed in   283
settings for   119
complex data types
arrays   147–148
strings   146–147
Component class   462
overriding methods   465

components   329–330, 332
 Button   333–334
 Canvas   334–335
 Checkbox   335–337
 CheckboxGroup   337–339
 Choice   340–341
 handling events   461
 hierarchy   462
 including   331–332
 inherited functionality to handle
  events   461
 Java-compatible   392–393
 Label   341–343
 List   344–346
 managing how they look in
  containers   330–331
 manually determining layout   384–385
 passed by corresponding event   463–464
 pixel location for   381–383
 placing   374
 referenced by geographical
  locations   374–76
 Scrollbar   347–349
 stacking   376–79
 TextComponent   349–354
compound document   674
computeSum() method   657
concurrent programming, independently
 executing entities   299
connect() method   613
Connection class   636
Connection interface   611–613
console I/O   534
const keyword   13, 40
Container class   417
containers   329–330
 Dialog   359–360
 FileDialog   360–364
 Frame   355–59
 inherited functionality to handle
  events   461

managing how components look
 330–331
 Menus   364–373
 Panel   359
 specialized   390–393
 tiling   379–381
Context | Add Method command   136,
 139–141
continue keyword   112
control-flow structures   77–79
 breaking out of loops   106–110
 diagramming   78–79
 do while loop   95–96, 98–99
 easier and smarter way to write
  code   89
 for loop   88–94
 goto keyword   106
 if conditional   80–87
 labeled break   111
 one inside another   92
 prematurely advancing in for loop   112
 spaces in code   93
 switch statement   99–105
 ternary (?) operator   87
 while loop   95–98
controlDown() method   486
controls   409
 adding   403–404
 deleting   403
 hash marks around   404–405
 properties   404–405
 static text   403, 405–407, 442–443
Controls toolbox   391–393, 403
Core API conformance level database
 functions   607–608
countItems() method   341, 345, 368
countMenus() method   367
countStackFrames() method   295
Create New Class dialog box   135, 150,
 161–162, 173, 187, 245, 300, 315, 467, 497
CreateControls() method   415, 417, 455, 509
CreateMenu() method   435, 437

CreateStatement() method   636
cross-platform independence   2
currentThread() method   295, 304
currentTimeMillis() method   194–195
CustApplet applet program   253–265
CustApplet class   254, 261
CustApplet.html page   263–264
customizable programs   242
Cycle applet   198–199
Cycle class   187, 194–195

D

daemon threads   323–324
data
    area for user to enter   351–352
    area for user to enter text   353–354
    byte-size packets   579
    sorting packets   579
data communication protocols   577–578
data source   619
data structure in LIFO (Last In First Out)
    format   220
data types
    boolean   50–52
    casting   50, 55–58
    char   52–54
    complex   146–148
    converting   50, 168
    declaring   46–48
    double   41, 54–55
    float   41–42, 54–55
    floating-point   54–55
    input stream   544
    int   41
    integer   44–50
    output stream   550
    platform-independence   50
    primitive   43–58
    single-precision   54
    string objects   42

DatabaseMetaData interface   611–612, 614
databases
    access errors   615–616
    access warnings   616
    client/server computing   618–619
    connecting Java applications to
        604–605
    data returned as result of SQL
        query   614
    dates   614
    drivers   611, 613–614
    executing single SQL statement   611,
        613
    executing stored procedures   611, 613
    fixed-point integer arithmetic   615
    implementation   616–617
    information about   611–612, 614
    sessions   611–613
    SQL timestamps   615
    SQL types   615
    storing and executing prepared SQL
        statement   613
    time   614–615
    truncating values   616
DataInputStream class   536, 542, 544
DataInputStream() method   575
dataio.java program   570–575
DataOutputStream class   545, 549–550
DataOutputStream() method   573, 575
DataTips   520
DataTruncation class   616
Date class   186, 232, 239, 241, 614
    constructors   220–222
    methods   222
    String variables   222
dates   614
    GMT (Greenwich Mean Time)   220–221
    UTC (Universal Time
        Coordinated)   220–221
db.close() method   637
dbWeb   666–667

DCOM (Distributed Component Object Model) 673, 680–681

Debug menu 519

debugging 277–287, 513–516

   accessing all variables 523–524

   adding variables 523

   breakpoints 119, 516–530

   Call Stack window 525, 526

   changing value in variable 521

   closing session 530

   compile-time bugs 513

   constantly watching value of variable or expression 523

   DataTips 520

   Disassembly window 527–528

   displaying programs on bytecode level 527–528

   dragging and dropping information between windows 524

   Exceptions window 529

   executing to breakpoint 516

   executing until cursor reached 516

   options 515

   QuickWatch dialog box 521–522

   run-time bugs 513–514

   Stack-based view of all calls to method 525–526

   starting session 514–516

   stepping through code 516

   Thread window 530

   threads 530

   variables and expressions information 519–530

   Variables window 523–524

   Watch window 523

DebugTest applet program 277–287

   errors in 281–286

   not including comments in 279

   Output window 282–283

Debug | Exceptions command 529

Debug | Stop Debugging command 530

decimal numerical system 41

declaring

   arrays 147–148

   data types 46–48

   interfaces 174

   methods 132

   strings 146

default project workspace 32–33

defining classes 129

delete() method 553

delItem(int index) method 345

delItems(int startIndex, endIndex) method 345

deliverEvent() method 461

dependency projects 114

deregisterDriver() method 614

descent() method 686

deselect() method 345

destroy() method 182, 185, 194, 240, 295, 307, 313, 712

   overriding 188–189

Developer Studio 24, 27, 135, 441

   Bitmap Editor window 389

   Build command 31

   editing and manipulating pictures 388–390

   File | New command 29

   Menu Editor window 394

   opening new text file 46

   project workspaces 114

   Resource Editors 387–394

   specifying arguments to be passed 249

   specifying class modifier 173

   Text Editor window 29–31

DHCP (Dynamic Host Configuration Protocol) 582

dialog boxes 359–360, 390, 401–410, 441–443

   check box buttons 444

   combo boxes 445–446

   editing properties 447

   modal 359–360

Dialog class 359–360

   methods 360

Dialog container 359–360
Dialog Resource Editor 390–393, 399–410, 441, 444, 447–448, 500–503
    closing 411–412
    Dialog units 393
    Properties window 410
    status bar 392
Dialog Resources 401
    porting to Java source 395
DialogLayout layout manager 398, 415
DialogLayout.java file 414, 451, 506
directories
    file descriptors 555–556
disable() method 370
Disassembly window 527–528
displayImage() method 713
dispose() method 356
division (/) arithmetic operator 59
DLL file extension 651
dllExample.h header file 654, 655–656
dllExample.stubs file 655–656
DLLs (dynamic link libraries) 605, 606, 651
    creation of 655–656
    loading 652–653
    Windows 3.1 651
    Windows 95 651
DNSs (Domain Name Services) 581
do while loop 95–96, 98–99
DOS windows 36
dot (.) operator 149–150
dotted octet 580, 582
double backslash (//) 48
double data type 41, 54–55
drawString() method 205–206, 213, 241, 281, 342, 455
driver classes 614–615
Driver interface 611, 613–614
driver manager 609
DriverManager class 614–615
DriverPropertyInfo class 615
drivers 618–619

properties 615
dumpStack() method 295

E

eat() method 160–162, 166–167
echoCharlsSet() method 352
echoing characters 352
Edit menu 427
editing preferences 119
Edit | Breakpoints command 518
Edit | Undo command 403
else keyword 82–85
embedding applets 200–203
encapsulated code 679
enumerate() method 295
equalsIgnoreCase() method 261
errors
    bugs 556
    due to situations 556
    potential 311
escape characters 42–43
Event class 462
event handling 459–460, 596
    action-based 495–510
    AWT (Abstract Window Toolkit) 460–464
    mouse 474
    techniques 465–510
event-driven programming 459, 460
Event.ALT_MASK constant 494–495
Event.CTRL_MASK constant 495
Event.META_MASK constant 495
Event._MASK constant 495
events
    management 461
    most common outside source 460
    passing to component or subcomponent 461
    passing to corresponding component 463–464

turning into objects   460

types of   472–473

UI component responsible for   509

EventTest class   467–471

EventTest program   466–472

exception handling   27, 311, 529, 556, 642, 656–662

catch block   658–659

catching exceptions   658–660

classes that throw exceptions   661

finally block   659

nested try blocks   660–661

rethrowing exceptions   661–662

throwing exceptions   657

try block   658–659

exceptions   27, 656–657

catching   658–660

class objects   556

java.io package   556–575

runtime   657

throwing   529, 657

exceptions program   657

Exceptions window   529

EXE file extension   651

executables   642–643

executeQuery() method   613, 637

executeUpdate() method   613

Execute I checkBal command   638

executing programs   35

exists() method   553

exit() method   470

explanatory comments   226

explicitly declaring variables   43

exponential notation   54

expressions

constantly watching value of   523

returning value of   239

extends keyword   156

F

FIFO (First In First Out) format   314

File class   533, 551–552

file descriptors accessing directories and files   555–556

file I/O streams   534

File menu   421–426

FileDescriptor class   533, 555–556

FileDialog class   360–364

methods   363

FileDialog container   360,–364

FileInputStream class   534, 539–541

methods   540–541

FileInputStream() method   561, 575

fileio.java program   557–564

FileOutputStream class   534, 545, 547–548, 561

FileOutputStream() method   561, 573, 575

files

attribute information about   551–552

file descriptors   555–556

project workspaces   118, 119

reading and writing data from random locations   553–554

reading input from   539–541

Files into Project dialog box   434, 450, 451, 506

FileView default project   116

File I Close command   411, 430, 448, 503

File I Close Workspace command   46

File I New command   29, 46, 121, 135, 150, 161, 187, 210, 224, 233, 244, 253, 268, 278, 292, 300, 315, 399, 439, 467, 475, 486, 497, 558, 564, 570, 586, 623

File I Open command   263

File I Save All command   195, 213, 241, 247, 263, 275, 293, 305, 319

File I Save command   31, 48, 265, 418, 437, 455

File I View command   414

fillOval() method   493

FilterInputStream class   536, 542–545

subclasses   536, 542–545

FilterOutputStream class   545, 549
    subclasses   545, 549
final classes   172
final keyword   170–171
final methods   171
final variables   171
finalize() method   541, 548
finally block   659–660
FineInputStream class   536
first() method   378
fixed-point integer arithmetic   615
float data type   41–42, 54–55
floating-point data type   54–55
    exponential notation   54
floating-point values   41–42
FlowLayout class   379–381
FlowLayout layout manager   379–381
flush() method   546
fly() method   686
Font class   207–208, 240
fonts   207
    attributes   207–208
    size   208
    supported by Java   207
for loop   88–94
    continue keyword   112
    declaring variable i in   148–149
    declaring variables inside   90
    infinite   91
    premature advancing in   112
Frame class   267, 355, 359, 471
    adding components to   358
    another class extending from   267
    instancing   356
    methods   355–356
    subclassing   357
Frame container   355–359
frames   355–359
    closing   466,–472
Fruit class   160–162, 165–167
function-oriented programming   125

functions   13
    stand-alone   132

G

GameLan site   8
generic environmental options   118
getAbsolutePath() method   552
getAlignment() method   343
getApplet() method   596, 598
getAppletContext() method   595–596, 598
getAppletInfo() method   240, 712
getApplets() method   598
getBackground() method   481
getCheckboxGroup() method   337
getCheckingBalance() method   635–636
getColor() method   205
getColumns() method   352, 354
getConnection() method   636
getContent() method   585
getCursorname() method   614
getCursorType() method   356
getDaemon() method   324
getDirectory() method   363
getEchoChar() method   352
getFD() method   541, 548
getFile() method   363
getFilenameFilter() method   363
getFilePointer() method   555
getFont() method   205
getFontMetrics() method   205
getHelpMenu() method   367
getIconImage() method   356
getInfo() methods   552–553
getInputStream() method   601–602
getItem() method   341, 345, 368
getLabel() method   334, 337
getLineIncrement() method   348
getLineNumber() method   545
getLocalHost() method   582
getLoginTimeout() method   615

getMaximum() method   348
getMenu() method   367
getMenuBar() method   356
getMinimum() method   348
getMode() method   363
getName() method   295, 304, 552
getOrientation() method   348
getOutputStream() method   601–602
getPageIncrement() method   348
getParameter() method   250–251, 262
getParameterInfo() method   252, 262
getParent() method   552
getPath() method   552
getPriority() method   295, 314
getPropertyInfo() method   613
getQueryTimeout() method   620
getRand() method   234, 235, 239–241
getRows() method   345, 354
getSelectedIndex() method   341, 346
getSelectedIndexs() method   346
getSelectedItem() method   341, 346
getSelectedItems() method   346
getSelectedText() method   350
getSelectionEnd() method   350
getSelectionStart() method   350
getState() method   337
getStatus() methods   553
getText() method   343, 350
getThreadGroup() method   295
getTitle() method   356, 360
getValue() method   349
getVisible() method   349
getVisibleIndex() method   346
gif file format   390
global variables   131
GMT (Greenwich Mean Time)   220, 221
Gosling, James   2
gotFocus() method   462, 473, 493
goto keyword   40, 106
grade variable   104
Graphic Resource Editor   388–390

graphics
    color   208–209
    coordinate system   205–207
    enhancing applets   203–214
    management   388–390
Graphics class   194, 203–204, 209, 213, 240, 481
    coordinate system   205–207
    drawing things from   334–335
    public methods   204–205
    setting font in   208
GridBagLayout layout manager   383
GridLayout class   381–383
GridLayout layout manager   381–383
GUI (Graphical User Interface)   603

H

handleEvent() method   461–462, 464–465, 468, 470–471, 473, 496–497, 499, 508, 586, 596–598
    overriding   465–472
    overriding supporting methods   473–474
Help | Search command   205
hexadecimal numerical system   41
hide() method   417, 509
hiding variables   149–154, 158
HotJava browser   2–3, 7
HTML (HyperText Markup Language)
    ActiveX objects   670–673
    browser interpretation of code   215
    case-sensitivity   265
    editing files in Visual J++   264
HTML pages
    alignment of applet display   202–203
    alternative text to applets   201
    applet residing in different directory   201–202
    applets   200–203
    automatically generating   227
    embedding applets   200–203

passing information to programs 249–250

passing parameters to applet 229–230

specifying how applet displays 202

HTTP/HTML (HyperText Markup Language/HyperText Transfer Protocol) model 665

I

I/O (input/out) processing 533–534

I/O streams 534

IANA (Internet Assigned Numbers Authority) 583

IDEs (Integrated Development Environments) 3–4, 20–22

IDL (Interface Definition Language) 688–689

IEEE (Institute of Electrical and Electronic Engineers) 54

if conditional 80–81, 86–87, 107

break statement 107

else keyword 82–85

IIS (Internet Information Server) 666

IllegalStateException exception 313

imageUpdate() method 713

implements keyword 175

import keyword 194

import statements 166

importing

awt packages 185

classes 185

packages 185

Information For Running Class dialog box 510

InfoView 116–117

more information on error 284

inheritance 155–167

extends keyword 156

method overriding 159–167

multiple 177

single 155, 177

subclass 155–157

super keyword 158–159

superclass 155–157

this keyword 157–158

init() method 182–184, 194, 197, 240, 251, 262, 267, 281, 451, 455, 492, 712

overriding 190

initialization 88

input streams

array of bytes as 538–539

buffered 542–543

closing 538

combining 541

data types 544

line numbers 542–543, 545

marking position in 538

parsing into tokens 556

processing and filtering 542–545

push back buffer 544

pushing byte back into 544

reading data from 537

returing to marked position in 538

skipping number of bytes 538

string source of 541–542

InputStream class 533–534, 536–538

blocking technique waiting for data 536

methods 537–538

subclasses 536

Insert Files into Project dialog box 413–414

Insert Resource dialog box 401–402, 421, 441, 500

insertText(String text, int pos) method 354

Insert | Files into Project command 413, 434, 450, 506

Insert | New Java Class command 135, 150, 161–162, 187, 210, 245, 300, 315, 400, 467, 497, 558, 564, 571, 586

Insert | Remove Breakpoint command 517–518

Insert | Resource command 401, 421, 441

instance variable 130

instanceof operator 131, 168

instancing
    arrays   147
    classes   129–131
    strings   147
int data type   41, 45, 48
int read() method   537
integer data type   44–50
    byte   44, 48
    int   45, 48
    long   45, 48
    short   45
integer literals   41
integers   44–50
    signed   72
    unsigned   72
integrated debugger   26, 27
interfaces   173–177
    behavior of   174
    declaring   174
    extending to another interface   174
    implementing   174–176
    java.sql package   611–614
    multiple classes   175–176
    multiple implementations of   176
    multiple inheritance   174
    related   171
    syntax for declaring   174
    UniversalButtons class   176
Internet
    ActiveX controls   691–696
    ActiveX model   665–667
    applets   180
    DNSs (Domain Name Services)   581
    IP addressing   581
    Java examples   7–10
    predefined port numbers   583
    URLs (Uniform Resource
        Locators)   581, 584–585
Internet Control Pack   669
Internet Explorer   215
    ActiveX   665, 677

    applets   180
    automatically loading   195–196
    automatically starting   241
    CustApplet applet   263
    JVM (Java Virtual Machine)   643
    status bar   197
Internet protocols, communicating
    with   584–595
interrupt() method   295
interrupted() method   295
IP (Internet Protocol)   579
IP addressing   580–582
    DHCP (Dynamic Host Configuration
        Protocol)   582
    dotted octet   582
    Internet   581
ipconfig.exe utility   582
isAbsolute() method   553
isAlive() method   295, 305, 309
ISAPI (Internet Server Application
    Programming) interface   667, 676
isDaemon() method   296
isDirectory() method   553
isEditable() method   350
isFile() method   553
isInterrupted() method   296
isModal() method   360
ISQL (Interactive SQL) utility   604
isResizable() method   356, 360
isSelected(int index) method   346

J

JARS (Java Applet Rating Service) site   9
Java
    24-bit abstract color model   208
    ActiveX COM objects   684–686
    ActiveX vs., 675–677
    APIs (Application Programming
        Interfaces)   3
    appletcations   5–6
    applets   5–6

applications 5–6
as object-oriented programming
  language 1–2
automatic memory management
  19–20
building ActiveX COM objects
  688–690
C model for 12–13
C++ model for 1–2, 12–13
class libraries 179
COM (Component Object Model) 681
const keyword 13
control-flow structures 77–112
coordinate system 206–207
cross-platform independence of 2
DCOM (Distributed Component Object
  Model) 681
dynamic 19–20
ease of use 2
fonts supported 207
functions 13
future of 3–4
history of 2–3
IDE (Integrated Development
  Environment) 3–4, 20–22
Internet examples 7–10
items not valid in 13
JDB 3
JDK (Java Development Kit) 21
keywords 40
linking C and C++ code to 173
literals 41–43
multithreaded 14–16
naming conventions 5
object-oriented programming 114,
  124–177
online documentation 30
operators 58–77
platform independence 18–19
pointers 12–13
power of 11–13
primitive data types 43–58

programs 5–6
RMI (Remote Method Invocation) 681
security 19
spaces in code 93
strongly typed 43
structure of 39–112
templates 13
types available in 4–6
version 1.1 328
Java applets 179–181
Java Class Library
  java.lang.Object class 312
  source code available for 526
Java Electric Commerce APIs (Application
  Programming Interfaces) 3
java file 688
java file extension 33
Java Resource Editor 392
Java Resource Wizard 394–395, 413–419,
  432–433, 448–449, 457, 504–505
  Binary Resource files (RES) 412
  building Java source files 396–397
  confirmation dialog box 397
  constructing classes 414–418
  constructing menus 435
  Dialog Resource source file 398
  DialogLayout source file 398
  editing files from 418
  locating resource template to port to
    Java 396
  Resource Template files (RCT) 411–412
  starting 395
  what is found in files 396
Java-compatible components 392–393
Java-compliant browsers 201, 643
java.applet package 186, 239, 261, 274
java.applet.Applet class 182–184, 187,
  250, 252
  subclassing 298
java.awt class 661
java.awt package 186, 239, 261, 267, 274,
  328–330

java.awt.Component class   328, 461, 493

java.awt.Container class   329–330

java.awt.Dialog class   415

java.awt.Event class   460–461, 470, 485

java.io class   661

java.io package   186, 533–556
    exceptions   556–575

java.io.ByteArrayInputStream class   567

java.io.ByteArrayOutputStream class   567

java.io.DataInputStream class   573

java.io.DataOutputStream class   573

java.io.Exception class   567

java.io.File class   560, 573

java.io.FileInputStream class   560, 573

java.io.FileOutputStream class   560, 573

java.io.IOException class   560, 573

java.lang class   661

java.lang package   186, 239, 303

java.lang.DriverManager class   635

java.lang.Exception class   657

java.lang.Integer class   252

java.lang.Object class   311–312

java.lang.Runtime class   652

java.lang.System class   560, 567, 573

java.lang.Thread class   295–296, 303, 525
    methods   295–296

java.net class   661

java.net package   186, 577, 581, 584–600

java.net.InetAddress class   581

java.sql package   610–616
    Callable Statement interface   611
    CallableStatement interface   613
    classes   614–616
    Connection interface   611–613
    DatabaseMetaData interface   611–614
    river interface   611–614
    interfaces   611–614
    PreparedStatement interface   613
    ResultSet interface   612, 614
    ResultSetMetaData interface   614
    Statement interface   611, 613

java.sql.Connection class   635

java.sql.ResultSet class   635

java.sql.Statement class   635

java.util class   661

java.util package   186, 232, 239
    classes   219–223

java.util.Stack class   220

java.util.Vector class   220

JavaClassSample class   686

javah utility   654–655

JavaScript   3, 669–670, 675
    working directory of examples   8

JavaSoft Web site   7, 21, 198-199, 611, 620

JavaWorld site   10

JDB   3

JDBC (Java Database Connectivity)   603–617,
  622–639
    advantages   619–620
    API and classes   610
    application   609
    architecture   609–610
    client/server computing   618–619
    disadvantages   620–621
    driver manager   609
    drivers   610
    implementation   616–617

jdbcCompliant() method   613–614

JDK (Java Development Kit)   7, 21
    AppletViewer   216–217
    javah utility   654–655
    lack of professional management
  capabilities   120
    version 1.1   328

Jeeves APIs (Application Programming
  Interfaces)   3

JIT (Just In Time) compiler   181, 644–645

join() method   296

jpeg file format   390

jview interpreter   35, 243
    running   276

JVM (Java Virtual Machine)   641
    bytecode verifier   648–650

bytecodes 645–650
executables 642–643
Internet Explorer 643
JIT (Just In Time) compilers 644–645
Netscape Navigator 643
platform-specific 642–643
runtime interpreter 644

K

kernel 17
keyboard 460
keyboard events 486
    overriding 483–495
keyDown() method 462, 483–485, 487, 492, 495
KeyTest applet program 486–495
    drawing circle onscreen 492–494
    focus 493–494
KeyTest class 487–492
keyUp() method 462–484
keywords 40
    color 32
    listing of 40

L

Label class 341
    input variables 342
    methods 343
Label component 341–343
labels 111, 341–343
last() method 378
lastModified() method 553
layout managers 330–331, 374
    adding components to 332
    avoiding usage of 384–385
    BorderLayout 374–376
    CardLayout 376–379
    default 380
    DialogLayout 398, 415

FlowLayout 379–381
GridBagLayout 383
GridLayout 381–383
user created 331
layoutContainer() method 331, 378, 381
LayoutManager interface 331
left shift (<<) bitwise operator 70–73
length() method 553, 555
Level 1 API conformance level database functions 608
Level 2 API conformance level database functions 608–609
LifeCycle applet program 186–200
LIFO (Last In First Out) format 220
    list of methods 525
lineno() method 556
LineNumberInputStream class 536, 542–543, 545
linking to system dialog boxes 360–364
list boxes 344–346
List class 344
    methods 345–346
List component 344–346
literals
    character 42
    integer 41
    non-numerical 42–43
    numerical 41–42
    string 42–43
loadLibrary() method 652–656
logical operators
    AND (&&) 64–65
    NOT (!) 64–65
    OR (| |) 64–65
long data type 45, 48
loops
    break statement 107–110
    breaking out of 106–110
    do while 95–96, 98–99
    for 88–94
    initialization 88

labeled breaks   111
  while   95–98
lostFocus() method   462
low-level I/O   534
lowerCaseMode() method   556

M

main(© method   141, 151, 163, 181–182,
  243, 245–246, 267, 274–275, 298, 300–301,
  304–305, 308, 310, 316, 318–319, 357,
  400, 414–417, 468, 471, 498, 508–509, 558,
  564–565, 571, 587–588
  argv() String array   243–244
  editing source code   434–437
  signature   243
  variables inside and outside   508
MAK (Project Workspace makefile) file
  118–119
makeVisible(int index) method   346
MalformedURLException class   584
Maple class   168–169
mark() method   538
markable streams   535
markSupported() method   538
Math class   239
Math.abs() method   239
MDP (Project Workspace) file   118–119
memory
  automatic management   19–20
  buffer streams   534
  leaks   19
menu bars   366–367
  editing   430
Menu class   367
  methods   368
menu items, naming convention for   34
Menu Resource Editor   394, 420–422, 424–430
  main menu bar representation   422
  Properties window   423
MenuBar class   366
  methods   367

MenuItem class   369–370
menus   364–368, 372–373
  adding items   369–370, 423–426
  adding to application   420–431
  disabling menu item   370
  managing   394
  resources   420–422
  separators   370
  submenus   371, 430
Menus container   364–373
metaDown() method   486
methodName() method   132
methods
  access modifiers   170–172
  classes   132–146
  common definitions   173
  Date class   222
  declaring   132
  definitions of   174
  final   171
  increasing/decreasing accessibility
    to   170–171
  input variables   133
  LIFO (Last In First Out) list   525
  native   650
  native modifier   173
  no modifier   171
  overloading   133–146
  overriding   159–167, 175, 183
  overriding supporting   473–474
  parentheses () and   133
  private   171
  protected   171
  public   171
  referencing within class   157
  return keyword   133
  return type   132–133
  several classes calling   132
  Stack-based view of all calls to   525–526
  static class   132
  synchronized   171

variables to enter data 133
MethodTest class 161
MethodTest.java program 161–167
Microsoft ActiveX home page 692–695
Microsoft ActiveX Web site 667
Microsoft site 584–585
minimumLayoutSite() method 331
minimumLayoutSize() method 378, 381
minimumSize() method 346, 352, 354
modal dialog boxes 359–360
modifiers 170–173
modulus (%) arithmetic operator 59
mouse 460, 474
mouse events
    overriding 475–483
    responding to 228–229
mouseDown() method 474, 481
mouseDrag() method 462, 474
mouseEnter() method 462, 474
mouseExit() method 462, 474
mouseMove() method 462, 474
MouseTest applet program 475–483
    setting pane to color 481
    toggling background color 482
MouseTest class 476–481
mouseUp() method 462, 474
mSQL database engine 622
multidimensional arrays 148
multiple inheritance 177
multiple-line (/* */) comments 48
multiplication (*) arithmetic operator 59
multitasking 16
    preemptive 17
multithreaded OS (operating system) 290
    32-bit 14–18
    queue 290
multithreading 14, 171, 289–294
    implementing Runnable interface 297, 306–308
    only one thread executing at a time 310

power of 299
programming 314–324
programming techniques 297–308
several threads based on same object 299
subclassing Thread class 297–306
support 228
thread priorities 314–320
MyAniApplet applet program 291–294, 702–717
    code generated for 293
    information about variables and expressions 519–530
    setting breakpoint in 519
MyAniApplet() method 712
myAppletThread thread 307
myArithOperatorTest.java program 60–61
myBitTest.java program 69–70
myBoolTest.java program 51
myBreakTest.java program 109–110
myByte integer variable 57
myCastTest.java program 56–58
myCharTest.java program 53–54
myComparisonTest.java program 63–64
myForText.java program 93–94
myIfTest.java program 85–87
myIntegerTest.java program 46–49
myShiftTest.java program 73–74
myShort integer variable 57
mySwitchTest.java program 103–105
myWhileTest.java program 97–98

N

naming conventions 332
    Java 5
naming projects 123
nanosecond.start() method 296
native methods 642, 650–651
    accessing Windows platform 652–653

calling 653
class header file 654
creation of 653–656
declaring 653
dllExample.h header file 654–656
dllExample.stubs file 655–656
stub C file 655
stubspreamble.h file 655–656
native modifier 173
negation (-) operator 59
nested try blocks 660–661
Netscape Navigator 215
applets 180
JVM (Java Virtual Machine) 643
SecondApplet applet program viewed in 215–216
viewing applets in 215–216
network programming 577–602
browser communications 594–595
communicating between applets 596–599
communicating with Internet protocols 584–595
communicating with servers 599–602
networks
data communication protocols 577–578
TCP/I– (Transmission Control Protocol/Internet Protocol) 578–583
New Class dialog box 210, 571
Net dialog box 29, 121, 135, 150, 161, 187, 210, 224, 233, 244, 253, 268, 278, 292, 300, 315, 399, 439, 467, 475, 486, 497, 558, 564, 570, 586, 623
Net Method dialog box 136, 139, 140–141, 151, 162–163, 172, ç188–190, 211, 235, 246, 301, 316, 400, 468, 487, 498–499, 558, 565, 571, 586–587
New Project dialog box 253, 558
Net Project Information dialog box 230–233, 253, 268, 278, ç292, 439, 475, 486, 623

Net Project Workspace dialog box 122–123, 150, 161, 224, 226, 233, 244, 278, 292, 300, 315, 399, 439, 467, 475, 486, 497, 564, 570, 586
new projects 114
next() method 378, 614
nextInt() method 240
nextToken() method 556
non-numerical literals
character literals 42
string literals 42–43
nonJava-compliant browsers 201
NOT (!) logical operator 64–65
NOT (~) bitwise operator 66–69
notify() method 311–322
notifyAll() method 311–322
numberOfPages integer variable 131
Numeric class 615
numerical literals
boolean literals 42
floating-point values 41–42
integer literals 41
numerical systems 41

O

Oak programming language 2
object-oriented programming 39, 113–114, 124–177
classes 129–146
communication between objects 126
complex data types 146–148
control-flow structures 78
inheritance 155–167
interfaces 173–177
Java 114
methods 132–146
modifiers 170–173
object casting 168–170
objects 128–129
scope 148–154
variables 131–132

object-oriented programming language 1–2
<OBJECT>...</OBJECT> tag 668, 671
    attributes 672
objects 2, 128, 679–680
    casting 168–170
    communication between 126
    implementing with classes 129
    instance of another class 131
    observing 220
    relationships of 128
Observable abstract class 220
Observer interface class 220
octal numerical system 41
OCX (OLE Controls) 671
ODBC (Open Database Connectivity)
    API conformance levels 607–609
    application 605–606
    architecture 605–606
    Core API level 607–608
    driver manager 605–606
    drivers 605–606
    Level 1 API level 608
    Level 2 API level 608–609
    pros and conts 607
    slow data retrievals and updates 606
odbc.dll driver manager 605
odbc.ini initialization file 606
odbcinst.dll installation file 606
OLE (Object Linking and Embedding) 4
    ActiveX and 674–675
    advantages 674
    compound document 674
online help 205
Open dialog box 360–361
openConnection() method 585, 591
operands 59
    bitwise operators 66
    default data type 59
    promoting 59
operator precedence

algebra 75–76
    Java 76–77
operators 58–77
    arithmetic 58–61
    assignment 62
    bitwise 66–74
    bitwise assignment 74–75
    boolean 64
    comparison 62–64
    logical 64–65
    precedence 154
    ternary (?) 87
    unary 68
Options menu 428–430
OR (|) bitwise operator 66–68
OR (| |) logical operator 64–65
Oranges class 160–167
organizing project workspaces 119–124
OS (operating systems)
    interrupting threads 17
    multithreaded 14–18
output streams
    array of bytes 547
    closing 546
    data types 550
    flushing 546
    printing in text form 550–551
    processing and filtering 549
    writing data to 546
    writing to buffer 549–550
    writing to file 547–548
Output Window 33, 282–283, 286
OutputStream class 533–534, 545–555
    methods 546
    subclasses 545
overloading methods 133–146
overriding
    methods 183
    paint() method 203–204

P

packages   166, 171
    importing   185
packets   579
paint(© method   187–188, 194–195, 207–208, 211, 262, 281, 335, 359, 455, 481, 483, 493, 495, 714
    overriding   203–204
Panel container   359
panels   359
Panels class   359
Paperback subclass   155–157
paramString() method   346, 350, 356, 360, 363
PARAM_Color String variable   262
parent class, referencing part of   158–159
parseInt() method   252
passing information to programs   242–265
    code in applet to retrieve
        information   249–252
    HTML page   249–250
passwords   352
pause() method   188, 194–195
pausing applets   194–195
PDAs (Personal Digital Assistants)   2
PipedInputStream class   535–536, 545
PipedOutputStream class   535, 545, 551
platform-independence   18–19
    applets   215
    data types   50
pointers   12–13
port I/O   534
ports   583
postEvent() method   461
preemptive multitasking   17
preferredLayoutSize() method   378, 381
preferredSize() method   346, 352, 354
PreparedStatement interface   613
previous() method   379
primitive data types   43–58
    boolean   50–52
    char   52–54

floating-point   54–55
integers   44–50
reading in portable fashion   542
Print() method   551
printing
    output stream in text form   550–551
    values of variables   48
println() method   48, 53, 61, 93
PrintStream class   545, 549–551
private keyword   170–171
private methods   171
private variables   170–171
procedure-oriented programming   125
process   15–16, 290
    threads   290
program exceptions   657
programming
    function-oriented   125
    object-oriented   113–114, 124–177
    procedure-oriented   125
    structured   113, 125–126
programming languages   1–2
programs   5–6
    customizable   242
    displaying on bytecode level   527–528
    executing   35
    internally multithreaded   294
    JIT (Just In Time) compilers   644–645
    making packages available to   166
    memory leaks   19
    multiple working together   114
    organizing files   33
    passing command-line argu-
ments   242–244
    passing information to   242–265
    reusable components   128
    Runnable interface   308
    steps for creation   27–28
    writing   28–31
Project Workspace window   114–115
    ClassView   116

FileView   116
InfoView   116–117
project workspaces   114–117
   breakpoints   119
   compiler settings   119
   creation of   120–124
   default   31–33
   default files   114
   default project   116
   displaying class organization   116
   displaying files and subprojects   116
   editing preferences   119
   files   118–119
   generic environmental options   118
   MAK (Project Workspace makefile)
     file   118–119
   MDP (Project Workspace) file   118–119
   name and location of source code
     files   119
   naming projects   123
   organizing   119–124
   outline of online information   117
   project management   115
   project-compiling configurations   115
   special directory   114
   WordAddition   134–141
projects
   checking which files belong to   414
   closing   46
   configuration set to Java Virtual
  Machine Debug   514–515
   default files belonging to   114
   directory   114
   extending from other projects   114
   naming   123
   new   114
Properties dialog box   501, 503
Properties window   404–405, 410
protected keyword   171
protected methods   171
protected variables   171

pseudo-random numbers   220
public classes   172–173
public keyword   171
public methods   171
public variables   171
pushBack() method   556
PushBackInputStream class   536, 542–544

Q

QuickWatch dialog box   521–522

R

radio buttons   337–339
random access file I/O   535
Random class   220, 232, 239–240
random integer-based value   240
RandomAccessFile class   533, 535, 553–555
read() method   537, 544, 554–555, 568, 570
readBoolean() method   544, 554
readChar() method   544, 554, 574
readDouble() method   544
readFloat() method   544
reading
   input from file   539–541
   number of bytes available to read   537
   streams   536–538
readInt() method   544, 554, 574
readLine() method   592
readLong() method   544, 554
readType() method   544
referredLayoutSize() method   331
registerDriver() method   614
relative URLs (Uniform Resource
  Locators)   585
remove() method   356, 367–368
removeLayoutComponent() method
  331, 379

repaint() method 204, 481
replaceItem() method 346
replaceString(method 354
requestFocus() method 493
reset() method 538
reshape() method 384
resize() method 240, 356, 455
Resource Compiler 395
Resource Editors 387–394
   developing UI (User Interface)
     398–438
   Dialog 390–393, 441, 447–448
   Graphic 388–390
   Java Resource Wizard 395–398
   Menu 394, 420–430
Resource Scripts (RC) 395
resource template (RCT) 392
Resource Template file (RCT) 401, 411–412
resources 388
   file 395
   menus 420–422
   threads and 18
ResultSet interface 612, 614
ResultSetMetaData interface 614
resume() method 296
rethrowing exceptions 661–662
return keyword 133, 239
right shift (>>) bitwise operator 70–73
RMI (Remote Method Invocation) 681
rollback() method 612
run(© method 296, 298, 301, 303, 305, 307,
  310, 313, 316, 318–319, 715–717
   animation algorithm 716
   automatically calling 304
   loading images 715–716
   pausing thread 716
run-time bugs 513–514
Runnable class 297
Runnable interface 295, 297
   applets 306–308
   implementing 306–308

   passing objects to Thread class
     constructor that implements 299
   programs 308
Running Class dialog box 247
runtime exceptions 657

S

s string variable 150
Save As dialog box 31, 48, 360–361
saving
   text files 48
   Welcome.java program 31
scientific notation 42
scope 148–154
   hiding variables 149–154
   resolution 149–150
ScopeTest class 150
ScopeTest.java program 150–154
Scrollbar class 347
   methods 348–349
Scrollbar component 347–349
scrollbars 347–349
SecondApplet applet program 210–214
SecondApplet class 210–211
security
   appletcations 267
   bytecodes 19
seek() method 553–555
select() method 341, 346, 350
selectAll() method 350
sequence of bytes 534
SequenceInputStream class 536, 541
servers 604
   communicating with 599–602
   programming 600–601
ServerSocket class 600–601
setAlignment() method 343
setBackground() method 481
setCheckboxGroup(CheckboxGroup
  mygroup) method 337

setColor() method   205, 209, 213, 240

setCursor() method   356

setDaemon() method   296, 324

setDirectory() method   363

setEchoCharacter() method   352

setEditable() method   350

setFile() method   363

setFilenameFilter() method   363

setFont() method   205, 208, 213, 240, 262, 285

setHelpMenu() method   367–368

setIconImage() method   356

setLabel() method   334, 337, 509

setLineIncrement() method   349

setLineNumber() method   545

setLoginTimeout() method   615

setMaxRows() method   613

setMenuBar() method   356, 367, 372

setMultipleSelections() method   346

setName() method   296

setPageIncrement() method   349

setPriority() method   296, 314

setQueryTimeout() method   613, 620

setResizable() method   356, 360

setState() method   337, 369

setText() method   343, 350

setTitle() method   356, 360

setTransactionIsolation() method   612

setValue() method   349

setValues() method   349

shiftDown() method   486

shoot() method   686

short data type   45

show() method   150–151, 356–357, 379, 417, 509

showDocument() method   594–595

showStatus() method   194

signature   243

signed integers   72

significant digits   54

single inheritance   155, 177

single-line (//) comments   48

single-precision data type   54

size() method   550

skip() method   537–539

skipBytes() method   544–555

sleep() method   296, 311

SMP (Symmetric Multiprocessing Systems)   16

Socket class   600–601

sockets   583

sorting packets   579

source code files

    editing to integrate it   414–418

    linking   33

    name and location of   119

    where to store   119

specialized containers   390–393

Sphere class   158–159

SQL (Structured Query Language)   603

    checkBal applet program   622–639

    delete command   621

    DML (data modification) statements   621

    insert command   621

    interaction with databases   3

    overview   621–639

    select command   621

    timestamps   615

    types   615

    update command   621

SQLException class   615–616

SQLException exception   635

SQLWarning class   616

stand-alone functions   132

stand-alone variables   131

start(© method   182–184, 194, 197, 199, 241, 263, 267, 304, 307–308, 310, 319, 714–715

    overriding   189–190

starting

    AppletWizard   224–225

    Java Resource Wizard   395

    Visual J++   27

Statement class   637

Statement interface   611, 613

static class methods   132

static text control   403, 406–407, 442–443

static variables   508

status bar   197

stop() method   182, 185, 194, 198, 241, 263, 296, 305, 307–308, 313, 714

    overriding   189

    viewing   199

streams   533–556

    buffered   534

    byte array I/O   534

    byte-size packets   579

    file I/O   534

    identifying if supports mark and reset capabilities   538

    markable   535

    marking position in   535

    memory buffer   534

    reading   536–538

    string buffer I/O   534

    unbuffered   534

    writing   545–546

StreamTokenizer class   533, 556

StreamTokenizer() method   556

String array   244

string buffer I/O streams   534

String class   186, 261

string literals   42–43

string object data type   42

String variables   222

StringBufferInputStream class   534, 536, 541–542

strings   146–147

    comparing   261

    declaring   146

    instancing   147

    source of input stream   541–542

strongly typed   43

structured programming   39, 113, 125–126

stub C file   655

stubspreamble.h file   655–656

subclasses   155–157

subinterfaces   174

submenus   371, 430

subprojects   114

subThreadGroup   323

subtraction (-) arithmetic operator   59

super keyword   158–159, 161, 167

super.handleEvent() method   473

superclasses   155–157

    accessing overridden method   161

    casting to subclass   168

    hiding methods   159–160

    method overriding   167

superinterfaces   174

SupermanJC class   686

superobjects   128

suspend() method   296, 312

switch statement   99–101, 103–105

    break keyword   100

    cases and constants   102

    common programming error   105

    comprising block   101

    default statement   100

switch-case flow control statement   484–485

synchronized keyword   171, 321

synchronized methods   171

System class   186, 470

system dialog boxes, linking to   360–364

T

TCP (Transmission Control Protocol)   579

TCP/IP (Transmission Control Protocol/Internet Protocol)   578–582

    IP (Internet Protocol)   579

    IP addressing   580–582

    ports   583

    sockets   583

    TCP (Transmission Control Protocol)   579

templates 13
ternary (?) operator 87
test.class class 649
TestClass class 157
testing applets 216
text, color 208–209
Text Editor window 29–32
text fields 351–352
text files 48
text string 341–343
textarea 353–354
TextArea class 349, 353
    methods 354
TextComponent class 349
    methods 350
TextComponent component 349–354
TextField class 349, 351
    methods 352
theColor variable 261–262
this keyword 157–158
Thread class 297, 308–309, 312, 314, 712
    constructing 297
    instance of 298
    MAX_PRIORITY constant 314, 318, 320
    MIN_PRIORITY constant 314, 318, 320
    NORM_PRIORITY constant 314
    passing objects to constructor that implements Runnable interface 299
    subclassing 295, 297–306
    Thread constructor 323
Thread window 530
ThreadGroup class 322–323
threads 14–16, 171, 290, 294–296
    animation running on 291–293
    attributes 290
    blocked state 310–313
    cars on highway and 291
    checking for daemon status 324
    daemon 323–324
    dead state 313
    debugging 530
    destruction of 294
    determining state of 309
    dying 313
    FIFO (First In First Out) format 314
    groups 322–323
    interrupting 17
    life cycle 308–313
    main body of program 294
    managing 322–323
    methods for wrong state 313
    multiple 14
    multiple waiting on object monitor 311
    only one executing at a time 310
    owner of object monitor 311
    passing objects to 297
    piped I/O communication between 535
    piped I/O streams 545
    priorities 18, 291, 314–320
    queue 314
    resources and 18
    returning JVM (Java Virtual Machine) threads 304
    Runnable interface 295, 297
    running state 310–311
    sending to back of queue 312–313
    sleeping 311
    slice of CPU time 16
    spawned 290
    spawned in start() method 307
    spawned state 310
    spawning 294
    start() method 304
    state exceptions 313
    stopping executing in synchronized method 322
    subclassing Thread class 295
    subThreadGroup 323
    supporting others executing 323–324

suspending and resuming 312
synchronization 321
unable to execute 313
user interface 294
ThreadTest.java program 315–320
throwing exceptions 529, 657
time 220–223, 614–615
Time class 614–615
Timestamp class 615
toByteArray() method 539, 547, 568
today's date 220
TODO comments 226
Tools | Java Resource Wizard command 395,
413, 432, 448, 504
toString() method 205, 241, 296, 379, 381,
539, 547
Tree class 168–169
Trojan Horse attack 6
try block 658–659
try keyword 311
TV class 175–176
Types class 615

U

UDP (User Datagram Protocol) 580
UI (User Interface)
applets 438–457
AWT (Abstract Window Toolkit)
328–385
compatible environment 327
designing 327–398
developing 398–457
Resource Editors 387–394
resource template (RCT) 392
UIApplet applet program 438–457
adding source files to 450–451
combo box 445–446
dialog box 441–447
editing source code 451–455

porting resource template to Java
448–449
resource 441
UIAppletDialog.rct file 448–449
UIApplet class 451–455
UIAppletDialog class 455
UIAppletDialog.java file 451
UIAppletDialog.rct file 448–449
UIApplication class 415, 418, 435–436
UIApplication program 399–438
adding controls 403–404
adding menu 420–431
adding radio buttons 407–409
adding source files to 413–414
control properties 404–405
controls 409
deleting controls 403
dialog box 401–410
DialogLayout.java file 414
Edit menu 427
editing menu bar 430
editing source code in main()
method 434–437
editing source code to integrate it
414–418
File menu 421–426
inserting files into 434
instancing 416
Options menu 428–430
resource creation 401
resource template 411–412
UIApplicationDialog.java file 414
UIApplicationMenu.rct file 431–433
UIApplication.java file 434
UIApplicationDialog class 396, 416–417
UIApplicationDialog.java file 414
UIApplicationDialog.rct file 411
UIApplicationMenu class 436
UIApplicationMenu.rct file 431–433
UIEventTest class 497–499, 508
UIEventTest program 497–499, 510

adding source files   506–509
porting UIEventTestDialog.rct
   file   504–505
resource creation   500–503
UIEventTestDialog class   508
UIEventTestDialog.java file   506
UIEventTestDialog.rct file   503–505
unary operator   68
Unicode   52
UniversalButtons class   176
unread() method   544
unsigned integers   72
unsigned right shift (>>>) bitwise operator   72
URL class   584–585
URLConnection class   585, 591
URLConnectionTest class   586
URLConnectionTest() method   587
URLConnectionTest.java program   585–593
URLs (Uniform Resource Locators)   581,
   584–585
      absolute   585
      actual network connection to   585–593
      relative   585
UTC (Universal Time Coordinated)   220–221

V

valid() method   556
values
      comparing relationship between   62–64
      number of significant digits in   54
variables   43–45
      access modifiers   170–172
      adding during debugging   523
      adding values to   62
      assigning and declaring   50
      boolean   50–51
      changing type of   55–58
      changing value in   521
      classes   131–132
      constantly watching value of   523

declaring inside for loop   90
effectively constants   174
explicitly declaring   43
final   171
global   131
hiding   149–154
increasing/decreasing accessibility
   to   170–171
inside and outside main() method   508
must be class member   131
naming   332
printing out values of   48
private   170–171
protected   171
public   171
referencing within class   157
scope   148–154
stand-alone   131
static   508
volitile   321
Variables window   523–524
VBScript   666, 669–670
VBX (Visual Basic Controls)   671
VCR class   175–176
Vector class   220
View | Call Stack command   525
View | Disassembly command   527
Visual Basic   679
Visual C++   223
Visual J+   20, 22–23
      ActiveX and   4
      ActiveX samples   690–691
      additional tools for   24–26
      AppletWizard   25, 223
      as object-conscious environment   114
      building project   31–33
      debugging   513–516
      default project workspace   32–33
      Developer Studio   24
      DOS windows   36
      editing HTML files   264

executing program 35
integrated debugger 26–27
jview interpreter 243
online documentation 30, 117, 205
Output Window 33
project workspaces 114–124
starting 27
steps for program creation 27–33, 35
wizards 24–25
writing programs 28–31

V

wait() method 311–322
Watch window 523
Welcome applet program 232–242
Welcome class 233–235, 239
    default constructor 240
    source code 234
Welcome.java program 28–33
while loop 95–98
windows 390
    constructing/destructing 274
Windows 3.1x 15
    DLLs (dynamic link libraries) 651
Windows 95, 14–16
    backward compatibility 15
    DLLs (dynamic link libraries) 651
    hybrid 32-bit operating system 290
    winipcfg.exe utility 582
    wizards 223
Windows NT 14–16, 290
    ipconfig.exe utility 582
    thread slice of CPU time 16
Windows platform
    accessing native methods 652–653
    DLLs (dynamic link libraries) 605–606
winipcfg.exe utility 582
WISQL (Windows ISQL) utility 604
wizards 24–25, 223–224
WordAddition application 134

WordAddition class 135–136, 138, 141, 151
WordAddition project workspace 134–141
WordAddition.java program 134–146
    automatically generated code 136
    executing 145
Workspace dialog box 623
write() method 546, 550, 555, 570
write() methods 554
writeBoolean() method 554
writeChar() method 550, 574
writeChart() method 554
writeDouble() method 550
writeFloat() method 550
writeInt() method 554, 574
writeLong() method 554
writeType() method 550

X

XOR (^) bitwise operator 66–68
XYZ class 170–171

Y

yield() method 296, 312–313

Z

ZD Net ActiveX files 696